CONFUCIUS AS A TEACHER

— Philosophy of Confucius with Special Reference to Its Educational Implications

CHEN JINGPAN

(A thesis submitted in conformity with the requirements
for the degree of Doctor of Philosophy at the
University of Toronto in 1940)

FOREIGN LANGUAGES PRESS   BEIJING

First Edition   1990
Second Printing   1994

ISBN 7-119-01007-7

© Foreign Languages Press, Beijing, 1990

Published by Foreign Languages Press
24 Baiwanzhuang Road, Beijing 100037, China

Printed by Beijing Foreign Languages Printing House
19 Chegongzhuang Xilu, Beijing 100044, China

Distributed by China International Book Trading Corporation
35 Chegongzhuang Xilu, Beijing 100044, China
P.O. Box 399, Beijing, China

Printed in the People's Republic of China

CONTENTS

ODE TO CONFUCIUS

(Sung by all Chinese today on the birthday
of Confucius, August 27th)

How lofty is Heaven! It leaves nothing uncovered;
How deep is Earth! It leaves nothing unsustained;
How bright the Sun and Moon! They leave nothing unlighted;
How great the Seas and Rivers! They leaven nothing
    unreceived;
How sublime and vast are they! No words can ever express
    them.
O my Master! His Tao is the culmination of all wisdom.
He spreads rays of Bright Virtues under Heaven!
And moves the world towards the State of Great Harmony,
He is the Pattern of Teachers for myriads of ages!
And transmits forever his undying spirit.

孔子歌

天高兮！無不覆；

地厚兮！無不載；

日月之明兮！無不照；

河海之大兮！無不容；

巍巍蕩蕩兮！莫之能名，

惟我夫子兮！道集大成；

明明德於天下兮！

進世界於大同；

師表萬世兮！

長留不死之精神

Chinese text of the "Ode to Confucius" in the author's own calligraphy.

CHAPTER I

INTRODUCTION

OUTLINE

A. The Importance of a Scientific Study of Confucius

B. The Place of Confucius in Chinese Civilization
1. Confucius as a preserver of Chinese civilization
2. Confucius as a creator of Chinese civilization
3. Confucianism as a preserving factor of Chinese civilization
4. Confucianism as a creating factor of Chinese civilization
5. Other schools of philosophy co-existent with Confucianism
6. Conclusion: Von der Gabelentz's appraisal of Confucius

C. Honours, Titles, and Ranks Conferred upon Confucius Throughout Chinese History

D. Modern Attitudes Towards Confucius
1. Vicissitudes of Confucianism since 1911
2. Arguments of those who oppose Confucianism
3. Arguments of those who favour Confucianism
4. Conceptions of some present leading Chinese scholars with regard to the character of Confucius

E. The Objective of This Thesis
To show the following through the study of the philosophy of Confucius, with special reference to its educational implications:
(a) The place of Confucius as a teacher,
(b) His contribution as a teacher

3

F. Source Material Used in This Study

(a) The difficulty of choosing the source material:

(1) The excessive quantity of the material,

(2) The unreliability of much of the material

(b) Confucius' sayings, according to his immediate disciples, as recorded in *The Analects* and other classics

(c) Confucius, according to Mencius and Hsün-tzu

A. The Importance of a Scientific Study of Confucius

The importance of a scientific study of Confucius can hardly be overstated. He has been the national ideal of the Chinese people for about 2,500 years. He has occupied a unique place in Chinese history. Numerous books have been written about him, and numerous titles and honours have been conferred upon him. But during recent years there have been new discoveries about Confucius through historical or more scientific ways of studying the Confucian classics and other ancient Chinese literature, and through archaeological discoveries which have shed much light directly or indirectly upon the study of this ancient sage. So there seems to be a great need today to re-examine scientifically this important personage in world history, and re-systematize his teachings according to the results gained from recent discoveries. Again, Confucianism today is challenged by great rivals with the advent of western thought and way of life, and a new social order, brought about by the industrial age. It seems necessary, on the one hand, to re-interpret Confucius' teachings according to present-day language, while keeping their original meanings intact, and present to the world Confucius' view-points towards the solution of world problems. "If China has anything to contribute to the world," says Dr. Leonard Shihlien Hsu, "Confucianism will be a part, not a small part indeed, of this contribution." (*The Political Philosophy of Confucianism*, Introduction, p. 21) On the other hand, through careful scientific study of Confucius, it will also bring to light the shortcomings of his teachings or the misinterpretation of the words of this great Master by his later followers. What is really dead or no longer appropriate, if any, in the Confucian system should be ruthlessly excised and cast away, and what is good in alien systems should be assimilated and absorbed, as has so successfully been done during the past 2,500 years. Assuredly, the Confucian system must continue to do so if it is to live and thrive in the new China and the new world. Sir R. F. Johnston, late Professor of Chinese at the University of London, has wisely advised the modern disciples of Confucius as follows: "What loyal Confucians must do, if they wish their Master to remain what he has been for two thousand years, the Sage and supreme Teacher of the Chinese people, is to act on the advice recently given to the followers of a very different teacher—Karl Marx. They must 'disentangle in his teaching, from what is dead or no longer appropriate, what remains alive and capable of that growth and adaptation which is the prerogative of living things'." (*Confucianism and Modern China*, p. 196) Only through a careful and scientific study of the life and teaching of Confucius can this work of "disentanglement" be expected to contribute to the glory of the Master and the country to which he belongs, as well as to the benefit of world civilization as a whole.

B. The Place of Confucius in Chinese Civilization

Confucius can be called both the preserver and creator of Chinese Civilization. Confucianism has for these 2,500 years summed up and included in its system nearly all that is good in the original Chinese cultural heritage, and has from time to time assimilated and absorbed good elements from alien systems, thus constituting what we have in Chinese civilization.

1. Confucius as a preserver of Chinese civilization

Confucius preserved what he thought to be the best of the original Chinese culture which had been handed down from the remote past. He was a diligent student all through his life, and "extensively studied all learning" (*The Analects*, Bk. 12, Chap. 15, Ver. 1). He called himself a "Transmitter" of the ancient culture and has been regarded as a Chi Ta Ch'en[1] or one who epitomized the great teachings of such ancient Sages and Sage-Kings as Yao[2], Shun[3], Yu[4], T'ang[5], Wen[6], Wu[7], and Chou Kung.[8] (See *Mencius*, 5.2.1.6; 7.2.38; *Chung Yung*,[9] 30.1; *Shih Chi*,[10] Chap. 180, p. 8; *Han Shu*, Chap. entitled: "I Wen Chi"[11])

2. Confucius as a creator of Chinese civilization

Although Confucius was anxious to preserve the ancient Chinese culture, yet he was by no means a blind conservative. He says, for example, "He who cherishes his old knowledge and is continually acquiring new is fit to be a teacher." (*Lun Yu* or *The Analects*, 2.11) Again, in *Chung Yung* or *the Doctrine of the Mean* he is made to say that calamity will inevitably befall the man who "while living in the present age is always harking back to the ways of antiquity." (*Chung Yung*, 28.1) He has generally been believed to have "selected, expunged, and rectified" the ancient materials for the exemplification of his own principles, which he believed would meet the need and solve the problems of his day. (See Chap. 3 below)

Before the time of Confucius, there had been already a group of scholars called Jü[12], who belonged generally to the aristocratic class of people. Confucius was also one of the Jü scholars, but he had thousands of able and faithful followers. He gave them a new spirit, a new set of teachings, and new reading materials worked out from the old, and thus he transformed Jü into a new social system, with no class distinctions, and with a special kind of work and way of living. They still retained the old name Jü, and when later on they, as followers of Confucius, came into power and became numerous and influential, the name Jü became exclusively attached to them. Up to the present, the name Confucianist is used as identical with Jü, and Confucianism is known in China as the religion or school of Jü, with Confucius as its honoured founder.

3. Confucianism as a preserving factor of Chinese civilization

Being loyal to their Master, the Confucianists have faithfully preserved the Chinese civilization as handed down from Confucius. They have met various kinds of difficulties and oppositions, but they have been able to surmount them all, and from time to time go on their way stronger than ever.

During the political chaos and battle of ideas in the centuries following Confucius, Confucianism won victories over Taoism, Mohism,[13] Naturalism, Legalism, Stoicism, Hedonism, and a host of other philosophies. When Ch'in Shih Huang[14] succeeded in the middle of the third century B.C. in subduing all the Chinese feudal princes and bringing the whole empire under unified control, he attempted to wipe out Confucianism by "The burning of the Books (Confucian) and the burying alive of Confucianists." But in doing so he only caused the ruin of his own empire, and before long Confucianism came back again to its full strength and power. Again, men like the founder of the Han dynasty, uneducated rustics, who looked down upon Jü scholar as impractical book-worms, came to the throne. There were tribes from outside the sphere of Chinese culture, like the Tibetans, the Mongols and

Manchus, who conquered China and established themselves as its masters. But one and all they were glad after a time to call in Confucian scholars to continue government of China in the time-honoured way, and were soon conquered and absorbed by the Chinese, not so much with material weapons as with the spiritual Confucian culture, preserved and handed down by Confucian scholars.

4. Confucianism as a creating factor of Chinese civilization

Being faithful to the creative spirit of Confucius, his followers have never been entirely blind conservatives. They have sometimes shown wonderful adaptability to new elements, and ability in absorbing new elements from other alien sources, adding new strength to their own system, while remaining always true and faithful to their Master. It is wrong to assume, as it has frequently been done, that Chinese civilization as represented by Confucianism has been entirely static and non-progressive, and that there is in it no vitality, no power of growth and adaptation. On the contrary, Confucianism is and has always been a living thing; it has the property shared by all living organisms—that of assimilation and absorption. Various modifications in Confucian thought can be distinctly traced to Buddhist, Taoist and other influences; and Confucius' teachings have been interpreted and commented upon again and again in the light of new truths as related in other systems of thought in various ages. It is interesting to note, for example, in the beginning of the T'ang dynasty (A.D. 618-907), although Confucianism was accepted as the State-cult, and occupied a position analogous, if not identical, with that of a national religion, various foreign religions were still allowed to co-exist with it. Islamism, Buddhism, Judaism, Christianity, Zoroastrianism, Manichaeism, etc. were all established on Chinese soil at that time, and some of them, like Buddhism and Christianity, were even propagated under imperial patronage. It is not the purpose here to describe the changes that Confucianism has undergone during the past as the result of its contact with new ideas emanating from native and foreign sources. It is sufficient to mention the fact that Confucianism is not, and never has been a closed system imper-

vious to new thought, but rather is and has been a closed system
with great capacities of tolerance, assimilation and absorption, the
essential characteristics of a creative living organism. Serious scholars of Chinese studies would readily agree with Rev. John Ross that
"there is in Confucianism nothing incompatible with the progress,
social, political or spiritual, of the Chinese people" (*China.* The
Quarterly Record of the Christian Literature Society for China, July
1913, p. 663), or with Professor R. F. Johnston that "Confucianism,
I maintain, is a living thing, and I doubt whether there is anything
in the Confucian teachings that is really dead." (*Confucianism and
Modern China,* p. 197)

5. Other schools of philosophy which co-existed with Confucianism

It is to be remembered that Confucianism is only one of the
many philosophical schools which originated in China. Ssu-ma
T'an (*d.* 110 B.C.), the father of Ssu-ma Ch'ien (145-86 B.C.), one of
the greatest Chinese historians, mentions six prominent schools in
Shih Chi or *The Historical Records* (chapter 130): the Yin-yang
school,[15] the Literati or Confucian school (Jü Chia),[16] the Mohist
school (Mo Chia),[17] the Name school (Ming Chia),[18] the Legalistic
school (Fa Chia),[19] and the Taoist school (Tao Teh Chia).[20] To these
six schools, Liu Hsin[21](53 B.C.-A.D. 18), one of the greatest Confucian scholars, added those of Agriculture (Nung Chia),[22] Diploma-
tists (Tsung Heng Chia),[23] Storytellers (Hsiao Shuo Chia),[24] and
Miscellaneous (Tsa Chia),[25] thus bringing the total up to ten. (*Han
Shu*[26] p. 61 f) Besides these, there are many other schools as
mentioned by Mencius and others, such as those of Yang Chu,[27]
Hsü Hsing,[28] Ch'en Hsiang[29] et al; and at the time of Mencius
(371-309 B.C.), for example, the most popular schools were those
of Yang Chu,[30] of the Mohist,[31] and of the Confucian.[32] (See *Mencius,*
3.9.9) All these schools, according to Han Mu (A.D. 22-92), the
father of Chinese dynastic histories, sprang from the same origin,
the "Six Disciplinary Arts" (Liao I),[33] each emphasizing certain
aspects of the common source. (See *Ch'ien Han Shu* 3, *The Official
History of the Former Han Dynasty,* Chap. entitled "I Wen Chi",[34] *The
Records of Arts and Literature*) When Confucianism became a

state-cult under the reign of Emperor Wu (140-85 B.C.) of the Han dynasty, Confucius' teachings, or the Confucian literature, as it was supposed to have been written, or to have been "expunged and rectified" from ancient literature by Confucius, began to monopolize the nation's intellectual world. All other independent heterodox philosophies of the different schools were overlooked or suppressed in the interest of political expediency or ethical uniformity, but, as a matter of fact, many of their ideas succeeded in creeping into the Confucian system, and in modifying it to a considerable extent.

In conclusion, it is safe to say, in general, that Chinese civilization, as such, owes its existence to Confucius and his followers of the different ages, and it is no wonder that Confucius should have been accepted as the "Unsceptred King", ruling over the Chinese intellectual world for over two thousand years. Von der Gabelentz, a German writer, says:

"Quite unique is the position occupied by him who, as no other man, was a teacher of his people; who, I venture to say, has become and continues to be a ruler of his people, the sage of the family K'ung in the State of Lu, whom we know by the name of Confucius. Unique is his position, not only in history of philosophy, but also in the history of mankind. For there is hardly any other man who, like Confucius, incorporated in his own person all the constituent elements of the Chinese type, and all that is eternal in his people's being. If we are to measure the greatness of an historic personage, I can see only one standard applicable for the purpose: the effectiveness of that person's influence according to its dimensions, duration, and intensity. If this standard be applied, Confucius was one of the greatest of men. For even at the present day, after the lapse of more than two thousand years, the moral, social, and political life of about one-third of mankind continues to be under the full influence of his mind. (*Confucius und seine Lehre*, p. 4 et seq., quoted from Friedrich Hirth's *The Ancient History of China*, pp. 242-3)

C. Honours, Titles and Ranks Conferred upon Confucius Throughout Chinese History

The position of Confucius in Chinese history has never been definitely established, his posthumous titles and ranks being sometimes very high, sometimes very low. The following are some of them:

(a) In Confucius' lifetime

In his lifetime Confucius was generally called Master. Once in *The Analects* he was called Chiang Sheng[35] or "Becoming Sage". He never allowed himself to be called a Sage; he wanted, however, to become a superior man or Chun-Tze,[36] a topic which he very frequently discussed.

The following are some quotations from *The Analects*:

"The Master said, 'A Sage and the man of perfect virtue;—how dare I rank myself with them?' " (*The Analects*, 7.33)

"The Master said, 'A Sage is not mine to see; could I see a Chun-tze, that would satisfy me'." (*The Analects*, 7.25.1)

"Tzu Kung said, 'Certainly Heaven has endowed him unlimitedly. He is a Chiang Sheng (Becoming Sage)'." (*The Analects*, 9.6.2)

(b) In the period of the Warring States (481-206 B.C.)

In the sixteenth year of Duke Ai of Lu (479 B.C.) Confucius died, and Duke Ai went to his grave and lamented for him and called him Ni Fu[37] or Father Ni, a name which was to be often mentioned later on.

In the next year (480 B.C.), Duke Ai turned Confucius' house into Confucius' Temple, in which he store Confucius' caps, robes, books, musical instruments, carriages, and sacred vessels for display. They were still in good condition when Ssu-ma Ch'ien visited the temple about four hundred years later. (See *Shih Chi*, "Life of Confucius"[38])

Generally speaking, Confucius was regarded as a Sage, in the sense of a great man with perfect virtues, and with the power of "exercising transforming influences upon man and nature." (*Mencius*, 7.2.25.6.-7) The following are some quotations from *Mencius* written in the latter part of this period.

Mencius said: "Confucius was the Sage of Time" (*Mencius*, 5.2.1.5) Again he said: "Since there were living men until now, there never was another Confucius." (*Mencius*, 2.1.2.23)

Tzu-Kung said: "Master (Confucius) you learn without satiety, that shows your wisdom, you teach without being tired, that shows your benevolence; benevolent and wise, Master you are a Sage." (*Mencius*, 2.1.2.19) Again he said: "From the birth of mankind till now, there has never been another like our Master". (*Mencius*, 2.1.2.27)

Tsai-Wo[39] regarded Confucius as "far superior to Yao and Shun", the two ideal Sage-kings of the ancients. (*Mencius*, 2.1.2.26)

Yu-Yao[40] said: "From the birth of mankind till now, there never has been one so complete as Confucius". (*Mencius*, 2.1.2.28)

Even Han Fei[41] who ridiculed Confucianism as one of the five "parasites",[42] called Confucius a "world-sage." (See "Wu Tu"[43])

(c) In the Han dynasty (206 B.C.-A.D. 221)

In the twelfth year of Emperor Kao-Tsu[44] (194 B.C.), the emperor went himself to worship and offer sacrifices to Confucius at Confucius' Temple in Ch'u-fu.[45] Thus he started the custom of State-offerings, and royal visits from new emperors, to Confucius, at Confucius' Temple in Ch'u-fu which continued down to the end of the Manchu dynasty. (A.D. 1911)

In the first year of Emperor P'ing[46] (A.D. 1), Confucius was canonized as Pao-Ch'eng-Hou Hsun-ni-kung[47] or "Marquis of Completed Praise, Illustrious Duke Ni."

In the second year of Yung P'ing[48] (A.D. 60) during the reign of Ming Ti[49] or Emperor Ming (A.D. 58-75), the picture or tablet of Confucius was introduced into every classroom throughout the empire, to be worshipped by all students and teachers generally, not so much as a god but as an ideal teacher. This practice also was followed continuously from that time to the early years of the Chinese Republic.

During this period Confucius was generally regarded as more than a human sage, and as sharing many qualities that were super-human. It was believed that he had had a miraculous birth and that at the time of his birth, two dragons had patrolled the sky, two fairies had spread a red mist in the air, five old men representing the spirits of the five planets had come down from heaven, and the Ch'i Lin, a strange animal which was believed to manifest itself in the world only when an emperor or other great historic personage was born, had appeared and vomited the Jade Books, while strange music came from a mysterious source and a voice from the sky announced the birth of an illustrious child. (See *Ch'i Ching Wei*[50] or *The Apocrypha of the Seven Classics*) He was sometimes called Ta Sheng[51] or "Great Sage", who "wrote *The Spring and Autumn Annals*, produced *The Book of Filiatry*, expunged and rectified *The Five Classics*, talked on the Ch'i Tz'u[52] of *The Book of Changes*, put in order the heaven and the earth, appraised the 'Bright Spirits' . . . and worked out a system for the Han dynasty." (The stone tablet put up in Confucius' Temple in the first year of Yung Hsing, (A.D. 153; see *Chin Shih Chuei Pien*[53], Vol. 8, Han Section, p. 5) He was believed to have known beforehand the persecution of the Confucianist by the First Emperor of Ch'in, and his own death at Sha Ch'iu[54]. (*Lun Heng*[55], by Wang Chung) When Prince Kung of Lu[56] wanted to tear down the house of Confucius in order to enlarge his palace, he was threatened and held back by strange music that came from the walls of Confucius' house. (See *Han Shu*, "Biography of Prince Kung of Lu") The literature in this period abounds with records of such super-human attributes of Confucius. He was believed to have been fathered by the "Black God", Hei Ti[57], and borne by the woman Yen[58], and he was practically raised from the rank of human sagehood to that of godhood, though never officially deified as God.

Sometimes he was called the Su Wang[59], or "Uncrowned King" who "had laid down a system for later kings to follow". (See the stone tablets put up at Confucius' temple in the second year of Yung Shou[60], A.D. 156, and in the second year of Chien Ning[61], A.D. 169, for commemoration of Confucius; *Chin Shih Chuei Pien*, Vol. 13[62], Han section, pp. 5 and 9)

From the fifteenth year of Yung P'ing[63] A.D. 72 up to the end of the Manchu dynasty the seventy-two favourite disciples of Confucius were also worshipped and sacrificed to, in company with their Master.

(d) During the Six Dynasties, A.D. 221-618 (including the Three Kingdoms, Wei and Sui)

In A.D. 220, the first year of Emperor Wen of Wei[64], every county or state was asked to have at least one temple to Confucius. In the same year a stone tablet was put up by the emperor at the Confucian temple in Ch'u-fu, on which Confucius was hailed as "a Great Sage in this Fateful World, and an Ideal Teacher for Myriads of Years"[65]. (See *Chin Shih Chuei Pien*, Vol. 23, Wei section, p. 1)

In A.D. 246, the seventh year of Cheng Shih of Wei[66], Confucius was honoured as Hsien Sheng[67] or the "Former Sage", and his favourite disciple Yen Yuan[68] as Hsien Shih[69] or "the Former Teacher." (See *Wei Chih*[70])

In A.D. 492, the sixteenth year of T'ai Huo 2 during the reign of Emperor Hsiao Wen[72] of the Northern Wei, Confucius was canonized as Wen Sheng Ni Fu[73] or the "Cultural Sage, Father Ni." (See *Pei Wei Shu*[74])

In A.D. 536, the third year of Hsing Huo[75] during the reign of Emperor Hsiao Ching[76] of the Northern Wei, the first image of Confucius was put up in his temple at Ch'u-fu together with the images of ten of his disciples. From this time on to the beginning of the Ming dynasty the worship of images became popular in the Confucian system—a marked influence of the Buddhist religion. In the same year a stone tablet was put up in the temple to commemorate this occasion, on which the chief works of Confucius were mentioned as "Correcting the music and odes, revising *The Spring and Autumn Annals*, and editing and expurgating the Six Classics." (See *Chin Shih Chuei Pien*, Vol. 31, Eastern Wei section, p. 2; see also *Ch'ueh Li Chih*)[77]

In A.D. 580, the second year of Ta Ch'eng[78] during the reign of Emperor Hsuan[79], of the northern Chou[80], Confucius was canonized as Tsou Kuo Kung[81] or "The Prince of Tsou". (See *Pei Chou Shu*[82])

In A.D. 581, the first year of K'ai Huang[83] during the reign of Emperor Wen of Sui[84], Confucius was given the title of Hsien Shin Ni Fu[85] or "Former Teacher, Father Ni". (See *Sui Chih*[86])

In A.D. 611, the seventh year of Ta Yie[87] of the Sui dynasty, a stone tablet was put up in Confucius' Temple at Ch'u-fu, on which he was honoured as Ta Sheng Hsuan Ni[88] or "Great Sages, Illustrious Ni", and Pei Wang Shih Piao[89] or "Ideal Teacher for Hundreds of Kings". (See *Chin Ts'ui Pien*, Vol. 40, Sui section, p. 3)

(e) In the T'ang dynasty. (A.D. 618-907)

In A.D. 624, in the seventh year of Wu Teh[93], Emperor Kao Tsu[91] offered sacrifices to both Chou Kung and Confucius. Chou Kung was honoured as Hsien Sheng[92] or the "Former Sage", while Confucius was called Hsien Shih[92] or the "Former Teacher." (See *T'ang Shu*)

In A.D. 628, the second year of Cheng Kuan[94] during the reign of Emperor T'ai Tsung[95], Confucius was elevated to Hsien Sheng, or "Former Sage." (See *T'ang Shu*[96])

In A.D. 630, the fourth year of Cheng Kuan, an imperial mandate was issued to the effect that Confucius' temples should be built in all Chou[97] or departments, and Hsien[98] or counties throughout the country. This was the beginning of the official worship of the Confucian temple in the Chou and Hsien. (See *Ch'ueh Li Chih*)

In A.D. 632, the sixth year of Cheng Kuan, the temple of Chou Kung was closed in the imperial city, and Confucius was elevated as Hsien Sheng, or "Former Sage", and Yen-tzu[99] as Hsien Shih or "Former Teacher." (See *T'ang Shu*)[100]

In A.D. 637, the eleventh year of Cheng Kuan, Confucius was honoured as Hsuen Fu or "Illustrious Father."[101] (See *T'ang Shu*)

In A.D. 650-655, during the period of Yung Hui[102] in the reign of Emperor Kao Tsung[103], Chou Kung was again honoured as "Sage" and Confucius as "Teacher." (See *Ch'ueh Li Chih*)[104]

In A.D. 657, the second year of Hsien Ch'ing[105], Confucius was honoured as "Former Sage." (*Chueh Li Chih*)

In A.D. 666, the first year of Chien Fung[106], Confucius was given the title of T'ai Shih Lu Kuo K'ung Hsuan Kung[107] or "Grand Teacher, Illustrious Prince K'ung of the State of Lu". (See *T'ang Shu*)

In A.D. 739, the 27th year of K'ai Yuan[108], during the reign of Hsuan Tsung[109], Confucius was canonized as Wen Hsuan Wang[110], or "Culture-spreading King." (See *T'ang Shu*) This was the first time that the title "King" was officially given to Confucius.

(f) In the Sung dynasty, A.D. 960-1280

In A.D. 1008, the first year of Ta Chung Hsiang Fu[111], Confucius was canonized as Yuan Sheng Wen Hsuan Wang[112] or the "First Holy Culture-spreading King", his father was canonized as Ch'i Kuo Kung[113] or the "Prince of Chi", his mother as Lu Kuo T'ai Fu Jen[114] or the "Great Lady of the State of Lu", and his wife as Huen Kuo Fu Jen[115] or the "Lady of the State of Huen". The name of his native town, Ch'u-fu[116] was changed to Hsien Yuan[117], or the "Spiritual Source." (See *Sung Shih*[118])

In A.D. 1012, the fifth year of Ta Chung Hsiang Fu, the title of Confucius was changed from Yuan Sheng Wen Hsuan Wang to Chih Sheng Wen Hsuan Wang[119], that is, the character Yuan[120] or "First" was changed to Chih[121] or "Most", so instead of being the "First Holy", Confucius became the "Most Holy" King[122]. The reason for the change was said to be that during this year the emperor Chen Tsung[123] built a temple for the worship of his ancestor, Chao Yuan Ming[124], and the character "Yuan" of the old title of Confucius became tabooed because of the second character in the name of the ancestor of the emperor. (See *Sung Shih*, Vol. 8, p. 6)

(g) In the Yuan dynasty, (A.D. 1280-1368)

In A.D. 1307, the eleventh year of Ta Teh[125], Confucius received an addition to his title; the two characters Ta Ch'eng[126] being added to Chih Sheng Wen Hsuan Wang. So his complete title became Ta Ch'eng Chih Sheng Wen Hsuan Wang, or "Great Perfect, Most Holy Culture Spreading King." (See *Yuan Shih, The Official History of Yuan*)

(h) In the Ming dynasty, (A.D. 1368-1644)

Throughout this long dynasty Confucius was almost entirely

officially called Hsien Shih or "Former Teacher". For example, it is repeatedly recorded in the *Ming Shih*[127], the official history of Ming, that whenever a new emperor came to the throne, he would, as a rule, visit and offer sacrifices to Hsien Shih Kung Tzu[128] or "Former Teacher Confucius."

In A.D. 1381, the fourteenth year of Hung Wu[129], an imperial mandate was issued to all parts of the country ordering the destruction of all images of Confucius, and the using of wooden tablets of Confucius in their stead. This was a marked reaction against the practice of Buddhism. (See *Ch'ueh Li Chi*) In the Sung dynasty, the philosopher Chucius[130] had already complained about the worship of the images of Confucius. He said "The Illustrious Sage (Confucius) really should not be put into images, for at the time of the Spring and Autumn Sacrifices, it is quite right just to use the wooden tablets." (See *Yu Lu*[131] or *The Records of Chucius' Sayings*) His idea was actually now put into practice and all the images of Confucius, together with those of his disciples, were destroyed, and wooden tablets were put up in their stead.

In A.D. 1530, the ninth year of Chia Ching[132], Confucius was canonized as Chih Sheng Hsien Shih K'ung Tzu[133] or "The Most Holy Former Teacher Confucius." (See *Ming Shih*, the Official History of Ming) The temple of Confucius was called Hsien Shih Miao[134] or "the temple of the Former Teacher". From that time on to the present the title "King" has never officially been given to Confucius. (See also *Ming Chi*[135], *The Record of the Ming*, Vol. 30, pp. 18-19)

(i) In the Ch'ing dynasty, (A.D. 1644-1911)

(All the following records have come from *Ta Ch'ing Hui Tien*[136], Vol. 90, section on Li)

In A.D. 1645, the second year of Shun Chih[137], Confucius was canonized as Ta Ch'eng Chih Sheng Wen Hsuan Hsien Shih K'ung Tzu[138] or "Great Perfect, Most Holy Culture Spreading Former Teacher Confucius."

In A.D. 1657, the fourteenth year of Shun Chih, Confucius was canonized as Chih Sheng Hsien Shih K'ung Tzu[139], or "The Most Holy Former Teacher Confucius."

In A.D. 1684, the twenty-third year of K'ang Hsi[140], the four characters, Wan Shih Shih Piao[141], or "The Ideal Teacher for a myriad generations", were written by the emperor himself to be carved in wooden tablets and hung at the front of Ta Ch'eng Tien[142] or "Great Perfect Palace", the Temple of Confucius in the Capital City, and at the Wen Miao[143] or the "Culture Temple", Confucius' temples in various provinces, counties, districts, cities, etc.

In A.D. 1723, the first year of Yung Cheng[144], the five generations of Confucius' ancestors were all canonized as "Kings."

In A.D. 1727, the fifth year of Yung Cheng, the 27th day of August, the birthday of Confucius, was fixed as a public holiday and a public feast day. No butchery was allowed on that day.

In the latter part of this dynasty there was a marked revival of the "Modern Text School", the Chin Wen Chia[145], whose scholars generally shared the view of the Han scholars about the nature of Confucius, that he was a super-human Sage. The chief exponent of this school in this period was K'ang Yu-wei (1858-1927), who wrote in his famous *K'ung Tzu Kai Chih K'ao*[146] or "Research on changing of the systems by Confucius" that "Confucius was the Chiao Chu[147] or the Lord of Religion, a Spiritual Holy King, comparable with the Heaven and the Earth, and fostering myriads of things. There is no man, no affair, no principle which is not included in the great Tao of Confucius; therefore, he has been regarded as the 'Great Perfect and Most Holy One', and never has there been one like him from the birth of mankind till now." (*K'ung Tzu Kai Chih K'ao*, Vol. 10)

D. Modern Attitudes Towards Confucius, Since the Revolution of 1911

Since the fall of the Manchu dynasty and the inauguration of the Chinese Republic in 1911, Confucianism has ceased to be a state religion, enjoying imperial patronage and support. Western ideologies and practices have come into full contact with those of the Confucian East, bringing about an intellectual upheaval that Chinese history has never experienced since the Ch'in dynasty in the 3rd century B.C. when there took place "the burning of books and the burying alive of Confucian scholars". The following are some facts regarding the fortunes of Confucianism during this period, and some reasons put forth by its proponents and opponents.

1. Vicissitudes of Confucianism Since 1911

1911. The Republic of China was established. Official state-sacrifices to Confucius were abolished, and Confucianism was no more the state-cult, as it had been since the time of Han Wu Ti[148].

1912. A provisional constitution was promulgated on March 11 guaranteeing the liberty of all religious beliefs.

1913. The Cabinet of the Republican Parliament issued the famous appeal for the prayers of Christendom on behalf of the New Republic. April 27 was the date appointed for the public prayer, and the day came to be known as "prayer Sunday."

The Confucian Church, K'ung Chiao Hui[149] was organized, the leading spirit of which was Dr. Ch'en Huan-chang, a follower and student of K'ang Yu-wei, author of *Economic Principles of Confucius and His School*, and editor of the periodical *Chen Shih Pao*[150]. In September, a memorandum was presented to the Parliament by members of the Confucian Church, in which the State-recognition of Confucianism was strongly advocated. The proposal was finally defeated by a narrow margin of nine votes, 264 against 255.

1914-1916. There was a reaction in favour of Confucianism during this period of presidency of Yuan Shih-kai[151], a great patron of Confucianism. The worship of Heaven and the sacrifices to Confucius were re-established, and the teaching of the Confucian classics was made compulsory in every primary and high school. On December 15, 1915, he established a constitutional monarchy with himself as emperor, which was to last a few months. However, the use he made of the Confucian system only tended to discredit Confucianism in the public eye.

1917. On July 1, Chang Hsun[152], a great patron of Confucianism, made a bold stroke to restore the Manchu regime and the Confucian system as the State-cult, but the transient monarchy lasted only ten days. Hsuan T'ung[153], the restored Manchu emperor, had to abdicate the second time after less than two weeks' reign.

1917-1927. Two big events took place during this period: the famous May Fourth Student Movement, sometimes called the Emancipation Movement, and the 1927 unification of China under the Kuomintang with the establishment of the Nationalist Government in Nanking, the capital city of China. This marked one of the greatest intellectual upheavals in the history of China. New thoughts and practices of all kinds flooded China in all directions. Old Chinese teachings, customs and beliefs were seriously criticized, and many of them ruthlessly discarded. Confucianism became one of the chief targets for attack, and Confucian scholars were generally regarded as conservative "old guards," despised and sometimes persecuted.

1927. The Ministry of Education under the Nationalist Government ordered the customary Spring and Autumn sacrifices to Confucius, which still lingered on in some districts after the Revolution, to be discontinued. All Confucian temples were to be converted into schools and their revenues diverted to purely educative uses. No Confucian classic was allowed to be taught in schools.

1932. The occupation of Manchuria by Japan was a serious blow to all Chinese people throughout the country. In many parts of China there were clear signs of something like a Confucian revival. Ch'en Chi-t'ang[154], the governor of Kwangtung Province, for example, was in active sympathy with a "revive-the-old-culture" movement with the slogan of "Back to Confucius." Describing the movement, a foreign observer declared that "supporters of the campaign hold the steady disappearance of the old virtues as taught by the 'Pattern of 10,000 generations' (Confucius) accountable for all the existing political and social chaos as well as the present national crisis. They maintain that had the Confucian teachings not been neglected, China would not be in the state she is in to-day." (*North China Herald*, Oct. 19th, 1932)

1934. In February, a new movement called the "New Life Movement" was officially inaugurated in Nanchang by Chiang Kai-shek, and soon spread all over the country. It has its roots in the old Confucian virtues, and has done much to revive the teachings of Confucius.

On June the fourth of the same year, it was ordered that the birthday of Confucius, the 27th of August, should be made a public holiday throughout China in commemoration of the great Sage. The following is a passage, from the *Shanghai Daily News*, of June 4, 1934, which shows clearly the attitude of the Kuomintang government towards Confucius.

"The birthday of Confucius has been included in the list of national holidays in China. This decision was adopted by the Central Executive Committee of the Kuomintang that held a meeting on June 1st, presided over by Sun Fo (son of Sun Yat-sen), chairman of the Legislative Council, Nanking. The observance of Confucius' birthday as a Chinese national holiday is significant. The Three People's Principles of the late Dr. Sun Yat-sen has been propagated throughout the country at the expense of Confucianism, which was the exclusive guiding spirit of Chinese moral principles. Importance is attached to the motive of the Kuomintang in reviving and supporting Confucianism."

1939. Teacher's Day was incorporated with the birthday of Confucius, and is now to be celebrated on the same day, August

27. Confucius has again been honoured as Wan Shih Shih Piao, the "Ideal Teacher for Myriads of Generations," but so far the study of the Confucian Classics is still excluded from the school curriculum of the present day.

2. Arguments of Those Who Oppose Confucianism

(a) Confucianism has been regarded by many Chinese people as the strongest bulwark of the monarchy which they have taken so much pains to get rid of. It has been used again and again by monarchs or militarists as an instrument to subdue and exploit the people. They argue, for example, that the Mongolian invaders, after their conquest of China, advocated Confucianism. The Manchus did the same thing when they conquered China, and such is the case in the present Manchuria under Japanese control. Yuan Shih-kai, the traitor of the Republic, was a great patron of Confucianism, and so were all the late discredited militarists, like Chang Hsun, Tuan Chi-Jui[155], Chang Ts'ung-ch'ang[156], and others. So there has been a strong belief, especially among Chinese political reformers between the years 1917-1927, that Confucianism is opposed to the Republican form of Government, and is a stumbling-block in the way of the nation's advancement.

(b) The modern "intellectual movements" in China have been unfavourable to Confucianism. In the last two decades, the Chinese nation has been in a state of rapid change and transformation, under which a series of literary, philosophical, historical and sociological polemics have taken place. All this contributed to the undermining of Confucianism. (See "Recent intellectual movements in China," by Monsheng Hsitien Liu: *China Institute Bulletin*, Vol. 3, No. 1, Oct. 1938) For example, as a result of the Literary Revolution of 1917 started by Hu Shih and Ch'en T'u-hsiu, aiming at "the overthrow of classical restrictions and repressions and the creation of a new, free, and living literature", the Confucian Classics have been banished from Chinese schools. With the revolution of Chinese Historical Studies in 1924, brought about by Ku Chieh-keng and others, the name of Confucius has been almost entirely dissociated from all the Classics. The conflict between Science and Philosophy in 1923 resulted in an overwhelming victory of Science over Philosophy, and by the debate on the materialistic interpretation of Chinese History in 1928-31, many teachings of Confucius have been discredited as old-fashioned, absurd, and even harmful. Confucianism was denounced, for example, by some writers as a "man-eating" religion because of its emphasis put upon the doctrine of chaste widowhood, and by others as a system of social and political philosophy aiming at the restoration of feudalism by emphasizing the virtues of loyalty to the kings, and filial piety to parents, etc. Wu Chih-hui, the famous philosopher of the "black-block" universe, even suggested once the burial of all the "thread-bound Chinese books," including of course all the Confucian Classics, for the next 3,000 years; and he suggested that only modern scientific works should be studied in the present scientific epoch. (See *Chih Hue Wen Ts'un*[157] or *A Collection of Writings by Wu Chih-hui*)

3. Arguments of Those Who Favour Confucianism

(a) Some favour Confucianism for ulterior motives, and not for the intrinsic value of the system.

The late militarists such as Yuan Shih-kai, Chang Hsun, Tuan Chi-jui, Chang Ts'ung-ch'ang, Chang Tso-lin[158] and others, were all in favour of Confucianism, and appealed for the study of the Confucian Classics. For them, Confucianism was more of a political instrument to pave their way to some ulterior selfish objective, or sometimes a veil to cover up their evil deeds. For instance, General Chang Ts'ung-ch'ang, under whose control Shantung was almost completely devastated, printed a million copies of Confucian classics for free distribution.

Many members of the "Confucian Church" who take Confucianism as a religion and raise Confucius from the rank of human sage-hood to that of Godhood, the Lord of Confucian Religion, do so with the ulterior motive of opposing other religions, especially the Christian Religion. They do not want China to be called a country without its own original religion. They endeavoured once to put in the Constitution of the Kuomintang government a stipulation declaring Confucianism to be the state religion, and they have tried every means to "rationalize" the teachings and life of Confucius in order to serve their own purpose. (See *Ku Shih Pien*, Vol. 1, "Autobiography of Ku Chieh Keng")

(b) Some favour Confucianism because its teachings are compatible in most cases with modern thought, political, social, economic, or moral, especially, because it is in perfect harmony with the foundations of the Three People's Principles put forward by Dr. Sun Yat-sen, the Bible of the Kuomintang government. As a matter of fact many of the principles of Dr. Sun have been found to be based on the teachings of Confucius. Tai Chi-tao[159], one of the ablest and most respected members of the Nationalist Government, points out clearly in his famous work entitled *The Foundations of the Philosophy of the Principles of Sun-wen*, (See *Sun-wen Chu I Chih Che Hsueh Ti Chi Chiu*[160]) that the "foundations" of the principles of Dr. Sun Yat-sen are Confucian. (See also Dr. Yuan Cho-ying's *La philosophie morale et politique de Mencius*, Paris, 1927. Dr. Yuan claims Dr. Sun as "Un defenseur de la Doctrine Confuceene")

(c) Some are in favour of Confucianism because they are convinced that the teachings of Confucius not only are in harmony with the current thought of the world but also offer valuable suggestions towards the solution of world problems. For example, the ethics which Confucius extolled have been regarded as the virtues which are in great need of being popularized to-day. The virtues, such as, Li, I, Lien, Chih[161], or Courtesy, Justice, Honesty, and Honour; and Chung-hsiao, Jen-ai, Hsin-i, Huo-p'ing[162], or Loyalty and Filialtry, Benevolence and Love, Honesty and Justice, Harmony and Peace, have been the cardinal virtues advocated by the New Life Movement.

(d) Some favour Confucianism because it has represented the Chinese spirit and culture for thousands of years, and has helped the country pass triumphantly through countless trials and difficulties. They think such a spirit and culture should be preserved and developed for the good of the country and for the benefit of the world.

Dr. K'ung Hsiang-Hsi[163], premier of the Kuomintang government, gave a speech on August 27, 1939, to a group of over 300 leaders of the present government, at a meeting held in Chungking to commemorate Confucius' birthday. The speech runs in part as follows:

"The establishment of any country, or the rising up of any nation in the ancient or in the modern world, must depend upon the existence of a certain spiritual force. Our country has been established for several thousands of years, and has passed through many trials and tribulations. The reason that we have been able to conquer all dangers and difficulties, and exist independently and unconquerably in the world up to the present day, is due to the preserving and binding strength of such a spiritual force, which has been generated through the teachings of Confucius." (See *Huang Chung Shih Pao*[164], *The Toronto China Daily News*, Oct. 13, 1939)

4. **Conceptions of Some Present Leading Chinese Scholars with Regard to the Nature of Confucius**

(a) Dr. Hu Shih. "Confucius was essentially a statesman and reformer." (*The Development of the Logical Methods in Ancient China*, p. 21) In another place he said that Confucius "was a historian of importance and did his work as a teacher." (*Encyclopedia of Social Science*, article on Confucius, by Hu Shih)

(b) Professor Ku Chieh-keng. "In the period of *The Spring and Autumn Annals*, Confucius was a Chun-tzu[165] or 'Superior Man'; in the period of the Warring States he was a Sheng Jen[166] or a 'Sage'; in Western Han he was a Chiao Chu[167] or the 'Lord of Religion'; after Eastern Han he was again recognized as Sheng Jen; and at present he is once more becoming a Chun-tzu." (*Ku Shih Pien*[168], Vol. 2, pp. 130-140)

(c) Dr. Leonard Shihlien Hsu. He regards Confucius as a great political philosopher. (See his great work *The Political Philosophy of Confucianism*, published in London, 1932)

(d) Dr. Ch'en Huan chang. He regards Confucius as a great Economist. (See his doctorate thesis at Columbia University, U.S.A. *The Economic Principles of Confucius and His School*, published in New York, 1911, in 756 pages)

(e) Dr. Fung Yu-lan. "Confucius was, in short, primarily an Educationalist." (See *A History of Chinese Philosophy* by Fung Yu-lan, translated by Derk Bodde, 1937, pp. 46-54)

(f) Dr. Lin Yutang. In his popular book of 1963, *My Country and My People*, he regards Confucius as merely a "good old school teacher", and not a "political thinker." "It is a queer irony of fate," he says, "that the good old school teacher, Confucius, should ever be called a political thinker, and that his moral molly-coddle stuff should ever be honoured with the name of a 'political' theory. The idea of a government by virtue and by benevolent rulers is so fantastic that it cannot deceive a college sophomore." (Lin Yutang, *My Country and My People*, 1936) In 1938 he published another book entitled *The Wisdom of Confucius*, in which he regards Confucius as a wise moral teacher whose "fundamental view-point concerning the conduct of life and society" he believes "will still hold its own" in the modern world. (*The Wisdom of Confucius*, published in New York, 1938, p. 4)

E. The Objective of This Thesis

From the above analysis the importance of Confucius in Chinese history and civilization can readily be seen. Different opinions about this great personage have been formed in different periods of the long history of China. At the zenith of his fame no high-sounding title or honour was too great for him; at the nadir of his fortunes he was accused of being responsible for all the sufferings of his country and his people.

The objective of this thesis is two-fold. In the first place, it is hoped that through the study of the philosophy of Confucius, with special reference to its educational implications, it may be clearly seen that Confucius was, above all else, an ideal teacher. His philosophy as implied in his treatment of teaching materials to be found in the Classics (See chapter "On Confucius in relation to the Classics"), and in the aims, substance and methods of his teachings, tends to show that he was primarily a great teacher.

In the second place, it is also hoped that through the study of such educational implications of his philosophy, a contribution may be made to the modern science and philosophy of education; and that it may also help to bring to the Occident a knowledge of the extent and the richness of the culture of China, and so produce a better appreciation and understanding of the Chinese people, as represented by one of their most respected teachers, Confucius.

The following chapters will deal separately with each of such implications, namely:

On the relation of Confucius to the Classics (his teaching materials)   .

On the aims of his teaching
On the substance of his teaching
On the methods of his teaching

28

F. Source Material Used in This Study

One of the most difficult problems in the study of Confucius, as well as any historical research in ancient Chinese philosophy, is the choice of source material. On the one hand, there is such a tremendous amount of material that the task of selection has become very difficult. For example, in the section on Classics, of *A Classified Catalogue of Chinese Books in the Sino-Japanese Library of the Harvard-Yenching Institute at Harvard University*,[169] there are listed already 3131 Chinese books on Confucian Classics, and these have been classified and catalogued by the Harvard-Yenching Institute at Harvard University. There are still many books on the Classics, and still more books written about Confucius, that have not been regarded as Confucian Classics, which are not included in that catalogue.

On the other hand, through modern scientific methods of the study of the Classics, the problem of the authenticity of the present-day Classics, as such, has become acute. It has been discovered that there are spurious passages and forged books in the so-called Classics. This problem will be dealt with more fully in Chapter Three of this thesis. It is sufficient to mention here the fact that it is impossible to study Confucius by using indiscriminately all the Confucian Classics without involving him in very serious inconsistencies. For example, Confucius' opinion about God as recorded in *The Book of Changes* was that of a rationalist. God, there, is almost identical with the impersonal natural law of the universe; while in *The Analects*, Confucius is depicted as a very religious gentleman, believing in a personal God and seeking to carry out His Holy Will. (See Chapter 5, "The substance of his teaching")

Most of the present texts of the "Six Classics", which have been traditionally believed to be the work of Confucius, either written, or "expunged and rectified" by him, have been much mutilated by later scholars, especially in the period of the Former Han, through careless or intentional adding or taking out of passages of the original books. It is very difficult if not impossible to study Confucius from his own works alone. These "Six Classics" together with their Commentaries were all valuable for the study of the thought and system of Confucianism, but they are not all equally valuable for the study of the teachings of Confucius himself. The best and most reliable way to study Confucius, the writer holds, is not primarily and directly from the "Six Classics" and their Commentaries, as most of the writers who have written on the life and teaching of Confucius have done; but rather, in the first place, from the more reliable records of his immediate disciples, concerning the life and teaching of their Master, and, in the second place, from the more genuine writings of some of the greatest Confucian scholars in the period nearest to Confucius' time, and such writings have been generally accepted as the most authentic interpretation of Confucius by the scholars in later generations.

So the scheme of this thesis is, in the first place, to take *The Analects* as the basis for the study of the life and teaching of Confucius as recorded and preserved by his immediate disciples. *The Analects* is the only book among the classics which nearly all sound scholars in different periods have accepted as the most authentic work of the age of Confucius. Even Chien Hsun-t'ung, one of the most critical of modern scholars, admits the authenticity of *The Analects*. "*The Analects*," he said, "is the only reliable source in the study of Confucius, yet even then it contains a large number of spurious statements." (*Ku Shih Pien*, Vol. 1, pp. 67-82) There are three slightly different versions of *The Analects*: namely, the Ancient Version[170], the Ch'i Version[171] and the Lu Version[172]. (See *Han Shu* "I Wen Chih"[173]) The best version, which is to be used in this study, is the Lu Version which was used in the State of Lu, the native state of Confucius, (See Kang Yu-wei's *Lun-yu Chu Hsu*[174]), and which differs in some important places from the Ku or Ancient Version, the version which has been commonly used. For example, in the Ancient Version, book seven, chapter 16, the word "I"[175], meaning "change", is written in the Lu Version as "I"[176], meaning "also", the same sound but with a different meaning. So the whole passage in the Lu Version instead of being translated as "If some years were added to my life, I would give 50 to the study of 'I' (Changes), and then I might come to be without great faults", should be translated as "If some years were added to my life I would study at fifty, and then 'also' I might come to be without great faults". Having taken *The Analects* as the basis, the writer is also drawing freely from Confucius' sayings in other classics and writings which agree with the ideas or spirit of the sayings of Confucius in *The Analects*. This will represent the teachings of Confucius according to his immediate disciples.

In the second place, the writer is taking Mencius (372-289 B.C.) and Hsun-tzu (308-213 B.C.) to represent the two distinct schools of interpretation of the teachings of Confucius which have developed from the death of Confucius up to the present. Mencius, like St. Paul in the Christian theology, Plato in the Greek philosophy, and Froebel in the modern educational theory, had the tendency to put more emphasis on the human mind—the motive, idea, or nature of man; while Hsun-tzu like St. James, Aristotle, and Herbart had the tendency to put more emphasis on human action in the outside world. They all followed the same masters and tried to be faithful to them: Mencius and Hsun-tzu to Confucius, St. Paul and St. James to Jesus, Plato and Aristotle to Socrates, and Froebel and Herbart to Pestalozzi; but they disagreed with each other about the interpretations of their respective masters. Professor Kuo Shao Yu[177], divided all followers of Confucius in different ages into two main groups: the Wu Wai[178] and the Chu Nei[179] or the "extrovert" and the "introvert." (*Ku Shih Pien*, Vol. w, pp. 253-254) Hsun-tzu best represents the former group, and Mencius the latter. In the later periods, Hsun-tzu's interpretation of Confucius was forcefully brought forward and amplified by Chucius[180] (1130-1200), and Mencius' position was ably defended and elaborated by Lu Hsiang Shan[181] (A.D. 1139-1192) and Wang Yang-ming[182] (A.D. 1472-1528). Neither of these two groups could fully represent its Master, Confucius, but both groups taken together would make a fairly justifiable representation of their Master.

Mencius' view can chiefly be found in the following works:

(a) The seven books of *Mencius*. *Meng Tzu* or *Mencius* has been generally considered a genuine product of the disciples of Mencius; and a large part of the book was probably edited by Mencius himself. The historian Ssu-ma Ch'ien states that Mencius, "with the disciples of Wan Chang[183], wrote prefaces to the *Books of Poetry* and *History*, set forth the meanings of Confucius, and prepared the works of Mencius in seven books." (Text in Legge's *The Chinese Classics*, Vol. 2, p. 1) Since the Sung dynasty it has been regarded as one of the "Four Gospels" of Confucianism.

(b) *The Chung Yung*. *The Chung Yung* or *The Doctrine of the Mean*, another of the four Confucian Gospels, can also be taken as representing the views of Mencius and his school. According to Ssu-ma Ch'ien, *The Chung Yung* was written by Tzu-ssu[184], one of the immediate disciples of Confucius. (See *Shih Chi*, Chap. entitled "The Life of Confucius"[185]), and Hsun-tzu spoke about Tzu-ssu and Mencius as belonging to the same school. (See *Hsun-tzu*, Chap. entitled "Fei Shih Erh Tzu"[186] or "Criticisms on Twelve Philosophers") Dr. Fung Yu-lan thinks that the first chapter, and the section from chapter 20, verse 17, to chapter 33, that is, the end of *The Chung Yung*, were probably the work of Mencius; the section from chapter 2 to chapter 20, verse 16 was probably the work of Tzu-Ssu; they both, however, belonged to the same school and shared more or less the same points of view. (See *Ku Shih Pien*, Vol. 4, pp. 183-184)

Hsun-tzu's view can chiefly be found in the following works:

(a) The 32 chapters of his own work now compiled in one book under his name, Hsun-tzu.

(b) *The Ta Hsueh*, or *The Great Learning*, one of the four Confucian Gospels. (See Fung Yu-lan's article: *Ta Hsueh Wei Hsun Hsueh*[187], or "*The Great Learning* as the Learning of Hsun-tzu's Schools", *Ku Shih Pien*, Vol. 4, pp. 176-182)

(c) Some portions in *Hs'ao Tai Li Chi*[188] or *The Younger Tai's Records of the Rites*, and *Ta Tai Li Chi*[189] or *The Elder Tai's Records of the Rites*. The following are some of the chapters in the two Tai's

Records which resemble the work of Hsun-tzu.

Ta Tai or Hsiao Tai Records	Names of the Chapters	Resembling Names of the Chapters in Hsun-tzu
Hsiao Tai	San Nien Wen 三年问	Li Lun 礼论
Ta Tai	Li San Pen 礼三本	
Ta Tai	Ai Kung Wen Wu I 哀公问五义	Ai Kung 哀公
Hsiao Tai	Yueh Chi 乐记	Yueh Lun 乐论
Hsiao Tai	Hsiang Ying Chiu I 乡饮酒义	
Hsiao Tai	P'in I 聘义	Fa Hsing 法行
		Yu Tso 宥坐
Ta Tai	Ch'uan Hsueh 劝学	Ch'uan Hsueh 劝学
		Hsiu Shen 修身
Ta Tai	Tseng-tzu Li Shih 曾子立事	Ta Lueh 大略

All the above resemblances should be interpreted to mean that the two Records incorporated Hsun-tzu's works, and not that Hsun-tzu copied the writings from the Records; because the *Records of Li* have been generally recognized to be a collection of works of different Confucian schools of the Han dynasty. (See *Ku Shih Pien*, Vol. 4, pp. 94-115).

CHAPTER II

THE BACKGROUND TO
THE TEACHING OF CONFUCIUS

OUTLINE

A. The Political Background
(A) Interstate relationship
1. Wars prevalent among different states
(a) Some reasons for wars
(1) The decline of the power of the central government
(2) The collapse of the feudal system
(3) The selfishness of different states
   a. Struggle for leadership
   b. Struggle for the expansion of territories
   c. Struggle for wealth
(b) The cruelty of wars
2. Treaties and alliances
(a) The treaty at Kuei Ch'iu
(b) The league of states at Sung
(B) Political systems
(a) The patriarchal system
(b) The feudal system
(c) The military system
(1) The development of more centralized control: in the States of Ch'i, Chin and Ch'u
(2) The expansion of army and military equipment
(3) Development of written regulations and laws

B. The Social Background
1. The gradual breakdown of feudalism
(a) The decline of aristocracy
(b) The rise of the lowly and unprivileged class
2. Some aspects of social evils
(a) General moral disorder
(b) The extravagance of the rich and the misery of the poor

(c) Corrupt government: numerous cases of regicide, heavy
    taxation, suffering of the common people
(d) Thieves and robbers prevalent
3. Increase of production, cities, wealth, and travelling facilities
   leading to the rise of the middle class people

C. The Intellectual Background
1. Educational background
. (1) Literature in the early Chou period
(2) Materials for writing
(3) School system
(4) Courses of study
(5) Respect for teachers
2. Philosophical background: unreliability of the traditional belief
   of the systems of philosophy before Confucius
(1) Pessimists
(2) Conservatives
(3) Reformers: Shu Hsiang, Tzu Ch'an, Yen Ying, and others
3. Religious Background
(1) The conception of God or Heaven
(2) The conception of spirits
(3) The means of communication with God and spirits: through
    the revelation of God, prayers, sacrifices, divination and
    magic

D. Life of Confucius

Four general backgrounds to the teaching of Confucius are to be considered in this chapter. They are the political background, the social background, the intellectual background, and the life history of Confucius himself. A study of them may help us to understand better some of the sources of the teaching of Confucius.

A. The Political Background

(A) Interstate Relationship

1. Wars Prevalent Among Different States

During the Spring and Autumn period (722-481 B.C.), in which Confucius lived, it is recorded in *The Spring and Autumn Annals* that there were 61 Cheng[1] or wars of invasion, 212 Fa[2] or wars of attack, 23 Chan[3] or battles, 44 Wei[4] or besiegements, and 27 Ju[5] or entrances, that is, of the conquering army into a conquered city or state.

As a result of these wars, many of the smaller states were conquered and their territories annexed by the few great powers. It has been estimated that at the beginning of the Chou dynasty, there were at least eight hundred vassal states, but at about the end of the fifth century before Christ, the numerous states were reduced to seven powers with a few buffer states subsisting between them. Toward the last quarter of the third century B.C. all the "contending states" were conquered by the State of Ch'in. Thus ended the long period of interstate warfare.

(a) Some reasons for the wars

(1) The decline of the power of the Central Government

After Wu Wang[6] conquered the Shang (Yin) empire, he parcelled out the kingdom to royal relatives. After the first strong Chou rulers, the dynastic house became enfeebled and power gradually passed to the feudal nobles of various states. In his time, Confucius, for example, murmured:

"It is now five generations since revenues of the states were left to the ducal house. It is now four generations since the powers of government have passed into the hands of the great officers. Therefore, the descendents of the three Huan (the great ancestors of the House of Chou) have lost all power and are now living in obscurity!" (*The Analects*, 16.3)

It is true that there was still a nominal emperor of the Chou empire, holding a theoretical sovereignty over the feudal states, but, in fact, he had little power even in the area directly under his rule. He became so insignificant, that neither Confucius in his time nor Mencius later, who went about drumming up support of various feudal state rulers for their doctrines, even bothered to go and see the emperor. This seemed to be a contradiction of Confucius' own political and social theory of an ideal social order, upholding loyalty to the highest authority. But the situation was so bad that the power of the emperor had long dwindled to nothing, and there was no point for either one of them trying to see the emperor at all.

(2) The collapse of the feudal system

The collapse of the feudal system which had been highly developed in China during the Western Chou period (1122-771 B.C.), with its moral standards and its social, economic and political principles and practices, was one of the important reasons for the interstate anarchy and wars.

Under the feudal system of ancient China, all land in the whole empire was ultimately the possession of the emperor. Thus *The Book of Poetry* says: "Under the whole heaven, every spot is the sovereign's ground; to the borders of the land, every individual is the sovereign's subject." (2,6,1,2) *Tso Chuan*, a commentary on *The Spring and Autumn Annals* by Tso Chiu-ming of the Chou dynasty also states: "The dominion of the Son of Heaven extends everywhere. The feudal lords have their own defined boundaries. Such is the ancient rule. Within the state and kingdom, what ground is there which is not the ruler's? What individual of all whom the ground supports is there who is not the ruler's subject?" So when the Royal House of Chou invested the male branches of its family with land grants, those so invested acted both as political rulers and as economic landholders. These feudal lords, in their turn, divided this land among their relatives, and these relatives again among the common people for cultivation. The common people could not themselves own land, and so were mere agricultural serfs of their political and economic overlords.

With the collapse of the feudal system during the Spring and Autumn period, came the decline of the sense of loyalty and faithfulness of the feudal princes towards their monarch, of the ministers towards their princes, or of the common people towards their overlords. So during the time of Confucius, not only the emperor had no power over the feudal princes, but also many of the feudal princes had little power over their barons or ministers. For example, the State of Lu, which was Confucius' native state, was actually ruled in his time by three families: Chi,[7] Meng,[8] and Shu-sun.[9] Again, in 505 B. C., the Baron of Chi was arrested by his minister, Yang Ho, and *The Historical Records* says, "Henceforth Yang behaved all the more arrogantly toward the Baron Huan of Chi, but on his part Baron Huan of Chi had also usurped the authority of the Duke". (*Life of Confucius*)

(3) The selfishness of the different states

The selfishness of different feudal states, especially of some more powerful states, eventually led to war. They struggled for leadership, for the expansion of their territories, and for the wealth of the other states.

a. Struggle for leadership

With the decline of the feudal system and the power of the central government, numerous duchies, baronics, and townships, which had emerged as independent states, fought against one another for supremacy. It seems there were five states more powerful than the rest, and they rose one after another to a place of supreme importance. As to which they were, historians never agree. But the common reckoning is of the principalities of Ch'i,[10] Sung,[11] Chin,[12] Ch'in,[13] and Ch'u.[14] These states were normally at war, with the invading barbarians and with one another. So this period, the Spring and Autumn period, was known as the period of the "Five Chiefs" or Wu Pa.[15] They were condemned by Mencius as sinners against the "Three Sage-kings" for, he says, "The Five Chiefs dragged the princes to punish other princes, and hence I say that they were sinners against the Three Sage-kings". (*Mencius*, 6,2,7,2)

   b. Struggle for the expansion of territories

   Han Fei-tzu[16] (*d.* 233 B.C.) said that during the rule of Chuang Kung[17] (612-589 B.C.), the state of Ch'u conquered 26 states and expanded the territory by 3,000 li; during the rule of Huan Kung[18] (683-641 B.C.) the state of Ch'i conquered 30 states and also expanded the territory by 3,000 li. (Vol. 2, Ch. 6, on Yu Tu)[19] And such was the case with other great states.

   c. Struggle for the wealth of other states

   One of the chief reasons for the constant wars was economic, a struggling for wealth. The customary way of evading an invasion was through various offerings. The following are some quotations from *Tso Chuan*:

   In the 14th year of Duke Hsuan[20] of Lu (594 B.C.), Meng Hsien-tzu[21] said to the Duke: "I have heard that the way in which a small state escapes a great one is by sending to it friendly missions and paying tribute, for which a hundred things are set forth in the court-yard."

   In the 24th year of Duke Hsiang of Lu,[22] (548 B.C.), "Fang Hsuan-tzu[23] was Chief Minister of Chin, and the offerings required of the different states became increasingly heavy, so that the people of Cheng were disturbed about it."

   In the 8th year of Duke Hsiang, (564 B.C.) Tzu Ssu[24] of Cheng said: "To pay the comer a reverent tribute of silks is the way for a small state. With cattle, gems, and silks, on our two borders, we can ingratiate ourselves with the stronger power, and thus protect the people. The enemy will then do us no harm, and the people will not be distressed."

(b) The cruelty of wars

Of the cruelty and suffering attendant upon the frequent wars, the following quotations from *The Spring and Autumn Annals* and *The Historical Records* will give some idea:

In the 28th year of Duke Hsi of Lu[25] (631 B.C.), "The Duke of Ch'in besieged the capital of Ts'ao,[26] and in an attack on one of its gates, many of his soldiers were killed. The people of Ts'ao took their bodies, and exposed them on the top of the wall."

In the 15th year of Duke Hsuan of Lu[27] (693 B.C.), Ch'u besieged Sung, "Hua Yuan of Sung[28] went up to the couch of Tzu Fan,[29] and roused him, saying, 'My master has sent me to inform you of our distress. In the city we are exchanging our children and eating them, and splitting up their bones for fuel'."

In the 8th year of Duke Hsiang of Lu[30] (564 B.C.), a messenger was sent from the State of Cheng to tell the Duke of Chin about the havoc made by the State of Ch'u to his State: "It (Ch'u) has burned all the stations on our borders; it has come insultingly up to our walls and suburbs. The multitudes of our people, husbands and wives, men and women, had no houses left in which to save one another. They have been completely destroyed, with no one to appeal to. If the fathers and elder brothers have not perished, the sons and younger brothers have done so. All were full of sorrow and distress, and there was none to protect them."

A song of a soldier: (*Ode*, number 234, verses 1 and 2)

"What leaves are not yellow!
What day do we not march!
What man is not wandering,
Serving in some corner of the kingdom!

What leaves have not turned purple!
What man is not torn from his wife!
Mercy be on us soldiers:
Are we not also men?"
(*The Book of Poetry*, Pt. 2, Bk. 8,10)

2. Treaties and Alliances

There were numerous treaties and alliances concluded between the various states during this period. *The Spring and Autumn Annals* and its *Three Commentaries* mention more than 600 times the term Meng,[31] a Treaty or Alliance. (See Harvard-Yenching Institute, Sinological Index series, supplement No. 2, "Combined Concordances to Ch'un-ch'iu, Kung-yang, Ku-liang and Tso-chuan," Vol. 3, 3/82877) They were formed sometimes for self-protection, as most of the small states did, sometimes for aggression, as most of the "Five Chiefs" did by "dragging the princes to punish other princes", and sometimes really for the sake of securing interstate peace and safety, as the famous League of States in 546 B.C., called by Hsiang Hsu[32] at the capital city of the State of Sung. Unfortunately, resembling conditions in modern Europe and Asia, their treaties were ultimately scrapped, and alliances and big and little ententes never lasted long. It is worthwhile to mention here one or two of those treaties in order to show something of their nature, and the reasons for their failure to bring about interstate peace. This would furnish not only problems which faced Confucius in his days, but also very similar problems facing the world to-day.

(a) The treaty at Kuei Ch'iu,[33] in the ninth year of Duke Hsi of Lu.[34] (651 B.C.)

Representatives from eight states came together in Kuei Ch'iu, for a solemn treaty, namely, "The Duke of Lu,[35] the king's chief minister the Duke of Chou,[36] the Marquis Ch'i,[37] the son (of the late Duke) of Sung,[38] the Marquis of Wei,[39] the Earl of Cheng,[40] the Baron of Hsu,[41] and the Earl of Ts'ao."[42]

According to *Mencius*, the treaty that was signed contained six articles: "The first injunction in their agreement was, 'Slay the unfilial; change not the son who has been appointed heir; exalt not a concubine to the rank of wife.' The second was, 'Honour the worthy, and maintain the talented, to give distinction to the virtuous.' The third was, ' Respect the old, and be kind to the young; be not forgetful of strangers and travellers.' The fourth was, 'Let not offices be hereditary, nor let officers be pluralists. In the selection of officers let the object be to get the proper man. Let not a ruler take it on himself to put to death a great officer.' The fifth was, 'Follow no crooked policy in making embankments. Impose no restrictions on the sale of grain. Let there be no promotions without first announcing them to the emperor.' (Sixthly), it was then said, 'All we who have united in this agreement shall hereafter maintain amicable relations.' " (*Mencius, 6,2,7,3*)

The chief reasons for its failure were, in the first place, that the treaty lacked universality; there were too few states represented, especially some of the most important like the State of Ch'u,[43] Chin,[44] and Ch'in.[45] In the second place, there was the selfish motive of the leader. It is recorded in *Tso Chuan* that when the Prime Minister of the king returned to the capital he met the Marquis of Chin on the way, and said to him: "You need not go on to the meeting. The Marquis of Ch'i (the leader of the league) does not make virtue his first object, and is most earnest about what is remote. Thus in the north he invaded the Hill Jung;[46] on the south, he invaded Ch'u; and in the west, he has assembled this meeting. . . . "

(b) The League of States at Sung

In the 27th year of Duke Hsiang of Lu,[47] (546 B.C.) when Confucius was still a small boy aged five, a minister of the state of Sung, named Hsiang Hsu[48] thinking of the cruelty and foolishness of war, decided to attempt to make an end of it. He was well acquainted with the leading ministers in several states, and presented his scheme to them. He began with Chin, the nominal leader, whose Prime Minister Han Hsuan Tzu[49] said: "War is a scourge of the people, an insect that eats up the resources (of a state), and the greatest calamity of the small states. If any one should try to put an end to it, though we think it cannot be done, we must sanction his proposal. If we do not, Ch'u will do so, and will proceed to call the states together, so that we shall lose the presidency of covenants." Chin agreed to the proposal, therefore, and was followed by Ch'u. The ministers of Ch'i at first opposed the plan, but one of their wise men, Ch'en Wen Tzu,[50] reminded them and said: "Since Chin and Ch'u have agreed, how can we decline? And men will say that we refused to sanction the stoppage of wars, which will certainly make our people disaffected. Of what use will it be for us to decline it?" So Ch'i agreed and was followed by the State of Ch'in. Delegates from fourteen states (including Sung) met at the capital of Sung, as if to be present at the meeting. Two months, however, were consumed in the negotiations, for the powerful states were all mutually jealous and wasted much time manoeuvering for precedence, and the result was that only nine states (not including Sung) actually took part in signing the covenant of preserving inter-state peace and order. Ch'i and Ch'in were exempted from it because of its peculiar nature and their own greatness, Chu[51] and T'eng[52] were exempted because of their weakness. The covenant was renewed five years later, but soon lost its force and utterly failed to achieve its announced purpose to put an end to war. (See *Tso Chuan*)

The chief weakness of this League was the jealousy and selfishness of some of the more powerful states. The following incident as recorded in *Tso Chuan* shows clearly the attitude of one of the most important members of the League, the State of Ch'u. "On the Hsin Chi[53] day they were about to convenant outside the western gate, when the men of Ch'u wore their armour under their outer clothes. Pei Chou Li,[54] (the Grand-administrator) said (to Tzu Mu,[55] the Prime Minister of Ch'u), 'The multitude of the states are assembled here, and is it not undesirable (now) to show them our want of good faith? The states expect good faith from Ch'u, and on that account they came to (indicate) their submission to it. If we do not keep faith, we are throwing away that by which we must effect the submission of the states.' He then earnestly begged that the armour might be put off; but Tzu-mu said, 'There has been no faith between Chin and Ch'u for long, we have to do merely with getting the advantage. If we get our will, what is the use of having good faith?' "

All the misery and suffering which resulted from wars, and the selfishness and unfaithfulness of different states, which were chief reasons for international troubles, came to the knowledge and direct experience of Confucius and influenced his teaching to a very great extent.

(B) Political Systems

At the time of Confucius there were three types of political systems already known to the world, namely, the patriarchal, the feudal, and the military systems.

(a) The patriarchal system

The political system before the Chou dynasty (1122-221 B.C.) can be regarded in general as patriarchal. The king was the sire, and his officers were responsible elders of different departments and districts, such as every father of a household is to its inmates. He derived his power chiefly from his forefathers, and people obeyed him because he was the descendant of those persons whom their forefathers had obeyed. So his chief duties were to offer sacrifices to his ancestors, and to protect his people, the descendants of the people of his ancestors, from their enemies or other calamities. In other words, the ancient Chinese people were ruled largely by the spirits of their ancestors—the early fathers of their families. When P'an Keng migrated his people to his new capital at Yin about 1400 B.C., and met the opposition of his people, he gathered them together and gave them his paternal admonition saying:

"Come, all of you; I will announce to you my instructions. Take counsel how to put away your selfish thoughts. Do not with haughty disregard of me follow after your own ease. . . . Formerly, the kings, my predecessors, and your forefathers and fathers, shared together the ease and labours of the state; how should I dare to lay undeserved inflictions on you? For generations the toils of your families have been approved, and I will not conceal your goodness. Now when I offer the great sacrifices to my predecessors, your forefathers are present to share in them. They observe the happiness I confer and the sufferings I inflict, and I cannot dare to reward virtue that does not exist. . . . Do I force you by my majesty? My object is to support and nourish you all. I think of the toils of my predecessors, who are now the spiritual sovereigns, for your ancestors; I would in the same way greatly nourish you, and cherish you. . . ."

The chief principle ruling such a system was the principle of filial piety or Hsiao.[56] The king in order to show his filial piety to his ancestors should try his best to protect his people who were the descendants of the people of his ancestors; and the people in order to show their filial piety to their ancestors should try their best to help their king who was the descendant of the kings of their ancestors. So it is natural through the love of their parents, that the rulers should act justly toward their people, and the people should be good to their rulers and to one another. This is what Mencius meant when he said: "Benevolence and righteousness were natural to Yao and Shun" (*Mencius*, 7, 1, 30, 1) the two ancient Chinese Sage-kings, as "their course was simply that of filial piety and fraternal duty." (*Mencius*, 6,2,2,4) They regarded their people as their own children or younger brothers and their people, in turn, regarded them as their fathers and elder brothers. So when Yao died, it was recorded, "The people acted as if they were mourning for a father or mother for three years, and up to the borders of the four seas every sound of music was hushed." (*Shu Ching*, "*Shun Tien*", cp. *Mencius* 5. 1. 4. 1)[57]

(b) The feudal system

The politico-social system founded on land-tenure of fiefs was prevalent in Europe from the ninth to the fifteenth century A.D., but in China it was actually carried out in the early part of the Chou dynasty. When the Chou people succeeded in overthrowing the Shang dynasty and subduing other hostile peoples, most of the conquered territories were given out as fiefs to members of the royal family, and to some great officials as compensation for military services. All the ministers and great officers within those feudal territories or states were also members, or those who were intimately related to members, of the ruling house, and held their offices in hereditary perpetuity, whereas the common people were denied all share in the political power, and were treated as serfs.

In the twenty-eighth year of Duke Chao of Lu (514 B.C.), Wei Tzu[58] said to Ch'eng Chuan:[59] "When Wu Wang[60] overthrew Shang and conquered the whole world, he gave fifteen (feudal) states to his brothers, and forty states to members of the House of Chi[61] (the

Royal House)." (See *Tso Chuan*)

Hsun-tzu said: "The Duke of Chou[62] established seventy-one (feudal) states, and members of the House of Chi alone occupied fifty-three of them." (*Hsun-tzu*, chapter entitled "Ju Shuo"[63])

Tso Chuan, under the seventh year of Duke Chao of Lu[64] (566 B.C.), states: "As the days have their divisions in periods of ten each, so men have their ten ranks. It is by these that inferiors serve their superiors, and that superiors perform their duties to the spirits. Therefore, the king[65] has the ruler[66] (of each feudal state) as his subjects; the rulers have the great prefects[67] as their subjects; the prefects have their officers;[68] the officers have their subalterns;[69] the subalterns have their multitude of petty officers;[70] the petty officers have their assistants;[71] the assistants have their employees;[72] the employees have their menials.[73] For the menials there are helpers;[74] for the horses there are grooms;[75] and for the cattle there are cowherds.[76] And thus there is provision for all things."

With a government thus maintained by a feudal aristocracy holding hereditary offices and fiefs, it was inevitable that the social organization should also be based on an elaborately graded patriarchy. The most important factors that bound together such an elaborate system were the controlling force, both spiritual and material, on the part of the superiors, and loyalty on the part of the inferiors. As soon as the superiors lost their controlling force, and the inferiors lost their sense of loyalty, the whole system collapsed.

(c) The military system

Beginning from the early part of the Spring and Autumn period there was the gradual collapse of the feudal system, and the ensuing development of the military system. This movement reached its climax in 221 B.C. when Ch'in Shih Huang succeeded in unifying all China by his military power, and regulated the royal families of all states except that of Ch'in to the level of the common people. Three outstanding characteristics which marked the development of the military system by the time of Confucius may be specially mentioned here.

(1) The development of centralized control over the political,

economic and military powers within the states. Instead of leaving whole districts or estates to the control of the feudal landlords or vassals, the rulers of many of the larger states began to exercise more direct control over them. The following are the three most powerful states by the time of Confucius:

   a. The State or Ch'i. When Kuan Chung[77] was the prime minister of Ch'i he introduced many reforms, one of which was that he "so organized the Interior Affairs as to facilitate the military orders".[78] His plan was as follows: "Five families were formed into a Kuei,[79] and the organization of five people (one from each family) was called a Wu,[80] and was led by a Kuei Chang.[81] Ten Kueis were formed into one Li,[82] and the organization of the fifty people (five from each Kuei) was called a Hsiao Jung[83] and was led by a Li Yu Ssu.[84] Four Lis made one Lien,[85] and the organization of the two hundred people (fifty from each Li) was called a Tsu,[86] and was led by a Lien Chang.[87] Ten Liens made one Hsiang,[88] and the organization of the two thousand people (two hundred from each Lien) was called a Lu,[89] and was led by a Hsiang Liang Jen.[90] Five Hsiangs made one Shih,[91] and the organization of the ten thousand people (two thousand from each Hsiang) was called a Chun,[92] and was led by the leaders or Shuai[93] of the five Hsiangs." (See *Ku Yu*, Vol. 6, *Ch'i Yu*, pp. 7-8) Thus the military power of the whole state was put under the control of the central government.

   b. The State of Chin. The following ways were used in order to obtain control of the central authority over the former feudal estates or districts

   First, by reducing the number of members of the royal families. *Tso Chuan*, under the 25th year of Duke Chuang of Lu,[94] (669 B.C.) states: "In winter, Duke Hsieng[95] of Chin[96] besieged Chu,[97] and slew all the sons of the former dukes." Under the second year of Duke Hsuan of Lu,[98] (607 B.C.) *Tso Chuan* says: "At the time of troubles occasioned by Li Chi,[99] and oath was taken in Chin that they would not maintain in the state any of the sons of their dukes; and from that time on they had no families in it which were branches of the ruling house."

   Secondly, by centralizing control over the military power under the central authority. For example, one of the reforms under Duke Wen of Chin[100] (636-628 B.C.) was that he put the military power of the "six armies" under the control of the "six civil administrators" of the central government.[101]

Thirdly, by separating the administrative control from the economic control over a given district. For example Hsien Chen,[102] who was captain of the Central Army[103] of the central government during the time of the Duke Wen of Chin, had the district Yuan[104] as his "eating district" or Shih I,[105] that is to say, he had economic control over that district but no power of control over the civil administration, which was given to Chao Shuai[106] who was the Tai Fu[107] or governor of that district. (See *Tso Chuan*, under the 25th year of Duke Hsi of Lu,[108] 635 B.C.)

c. The State of Ch'u

The administrative system in the State of Ch'u was from the beginning considerably different from that of most of the other states. Instead of giving out districts to members of the aristocratic families as land-tenure of fiefs, the rulers of the State of Ch'u chose rather to create local administrative units like Hsien[109] or "districts" (See *Tso Chuan*, under the 11th and 12th years of Duke Hsuan of Lu[110]); some of the offices were hereditary (See *Tso Chuan*, under the 13th year of Duke Chao[111]). There were also several administrative organs in each local unit, like civil and economic organs, as those in the state of Chin. The central power had authority directly over the internal affairs of each of the administrative units. *Tso Chuan*, under the seventh year of Duke Ch'eng of Lu[112] (594 B.C.), states:

"After the siege of the capital of Sung by Ch'u in the 14th year of Duke Hsuan[113] (595 B.C.), when the army returned, Tzu-chung[114] requested that he might receive certain lands of Shen[115] and Lu,[116] as his reward (Shang T'ien),[117] to which the king consented. Wu Ch'en,[118] the governor of Shen (Shen Kung),[119] however, declared the impropriety of the grant, saying, 'It is these lands which make Shen and Lu the states they are. From them they derive the levies with which they withstand the states of the North. Take them away, and there will be no Shen and Lu'. . . ."

(2) The expansion of army and military equipment

It was natural, with the greed and jealousy between the more powerful states and the constant worry of the smaller states about invasions by the powerful neighbouring states, that the army and military equipment should be much increased, and be taken as the chief concern of all the states. The following figures about the number of chariots of war which were actually engaged in wars in different periods would give some idea of the expansion of military preparation.

In the first year of Duke Yin of Lu,[120] 722 B.C., "Duke Chuang of Cheng[121] led 200 chariots to fight against Ching.[122]"

In the second year of Duke Ming of Lu,[123] 660 B.C., Prince Wu Kuei[124] of Ch'i invaded Chao[125] with 300 chariots.

In the 25th year of Duke Chuang of Lu,[126] 666 B.C., Tzu Yuan,[127] the minister of Ch'u,[128] invaded Cheng[129] with 600 chariots.

In the 28th year of Duke Hsi,[130] 632 B.C., Chin used 700 chariots to fight against Ch'u in the battle of Ch'eng P'u.[131]

In the second year of Duke Ch'eng of Lu,[132] 589 B.C., Ch'ueh Keh[133] of Chin used 800 chariots to invade Ch'i.

In the 18th year of Duke Hsiang of Lu,[134] 555 B.C., both Lu and Wei used 1,000 chariots to fight against each other.

In the 25th year of Hsiang, 548 B.C., Tzu Ch'an of Cheng[135] invaded Ch'en with 700 chariots.

In the 13th year of Duke Chao of Lu,[136] 529 B.C., Chin displayed 4,000 chariots in the south of Chu.[137] In the same year Shu Hsiang,[138] prime minister of Chin, also mentioned that there were 4,000 chariots of war in his country.

In the eleventh year of Duke Ai of Lu,[139] 484 B.C., Lu and Wu invaded Ch'i and captured 800 chariots. The actual number of chariots which were engaged in fighting must be several times more than that.

One chariot generally took about ten soldiers, so the number of soldiers engaged in fighting also increased tremendously. With the increase of fighting forces, there developed also military tactics, the methods of attack and defence, etc. Mo Ti,[140] a contemporary of Confucius, for example, was famous for being "skilful in maintaining military defences." (*The Historical Records*, Chap. 74, p. 6)

(3) Development of written regulations and laws

One of the most important characteristics of a military organization is that social order is maintained not by emphasizing primarily the virtue of filial piety, as in a patriarchal organization, nor by putting emphasis upon the virtue of loyalty, as in a feudal organization, but by encouraging people to obey the laws as set up by the rulers. Virtues in the military system, are not so much of personal relationships, as in the case of the other two systems, as of legal dealings.

Tso Chuan, under the sixth year of Duke Wen of Lu, 621 B.C., states that when Chao Tun[141] was in power in the State of Chin, he "appointed regular rules for the various departments of business; adjusted the laws for the various degrees of crime; regulated all criminal and civil actions at law; searched out runaways; ordered the employment of securities and bonds; dealt with old ordinances that had fallen into foul disorder; restored to their original order the distinctions of rank; renewed, according to their normal pattern, offices that had fallen into disuse; brought out men whose path had been stopped, and who were in obscurity."

In the sixth year of Duke Chao of Lu,[142] 536 B.C., Cheng Tzu-ch'an,[143] prime minister of the State of Cheng, ordered "the descriptions of crimes and their punishments to be cast in bronzes."(*Tso Chuan*)

Tso Chuan, under the 29th year of Duke Chao of Lu, 513 B.C., states: "In winter, Chao Yang[144] and Hsun Yin[145] of Chin led a force, and walled Ju Pin,[146] after which they had the (districts of the) state contribute a Ku[147] (equal to 480 catties) of iron, in order to cast penal tripods, on which to inscribe the penal laws prepared by Fan Hsuan-tzu."[148]

Confucius was born and lived during the time when all these political systems, patriarchal, feudal and military were much talked about among the intellectual circles, and practiced in one form or another in different states in different periods. There was no definite theory of political organization that was put into practice by all states, nor was it entirely adopted by any one state in two or three generations. It was a period of rapid political and social upheavals and transformations.

Confucius had no sympathy with the newly developed military system, with its unlimited military preparation, and its emphasis on written laws and regulations, and neglecting the moral codes under the patriarchal and feudal systems. He says: "If the people be led by laws, and uniformity sought to be given them by punishments, they will try to avoid the punishment, but have no sense of shame. If they be led by virtue, and uniformity sought to be given them by Li[149] or rules of proper conduct, they will have a sense of shame, and moreover will become good." (The Analects, 2.3) He was more in sympathy with the feudal system and its patriarchy of political and social grades, but the evils which existed between the different grades of people, he thought, should be modified by the theory and practice of the patriarchal system. So he taught, on the one hand, the Li[150] or the rules of proper conduct, in different ranks and in different places, with the "rectification of names", that is, making the actual in each case to correspond to the name, etc.; but on the other hand, he taught filial piety and paternal love, the chief characteristics of the feudal system, as the essential principles for a good government. These points will be dealt with more fully in later chapters.

B. The Social Background

1. The Gradual Breakdown of Feudalism

The chief reason for the gradual breakdown of feudalism could be attributed to the chaotic condition of the interstate relationship as mentioned above, namely, the numerous wars between states, and the frequent transfer of political allegiance under different treaties and alliances. The lords or members of the aristocratic families of the vanquished states were naturally degraded; while on the other hand, the wars, the demand for diplomatic talents, and for domestic statesmanship, elevated many men of great talent from lowliness and obscurity.

(a) The decline of aristocracy

The Book of Poetry, Tso Chuan and many other records of this period, give many evidences of how the nobles were gradually losing their position and becoming merged with the common people. *Tso Chuan*, for example, under the third year of Duke Hsiang of Lu, 539 B.C., makes the statement: "The Luan,[151] the Ch'ueh,[152] the Hsu,[153] the Yuan,[154] the Hu,[155] the Hsu,[156] the Ch'ing,[157] and the Po[158] (all descendants of great families of the State of Chin) are reduced to the position of menials." Confucius himself originally belonged to the nobility of the State of Sung, and his early ancestor, according to *The Historical Records*, was K'ung Fang-shu, who was a ninth-generation descendant of a king of Sung, and the fourth-generation ancestor of Confucius, who had moved to Lu where the family became impoverished.

The following odes are supposed to be the utterances of an officer who had followed his prince into exile after the downfall of his principality:

"Reduced! Reduced!

Why not return?
If it were not for your person, O Prince,
How should we be here in the mire?''
    (The Book of Poetry, pt. 1, Bk. 3,11)

''Fragments and remnant,
Children of dispersion are we!''
    (The Book of Poetry, pt. 1, Bk, 3,12)

(b) The rise of the lowly and unprivileged class to wealth and positions of power

It is recorded in *Tso Chuan*, for example, that Ning Hsi,[159] a mere carter, while feeding his oxen, attracted the attention of Duke Huan of Ch'i (685-643 B.C.), and so he obtained office; and that Po-li Hsi,[160] while a prisoner of war, was ransomed by Duke Mu of Ch'in. (659-621 B.C.) Many of the disciples of Confucius, who had come from unprivileged classes, rose to wealth and positions of power.

''The sons of boatmen
Are wrapped in furs of the bear and the grisly bear!
And sons of servitude
Form the officers in public employment!''
    (The Book of Poetry, pt. 2, Bk. 5,9)

Through the opportunity of the moment, and the persistent work of Confucius and his followers, education became more popularized. The so-called "Six Disciplinary Arts" (Liao I[161]), the cultural heritage from ancient China, which had been exclusively the possession of the ruling class, were now equally taught to the common people. This gave the common people a better chance to rise to positions of power.

The merchants, who had been despised in society, now through the power of their wealth, gradually rose till they became a very influential body of people in society, and some of them even succeeded in securing very high government positions. Thus *Ch'ien Han Shu* (*History of the Former Han Dynasty*) says:

"With the decline of the House of Chou, the rites (Li[162]) and laws fell into decay. . . . This falling away (from the old standards) reached the point where, among the officials and common people, there was none who did not set the (old) regulations aside and spurn what is fundamental (i.e., agriculture). The peasants became few and the merchants numerous. Of grain there was an insufficiency, and of (commercial) goods a superfluity. . . . Thereupon the merchants circulated goods difficult to obtain (i.e., rare and expensive luxuries); the artisans produced objects of no real utility; and the scholars instituted conduct subversive to morality, in their pursuit for immediate benefits and search for worldly wealth. . . . The grounds and groves of the rich underwent elaborate adornment, and their dogs and horses had a superabundance of meat and grain. . . . While among the common people, though all were (theoretically) of equal rank, some by the power of their wealth could become masters of others". (Chap. 91, p. 3)

The rise of the merchant class may be illustrated by such men as Hsuan Kao, who, while a mere merchant, successfully protected the State of Cheng from the surprise attack of the State of Ch'in in 627 B.C., and Lu Pu-wei,[163] who, from the position of a great trader, became minister of Ch'in, and died in 235 B.C.

2. Some Aspects of Social Evil

(a) General moral disorder

"The world has long been without the principles of truth and right" is a saying characteristic of the time. (*The Analects*, 4.24) Mencius (372-289 B.C.) describes the age of Confucius in these words: "The world had fallen into decay, and truth had faded away. Perverse doctrines and violent deeds had arisen. There were instances of ministers murdering their sovereigns and of sons murdering their fathers. Confucius was afraid." (*Mencius*, 3,2,9,7)

(b) The extravagance of the rich and powerful, and the misery of the poor and oppressed

"The palace of T'ung T'i[164] extends over several li". (*Tso Chuan*, under the 31st year of Duke Hsiang, 542 B.C.)

"Po Yu[165] of Cheng built an underground mansion for the purpose of drinking wine in the night." (*Tso Chuan*, under the 30th year of Duke Hsiang, 543 B.C.)

"Ch'u built the palace of Chang Hua."[166] (*Tso Chuan*, under the seventh year of Duke Chao, 535 B.C.)

"The grain in the ducal stores rots and is eaten by insects while the three classes of the old are cold and starving". (*Tso Chuan*, under the third year of Duke Chao, 539 B.C., the condition in the State of Ch'i as described by Yen P'ing Chung of Ch'i)

"The multitudes of the people are weary and worn, while the duke's mansions are multiplied and most costly." (*Tso Chuan*, under the third year of Duke Chao, 539 B.C., the condition of Chin as described by Shu Hsiang of Chin)[167]

> *"Some enjoy their ease and rest,*
> *And some are worn out in serving the state!*
> *Some lie and loll upon their couches,*
> *And some never cease marching about."*
> *(The Book of Poetry, Pt. 2, Bk. 6, 1)*

> *"The flowers of the bigonia*
> *Are in glorious yellow,*
> *But my heart is sad,*
> *I feel its wound.*

> *The flowers are now gone;*
> *There are only the leaves full green.*
> *Ah! Had I known it would be thus with me,*
> *I had better not have been born.*

> *Hunger has swollen the ewes' heads;*
> *There is nothing but the reflected stars in the fish-trap.*
> *If some men have aught to eat,*
> *Few can get their fill."*
> *(The Book of Poetry, Pt. 2, Bk. 8, 9)*

(c) Corrupt government: numerous cases of regicide, heavy taxation, suffering of the common people

The Spring and Autumn Annals records no less than thirty-six cases of regicide during a period of 234 years, (B.C. 719-485). Take, for example, the general social and political conditions in the native state of Confucius, the State of Lu. During the time when

Confucius lived, the whole state was in virtual chaos. Three families ran things and each strove for advantage; there were dissensions even within these families; plottings and intrigues were so rife that a man of principle would have little inclination to enter politics.

Tso Chuan, under the third year of Duke Chao of Lu, 539 B.C., states how in a long conversation between two leading officials of the states of Ch'i and Chin, namely Yen P'ing Chung of Ch'i,[168] and Shu Hsiang of Chin,[169] they brought out the corruption of their respective government, and the sufferings of their people. Ch'i and Chin, being the most powerful and progressive states of the time, could represent the general condition prevailing in most of the other states. Yen P'ing Chung of Ch'i started first, saying: "The produce of the people's strength is divided into three parts, two of which are paid to the state while only one is left to them for food and clothes (heavy taxation). The grain in the ducal stores rots and is eaten by insects, while the three (classes of the) old suffer hunger and cold. In all the markets of the states (ordinary) shoes are cheap, while those for criminals whose toes have been cut off are expensive. The common people are groaning under all this."

Shu Hsiang of Chin said: "The war-horses are not yoked; the ministers never take the field. There are no men over the duke's chariots, no proper officers over the soldiers. The multitudes of the people are weary and worn while the duke's mansions are multiplied and most costly. The people feel, when they hear the duke's commands, as if they must escape from robbers and enemies. . . . . The rulers go on from day to day without stop, buying all sorrow in pleasure."

Here is a bard who, disgusted with corrupt government and heavy taxation, was leaving his own state with this bitter farewell:

> *"Large rats! Large rats!*
> *Do not eat our millet.*
> *Three years we have tolerated you,*
> *But you have shown no regard for us,*
> *So we will leave you,*
> *And go to that happy land—*

Happy land! Happy land!
Where we shall find our peace."
(*The Book of Poetry*, Pt. 1, Bk. 9, 7)

(d) Thieves and robbers prevalent

With the general dissatisfaction and suffering of the common people, caused by corrupt officials, social injustice and inequality, and wars, together with the general political and social chaos and the breakdown of the moral standards, it is no wonder that there should have been so many cases of murder, theft and robbery during the age of Confucius.

Tso Chuan, under the 31st year of Duke Hsiang, 542 B.C., records what Shih Wen Po of the State of Chin[170] said about the condition of his own state as follows, "Our humble city, owing to the neglect of penal measures, is now full of thieves and robbers." Cheng Tzu-Ch'an[171] of the State of Cheng, also said that in Chin "robbers and thieves move about openly."

It is recorded in *Tso Chuan* under the 21st year of Duke Hsiang of Lu, 552 B.C., that "Consequently, the robbers are rampant in the State of Lu." (See also *The Analects*, 12, 18)

Under the 20th year of Duke Chao of Lu,[172] 522 B.C., *Tso Chuan* states, "The robbers are rampant in the State of Cheng."

In order to punish and guard against thieves and robbers, there was a marked development, as mentioned above, of the penal codes and written laws in some of the states during this period.

3. Increase of Production, Cities, Wealth, and Travelling Facilities Leading to the Rise of the Middle Class People

Pan Ku,[173] writer of *Han Shu*, described this age as an age of marked decrease of farmers, and increase of merchants and artisans. He complained: "With the decline of the House of Chou . . . the peasants became few and the merchants numerous. Of grain there was an insufficiency, and of (commercial) goods a superfluity". Those merchants and artisans produced and circulated many new and luxurious goods which Pan Ku termed as "goods difficult to obtain" and "object of no real utility."

Cities, as centres for circulating merchandise, developed rapidly.

There were several tens of Ch'eng[174] or "cities", which were mentioned in *The Spring and Autumn Annals*. Wealth of the states, as a whole, was also increased. Not only most of the aristocratic families lived luxurious lives but big merchants like Hsuan Kao, Lu Pu-wei, as mentioned above, all accumulated great wealth. *Tso Chuan*, under the year 526 B.C., gives an account about Han Hsuan-tzu, a minister of Chin, who "had a ring of jade, the mate of which belonged to a merchant of Cheng." One of the favourite disciples of Confucius, Tzu-kung,[175] was also a successful merchant. Confucius remarked: "His (commercial) goods are increased by him, and his (business) judgments are often correct." (*The Analects*, 11, 18)

Communication between different states was greatly facilitated, chiefly for military purposes. There were large and well-built roads leading to most of the big cities of different states, on which war-chariots, ox-carts, soldiers, merchants, scholars, officials, etc. could be seen passing to and fro in large numbers. Even the remote northwestern State of Ch'in which had not had much communication with other states in the early part of the Spring and Autumn period, is recorded in *Tso Chuan*, under the first year of Duke Chao of Lu,[176] 541 B.C., as having 1,000 chariots travelling from Ch'in to the State of Chin. Confucius spent a great deal of his lifetime travelling in his cart to and from different states. *Tso Chuan*, under the first year of Duke Chao, also states that the Duke of Chin built a great many river boats for travelling purposes. In *The Spring and Autumn Annals* there are numerous phrases like Kung Ju Chin[177] or Kung Chih Tzu Chin,[178] that is, "Duke going to Chin" or "Duke coming back from Chin". Indeed, judging from these phrases, the dukes in most of the smaller states had frequently to travel from one state to another. The travelling facilities enabled them to do so.

All this—the increase of production, cities, wealth, and travelling facilities—gave rise to the number and importance of the middle class people in society. Strictly speaking, under the feudal system of the early Chou Empire, there were only two classes of people —the overlords, including the emperors (Sons of Heaven), feudal lords and ministers and great officers, and the common people, who being landless, were mere agricultural serfs of their political and economic overlords, serving them in the fields in time of peace, an in the army, if necessary, in time of war. With the decline of the feudal system, the middle class, that is, people between the overlords and the agricultural serfs, gradually came into being and increased rapidly as production, cities, wealth, travelling facilities, etc. increased. This class of people was generally composed of merchants, artisans and unemployed scholars. That is what Pan Ku[179] meant when he said: "With the decline of the House of Chou ... the peasants (agricultural serfs) became few. ... The merchants circulated goods difficult to obtain; the artisans produced objects of no real utility; and the scholars instituted rules of conduct subversive of morality, in their pursuit after immediate benefits, and their search for worldly wealth." (*Han Shu*, Chap. 91, p. 3) This group of scholars or Shih,[180] who "were neither farmers, artisans, nor merchants, and who did not engage in any kind of productive activity, but depended entirely upon others for their support", later on developed into the most influential class of people in Chinese society even up to the present time. (Fung Yu-lan, *History of Chinese Philosophy*, translated by Derk Bodde, p. 52) Confucius, for example, is reported to have had over 3,000 of such scholars as his disciples. His contemporaries, Lao-tzu and Mo-tzu, and later in the period of the Warring States, Mencius, Yang-Chu,[181] Chuang-tzu,[182] and others, had also a great number of followers.

C. The Intellectual Background

Beginning from the time of Confucius, down to the end of the period of the Warring States (221 B.C.), there is to be marked one of the greatest intellectual upheavals in Chinese history. The general political, social and moral chaos, that allowed the greatest freedom of thought, created the situation of a great demand for scholars, and set every keen mind thinking about the best way of bringing about peace and order, which all had a great deal to do with the intellectual upheaval. Another cause for all the vigorous thinking of this age could be attributed to the rich cultural heritage that had come down from the remote past of Chinese civilization. Confucius mentioned many times in *The Analects* the culture of Hsia (*circa* 2205 B.C.-*circa* 1766 B.C.), Shang (*circa* 1766 B.C.-*circa* 1122 B.C.), and the early Chou, which formed the general intellectual background of Confucius' teaching, as well as the teachings of all later philosophers.

"Confucius said: 'The Yin (Shang) dynasty followed the regulations of the Hsia: wherein it took from or added to them may be known. The Chou dynasty has followed the regulations of the Yin: wherein it took from or added to them may be known'." (*The Analects*, 2,23)

"The Master said: 'I could describe the civilization of the Hsia dynasty, but the State of Ch'i[183] cannot render adequate corroboration. I can describe the civilization of the Yin dynasty, but the State of Sung[184] cannot render adequate corroboration. And all because of the deficiency of their records and wise men. Were those sufficient then I could corroborate my views'." (*The Analects*, 3. 9)

"Yen Yuan[185] asked how the government of a country should be administered. The Master said: 'Follow the seasons of the Hsia,

ride in the state carriage of Yin, and wear the ceremonial cap of
Chou. . . .' " (*The Analects*, 15, 10)

But since Confucius was living in the Chou period with its
culture well preserved, it is no wonder that he should have taken
the Chou culture as the chief background of his teaching. "The
Master said: 'Chou had the advantage of viewing the two past
dynasties. How complete and elegant are its regulations! I follow
Chou'." (*The Analects*, 3, 14)

At present we are in possession of a vast amount of literature
which is supposed to have come down from those early ages, Hsia,
Shang and the early Chou and has been incorporated in the Five
Classics. Although most modern critical scholars have doubted the
authenticity of much of that transmitted literature, still a large part
of it has been proved to be genuine, through a very careful
and scientific study. Modern archaeological discoveries of ancient Chinese pottery, oracle bones, bronze vessels, jades, stone
implements, shells, etc. have very much helped the discrimination
and verification of the traditional literature. There are many thousands of inscribed oracle bones of the Shang period that have been
discovered, and about 2,500 different inscribed Shang characters
have already been studied and deciphered. Many bronze vessels
with inscriptions have also been found and carefully investigated.
For example, Dr. H.G. Creel says in his *Birth of China*, "My study of
bronze inscriptions is based on detailed analyses of 219 inscriptions from the Western Chou and 113 Eastern Chou inscriptions".
According to the result of his investigations he says: "Such study
shows that much of the literature corresponds exactly with what
we find on the bronzes." (H.G. Creel, *The Birth of China*, p. 266)
With this transmitted literature, and the data of the archaeological
discoveries in mind, the following three intellectual backgrounds
of Confucius' teaching may be considered, namely, the educational
background, the philosophical background, and the religious background.

1. Educational Background

Both *Li Chi* and *Chou Li* give an elaborate system of education
in the early part of the Chou Empire, but most of it has been

discredited by modern critical scholars, as being only an ideal system wrought out by the scholars of the Han Empire. Nevertheless, judging from the cultural data of the early Chou period, obtained from recent excavations and from the transmitted literature, we must recognize that some form of fairly well organized educational system, more or less similar to that depicted in the Classics, must have existed in the early Chou period. But the fact that education at that time was chiefly concerned with the ruling class, or the aristocratic families, can hardly be denied. Confucius was, in fact, the first great teacher who sought to popularize education.

(1) Literature in the early Chou period (prior to Confucius)

Modern excavations have shown that the Shang and the early Chou people were very fond of writing. We have already obtained many thousands of pieces of bone and tortoise shell of the late Shang dynasty inscribed with characters, and of these Dr. H.G. Creel tells us that "Every important principle of the formation of modern Chinese characters was already in use, to a greater or less degree". (*The Birth of China*, p. 160) Many bronze vessels of the early Chou period which have been discovered carry inscriptions with characters of from several hundred down to only one or two characters. As Dr. Creel points out, "It has sometimes been thought that the Chinese of the Chou dynasty used writing but little, producing books by laborious and time-consuming methods. This is not true at all. The number of documents written even during early Chou times must have run into tens or hundreds of thousands". (*The Birth of China*, p. 254) All the writings said to have been produced during this period are generally grouped under six headings, known as The Liu I[186] or "Six Disciplinary Arts."

(a) *Poetry.*   The Chou people were fond of singing. They sang when they were in sorrow, about the death of relatives, the trials of military service, the evils of society, or personal hardships; in happy moods, about feasting, dancing, ceremonial offerings, or thanksgiving sacrifices to ancestors or to other spirits. There were songs of love between man and woman, songs of admonition, praise and prayer, and songs of the chase and the court. These were collected and selected, and possibly revised, by Confucius and others, until the present form of *The Book of Poetry*, Shih Ching,[187] was reached.

(b) Documents. They were composed of speeches made at various crises by kings and other rulers, exhorting their subjects to support them; political proclamations, such as denouncing the use of intoxicating liquor; moral and admonitory communications and exhortations, and other miscellaneous documents. They were later collected and selected, "expunged and rectified", by Confucius and others until they assumed the present form of *Shu Ching*,[188] generally known as *The Book of History*.

(c) Rites. The early Chou people were very careful in respect to the various ceremonial rites and observances on important occasions, such as marriage, birth, death, burial, offering of sacrifices, ceremonial visits and feasts; and also in everyday life, such as eating, walking, speaking, sleeping, etc. These were later on collected and selected, as were the previous writings, until the present form of I Li[189] or *The Rites* was obtained.

(d) Music. Music was used to a very great extent by the early Chou people especially in singing, dancing, feasting, and in different kinds of religious practices. There are many kinds of musical instruments mentioned in the transmitted literature, and some of these have been discovered by modern archaeologists. They can be generally classified into three groups: those to be held in the hand when beaten, such as, Nao[190] and Cheng;[191] those to be hung up when beaten, such as, Chung[192] and Po;[193] those with clappers, such as, Ling[194] and To.[195] (See the *Illustrated Catalogue of Chinese Government Exhibits for the International Exhibition of Chinese Art in London*, 1985, Vol. 1) There were also stone chimes, and wind and string instruments. Confucius is recorded as having been very much interested in music. He must have composed, selected and revised some of the music of his time, and talked much about music, and very likely wrote treatises on music. Traditionally, it is believed there was a collection of ancient music, known as *Yueh Ching*,[196] or *The Book of Music*, but unfortunately it was lost during or before the Han dynasty, probably after A.D. 85, so that all we

have today is a chapter on music in *Li Chi*, or *The Book of Rites*.

(e) I or "Changes".   This is a name given by the early Chou people, and had to do with methods of divination which were very commonly practised in the early Chou and the Shang periods. Most of the inscriptions of the oracle bones were connected with divination. Later on the methods or techniques of divination of different sorcerers' manuals were collected, selected and commented on until the present form of *I Ching*[197] or *The Book of Changes* was obtained. *The I Ching* in its original form, that is, without its commentaries, is possibly the first complete work of Chinese literature and it doubtless existed completely in its original form before the time of Confucius. There is much in it which is in common with the inscriptions of the oracle bones. Confucius might have read or known much about it, and was impressed especially by its principle of "change", as that "which is passing is just like the stream—never ceasing day or night." (*The Analects*, 9, 16)

(f) Annals of different states.   Detailed annals were kept at the courts of the different feudal states.

Tso Chuan under the 23rd years of Duke Chuang of Lu (670 B.C.) states what Ts'ao Kuei[198] said in protesting against the licentious actions of Duke Chuang of Lu,[199] "Every action of a ruler must be recorded. If your recorded actions are unlawful, how will your descendants look upon them?" Again, under the second year of Duke Hsuan[200] of Lu (607 B.C.), at the time when Duke Ling of Chin[201] was murdered, *Tso Chuan* states:

"The Grand Historian[202] (of Chin) wrote the entry, 'Chao Tun[203] has murdered his prince,' and showed it to the court. Hsuan Tzu (i.e., Chao Tun) said that this was not true. (The historian) replied, 'Sir, you are the highest minister. Flying from the state, you did not go beyond its frontiers. When you returned you did not punish the assassin. If it is not you (who are responsible), who is it?' . . . . Confucius said of this: 'Of old, Tung Hu was an excellent historian. In his writings he had the rule of not concealing (the truth)." Again, under the 25th year of Duke Hsiang (548 B.C.),[204] when Duke Chuang of Ch'i was murdered:

"The Grand Historian (of Ch'i) made a record of the fact saying: 'Ts'ui Tzu[205] has murdered his prince.' Ts'ui Tzu thereupon had him executed. Two of his brothers did the same after him, and were also executed. A third wrote the same and was spared. The historian in the south, learning that the Grand Historian and his two brothers had died in this way, took his tablets and went (to record also that Ts'ui Tzu had murdered his prince). But learning on the way that the affair had already been recorded (by the third brother), he returned."

The annals of different states sometimes had different names, for example, that of Chin was sometimes called *Ch'eng*,[206] that of Ch'u was called *Tao Wu*,[207] and that of Lu, *Ch'un Ch'iu*.[208] Mencius said: "The *Ch'eng* of Chin, the *Tao Wu* of Ch'u and the *Ch'un Ch'iu* of Lu were books of the same character. Their subject was the affairs of (Dukes) Huan of Ch'i and Wen of Chin, and their style was historical. Confucius said: 'Their righteous principles I ventured to take.' " (*Mencius*, 4,2,21)

It is very likely that Confucius wrote something down for his lectures on the "current histories" of his days, basing them primarily on the annals of his own state, i.e., the Ch'un Ch'iu of Lu, but centreing around certain basic Principle which he derived largely from the annals of different states. They were such as the "Righteous Principle", "the rule of not concealing the truth", and the principle of "Rectification of Names". His *Ch'un Ch'iu* was later on commented upon and possibly a little bit modified or expunged, until it assumed the present form of *Ch'un Ch'iu*, or *The Spring and Autumn Annals*.

A large part of the original materials of the annals of different states have been preserved in *Tso Chuan* and *Kuo Yu* as we have them at present.

The "Six Disciplinary Arts", namely, Poetry, Documents, Rites, Music, Changes, and Annals, formed the basic literature at the time of Confucius. *Kuo Yu* informs us that a crown prince of Ch'u, son of King Chuang of Ch'u (613-591 B.C.), was given instruction in such works as *'Poetry'*, *'Rites'*, *'Music'*, *'Spring and Autumn'* and *Ku Chih*[209] or *'Old Documents'*. (See *Ch'u Yu*, 1,1) Both *Kuo Yu* and *Tso*

Chuan give numerous references to these six important Disciplinary Arts in the early part of the Spring and Autumn period.

Besides this basic literature, there were also writings about the arts of archery, charioting, fencing, writing, counting, medicine, handicraft, etc., which were all important arts of the early Chou people.

(2) Materials for writing

From the inscribed oracle bones, we know there already existed a kind of book during the Shang dynasty. Bound together with cords, they were strips of wood or bamboo on which characters were written with brushes dipped in ink, or were carved with knives made of metal, or jade or other material. The character "book", or 冊 , is found on the oracle bones. The verticle lines represent the slips of wood or bamboo on which characters are written or carved, and the horizontal lines in the form of a loop represent a piece of cord. Bones with characters written with ink and brush have also been found.

The early Chou people took over the technique of writing and the materials for writing from the Shang people. They generally preferred to write with brush or carve with knives on slips of wood or bamboo, which they could easily carry around with them. The I Li[210] or *The Rites*, lists a bamboo writing-slip among the articles with which the corpse of every member of a certain class had to be provided. It was apparently worn at the girdle and used as a sort of note-book. When there were a number of these slips, they were strung together to form a book, as in Shang times. Sometimes they used silk or other kind of fabric to write on, and these would be rolled up to form a book or a part of a book. It is not surprising, that although the early Chou people wrote much, only a very small proportion of the literature has come down to us, because the materials which they used for writing on were generally fragile and easily destroyed.

(3) School system

School education was a rule limited to the aristocratic families. It was, in general, according to the Classics, divided into three grades, namely, the Shu[211] or Infant Schools, the Hsiao Hsueh[212] or

Lower Schools, the Ta Hsueh[213] or Higher Schools.

(a) Infant schools

They were generally for children under seven years of age, and held in the homes of aristocratic families.

(b) Lower schools

They were generally for boys between 8 and 15 years of age.

(c) Higher schools, or Grand Colleges

They were generally for men between 16 and 24 years of age. Those established in the Imperial city were called P'i Yin,[214] and those in the capital cities of the feudal lords were called P'an Kung.[215]

These schools theoretically were all under the direct control of the central government.

The following are a few quotations to illustrate the above briefly outlined school system.

Mencius says: "By the Hsia dynasty, the name Chiao[216] was used; by the Yin (Shang) dynasty, that of Hsu,[217] and by the Chou, that of Hsiang.[218] As to Hsueh,[219] it belonged to the three dynasties, and by that name." (*Mencius*, 3,1,3,10) Chucius,[220] the famous scholar of the Sung dynasty, commented on this saying that Chiao, Hsu, and Hsiang were all local district schools and were of the lower grade; while Hsueh was Kuo Hsueh[221] and was of the higher grade.

The Book of Rites, in the chapter on Hsueh Chi,[222] states:

"The ancient educational system was as follows: there were Shu[223] (infant schools) in the homes or Chia,[224] Hsiang[225] and Hsu[226] (lower schools) in the Tang[227] and Shu[228] (local districts), and Hsueh[229] (higher schools) in the Kuo[230] (the state capitals)."

The Book of Rites, in the chapter on Wang Chih,[231] states:

"The Hsiao Hsueh[232] or lower schools were situated at the left-hand side in the south of the royal palace; while the Ta Hsueh[233] or the "Grand Colleges" (higher schools) were situated in the suburbs of the state capitals; those which were in the imperial city were called P'i Yin,[234] and those in the state capital of the feudal lords were called P'an Kung."[235]

Han Shu, "I Wen Chih"[236] states:

"In the ancient system, eight years of age was the age to go to

Hsiao Hsueh[237] or the lower school."

Elder Tai's *Records of Li*, in the chapter on Pao Fu,[238] commented on by Pai Hu T'ung,[239] states:

"Eight years of age was the age to go to Hsiao Hsueh, and fifteen years old was the age to go to Ta Hsueh."

(4) Courses of study

According to the traditional literature, the following courses of study were offered in different grades of schools.

(a) Infant schools:

The children were taught the practice of the common knowledge of their daily lives, such as eating, talking, counting, etc.

(b) Hsiao Hsueh or lower schools:

a. Moral education:

Right conduct was emphasized, such as, "Sprinkling and sweeping the ground, answering and replying, advancing and receding." (*The Analects*, 19, 19)

b. Intellectual education:

This included reading, singing, writing, and mathematics.

c. Physical education:

This included archery, dancing, fencing, horse-riding, charioting.

(c) Ta Hsueh, or higher schools (Grand Colleges).

a. Moral education:

This included the cultivation of "right-mindedness and sincerity of thought", and all virtues and conduct which were necessary for self-cultivation and for the control of others.

b. Intellectual education:

This included the learning of the "Six Disciplinary Arts", and the cultivation of all the necessary habits, knowledge, and skill for the further "investigation of things and the extension of knowledge."

c. Physical education:

This included the more advanced forms and complicated practices of all those which were taught in the lower schools.

The following are some quotations to illustrate the above brief outline of the courses of study in schools of the early Chou period.

"When the children can eat by themselves, teach them how to use the right hands; when they are able to speak, the boys should be taught to talk smartly, and the girls to talk gently, boys wear skin and girls wear silk; when they are six years old, they should be taught how to count and to recognize the directions." (*Li Chi*, on Nei Tse)

"In the Chou system . . . boys went to the Hsiao Hsueh, or lower schools, when they were eight years of age, and were taught the manners of sprinkling and sweeping the ground, answering and replying, advancing and receding, and the arts of rites, music, archery, charioting, writing and mathematics. When they were fifteen years old, they entered the Ta Hsueh or the Grand Colleges (higher schools), and were taught lessons on the extension of knowledge and the investigation of things, and right-mindedness and the sincerity of thoughts." (*Yu Hai*[241])

"Ta Shih T'u[242] or the Chief Minister of Education taught three things to the milliards of people. . . .

a. Six virtues:[243] wisdom,[244] benevolence,[245] sagacity,[246] righteousness,[247] truthfulness,[248] and harmony;[249]

b. Six rules of conduct:[250] filial piety,[251] brotherly love,[252] conduct of love for relatives of the same clan,[253] conduct of love for relatives by marriage,[254] conduct of willingness to take responsibility,[255] and conduct of helping the poor and sick;[256]

c. Six arts:[257] ritual,[258] music,[259] archery,[260] charioting,[261] writing,[262] and mathematics."[263] (*Chou Li*, on Ti Kuan Ssu T'u[264])

Under each of the three main divisions there were numerous sub-divisions. Under the Six Arts, there were 5 kinds of rituals, 6 kinds of music, 5 kinds of archery, 5 kinds of charioting, 6 kinds of writing, and 9 kinds of mathematics. Each sub-division was again divided into different lessons. For example, under the five kinds of rituals: in Chi Li[265] there were 55 lessons, Pin Li[266] 6 lessons, Chun Li[267] 23 lessons, Chia Li[268] 50 lessons, Hsiung Li[269] 18 lessons, a total of 152 lessons. (*Chou Li*, "Ti Kuan Ssu-T'u"; and *P'ei Wen Yun Fu*,[270] Vol. 38, p. 3)

(5) Respect for teachers

Chinese people have from the very beginning of their cultural history shown much respect for teachers. King Wu[271] in his famous political address, delivered about 1123 B.C., says: "Heaven, out of compassion to the people below, has appointed over them princes, and given them teachers, that they may assist God on High in cherishing and tranquilizing the four quarters (of the world)." (*Shu Ching*, the first part of the Great Oath[272])

Teachers were regarded as divine commissioners or representatives from God to carry out the will of God and bring people back to Him. "There are three essentials in our lives, and they should be regarded as the same in importance: parents who beget us, teachers who teach us, and the kings who feed us." (*Kuo Yu*, Chapter on Chin Yu) Here teachers were put on the same level as parents and kings. Even the kings of the early Chou period, according to classical literature, paid very high respect to teachers. *Li Chi* says: "There are only two classes of people that the king dare not regard as his subjects: his teachers and the Shih (Children representing the spirits of the deceased at the sacrifices). According to the custom of the Grand College, a teacher does not have to stand facing north even when receiving an edict from the king, which shows great respect for the teacher." (*Li Chi*, chapter on Hsueh Chi[273]) Nearly all the great teachers of the Eastern Chou dynasty, including Confucius, Micius,[274] Mencius and others, shared the same traditional view of the dignity and respectability of teachers. They themselves were all conscious of their sacred vocation and divine commission as teachers of others. They assumed their responsibilities, and carried out their duties so honestly and enthusiastically that the traditional respect for teachers was still more enhanced, and has continued down to present China throughout these many centuries.

2. Philosophical background

It has been traditionally believed that all the philosophical schools that flourished in the periods of the Warring States and the early Han dynasty, and mentioned in the "I Wen Chin" ("Catalogue of the Imperial Han Library," chapter 30 of *Ch'ien Han Shu*), had all a common origin in the governmental office and under the royal control of the early Chou period. "I Wen Chin" states: "The various philosophers belonged to ten schools, but there are only nine worthy of notice. They all began when royal control (of the early Chou) was lessening and the feudal nobles were becoming more powerful and differed widely in what they preferred and disliked. . . ."

This conception of the pre-Confucian origin of the later philosophical schools was first repudiated by Dr. Hu Shih in his article *"The Various Philosophers Did Not Originate in the Imperial Offices"*[275] (*Ku Shih Pien*, Vol. 4, pp. 1-5), and his view has now been generally accepted by modern scholars. Dr. Hu Shih, however, maintains, in his *The Development of the Logical Method in Ancient China*, that there were certain philosophical schools which existed before Confucius and greatly influenced his teaching. He regarded, for example, the philosophy of Shao Cheng Mao[276] as recorded in *K'ung Tzu Chia Yu*,[277] the philosophy of Teng Shih as recorded in Lieh Tzu,[278] and the philosophy of Lao Tzu as recorded in *Tao Teh Ching*,[279] as pre-Confucian philosophies. (*The Development of the Logical Method in Ancient China*, pp. 11-20). *K'ung Tzu Chia Yu*, or *The Family Conversations of Confucius*, has now come to be generally regarded as the production of the Han scholars, and some modern scholars have even doubted that this man, Shao Cheng Mao ever actually existed. (See *A History of Chinese Philosophy*, by Fung Yu-lan, translated by Derke Bodde, p. 50) Again, *Lieh Tzu*, according to modern critical scholarship, has now determined that it "must in all probability be assigned rather to the Wei (A.D. 220-265) or Chin (A.D.265-420) dynasties, and, as such, may be used to exemplify the thought of that time, rather than of the Chou period." (*ibid.*, p. 19) Although there have still been lots of disputes about the date of Lao-tzu among Chinese scholars (See *Ku Shih Pien*, Vols. 4 and 6), yet the consensus of opinion seems to indicate that it might be possible that such a man, Lao-tzu, lived contemporaneously with Confucius, with whom Confucius might have had an interview, as it has been traditionally believed. Nevertheless, *Tao Teh Ching*, in its present form could never have been written by him before or during the time of Confucius, and it cannot be used to represent pre-Confucian thought.

Both Fung Yu-lan and Lo Ken-Tse[280] have strongly held the view that before Confucius there had not been any one who had composed any sort of literary work in a private capacity rather than an official one. The historian Chang Hsueh-Tseng (1738-1801) has also pointed out the same idea as follows:

"During the early period there were no instances of the (private) writing of books. Officials and teachers kept literary records, and historians made records of the passage of events. The purpose of written words was already sufficiently fulfilled, if by their means various officials might govern, and the common people be kept under surveillance.... It was only when the times were out of joint that teachers and scholars set up their (own private) teaching, and it was in so doing that our Master (Confucius) was superior to Yao and Shun (the legendary Emperors)." (Cf. Wen-shih T'ung-i, Shih-chiao section, pt. 1, in the Chang-shih I-shu, Vol. 1, p. 23)

Lo Ken-Tse gives four reasons why there had not been any sort of literary work in a private capacity before Confucius:

(1) "Before Confucius books had been kept within official circles."

(2) "Before the period of the Warring States there had been no need to produce the philosophies of different schools."

(3) "By attributing the works to the ancient authority, the faith of the people might be strengthened."

(4) The rise of the wealthy middle-class people, after the collapse of the feudal system, made learning more popular, and private writing developed for the sake of self amusement, or because of the struggle for power or prestige in society.

(See *Ku Shih Pien*, Vol. 4, pp. 8-68)

"Philosophy", as Fung Yu-lan points out, "if it is to be the systematic manifestation of thought, must necessarily find expression in the writings of private individuals. Prior to Confucius there were no such writings, and we, to-day, cannot know whether or not any kind of systematic philosophy actually did exist. So in his *A History of Chinese Philosophy*, he began with the philosophy of Confucius, because, he says: "Prior to him there existed, in all probability, no system of thought worthy of being called philosophy." (Fung Yu-lan, *A History of Chinese Philosophy*, translated by Derke Bodde, p. 8)

It is beyond the scope of this thesis to discuss in detail the complicated problems of philosophy before the time of Confucius. It is sufficient here just to mention some of the important current thoughts that were apparent during the time of Confucius, and that had, more or less, influenced the teachings of Confucius. Three kinds of people with their philosophies are to be considered briefly in the following, namely, the pessimists, the conservatives, and the reformers.

(1) Pessimists

The pessimists were those who grew weary of the deplorable conditions of the time, and felt no hope of salvation for the corrupt social order. They repudiated altogether the so-called civilization of their time, and "fled the world" to "conceal" themselves as porters, farmers, labourers, or "madmen". Men of this type are frequently mentioned in *The Analects*. There are three interesting anecdotes concerning these men, as recorded in the 18th book of *The Analects*, from which we may learn something about the pessimists.

(a) In the fifth chapter, it states: "The madman of Ch'u, Chieh-yu,[281] passed by Confucius, singing:

'O Phoenix! O Phoenix!
How has your virtue degenerated!
Let alone what you have been;
Think of what you will be!
Cease your toil! Cease your toil!
Peril awaits those who now engage in government.'

Confucius alighted from his carriage and wished to speak to him, but (the madman) hastened away, so that he could not talk with him."

(b) In the sixth chapter, it states: "Chang Chu,[282] and Chieh Ni[283] were at work in the field together, when Confucius passed by them, and sent Tzu Lu to inquire for the ford.

"Chang Chu said, 'who is he that holds the reins in the carriage there?' Tzu Lu told him, 'It is K'ung Ch'iu.' 'Is it not K'ung Ch'iu of Lu? asked he. 'Yes' was the reply, to which the other rejoined, 'He knows the ford.'

"Tzu Lu then inquired of Chieh Ni, who said to him, 'who are you, Sir?' He answered, 'I am Chung Yu.' 'Are you not the disciple of K'ung Ch'iu of Lu?' asked the other. 'I am', replied he, and then Chieh Ni said to him, 'The world is one seething torrent, and who is he that can change it? Would it not be better for you to follow a master who flees the world, than a master who merely flees from this man and that man?'; with this he went on hoeing."

(c) In the seventh chapter it states another incident:

"Tzu Lu, following the Master, happened to fall behind, when he met an old man, carrying across his shoulder on a staff a basket for weeds. Tzu Lu said to him, 'Have you seen my master, Sir?' The old man replied, 'Your four limbs are unaccustomed to toil; you cannot distinguish the five kinds of grain. Who is your master?' With this, he planted his staff in the ground, and proceeded to weed.

"Tzu Lu joined his hands across his breast, and stood before him.

"The old man kept Tzu Lu to pass the night in his house, killed a fowl, prepared millet, and feasted him. He also introduced to him his two sons.

"Next day, Tzu Lu went on his way, and reported his adventure. The Master said, 'He is a recluse', and sent Tzu Lu back to see him again, but when he got to the place, the old man was gone."

In the eighth chapter of the same book, book eighteen, seven names are mentioned of those who had retired into privacy from the world. They were: Pai I,[284] Shu Ch'i,[285] Yu Chung,[286] I I,[287] Chu Chang,[288] Liu Hsia Hui[289] and Shao Lien.[290]

Lao-tzu[291] might also be accounted one of the hermits.

The main reasons for those who took the pessimistic view and stood aloof from worldly affairs, as the above incidents show, are:

(a) That society was so corrupt that it was impossible to make it better. "The world is one seething torrent, and who is he that can change it?";

(b) That not only the corrupt world could not be made better, but also it was hostile to any reform. "Peril awaits those who now engage in government";

(c) That to cultivate the ground privately was regarded as more important and profitable than to engage in any hopeless social reform.

The attitude of Confucius towards these pessimists who shunned the world was one of sympathetic disapproval. For example, he spoke of Yu Chung and I I, the two hermits, "That while they hid themselves in their seclusion, they gave a license to their words; but in their persons, they succeeded in preserving their purity, and, in their retirement, they acted according to the exigency of the times." He was sympathetic towards these people, and sometimes called them "Hsien Jen"[292] or "worthy people" (*The Analects*, 14,39), though he disapproved of their philosophy of life. He felt he had a divine mission in carrying out the Truth of Heaven, and converting the people and changing society in accordance with the Truth. When Confucius was in danger in the city of K'uang,[293] and his disciples were all very much afraid, he spoke very calmly, "After the death of king Wen, was not the cause of truth lodged here in me? If Heaven had wished to let this cause of truth perish, then I, a future mortal, should not have got such a relation to that cause. While Heaven does not let the cause of truth perish, what can the people of K'uang do to me?" (*The Analects*, 9,5; cp. *Shih Chi*, "The Life of Confucius") In order to carry out his duty he had to live in society, so once he said with a sigh: "It is impossible to associate with birds and beasts. If I associate not with these people—with mankind, with whom shall I associate?" (*The Analects*, 18, 6, 4)

The Book of Poetry also gives many incidents of pessimists bemoaning the social evils:

> *"When I was young,*
> *Peacefully did time pass.*
> *But since my youthful days,*
> *All these evils have befallen me.*
> *I would that I might sleep, and never more awake!"*
> *(Pt. 1, Bk. 6,7)*

> *"The flowers are now gone;*

There are only the leaves full green.
Ah! Had I known it would be thus with me,
Better I had not been born."
     (Pt. 2, Bk. 8,9)

They cursed their birthdays for all the misfortunes that befell them; but they just wanted to live a sort of "sleeping" life, and cared not for any kind of social reform. Others attributed their fate to the decree of Heaven, which could not be altered by any human endeavour, and took a more epicurean view of life—to "eat, drink, and be merry".

"I go out at the North gate,
With my heart full of sorrow.
Straitened am I and poor,
And who cares for my distress?
So be it!
Heaven has done it:
Wherefore should I complain?
     (Pt. 1, Bk. 4,15)

"You have spirits and viands,
Why not daily play your lute,
To make yourself merry
And to prolong the day?
You will ere long die,
.And others will enter your chamber."
     (Pt. 1, Bk. 10,3)

Confucius reacted very strongly against all those pessimists. He said of himself that, "He was simply a man, who in his enthusiasm (of his work) forgets his food, who is optimistic, forgetful of his sorrows, and who does not perceive that old age is coming on." (*The Analects*, 7,18)

(?) Conservatives

Conservatives were those who were satisfied with the existing social order, and did not care for any reform. Two kinds of such people are to be considered here: the so-called Hsiang Yuan,[294] or "the good careful people of the village", who purposely opposed all reforms, and the majority of the common people who lived purposelessly and did not care for any reform.

(a) The Hsiang Yuan,[295] or the "good careful people of the village"

They were generally men of society, who were honoured and praised by village people for their pharisaic manners. They appeared to be good, and were proud of their own behaviour. They were satisfied with their own social order, and refuse purposely all new ideas and reforms. They were the great stumbling-block to social progress, and dangerous enemies to new truths and reforms. That is why they were the people whom Confucius hated most. He called them "the thieves of virtue" (*The Analects*, 17,13), and they were the only kind of people with whom Confucius did not want to have anything to do. "I do not feel sorry", he said, "when they pass my door without entering my house." (*Mencius*, 7,2,37,8)

Mencius gave a nice account about some of the characteristics of such "good careful people of the village". When he was asked "What sort of people were they who could be styled 'Your good careful people of the villages?' ", Mencius replied, "They are those who say, 'Why are they so magniloquent? Their words have not respect to their actions and their actions have not respect to their words, but they say,—The Ancients! The Ancients! Why do they act so peculiarly, and are so cold and distant? Born in this age, we should be of this age, to be good is all that is needed.' Eunuch-like, flattering their generation;—such are your good careful men of the villages." Wan Chang (Mencius' disciple) said, "Their whole village styles those men good and careful. In all their conduct they are so. How was it that Confucius considered them the thieves of virtue?" Mencius replied, "If you would blame them, you find nothing to allege. If you would criticize them, you have nothing to criticize. They agree with the current customs. They consent with an impure age. Their principles have a semblance of right-heartedness and truth. Their conduct has a semblance of disinterestedness and purity. All men are pleased with them, and they think themselves right, so that it is impossible to proceed with them to the principles of Yao and Shun. On this account they are called 'The thieves of virtue'. Confucius said, 'I hate a semblance which is not the reality. I hate the darnel, lest it be confounded with the corn. I hate glib-tonguedness, lest it be confounded with sincerity. I hate music of Cheng, lest it be confounded with the true music. I hate reddish blue, lest it be confounded with vermillion. I hate your good careful men of the villages, lest they be confounded with the truly virtuous.' The superior man seeks simply to bring back the Ching[296] or standard, and that being rectified, the masses are roused by virtue. When they are so aroused, forthwith perversities and glossed wickedness disappear." (*Mencius*, 7.2.37, 9-13)

According to Mencius, then, the reasons why the "good careful people of the village" were called "the thieves of virtue" by Confucius were as follows:

a. They were too conservative to receive any new idea or reform. They argued, for example, that "Born in this age, we should be of this age, to be good is all that is needed."

b. They were the "flatterers of the age", agreeing with the "current customs", and consenting with their 'impure age".

c. They were proud of being constantly praised and honoured, and they thought that "they themselves were right".

d. They were too obstinate, proud and conservative, to receive the real truth or "true virtue" of Yao and Shun.

e. To crown all, they were hypocritical. They had only a "resemblance" of virtue, so that there was a true danger of its being "confounded" with the real virtue. In short, they were the "Pharisees" to Confucius who condemned them with no less severe terms than those given by Jesus of Nazarreth to those Pharisees of his days.

(b) The majority of the common people

The majority of the common people during the time of Confucius, as they have always been in any time, were conservative in the sense that they were disinterested in any kind of social or political problems, and did not care whether there would be any reform or not in the political or social order. They were so much involved with their daily routine of living that they became indifferent to any kind of political and social system. They sang, for example,

> *"I rise at break of day,*
> *And rest at set of sun.*
> *I dig my well and drink,*
> *I till my field and eat.*
> *What has the power of the king to do with me?"*
> (*Ku Shih*, "Song of the Peasant of Yao")

They lived purposelessly and quietly, "without praise or blame", "taking part neither for God nor for his enemies". These "characterless souls" also hover in Dante's imagination on the hither side of Acheron at the outset of his journey. "The world suffers no rumour of them to survive; mercy disdains them, and justice too. Let us not talk of them, but look and pass." (See A.S. Pringle-Pattison, *The Idea of Immortality*, p. 197)

Confucius said, "The Chun-tzu[298] (Superior Man) is sick of the thought of his name not being mentioned after his death."(*The Analects*, 15,19) He had no sympathy with those "characterless souls" who did nothing worthy of being handed down. He disliked them and called them Tsei[299] or "Pest". One day Confucius met a certain men of this type, named Yuan Jang,[300] who "was squatting on his heels, and so waited the approach of the Master, who said to him, 'In youth, not humble as befits a junior; in manhood, doing nothing worthy of being handed down; and living on to old age: —this is to be a pest.' With this he hit him on the shank with his staff." (*The Analects*, 14,46)

(3) Reformers

During the time of Confucius there were many great scholars and politicians in various states, who were dissatisfied with the existing social and political orders, and endeavoured to find means to reform them. *Tso Chuan* under the 29th year of Duke Hsiang of Lu (544 B.C.), mentions one of the members of the royal family of the State of Wu, a noted politician, named Chi Cha of Wu,[301] who visited many scholars and politicians in different states. For example, in the State of Lu, he visited Shu Sun Mu Tzu;[302] in the State of

Ch'i, he visited Yen P'ing Chung;[303] in the State of Cheng, he visited Tzu Ch'an of Cheng;[304] in the State of Wei,[305] he visited Chu Wan,[306] Shih Kou,[307] Shih Yu,[308] Kung Tzu Ching,[309] Kung Shu Fa,[310] and Kung Tzu Chao;[311] in the State of Chin, he visited Chao Wen-tzu,[312] Han Hsuan-tzu,[313] Wei Hsien-tzu,[314] and Shu Hsiang of Chin.[315] Besides these there were many other politicians and scholars, such as Hsiang Hsu of the State of Sung,[316] who organized the famous league of states in 546 B.C.; Wei Yen,[317] and Tzu Mu,[318] in the State of Ch'u, who introduced many reforms to the State of Ch'u in the 25th year of Duke Hsiang of Lu, 547 B.C.; and various other reformers.

They had access to many ancient literary productions as their guide and reference. For example, they had nearly all the 29 chapters of *The Book of History* (Shu Ching[319]), accepted by the "Modern Text" school, all the 305 odes of *The Book of Poetry* (Shih Ching[320]), *The Book of Changes* (I Ching[321]) in its original form without the commentaries, the annals of various states, *The Book of Music*, and the records of ancient rites including the greater part of *The Rites* (*I Li*[322]). (Cp. Wang Kuo Wei, *Ku Shih Hsin Cheng*,[323] or "The New Evidence of Ancient History", incorporated in the *Ku Shih Pien*, Vol. 2, pp. 264-267; H.G. Creel, *The Birth of China*, Book 3, Chapter 29)

Those ancient materials, which already existed during the time of Confucius, were very rare and scattered among different states. Some states might have preserved some parts of some classics, while other states might have preserved other parts. So very few scholars had the opportunity of reading all of the ancient literature, and to the common people most of the material was almost inaccessible. *Tso Chuan*, for example, under the second year of Duke Chao, 540 B.C., states of Han Hsuan Tzu, a hereditary minister of the State of Chin, that it was only after he came on a diplomatic mission to the State of Lu, one of the most cultured regions in China, that he 'examined the books of the Grand Historian' and saw 'the symbols of the I' and the 'Ch'un Ch'iu of Lu'. Again, under the 29th year of Duke Hsiang of Lu, 544 B.C., it says of a member of the Royal House of Wu, Chi Cha[324] of Wu, that he had to come to Lu before he could hear the odes and music of the various states. When Confucius wanted to learn the "ancient rites and ceremonies" he had to leave his native state, Lu, and go to Chou, where he met Lao-tzu and others. (*Shih Chi*, "Life of Confucius") So one of the chief works of those reformers in the Spring and Autumn period, including Confucius, was to gather those rare materials together, make them known to society or to the government which they served, apply them to the specific occasions which arose during their service, and interpret them in such a way that they might solve or help to solve the problems which were brought forth by those occasions.

Nearly all the reformers in the Spring and Autumn period used the same method and adopted the same principles for their social and political reforms. The method which they all used was reformation through political measures. They all took office, and carried out their reform measures through good execution of their official duties. The belief that "The scholars, having completed his learning, should apply himself to be an officer" (*The Analects*, 19,13) was almost universal among the scholars. Confucius, however, through his unsuccessful attempts to hold office, hit upon a new method of carrying out the social and political reforms, that is, through the method of public education, which, later on, became very popular, especially among unemployed scholars.

The principle which those reformers generally adopted in the Spring and Autumn period in order to carry out their reforms was chiefly the principle of *li*.[325] The Chinese word *li*, as Dr. Lin Yu-tang has rightly pointed out, cannot be rendered by an English word. It has many meanings. He said, "On one extreme, it means 'ritual,' 'propriety'; in a generalized sense, it simply means 'good manners'; in its highest philosophic sense, it means an ideal social order with everything in its place, and particularly a rationalized feudal order, which was breaking down in Confucius' days." (Lin Yu-tang, *The Wisdom of Confucius*, p. 13). It was the *li* in the sense of the "ideal social order" that was generally used by those reformers, and that ideal social order was believed to have been recorded in the ancient literature supposedly handed down from the ancient 'sage kings" or ideal rulers, such as, Yao,[326] Shun,[327] Yu,[328] T'ang,[329] Wen,[330] Wu,[331] and Chou Kung.[332] So all the actions of the individual or the rules of the government that were spoken of as being according to *li*, were those which were in accordance with the "ideal social order" as recorded in the ancient literature. But the ancient literary materials, as mentioned above, were so rare, and so scattered, and their meanings were in most cases so obscure, that it was really the reformers' interpretation of the meanings of the ancient literature that was the most important factor in deciding the nature of the rules or conduct of the ideal social order, or, in other words, the nature of the rules or conduct in accordance with *li*.

It is impossible to give the views of all reformers during the time of Confucius. It suffices here just to mention three of the best known ones who had a great influence upon the thought of Confucius.

(a) Shu Hsiang of Chin[333]

Tso Chuan, under the 14th year of Duke Chao, 528 B.C., tells of Confucius' appreciation of the justice, straight-forwardness, and righteousness of Shu Hsiang.[334] He said:

"The justice of Shu Hsiang was that which was transmitted from antiquity. In the government of the state, and determining the punishment (for the assigned crime), he concealed nothing in the case of his own relative. Thrice he declared the wickedness of Shu Yu[335] without making any abatement. Whether we may say that he was righteous (is doubtful), but he may be pronounced to have been straightforward. At the meeting of P'ing Ch'iu,[336] he declared his (brother's) craving for bribes:—this was to give relief to Wei, and save Chin from the practice of cruelty. In getting Chi Sun[337] to return to Lu, he declared his (brother's) deceit:—this was to relieve Lu, and save Chin from the exercise of oppression. In the legal action of Hsing Hou,[338] he mentioned his (brother's) covetousness: —this was to keep the records of punishment correct, and save Chin from partiality. By his three declarations he took away three evils, and secured three advantages. He put his brother to death and increased (his own) glory:—this has the semblance of righteousness."

He regarded *li* as the most important for the individual as well as for the government, and the neglect of *li* was, according to him, the chief reason for the social and political disorder. In *Tso Chuan*, under the twenty-first year of Duke Hsiang, 552 B.C., it states:

"The meeting at Shang Jen[339] was to prevent Luan[340] from being harboured anywhere. The dukes of Ch'i and Wei behaved disrespectfully at it, which made Shu Hsiang say, 'These two princes are sure not to escape an evil end. These meetings and visits at courts are the essentials of *li*; *li* is the vehicle of government; it is through government that men's persons are guarded. When *li* is dishonoured, government is lost; and when government is not firmly established, disorder must ensue.' "

According to Shu Hsiang, *li* was set up by the ancient sage-kings and rulers, as the standard of government, for the prevention of crimes and for the encouragement of good conduct. They ensured the success of *li*, which they set up, by living up to that standard themselves, selecting the best men in their country to fill offices, and educating the people to observe *li*. So what the government of the later generations should do was simply to put *li* into practice and follow the examples of the sage-kings and rulers. With this pre-conceived view-point, he opposed very strongly the idea of government by written laws instead of by *li*, as introduced into the State of Cheng by its famous statesman, Tzu Ch'an.[341] So in the sixth year of Duke Chao of Lu, 530 B.C., he wrote a long letter to Tzu Ch'an, trying to persuade him to give up the idea of running the government by a set code instead of by *li* as handed down from the ancient past. He said:

"At first I regarded you (as my model), but now I have ceased to do so. When the ancient kings deliberated on (all the circumstances), and determined (on the punishment of crimes), they did not make general laws of punishment, fearing lest it should give rise to a contentious spirit among the people. But still, as crimes could not be prevented, they set up for them the barrier of righteousness, sought to bring them into conformity with their own rectitude, set before them the practice of *li*, and the maintenance of good faith, and cherished them with benevolence. They also instituted emoluments and places to encourage them to follow (their example), and laid down strict punishments and penalties to awe them from excesses. Fearing lest these things should be insufficient, they therefore taught the people (the principles) of sincerity, urged them by (discriminations of) conduct, instructed them in what was most important, called for their services in a spirit of harmony, came before them in a spirit of reverence, met exigencies with vigour, and gave their decisions with firmness. And in addition to this, they sought to have sage and wise persons in the highest positions, intelligent discriminating persons in all offices, that elders should be distinguished from true-heartedness and good faith, and teachers for their gentle kindness. In this way the people could be successfully dealt with, and miseries and disorder be prevented from arising.

"When the people know what the exact laws are, they do not stand in awe of their superiors. They also come to have a contentious spirit, and make their appeal to express words, hoping peradventure to be successful in their argument. They can no longer be managed. When the government of Hsia had fallen into disorder, the penal code of Yu was made; under the same circumstances of Shang, the penal code of T'ang; and in Chou, the code of the 'nine punishments':—those three codes all originated in ages of decay. And now in your administration of Cheng, you have made (your new arrangements for) dykes and ditches, you have established your (new system of) governmental (requisitions), which have been so much spoken against, and you have framed (this imitation of) those three codes, casting your descriptions of (crimes and their) punishments:—will it not be difficult to keep the people quiet, as you wish to do? The odes (4,1, ode 7) says,

> 'I imitate, follow, and observe the virtue of King Wen,
> And daily there is tranquility in all the regions';

And again, (3.1, ode 1.7),

> 'Take your pattern from King Wen,
> And the myriad states will repose confidence in you.'

In such a condition, what need is there for any code? When once the people know the grounds for contention, they will cast *li* away, and make their appeal to your descriptions. They will all be contending about a matter as small as the point of an awl or a knife. Disorderly litigations will multiply, and bribes will walk abroad—Cheng will go to ruin, it is to be feared, in the age succeeding yours. I have heard the saying that 'when a state is about to perish, there will be many new enactments in it'. Is your , proceeding an illustration of it?"

(b) Tzu Ch'an of Cheng[342]

There was no person in the Spring and Autumn period to whom Confucius showed greater respect and appreciation than Tzu Ch'an of Cheng. In *The Analects*, it is recorded that, "The Master said of Tzu Ch'an that he had four of the characteristics of a superior man: —in his conduct of himself, he was humble; in serving his superior, he was respectful; in nourishing the people, he was kind; in ordering the people, he was just." (*The Analects* 5,15) In the 21st year of Duke Chao, 521 B.C., when Confucius was 30 years old, Tzu Ch'an died. *Tso Chuan* under that year states, "When Tzu Ch'an died and Confucius heard of it, he shed tears and said, 'He afforded a specimen of the love transmitted from the ancients!' " In *Tso Chuan*, it is recorded again and again that the works of Tzu Ch'an received much praise from Confucius. For example, in the 31st year of Duke Hsiang, 548 B.C., Tzu Ch'an refused to destroy certain village schools, and, it is recorded, "When Confucius heard of this, he said, 'Looking at the matter from this, when men say that Tzu Ch'an was not benevolent, I do not believe it.' " Again in the 13th year of Duke Chao, 529 B.C., when the different states came together to make a covenant, Tzu Ch'an "disputed about the amount of the contributions required from Cheng. . . . The contention was continued from midday till dark", when he got what he wanted. Confucius said: "On this occasion Tzu Ch'an proved himself fit to be the foundation of his state. . . . When the states were assembled, to adjust the business of their contributions was according to *li*. "

Tzu Ch'an was, as a matter of fact, one of the greatest scholars and statesmen in the Spring and Autumn period. He was legalistic in mind and realistic in temperament. Being one of the early pioneers of one of the most important schools of philosophy in the period of the Warring States, namely, the Legalistic School (Fa Chia),[343] he had a tremendous influence upon the general trend of thought during and after his time. He introduced many social and political reforms during his prime-ministry in the State of Cheng, from the 30th year of Duke Hsiang to the 21st year of Duke Chao, that is, from 543 to 521 B.C. For example, *Tso Chuan*, under the 13th year of Duke Hsiang, 543 B.C., states: "Tzu Ch'an made the central cities and border lands of the state be exactly defined, and enjoined on the high and inferior officers to wear (only) their distinctive robes. The fields were all marked out by their banks and ditches. The Lu[344] and Ching[345] (social units) were divided into five, responsible for one another. . . ." In the third month of the sixth year of Duke Chao, 536 B.C., Tzu Ch'an asked that bronze vessels should be cast with the descriptions of crimes and their punishments upon them. In the fourth year of Duke Chao, 538 B.C., he made new and harder regulations for the contributions from the people in certain districts in the State of Cheng. With all these reforms, it is recorded that "great peace came to the State of Cheng".

Although he met with great success for his reforms, and was praised by Confucius and many others, yet he met also plenty of opposition and criticism, sometimes even from his best friends. For example, for the inscription of the penal laws on the bronze vessels, he was severely opposed by his friend Shu Hsiang, as already mentioned; and for the new regulations for contributions he was strongly criticized by his friend Tzu K'uang,[346] saying, "The superior man makes laws with slight requirements. The danger is of his still desiring more. . . . If the government does not follow the (established) laws and one can make new ones according to his own mind with every one of the people having a mind of his own, what place will be left for the ruler?" (*Tso Chuan*, under the 4th year of Duke Chao)

As a faithful, strong and far-sighted statesman, he did not care for criticism or opposition; he did what he thought right, good for the country, and for the people as a whole. For example, when his friend Tzu Kuan reported to him the criticisms of the people about his new regulations for contributions, he answered in a most unbiased and statesmanlike way: "There is no harm in it. If it only benefit the altar (country), I would either live or die. Moreover, I have heard that when the good doer does not change his measures, he can calculate on success. The people are not to be gratified in this; the measure must not be altered. The ode (a lost ode) says, 'If one's rules and righteousness be not in error, why regard the words of people.' I will not change it." (*Tso Chuan*, under the fourth year of Duke Chao, 538 B.C.)

Realistic in temperament, he believed in force and severity, law and punishment. He knew that they were not the best way to govern the people; but, in order to meet the immediate circumstance of his country and the general behaviour of his people, he thought that they were the best possible way. So in *Tso Chuan* under the 20th year of Duke Chao, 522 B.C., it is recorded, "Tzu Ch'an was ill, and said to Tzu Ta Shu,[347] 'When I die, the government is sure to come into your hands. It is only the (perfectly) virtuous, who can keep the people in submission by clemency. For the next class (of rulers) the best thing is severity. When fire is blazing, the people look to it with awe, and few of them die from it. Water again is weak, and the people despise and sport with it, so that many die from it. It is difficult, therefore, to carry on a mild government.' " Again, when Tzu Ch'an received the long letter from his friend Shu Hsiang about the laws inscribed on the bronze vessels, he returned the following reply, "As to what you say, I have not the talents nor the ability to act for posterity; my object is to save the present age. I cannot accept your instructions, but I dare not forget your great kindness."

While believing in new laws and regulations and, in general, a new social order, he did not lose sight of *li*. But his conception of *li* was somewhat different from that of many of his contemporaries. Instead of being conceived as originated only from the ancient sage-kings and rulers, the conception of *li* was, according to him, derived from the human imitation of the natural phenomena of heaven and earth. So to act in accordance with *li* came to mean to act in accordance with the natural laws of the universe, as interpreted by the ancient sages as well as by men of different generations in their imitation of the nature of heaven and earth. To live in "harmony" (Hsieh)[348] with the nature of heaven and earth was to him the real meaning of *li*. So he was not entirely satisfied with the conception of many of his contemporary reformers that the government should act entirely in accordance with the stereotyped form of the "ideal social order", or the *li* as handed down from the sage-kings and rulers. To rule by *li*, was to him to rule in accordance with the "ideal social order", which was in harmony with heaven and earth. The law and order of heaven and earth should be the chief criterion of right and wrong, and not the set regulations of the ancient sages, who derived their ideas of those regulations also from the law and order of the universe. Therefore, he believed that the new changes which he introduced into his own state were in harmony with the natural law and order working in man and the universe, and so they were not contrary to the spirit of the set regulations as handed down from the ancients. *Tso Chuan*, under the 25th year of Duke Chao, 517 B.C., gives the following passage which will illustrate the point of view of this great reformer:

"Tzu Ta Shu (a believer and successor of Tzu Ch'an)[349] had an interview with Chao Chien Tzu,[350] and was asked about the *li* of bowing, yielding precedence, and moving from one place to another. 'These, said Tzu Ta Shu, 'are matters of deportment, and not of *li*.' 'Allow me to ask', said Chao Chien Tzu. 'What we are to understand by *li*?' The reply was, 'I have heard our late great officer Tzu Ch'an say that *li* is founded in the regular procedure of heaven, the right phenomena of earth, and the actions of men. Heaven and earth have their regular ways, and men take these for their pattern, imitating the brilliant bodies of heaven, and according with the natural diversities of the earth. . . . There were ruler and minister, high and low, in imitation of the distinctive characteristics of the earth. . . . Life is a good thing; death is an evil thing. The good thing brings joy; the evil thing gives grief. When there is no failure in the joy and the grief, we have a state of harmony with the nature of heaven and earth, which consequently can endure long.' Chien Tzu said, 'Extreme is the greatness of *li*!' '*Li*', replied Tzu Ta Shu, 'determines the relation of high and low; it is the warf and woof of heaven and earth; it is the life of the people. Hence it was that the ancient kings valued it, and hence it is that the man who can now bend, now straighten himself so as to accord with *li*, is called a complete man. Right is it that *li* should be called great!"

(c) Yen P'ing-chung[351]

Yen P'ing-chung, or Yen Ying, was the prime minister of Ch'i during the time of Confucius. According to *Shi Chi*,[352] or *The Historical Records* written by Ssu-ma Ch'ien, it was due to the interference of Yen Ying that Confucius was not able to get a position in the State of Ch'i. It states that when the duke of Ch'i wanted to use Confucius, the "Minister Yen Ying spoke to the duke, 'The Ju (later identified with Confucianists) are bad models to follow because of their garrulousness, and they make bad subjects because of their pride and egotism. Their doctrines should hardly be applied to the people because of their emphasis on funerals, and their habit of letting a family go bankrupt in order to provide an expensive burial. They also make bad rulers because they go about preaching and begging and borrowing. Since the great men have died and the imperial dynasty of Chou is in decline, our *li* and music to-day have degenerated or been partly forgotten. Now comes Confucius with his insistence on ceremonial robes and the details of ceremonial processions and court etiquette. One can spend a lifetime and not be able to master the details of ceremonies. I rather question whether it is advisable for you to put him in power and change the customs of the country, bearing in mind the importance of considering the common people.' Therefore, the Duke always received Confucius politely, but did not ask him questions regarding *li* and ceremonies. In *The Analects*, Confucius praised him saying, "Yen P'ing-chung knew well how to maintain friendly intercourse. The acquaintance might be long, but he showed the same respect as at first." (*The Analects*, 5,16) He was one of the greatest scholars and statesmen of his time.

Though he had little sympathy with the extravagance and minute details of the ceremonial rites in which some followers of Confucius were apparently very much interested, yet he had very high regard for *li*. In fact, he held that the most effective method of social reforms was through the uplifting of *li*. *Li* was, according to him, derived from the ancient sage-kings who received it from the natural order of heaven and earth. According to *li*, every thing had its proper place in the universe, and everybody had his proper position in society under the patriarchy of the feudal system. Those who acted according to what they were were said to be acting in accordance with *li*, and vice versa. *Li* then was the rationalized feudal order which was gradually breaking down in his days. If everybody acted according to *li* or the rationalized feudal order, as handed down from the ancient sage-kings and rulers, all the troubles in society, he maintained, would easily be eliminated. *Tso Chuan*, under the 26th year of Duke Chao, 516 B.C., gives an account of the conversation between Yen Ying and the Duke of Ch'i about *li*. Yen Yzu said to the Duke:

"It is only an attention to *li* which can stop (the trouble). By *li*, the bounties of a family cannot extend to all the state. Sons must not change the business of their fathers—husbandry, some mechanical art, or trade; scholars must not be negligent; officers must not be insolent; great officers must not take to themselves the privileges of the ruler." "Good," said the Duke. "I am not able to attain to this; but henceforth I know how a state can be governed by *li*." "Long has *li* possessed such a virtue", was the reply. "Its rise was contemporaneous with that of heaven and earth. That the ruler order and the subject obey, the father be kind and the son filial, the elder brother loving and the younger brother respectful, the husband be harmonious and the wife gentle, the mother-in-law be kind and the daughter-in-law obedient; these are things in *li*. That the ruler in ordering order nothing against the right, and the subject obey without any duplicity; that the father be kind and at the same time be able to teach, and the son be filial and at the same time be teachable; that the elder brother, while loving, be friendly, and the younger docile, while respectful; that the husband be righteous, while harmonious, and the wife correct, while gentle; that the mother-in-law be condescending, while kind, and the daughter-in-law be winning, while obedient—these are excellent things in *li*." "Good," said the Duke, adding, "Henceforth I have heard the highest style of *li*." Yen Tzu replied, "It was what the ancient kings received from heaven and earth for the government of their people, and therefore they ranked it in the highest place."

Not only was *li* regarded as the most important for the government by Yen Tzu and others, but also *hsin*,[353] or good faith, was generally very highly esteemed by scholars and politicians in The Spring and Autumn period. As most of the inter state troubles arose from the breaking of promises between different states, it is no wonder that the virtue of good faith should be so much emphasized. For example, during the League of States in 546 B.C., *Tso Chuan*, under the 27th year of Duke Hsiang, states that "the men of Ch'u wore their armour under their outer clothes. Pai Chou *Li*[354] (the Grand administrator of the League) said (to Tzu Mu,[355] the prime minister of Ch'u), 'The multitude of the states are assembled here, and is it not desirable (now) to show them our want of good faith? The states expect good faith from Ch'u, and on that account they came to (indicate) their submission to it. If we do not keep faith, we are throwing away that by which we must effect the submission of the states.' He then earnestly begged that the armour be put off." In the same manner, Yen P'ing Chung also, in *Tso Chuan* under the 22nd year of Duke Hsiang, 551 B.C., spoke to the Duke of Ch'i about good faith. He said,

"At the meeting of Shang Jen,[356] you received the command of Chin (not to harbour Luan);[357] if you now receive him, what will be the use of that meeting? It is by good faith that a small state serves a large one. If its good faith be lost, it cannot stand. Let your lordship consider it." The Duke would not listen to him, and P'ing Chung withdrew and told Ch'en Wen-Tzu,[358] saying, "Rulers should hold fast good faith, and their subjects reverence and loyalty. It is the rule of Heaven that high and low should all observe true-heartedness, good faith, sincerity, and reverence. Our ruler is throwing himself away. He cannot continue long." In short, generally speaking all the reformers during the Spring and Autumn period took *li* as the standard of all human conduct, in government, family, and society, as well as in the daily life of an individual. "It is the stem of a man", said Meng Hsi-tzu.[359] "Without it, it is impossible for man to stand firm." (*Tso Chuan*, under the 7th year of Duke Chao, 535 B.C.) Virtues, such as benevolence, righteousness, sincerity, loyalty, and especially good faith, were much emphasized, because they were the important means of achieving and uplifting *li*, the ideal social order.

But during the time of Confucius, there was already a marked tendency towards a more realistic interpretation and theory of human conduct. The expediency and the immediately desirable results of conduct were taken as the chief concern by some great scholars during this period.

According to the more realistic scholars, such as Tzu Ch'an of Cheng, *li* was different from *i*[360] (deportment), and the chief standard for judging whether *li* was good or bad, right or wrong, was, sometimes, considered by those scholars, not to be the *li* itself, but the result which came out of it. The following passage from *Tso Chuan*, under the 5th year of Duke Chao of Lu, 547 B.C., can be cited as a good example.

"The Duke (Chao of Lu) went to Chin; and from his reception in the suburbs, to the gifts at his departure, he did not fail in any point of *li*. The Duke of Chin said to Nu Shu-ch'i,[361] 'Is not the Duke of Lu good at *li*?' 'How does the Duke of Lu know *li*?' was the reply. 'Wherefore (do you say so)?' asked the Duke. 'Considering that, from his reception in the suburbs to the gifts at his departure, he did not err in a single point, why should you say that he does not know *li*?' 'That was deportment (*i*[362]),' said Shu-chi, 'and should not be called *li*. Li is that by which (a ruler) maintains his people. Now the government (of Lu) is ordered by the (three great) families, and he cannot take it from them and there is Tzu Chia Ch'ien[363] and he is not able to employ him. He violates the covenants of our great state, and exercises oppression on the small state. He makes his gain out of the distresses of others, and is ignorant of his own. The (patrimony) of his House is divided into four parts, and (like one of) the people he gets his food from others. No one thinks of him, or takes any consideration for his future. As the ruler of a state, he will meet with calamity, and he has no regard as to what is proper for him to do. The beginning and end of his *li* should be in these matters; and in small particulars he practices *i* (deportments), as if that were all-important—is it not far from correct to say that he is well acquainted with *li*?' The superior man will say that Shu Hou[364] (Shu-chi) showed by these remarks that he knew *li*."

According to this passage, *li* became identified with the general success of a person. Its meaning or value was to be determined by its consequences. With the changing conception of *li*, the conception of virtues, which had been inseparably connected with *li*, was also changed. Virtues were accepted not so much for the sake of virtues themselves, but rather for the sake of expediency. If the virtue could not give a desirable result, it was to be discarded, according to the conception of some of the realistic scholars. For example, when Tzu Mu,[365] the prime minister of Ch'u, one of the greatest scholars and politicians of his time, was asked to keep the virtue of good faith, during the League of States in 546 B.C., he answered frankly, "There has been no good faith between Chin and Ch'u for long. We have to do merely with getting the advantage. If we get our will, what is the use of having good faith?" (*Tso Chuan* under the 27th year of Duke Hsiang of Lu).

The use of force or war was sometimes justified by these scholars, in order to secure desirable results. So Hsiang Hsu[366] of Sung, the originator of the League of States with the view of maintaining international peace, was very much criticized by the famous scholar and politician Tzu Han,[367] saying:

"It is by their arms that Chin and Ch'u keep the small states in awe. Standing in awe, the high and low in them are loving and harmonious; and through this love and harmony they can keep their states in quiet and thereby serve the great states. In this, is the way of preservation. If they were not kept in awe, they would become haughty. That haughtiness would produce disorder; that disorder would lead to extinction. This is the way to ruin. Heaven has produced five elements which supply men's requirements, and the people use them all. Not one of them can be dispensed with. Who can do away with the instruments of war? They have long been in requisition. It is by them that the lawless are kept in awe, and accomplished virtue is displayed. Sages have risen to their eminence, by means of them; and men of confusion have been removed. The courses which lead to decline or to growth, to preservation or to ruin, of blindness on the one hand, of intelligence on the other, are all traced to these instruments. And you have been seeking to do away with them. Is not our scheme a delusion?"

Not only was war praised and justified, written laws with punishments were also gradually introduced to take the place of the decaying moral and religious sanctions. Different schools of philosophy began to spring up to interpret the traditional political, social, ethical and religious beliefs. That led to the glorious period of Chinese philosophy, right after the death of Confucius, 479 B.C., up to the unification of China under the First Emperor of the Ch'in dynasty, 221 B.C.

3. Religious Background

Three points may be considered in relation to the religious background of the teaching of Confucius:

(1) The conception of God or Heaven,

(2) The conception of spirits,

(3) The means of communication with God or spirits.

(1) The conception of God or Heaven

From the very ancient days of Chinese history, down through the time of Confucius to the present, we have records about the Chinese belief in one supreme God, the ruler over heaven and earth.

From the old divination bones of the latter part of the Shang dynasty, we have the name of god written as 帝 , hence comes the modern Chinese character 帝 [368] or Ti, meaning God. According to James M. Menzies, the ancient character Ti is made up of three parts: first, 朿 , a bundle of wood; second, Ｈ, a thong which binds the wooden faggots together; third, 二 , the two lines that represent the conception, "above". So the whole character would mean to gather together the strips of wood and bind them together into a faggot for the burnt offering to "Above", or Heaven. (See James M. Menzies, *Old Bones of the Shang Dynasty, China*, 1933) It is interesting to note that the Latin origin of the word religion, religio or relligio, has much in common with the ancient Chinese idea about God. Two alternative derivations have been given to that Latin origin, viz. from relegere, to gather together, to collect (re = back, legere = gather), and religare, to bind back, to fasten (re = back, ligare = bind). Although there have been many interpretations and discussions about these derivations since the time of Cicero, yet there is no denying the striking similarity between the religious belief of the ancient Chinese people, as represented by the character 朿 , and that of the ancient Western people as represented by the origin of the Latin word religio or relligio.

The character for Heaven or T'ien was written as 吳 in the divination bones of the Shang people. According to Mr. Menzies it is made up of two parts: first, 口 , which indicates a city, and the second 大 or Ta,[369] which means great or important, a title generally given by the Shang people to the spirits of their great ancestors and God on high. So the whole character would mean the city in which the great spirits dwell.

After the Chou conquest in 1123 B.C., however, T'ien and Ti or Heaven and God, became identified. From the old bronze inscriptions and the transmitted literature of the early Chou period, we know that the Chou people used interchangeably the two words, T'ien and Ti. Hence we have the common expression in Chinese literature Huang T'ien Shang Ti[370] "August Heaven, God on High", in which T'ien and Ti are mentioned together to mean the same Deity, God, the Supreme Ruler of the universe.

The following are some quotations from ancient Chinese literature which were probably very familiar to Confucius, about the nature of God or Heaven, as conceived by the early Chinese people.

(a) Parent of man

"Oh, vast and distant Heaven, who are called our parent."
(The Book of Poetry, 2,5,4,1)

"Heaven gave me birth"
(The Book of Poetry, 2,5,3,3)

"Heaven gave birth to the multitudes of the people"
(The Book of Poetry, 3,3,1,1)

"Heaven, in giving birth to the multitudes of the people,
To every faculty and relationship annexed its law.
The people possess this normal nature,
And they (consequently) love its normal virtue."
(The Book of Poetry, 3,3,6,1)

(b) Loving

"Heaven loves the people, and the rulers should reverence this
mind of Heaven."
(The Book of History, 2,4)

"How great is the love of Heaven towards the people."
(Tso Chuan, under the 14th year of Duke Hsiang of Lu)

(c) Author of blessing

"Heaven protects and establishes thee, with the greatest security;
Makes thee entirely virtuous, that thou mayest enjoy every
happiness."
(The Book of Poetry, 2,1,6,1)

"The king Wen, watchful and reverently with entire intelligence
served God;
And so secured the great blessing."
(The Book of Poetry, 3,1,2,3)

(d) Author of calamity

"Compassionate Heaven is arrayed in angry terrors;
Heaven is indeed sending down ruin."
(The Book of Poetry, 3,3,2)

"What crime is chargeable on us,
That Heaven (thus) sends down death and disorder?

Famine comes again and again.''
    (The Book of Poetry, 3,3,4,1)

(e) Just moral judge

"The way of God on high (Shang Ti) is not invariable,
(for He rewards a man according to His action),
On the good doer He sends down all blessings,
And on the evil doer He sends down all miseries."
    (The Book of History, chap. on I Shun, 8)

"Heaven graciously distinguished the virtuous; . . .
Heaven punishes the guilty. . . ."
    (The Book of History)

(f) Majestic

"Great is God, beholding the lower world in majesty."
    (The Book of Poetry, 3,1,7)

"The bright and glorious God on high."
    (The Book of Poetry, 4,2,1)

(g) Mysterious

"The ordinances of Heaven—how deep are they and
unintermitting."
    (The Book of Poetry, 4,1,2)

"The doings of high Heaven have neither sound nor smell."
    (The Book of Poetry, 3,1,1)

(h) Intelligent

"Great Heaven is very intelligent."
    (The Book of Poetry, 3,3,2)

"Great Heaven makes no mistake."
    (The Book of Poetry, 3,3,2)

"O bright and high Heaven, who enlighteneth and ruleth this
lower world."
    (The Book of Poetry, 2,6,3)

"Great Heaven is intelligent, and is with you in all your doing,

*Great Heaven is clear-seeing, and is with you in your wanderings
and indulgences.''*
(The Book of Poetry, 3,2,10,8)

(i) All-ruling

"Could Heaven be escaped?''
(Tso Chuan, under the 4th year of Duke Hsuan)

"Could Heaven be evaded?''
(Tso Chuan, under the 15th year of Duke Hsuan)

(j) Powerful to be appealed to for help

"The troops of Yin-Shang
Were collected like a forest,
And marshalled in the wilderness of Mu.
We rose to the crisis;—
'God is with you' (said Shang-fu to the king),
'Have no doubts in your heart'.''
(The Book of Poetry, 3,1,2,7)

"The proud are delighted and the troubled are in sorrow.
O azure Heaven, O azure Heaven,
Look on these proud men,
Pity these who are troubled.''
(The Book of Poetry, 2,5,6)

(k) Immanent and transcendent

The famous prayer of King Ching in his ancestral temple:

*"Let me be reverent, let me be reverent, (in attending to my
duties);*
(The way of) Heaven is evident,
And His appointment is not easily (preserved).
Let me not say that He is high aloft above me,
He ascends and descends about our doings;
He daily inspects us wherever we are.

I am (but as) a little child,
Without intelligence to be reverently (attentive to my duties)

But by daily progress and monthly advance,
I will learn to hold fast the gleams (of knowledge),
Till I arrive at bright intelligence.
Assist me to bear the burden (of my position),
And show me how to display a virtuous conduct."
        (*The Book of Poetry,* 4,1,3,3)

The word T'ien or Heaven was sometimes used with a very different meaning. It was sometimes used merely to denote the material or physical sky, such as:

"Things cannot grow with heaven alone (earth is needed)".
        (*Tso Chuan,* third year of Duke Chuang of Lu)

"The beauty of heaven and earth is perfect".
        (*Tso Chuan,* 22nd year of Duke Chuan)

With the exception of these references to the purely physical sky, references to T'ien in *Shih Ching, Shu Ching, Tso Chuan,* and *Kuo Yu* seem generally to designate the ruling or presiding personal T'ien or God, which also seems to be meant by Confucius in *The Analects.*

(2) The conception of spirits

Besides believing in one supreme personal Deity, both the Shang and Chou people believed a host of spirits. They termed them as Kuei[371] "demons", or Shen,[372] "spirits". Both terms were used interchangeably, indicating deities of a lower order and of subordinate rank. They formed a celestial hierarchy around Shang Ti, God on High, like that of the dignitaries around the king in the feudal system. There were spirits of heavenly bodies, mountains, rivers, grains, territories, down to those of the furnace, and the "southwest corner" of a house, etc. (*The Analects,* 3,13) Every family had its ancestors for its tutelary spirits, thus kings Wen and Wu were the tutelary spirits of the family of Chou. (*The Book of Poetry,* 2,6,5; 3,3,4) The spirits were classified into different ranks according to the system of human society. Thus in the Spring and Autumn period: "The son of Heaven performed all-inclusive sacrifices to various divinities and various classes of creatures. The feudal lords

sacrificed to Heaven and Earth, and the three luminaries (the sun, moon and stars), as well as to mountains and rivers in their territories. The ministers and great officials performed sacrifices to the spirits of the house and to the ancestors. The lesser officers and common people did not more than sacrifice to their ancestors. . . ."
(*Kuo Yu*, on Ch'u Yu, 2,2)

These spirits were generally supposed to inhabit the air and to survey the actions of men.

> *"Do not say, 'this place is not public;*
> *No one can see me here'.*
> *The approaches of spiritual beings*
> *Cannot be calculated (beforehand);*
> *But the more should they not be slighted."*
> (*The Book of Poetry*, 3,3,2,7)

Sometimes the departed great and good were supposed to dwell in heaven in the immediate presence of God, and to be able to come and go.

> *"King Wen is on high,*
> *Oh! bright is he in heaven.*
> *He ascends and descends,*
> *On the left and the right of God."*
> (*The Book of Poetry*, 3,1,1,1)

They were invariably represented as subordinate to God and engaged in carrying out His will. God was conceived as a moral Deity who would reward the good and punish the wicked, so all the spirits were believed to do the same. Even the spirits of ancestors could show no partiality in favour of their descendants who did evil, but, on the contrary, would join in their chastisement. *Tso Chuan*, under the 5th year of Duke Hsi, 655 B.C., states:

"The spirits, regardless of who the man is, accept only virtue; therefore, the Book of Chou says, 'The Imperial Heaven has no partiality, he helps only those who are virtuous' . . . . Thus without virtue, the people will not be harmonious and the spirits will not accept the offerings. If the State of Chin seize Yu, and with illustrious virtue present fragrant offerings, will the spirits indeed reject them?".

In the *Kuo Yu*, under the year 647 B.C., it is said that the ruler should:

"Pacify the multitude of spirits and put in harmony the myriad of people. Therefore the Ode (3,1,6,6) says: 'He conformed to the example of his ancestors, and the spirits had no occasion for complaint!" (*Chin Yu*, 4,2)

During the Spring and Autumn period there were already men who took a more skeptical attitude towards the supernatural spirits and the so-called "Way of Heaven". *Tso Chuan* records speeches of several of such men, as for example under the 32nd year of Duke Chuang of Lu, 622 B.C.:

"Shih Yin[373] said: 'Is Kuo[374] going to perish? I have heard that it is when a state is about to flourish that (its ruler) listens to his people; when it is about to perish, he listens to the spirits.' "

Under the 18th year of Duke Chao, 527 B.C.:

"Tzu Ch'an[375] said: 'The Way of Heaven is distant, while the Way of Man is near. We cannot reach to the former; what means have we of knowing it? How should Pi Chao know the Way of Heaven? He is a great talker, and we need not wonder if his words sometimes come true.' "

And under the first year of Duke Ting, 509 B.C.:

"Shih Pai[376] said to Han Chien Tzu,[377] 'The State of Hsieh makes its appeal to men, while the State of Sung makes its appeal to spirits. The offence of Sung is great."

Confucius, though he believed in a personal God or Heaven, adopted more or less the same skeptical attitude towards the spirits. For example, he said: "To give one's self earnestly to the duties due to men, and, while respecting the spirits, to keep them at a distance, may be called wisdom." (*The Analects*, 6,20)

(3) The means of communication with God and spirits

(a) God revealed Himself to man

a. Through nature

"The Master said: 'Does Heaven speak? The four seasons pursue their courses, and all things are (continually) being produced, (but) does Heaven say anything?' " (*The Analects*, 17,9)

"It is Heaven which is all-intelligent and observing. Let the sage take it as his pattern." (*The Book of History*, Yueh Ming,[378] Charge of Yue)

> "*Heaven, in giving birth to the multitudes of the people,*
> *To every faculty and relationship annexed its law.*
> *The people possess this normal nature,*
> *And they (consequently) love its normal virtue.*"
>   (*The Book of Poetry*, 3,3,6,1)

b. Through rulers and teachers

"Heaven, out of compassion for the people below, has appointed over them princes, and give them teachers, that they may assist God on high in cherishing and tranquilizing the four quarters (of the world). Thus with regard to the guilty or the innocent how dare we transgress his will."

(*The Book of History*, Tai Shih Shang,[379] the first part of the "Great Oath"); (see also The *Book of Poetry*, 3,1,7,1)

c. Through the general opinion of the people—"vox populi vox Dei"

"Heaven shows compassion towards the people, what the people desire, Heaven will grant it to them."

(*The Book of History*, Tai Shih Shang,[380] the first part of the "Great Oath")

"Heaven sees as my people see, and hears as my people hear." (*The Book of History*, Tai Shih Chung,[381] the second part of the "Great Oath")

(b) Prayers

a. Prayers for wisdom, virtue

> *See King Ching's prayers in the ancestral temple.*
>   (*The Book of Poetry*, 4,1,3,3)

b. Prayers for self sacrifice for the death and sins of others

When King Wu was seriously sick, his brother Chou Kung[382] prayed to the spirits of his ancestors to spare the life of his brother, the king; "But if it cannot be otherwise, then take me Tan[383] instead of such a one's person (King Wu)." He was willing to die for his brother. That prayer, it is recorded, was then laid up in the metal-bound casket.

(*The Book of History*, Chin T'eng[384] or the "metal-bound casket")
The prayer of T'ang for the sins of his people.

"I, the child of *li*, presume to use a dark-coloured victim, and presume to pray frankly to Thee, O most great and sovereign God, that the sinner I dare not pardon, and thy ministers, O God, I do not keep in obscurity. The examination of them is by thy mind, O God. If, in my person, I commit sins, they are not to be attributed to you, the people of the myriad regions. If you in the myriad regions commit sins, these sins must rest on my person."

(*The Analects*, 20,1,3)

c. Prayer for help

> "*O azure Heaven, O azure Heaven, look on these proud men, pity these who are troubled.*"
> (*The Book of Poetry*, 2,5,6)

d. Prayers of praise and thanksgiving
They were generally connected with sacrifices.
(See the following section on sacrifices)
(c) Sacrifices

> "*I have brought my offerings, a ram and a bull, May Heaven accept them!*"
> (*The Book of Poetry*, 4,1,7 and also 3,2,1)

Sacrifices to God and spirits, especially ancestors' spirits, were very commonly practiced and were regarded as one of the most important duties of kings and their ministers as well as the common people. Most of the bronze vessels of the Shang and Chou dynasties that have been preserved were mainly used for sacrificial or ceremonial purposes, and ancient literature is full of instances of sacrifices and regulations and ceremonies concerning them.

The motives underlying those sacrifices varied considerably between different individuals on different occasions.

a. The most common motive was perhaps to serve God or spirits, in order to please them and receive blessing from them.

"How is it I am afflicted with drought?
I cannot ascertain the cause of it.
In praying for a good year I was abundantly early;
I was not late in sacrificing to the spirits of the four quarters of
the land.
God in the great Heaven does not consider me."
(The Book of Poetry, 3,3,4,6)

b. For thanksgiving

"The spirits conferred prosperous harvest upon them and the people offered things up out of gratitude."
(Kuo Yu, Chu Yu, 2,1)

"The great sacrifice, the suburban sacrifice (made to Heaven in winter and Earth in summer), the sacrifices to those ancestors who have done great deeds, and to those who have displayed remarkable virtue, and sacrifices performed to show gratitude—these five are the sacrifices on the statute books of the state. In addition there are spirits of the soil and grain, and of mountains and rivers, all of whom have accomplished outstanding deeds on behalf of the people. As to the sages and virtuous men of former times, it is through them that shining sincerity has been created. As to the three luminaries in heaven, they are what the people look up to with reverence. As to the Five Elements on Earth, these are what induce life and propagation. As to the famous mountains, rivers and marshes of the nine provinces, it is from these that useful natural resources are derived. Anything not in the above classes is not put in the records to be sacrificed to." *(Kuo Yu, Lu Yu, 1.9)*

c. For social and political reasons

"Sacrifice is that through which one can show one's filial piety and give peace to the people, pacify the country and make the people settled. . . .

"Among the common people, men and women, according to days of good fortune, offer their sacrificial victim. They are reverent with the sacrificial grain contained in the vessels, show care in cleaning up, are prudent in the decorations of their clothing, and cautious in their wine offering. They give guidance to their sons and blood relatives, follow the seasonal sacrifices, are pious in their ancestral worship, and conduct their words along harmonious paths, so as to make illustrious their sacrifices to the early ancestors. They are reverent and solemn as if someone were overlooking them.

"Thereby local friends and relatives through marriage elder and younger brothers and blood relations are united. Thereby all sorts of abuses are stopped; the evils of slander are rooted out; those who are friends are united; relatives are drawn into a common bond; and both superior and inferior are put at rest, so as thus to extend and strengthen the family. It is through these sacrifices that those above teach the people proper respect, and those below make manifest their service to their superiors. . . . It is through the sacrifices that the unity of the people is strengthened, and why, then, should they abandon them?" (*Kuo Yu*, Ch'u Yu, 2,2)

Looked at from this viewpoint, sacrifice becomes the sort of thing which the Confucian philosopher, Hsun Tzu,[385] describes as follows: "Among superior men it is considered to be a human practice; among common people it is considered to be a serving of the spirits." (*Hsun Tzu*, p. 245)

There was no image of any shape, nor idol worship of any kind. Sacrifices were, as a rule, performed in the open air to the invisible spirits of Heaven or God. There was, however, a temple dedicated to the worship of ancestors. It was styled "Miao",[386] and in this temple clan ancestors were worshipped and sacrificed to.

No man was separated to be a priest. The heads of every family, village, district, and state, were supposed to be the representatives to offer sacrifices to the spirits of the family, village, district and state, respectively. "For a man to sacrifice to a spirit which does not belong to him", said Confucius, "is flattery". (*The Analects*, 2,24)

The only assurance for the acceptance of any sacrifice to Heaven or spirits was the moral conduct on the part of those who offered it. Thus *Tso Chuan* states: "The spirits, regardless of who the man is, accept only virtue. . . . Without virtue the people will not be harmonious and the spirits will not accept the offerings." (*Tso*

Chuan, under the fifth year of Duke Hsi, 655 B.C.) Again, under the 10th year of Duke Chuang, 684 B.C.: "When there is but small sincerity, which is not perfect, the spirits will not give you happiness." *Kuo Yu* records a speech made concerning the descent of a divine being which occurred in Hsin in 662 B.C.:

"When a state is about to flourish, its ruler is equable, perspicacious, sincere and upright. He is refined, pure, kind and in harmonious equilibrium. His virtue is sufficient to make his sacrifices manifest, and his kindness is sufficient to unify the people. The spirits enjoy his offerings, and the people listen to him. People and spirits are without resentment. Therefore illustrious spirits descend in it (his state), to survey his virtuous government, and scatter happiness to all alike." (*Kuo Yu*, Chou Yu, 1.12)

(d) Divination and magic

Divination and magic were important means of communication with God and spirits as practiced by the Shang and Chou people.

Ch'ien Han Shu, "I Wen Chih"[387], gives six classes of the arts of Divination and Magic, which were commonly practiced in ancient China. They were *T'ien Wen*[388], Astrology; *Li Pu*[389], Almanacs; *Wu Hsing*[390], Five Elements; *Shih Kuei*[391], Divination Plant and Tortoise Shell; *Tsa Chan*[392], Miscellaneous Divination; and *Hsing*[393], System of Forms. All these six kinds of divination and magic were all mentioned in *Tso Chuan* in the Spring and Autumn period, the period of Confucius. (See Fung Yu-lan's *A History of Chinese Philosophy*, translated by Derk Bodde, pp. 26-29)

D. Life of Confucius

The name Confucius is a Latinization of K'ung Fu Tzu,[394] meaning K'ung the Master; his given name is Ch'iu;[395] and his cognomen Chung-ni.[396] Very few dates of the early Chinese philosophers have been accepted so confidently by modern critical Chinese scholars as that of Confucius. In 1917, for example, Dr. Hu Shih wrote in his preface to *The Development of the Logical Method in Ancient China*, "Chinese historians have been very careless in assigning the dates of the philosophers dealt with in this essay. I have accepted only one date without question—that of Confucius." Although a life history full of romance has been painted for this great teacher by Chinese historians and Western writers, a large part of the story has been questioned by modern critics. Perhaps the best and comparatively reliable life history of Confucius is the long chapter (chap. 47) devoted to him in *Shih Chi* or *The Historical Records* by Ssu-ma Ch'ien in the first century B.C. Even that, according to modern critics, is not entirely free from unreliability. In order to make it as reliable as possible, the story here presented has to be very sketchy. For the sake of clearness, the life of this great historical personage is briefly summarized as follows:

Date	Age	Important events
551	Birth	21st year of King Ling of Chou. 22nd year of Duke Hsiang of Lu. Born in the town of Tsou,[397] the present Ch'u-fu, in the State of Lu, which is now a part of Shantung Province. His ancestors were of the Royal House of Sung, but his great grandfather had moved to Lu, where the family became impoverished. His father, Shuliang Ho, was once a city major and a man of great strength and

courage. His mother, Yen Cheng-tsai, was well educated and of good character, and appears to have stimulated his ambition and encouraged his studies. (*Li Chi* Bk. 2, Sec. 1, pt. 1) His father probably died soon after he was born.

544	8	When he was a child, he used to play at making sacrificial offerings and performing the ceremonies. Chi Cha[398] of Wu visited scholars and politicians of different states. Next year Tzu Ch'an became the prime-minister of Cheng.
537	15	He decided to be a student, and learned very hard from great masters of different subjects.
531	19	He married, and about the same time entered upon his official career in Lu, being first a keeper of grain stores and then in charge of public lands. (*Mencius* 5,2,5)
525	27	T'an Tzu[399] came to Lu, Confucius saw him and learnt the ancient official systems from him. (*Tso Chuan*, under the 17th year of Duke Chao) Three years afterwords Tzu Ch'an died, Confucius wept for his death.
518	34	Baron Meng Hsi[400] of Lu died. Before his death he advised his two sons, Baron Meng Yi,[401] and Nan Kung Ching Shu,[402] to study *li* under Confucius. Probably this year he went to Chou to learn *li* from Lao-tzu. After he returned to Lu, "More and more disciples came to study under him." (*The Historical Records*)
517	35	Confucius went to Ch'i[403] with Duke Chao of Lu whose troops were defeated by the joined forces of three barons of Lu, namely, Baron P'ing of Chi,[404] Baron Meng[405] and Baron Shu-sun.[406] Baron P'ing of Chi ran the government for seven years until Duke Ting[407] was elected to be the ruler of Lu.

Confucius was dissatisfied with the political and social order of Ch'i. He said, "Ch'i by one change, would come to the State of Lu. Lu by one change, would come to Tao (a state where true principles dominated)." (*The Analects*, 6, 22) Duke Ching of Ch'i wanted to put him in power, but the plan was interrupted by Yen Ying.[408] He spent most of his time in teaching his disciples, and especially indulged himself in music. "When the Master was in Ch'i he heard the Shao, and for three months did not know the taste of meat. 'I did not think,' he said, 'that music could have been made so excellent as this.'" (*The Analects*, 7,13)

510   42   Duke Chao of Lu died an exile in Ch'i, his son Duke Ting[409] succeeded him, but the real power was in the hands of the Chi, Meng and Shu-sun families.

About this time Confucius returned to Lu, but owing to the chaotic conditions there, politically, socially, and morally, Confucius "decided not to go into the government, but retired to study, or edit the books of poetry and history and ritual and music. The number of disciples rapidly grew, and there were many who came from distant parts of the land." (*The Historical Records*) Baron P'ing of Chi died; his son Baron Huan succeeded him.

505   47   Yang Yu (also referred to in *The Analects* as Yang Ho)[410] arrested his master Baron Huan of Chi, put him in prison, and made him sign a pledge before releasing him.

502   50   Kung-Shan Pu Ch'ou, who did not get along with Baron Huan of chi, started a rebellion in the city of Pi,[411] and allied himself with Yang Hu; but in the following year they were defeated, and Yang Hu escaped to Ch'i. Confucius was then put in power

by Duke Ting of Lu, first as the magistrate of Chung-tu, then promoted to the office of secretary of Public Works, and finally became the Grand Secretary of Justice.

500   52   When Duke Ting of Lu went to attend a good-will conference with Duke Ching of Ch'i at Chia-ku,[412] Confucius was asked to go with Duke Ting as acting Chief Minister. He persuaded the Duke to take along with them the Right and Left Secretaries of War. As the result of the conference, the Duke of Ch'i returned the lands of Yun,[413] Wen Yang[414] and Kuei-t'ien,[415] which he had taken away from Lu.

497   55   Baron Huan of Chi put his trust in Confucius, and made Tzu-lu, Confucius' disciple, Secretary of his Barony. Confucius suggested to Duke Ting, "A subject ought not to keep a private army, and a lord ought not to have a town with over a hundred parapets (each parapet representing 30 feet of length)." (*The Historical Records*) With the help of Baron Chi, Baron Shu-sun's city of Hou, and Baron Chi's city of P'i,[416] where rebellion under Kung-Shan Pu Ch'ou had taken place, were razed by the Duke, who did not succeed in razing the city of Ch'eng,[417] the stronghold of Baron Meng.

496   56   In the 14th year of Duke Ting, he was promoted to the position of Prime Minister. After three months of premiership, he found that he could not get along with the Duke. When the Duke neglected his duty of sending burnt offerings to the ministers after the public worship and sacrifice to Heaven, he left his position and went to Wei. Thus began his 13 years of wandering life among the different states (496-484), teaching his disciples and preaching his doctrines. The states which he

travelled through, as mentioned in *The Historical Records*, were Wei,[418] Ch'en,[419] Ts'ai,[420] Ts'ao,[421] Sung,[422] Cheng,[423] and to the border of Chin.[424] He underwent hardships and dangers staying now in one state and then in another.

484   68   Confucius returned to his own State of Lu in the 11th year of Duke Ai of Lu,[425] and there spent most of his time teaching.

481   71   When Baron Chen Heng[426] killed his master Duke Chien[427] of Chi, "Confucius bathed, went to court, and informed Duke Ai, saying, 'Chen Heng has slain his sovereign. I beg that you undertake to punish him.' " (*The Analects* 14, 22)

     The same year two of Confucius' most favourite disciples Yen Hui[428] and Chai Yu[429] died.

480   72   Another favourite disciple of Confucius Chung Yu,[430] or better known as Tzu Lu,[431] died in Wei. Confucius fell sick.

479   73   When Tzu Kung heard that his beloved Master was very ill he hurried to see him. Confucius was just then walking slowly around the door, supported by a walking stick, and said to him, "Ah Sze, why do you turn up so late?" Confucius then sighed and sang a song:

     "Ah! the T'ai-shan (the sacred mountain) is decaying!

     The roof beam is breaking!

     The wise man is weakening!"

He then shed tears and spoke to Tzu-kung, "For a long time the world has been living in moral chaos, and no ruler has been able to follow me. . . ." Seven days afterwards he died, aged 73. This was on the day Chi-ch'ou of April, in the 16th year of Duke Ai of Lu. He was buried in his native village,

Ch'u-fu. His students stayed near his tomb until the end of the three years mourning, and Tzu-kung stayed there three additional years. (*Mencius,* 3,1,4)
Regarding himself and his intellectual progress, the Master said: "At 15, I bent my mind on learning; at 30, I stood firm; at 40, I was free from doubts; at 50, I understood the way of Heaven; at 60, my ear was an obedient organ for the reception of truth; at 70, I could follow the desires of my heart without transgressing what was right." (*The Analects,* 2,4)

The great historian, Ssu-ma Ch'ien, wrote in the first century before Christ the following famous appraisal of the life and teaching of Confucius that can best describe the position then held and still held by the great Teacher in the hearts of the Chinese people:
The Book of Poetry says, 'High is the mountain I look up to, and bright is the example for our emulation! Although I cannot reach the top, my heart leaps up to it.' As I read the books of Confucius, I thought to myself how he must have looked. When visiting Lu, I saw the carriages, robes and sacred vessels displayed at the Temple, and watched how the Confucian students studied the historical systems at his home, and lingered on, unable to tear myself away from the place. Countless are the princes, rulers and great men in history, that the world has seen in its time: glorious in life, forgotten in death. But Confucius, though only a humble member of the cotton-clothed masses, remains among us as the acknowledged Master of scholars for over ten generations. By all, from the emperors, kings and princes down, who discuss the 'Six Arts', the final authority of the Master is fully and freely admitted. He indeed may be pronounced the 'Holiest Sage'."

CHAPTER III

CONFUCIUS IN RELATION TO
THE CLASSICS

OUTLINE

A. The Names and Various Groupings of the Classics
(A) The names of the Classics
(B) The various groupings of the Classics
1. Pre-Ch'in period—The formation of the "Six Classics"
2. Post-Ch'in period
  a. The five Classics of *The Historical Records*
  b. The nine Classics of *Han Shu*
  c. The six "stone classics" of the Han dynasty
  d. The twelve "stone classics" of the Tang dynasty
  e. The twelve Classics in the Ching Tien Shih Wen
  f. The first edition of the nine Classics from blocks in the Five
    Dynasties (A.D. 907-960)
  g. The thirteen "stone classics" of Kuo Tzu Chien in the Chien
    Lung period of the Ch'ing dynasty
  h. The "four books" and the "five classics"

B. The Controversies Between the Modern Text School and the
  Ancient Text School
(A) Controversies about the texts of the Classics
1. About the written characters used in the classical texts
2. About the contents of the Classics
  a. *The Book of Poetry*
  b. *The Book of History*
  c. *The Book of Changes*
  d. *The Book of Rites*
  e. *The Spring and Autumn Annals*
  f. *The Analects*
  g. *The Book of Filial Piety*
(B) The interpretation of the Classics

C. Some Views of Modern Higher Critics with Regard to the Relation of Confucius to the Classics

(A) The backgrounds of the modern higher critics

1. The general sceptical spirit of the modern age

2. The modern archaeological discoveries

3. Higher critics of the earlier periods

(B) The views of some of the modern higher critics

D. The Conclusions of the Present Writer

The Chinese Classics, like Greek and Roman models of antiquity, were, until recently, objects of an almost exclusive veneration. The name Confucius was in one way or another connected with them, and when Confucianism became a state cult the Classics were taken to sum up almost the whole of Chinese culture. Nevertheless, Chinese scholars, for more than two thousand years, have never entirely agreed with one another upon the problem of how the Classics were related to Confucius. The place of Confucius in Chinese history, as a matter of fact, has always fluctuated in accordance with the belief as to the nature of this relationship.

The problems of this chapter are these: What are the Chinese Classics? Did Confucius write them or compile them, or have anything to do with them? Was Confucius an originator, or a transmitter, or neither an originator nor a transmitter, or both an originator and a transmitter of the Classics? These are fundamental problems with regard to the position of Confucius in Chinese history.

Roughly speaking, all different opinions in Chinese history with regard to the Classics can be grouped under the following three headings, namely, "the modern text school" (Chin Wen Chia), "the ancient text school" (Ku Wen Chia), and the Modern Higher Critics. The following are chief topics for discussion in this chapter:

1. The names and various groupings of the Classics
2. The controversies between the Modern Text School and the Ancient Text School
3. The views of some of the Modern Higher Critics
4. The conclusions of the present

A. The Names and Various Groupings of the Classics

(A) The Names of the Classics

(1) *Shih Ching* or *The Book of Poetry*

This is a collection of 305 odes in various metres, besides six with music and title but without text, written generally in the early part of the Chou period before the time of Confucius.

(2) *Shu Ching* or *The Book of History*

It is a collection of historical documents, chiefly kings' proclamations, from Yao the Great (traditionally c. 2757-c.2258 B.C.) to Duke Mu of Chin (659-621 B.C.).

(3) *I Li* or *The Rites*

It treats of the ceremonial rites and the rules of proper conduct of everyday life in feudal China.

(4) *I Ching* or *The Book of Changes*

This deals with the principles of cosmic and social evolution. Originally it was a divination system based on changing arrangements of lines of an octogram.

(5) *Yueh Ching* or *The Book of Music*

It was lost during or before the Han dynasty. The chapter on Yueh Chi or *The Records of Music*, in the present Li Chi, is said to be a portion of the lost book.

(6) *Ch'un Ch'iu* or *The Spring and Autumn Annals*

It is a historical critique on politics during the reign of twelve dukes of the Lu State, 722-481 B.C.

The above six books are frequently called the 'Six Classics'.

(7) *Lun Yu* or *The Analects*

It is a collection of records of the conversations between Confucius and his disciples on a variety of subjects.

(8) *Hsiao Ching* or *The Book of Filial Piety*

This is a short book of less than 2,000 characters, dealing with the subject of filial piety, and is said to be the record of the conversations between Confucius and his disciple, Tseng-tzu.

(9) *Chou Li* or *The Official System of Chou*

It is said to be a record of the constitutional matters of the Chou dynasty.

(10) *Li Chi* or *The Book of Rites*

It is a collection of records of the ancient rites, and some of the sayings of Confucius and his disciples, but they were revised again and again by the Han scholars, such as, Tai Te, known as the Elder Tai, Tai Shen or the Younger Tai and the scholars of the later Han period, such as Ma Yung, Lu Chih and Cheng Hsuan. It is sometimes called Hsiao Tai Li Chi or the Younger Tai's Records of Rites, because it was chiefly on this record that the final revision by the scholars of the later Han was based.

(11) *Tso Chuan* or *Tso's Commentary*

It is said to be an interpretation of *The Spring and Autumn Annals* written by Tso Ch'iu-ming, a disciple of Confucius.

(12) *Kung-yang Chuan* or *Kung-yang's Commentary on The Spring and Autumn Annals*

(13) *Ku-liang Chuan* or *Ku-liang's Commentary*

Both Kung-yang's and Ku-liang's Commentaries are said to be the oral interpretations or detailed explanations of Confucius, of his own book, *The Spring and Autumn Annals*, transmitted by his disciples, and reduced to writing during the Han dynasty.

(14) *Erh Ya*

This is a dictionary for the study of the Classics, and has been considered to be the oldest dictionary in China.

(15) *Meng-tzu* or *Mencius*

It is a collection of the sayings of Mencius, probably gathered by his disciples. It was not included as a classic until the 11th century.

(16) *Ta Hsueh* or *The Great Learning*

(17) *Chung Yung* or *The Doctrine of the Mean*

Both *Ta Hsueh* and *Chung Yung* were originally two of the forty odd books in *Li Chi* or *The Book of the Rites*. They were singled out from the collection by philosophers of the Sung dynasty to form part of the so-called 'Four Books' with *Mencius* and *The Analects*.

(18) *Hsiao Hsueh* or *The Small Learning*

This is included as one of the Classics in *The Han Shu* or *The Official History of the Han Dynasty* written by Pan Ku (22-92 A.D.). It deals primarily with the various types and methods of writing and was taken as a primer for children in the Han and some other periods.

(19) *Lao-tzu*

This is a collection of the doctrines taught by Lao-tzu, the founder of the Taoist School. It was included as one of the Confucian Classics in the famous Ching Tien Shih Wen K'ao or *The Commentary on the Literature of the Classics*, written by the famous scholar, Lu Teh-ming, in the Tang dynasty. Lao-tzu was exceedingly popular in the T'ang period and is said to have been a teacher of Confucius.

(20) *Chuang-tzu*

This is said to be the work of Chuang-tzu, the most famous disciple of Lao-tzu and the greatest advocator and ablest exponent of Taoism. This is also included as one of the Confucius Classics in *The Ching Tien Shih Wen K'ao*.

(B) The Various Groupings of the Classics

1. The Pre-Ch'in Period—the formation of the 'Six Classics'

The following authoritative sayings by Confucius and others show something of the appearance and formation of the Liu Ching or "Six Classics".

a. "The Master said: 'It is by the Shih that the mind is aroused, it is by the *li* that the character is established, it is from the Yueh that the finish is received.' " (*The Analects*, 8, 8) Here we have the combination of Shih or *The Book of Poetry*, Li or *The Book of Rites*, and Yueh or *The Book of Music*.

b. "The Master's frequent themes of discourse were *Shih, Shu* and the maintenance of *Li*. (*The Analects*, 7, 17) Here we have the combination of *Shih* or *The Book of Poetry*, *Shu* or *The Book of History*, and *Li* or *The Book of Rites*.

c. "The Master said: 'If some years were added to my life I would give fifty to the study of the *I*, and then I might come to be without great faults.' " (*The Analects*, 7,16) Here *I* or *The Book of Changes* is added.

d. Mencius says, "Confucius was afraid, and made the Ch'un Ch'iu or *The Spring and Autumn Annals*." (*Mencius*, 3.2.9.8) So here we have *The Spring and Autumn Annals* added to the work of Confucius.

e. The first appearance of all the Six Classics mentioned together in Chinese literature is in the work of Chuang-tzu (369-286 B.C.). For example, he says: "Confucius told Lao-tzu, 'I have worked on the Shih, Shu, Li, Yueh, I and Ch'un Ch'iu for a long time. . . .' " Again he says with reference to the six books used by the Confucius: "The Shih describes aims; the Shu describes events; the Li describes conduct; the Yueh secures harmony; the I shows the principles of Yin and Yang; the Ch'un Ch'iu shows distinctions and duties."

So the complete formation of the Six Classics was very likely in the latter part of the period of the Warring States. (481-221 B.C.)

2. The Post-Ch'in Period

At the "Ch'in Burning" of 213 B.C., *The Book of Music* was almost completely destroyed. What was left was made a chapter of *Li Chi*, called *Yueh Chi* or *The Records of Music*. Hence the name of Wu Ching or "Five Classics" of the Confucian School.

Later on, owing to the controversies over the interpretation of the Classics and to the higher esteem of Confucius, the Commentaries on the Classics, such as the Three Commentaries of the Spring and Autumn Annals, namely, the Tso Commentary, the Kung-Yang Commentary and the Ku-Liang Commentary; the Dictionary of the Classics, that is the Erh Ya; the writings of famous Confucianists, such as, *The Analects, Mencius, The Great Learning, The Doctrine of the Mean, The Book of Filial Piety, The Small Learning, Lao-tzu* and *Chuang-tzu*, all became recognized as classics in one period or another. So there have been such terms as Five Classics, Six Classics, Seven Classics, Nine Classics, Eleven Classics, Twelve Classics, Thirteen Classics, etc.

It is impossible to date the exact period or dynasty in which certain groupings were made, as some writers have tried to do, because the groupings have frequently been arranged differently in the same period by different scholars, or sometimes by the same scholars under different conditions. But the groupings in the following works which have had a great influence on the spread and standardization of the classical studies, may be specially mentioned:

a. Shih Chi or *The Historical Records*, by Ssu-ma Ch'ien (140-80 B.C.), "father of Chinese history."

The Five Classics he mentioned were: *The Book of Poetry, The Book of History, The Book of Rites, The Book of Changes*, and *The Spring and Autumn Annals*.

b. *Han Shu* or *The Official History of the Han Dynasty* by Pan Ku (A.D. 22-92), "father of the Chinese dynastic histories."

Pan Ku here followed the number of Classics as given in the *Ch'i Lueh* or *The Seven Summaries* written by Liu Hsin. Nine Classics were mentioned. They were divided into 103 schools, and altogether 3,123 chapters were written on the Nine Classics. The following is a summary of them:

Nine Classics	No. of schools	No. of chaps.
Book of Changes	13	294
Book of History	9	412
Book of Poetry	6	416
Book of Rites	13 (Includes I Li, Chou Li and Li Chi)	555
Book of Music	6	165
Spring and Autumn Annals	23 (Includes Three Commentaries: Kung-yang, Ku-liang, Tso)	948
Analects	12	229
Book of Filial Piety	11 (Includes Erh Ya)	59
Hsiao Hsueh (Small Learning)	10	49
	103	3,123

So actually the Classics as accepted in part or in full in later periods were given here, except that in and after the Sung dynasty the *Ta Hsueh* and *Chung Yung* have been regarded as two separate Classics and formed part of the "Four Books" with *Mencius* and *The Analects*; and in *The Ching Tien Shih Wen* in the T'ang dynasty when the Taoist Classics, *Lao-tzu* and *Chuang-tzu*, were also taken into the group of the Confucian Classics.

c. The Stone Classics of the Han dynasty

Between A.D. 175 and 183, under the reign of Emperor Ling, an imperial order was issued for the engraving in stone of the complete text of the Six Classics. The task was entrusted to Ts'ai Yung (A.D. 133-192) who wrote the text himself in red ink on stone tablets for the workmen to cut. It is reported that when the whole work was finished and the tablets were set up at the gates of the Grand College at Lo-yang, "the people who came to see them or copy from them were so many that there were more than one thousand carts every day, and the streets and avenues of the city were blocked by them. They were destroyed about a century later, probably due to political intrigue. At present the National Library of Peiping has acquired an oblong fragment measuring 24 x 12 inches, which was unearthed near Lo-yang in the summer of 1929. The two faces bear 120 characters beautifully executed in the Li Shu style, which was the prevailing form of writing at that time. The texts selected were all from the Modern Text School, as distinguished from the Ancient and Archaic Text School. The following are the names of the Classics and the texts used:

Six Classics	*Version*
Book of Poetry	Lu version (Lu Shih)
Book of Rites	Elder Tai Records (Ta Tai Li Chi)
Book of Changes	Ching Shih version (Ching Shih I)
Ch'un Ch'iu, with Kung-yang Commentary	Yen-yen version
Book of History	Ou-yang text (Ou-yang Shang Shu)
Analects	Chang Hou version

d. *The Ching T'ien Shih Wen* written in A.D. 583 by Lu Teh-ming of the T'ang dynasty.

The following twelve Classics were mentioned:

Chou I (The Book of Changes of Chou)
Shang Shu (The Book of the Ancient Records)
Mao Shih (The Book of Odes of the Mao Version)
San Li (Three Records of Rites)
I Li (The Rites)
Chou Li (The Official System of Chou)
Li Chi (The Book of Rites)
Ch'un Ch'iu (The Spring and Autumn Annals)
Hsiao Ching (The Book of Filial Piety)
Lun Yu (The Analects)
Lao-tzu
Chuang-tzu
Erh Ya

e. The Stone Classics of T'ang dynasty

They were engraved between 836 and 841 under the supervision of Cheng T'ang.[1] The style of writing used was similar to the modern simple K'ai Shu or "model script". Chavennes has published clear photographs taken in 1907 from the stelae which are now in the Pei Lin or "Forest Tablets" at Hsi-an. These include only five of the 12 Classics, namely, the books of Changes, Poetry, History, Analects and Erh Ya. Not produced by him are the *Three Rites, Three Commentaries of the Spring and Autumn Annals*, and *The Book of Filial Piety*. About 1928 Chang Ts'ung-ch'ang, then governor of Shantung Province, sponsored a splendid wood-block edition in 74 large volumes, based upon rubbings from the tablets before they had been damaged in the great earthquake of January 23, 1556. This edition, entitled *Tang K'ai-Cheng Shih Pei Erh Ching* or the *Twelve Classics on the Stone Tablets of the K'ai-Cheng Year of the T'ang Dynasty*, bears the imprint of the Pi Jen T'ang. The following is a list of the names of the twelve Classics, the number of stones cut, the number of volumes, the texts, and the number of words.

Twelve Classics	No. of Tablets	No. of vols.	The Texts	No. of words
Shang Shu (The Book of History)	10	13	Kung Shih	27,134
Chou I (The Book of Changes)	9	9	Wang Pi's Commentary	24,437
Mao Shih (The Book of Poetry)	16	20	Cheng's Commentary	40,848
Chou Li (Official System of Chou)	17	11	Cheng's Commentary	49,516
I Li (The Rites)	20	17	Cheng's Commentary	57,111
Li Chi (The Book of Rites)	33	20	Cheng's Commentary	98,994
Ch'un Ch'iu Tso Chuan (Tso's Commentary)	67	30	Tu's Commentary	198,945
Ch'un Ch'iu Kung-yang Chuan (Kung-yang's Com.)	17	12	Ho Hsiu's Commentary	44,748
Ch'un Ch'iu Ku-liang Chuan (Ku-liang's Com.)	16	12	Fan Ning's Commentary	42,089
Hsiao Ching (The Book of Filial Piety)	1	1	Emperor Ming's Commentary	
Lun Yu (The Analects)	7	10	Ho Yen's Commentary	16,509
Erh Ya	5	3	Cheng Po's Commentary	10,791

f. The first edition of the Nine Classics from blocks in the Five Dynasties (A.D. 907-960)

In 932 Emperor Ming Tsung of the short Posterior T'ang dynasty ordered the Nine Classics to be cut in wood, printed and sold to the public under the supervision of Feng Tao. The work of editing and of printing lasted for 21 years, and 21 years of civil war at that, during which four dynasties, three of them founded by Turkish or Uigur adventurers, followed one another in rapid succession. But somehow or other Feng Tao retained his post as head of the civil administration, while T'ien Min, head of the whole undertaking for printing and editing, and his associates, worked steadily on at the Classics. Finally in 953 the whole work was completed in 130 volumes containing the Nine Classics and their commentaries, the text of which was based avowedly upon that cut in stone about a century before. The following are the names of the Nine Classics printed:

> *The Book of Changes*
> *The Book of History*
> *The Book of Poetry*
> *I Li* or *The Rites*
> *Chou Li* or *The Official System of Chou*
> *Li Chi* or *The Book of Rites*
> Tso's *Commentary on the Spring and Autumn Annals*
> Kung-yang's *Commentary on the Spring and Autumn Annals*
> Ku-liang's *Commentary on the Spring and Autumn Annals*

g. The thirteen stone-classics of Kuo Tzu Chien[2] put up in the 56th year of Ch'ien Lung[3] of the Ching dynasty (1791 A.D.)

They were copied and cut in stone from the *Shih San Ching Chu Su* or *The Thirteen Classics with Their Commentaries*[4] published in the 12th year of Ts'ung Chen[5] of the Ming dynasty (A.D. 1639), all except two, the commentary of *Mencius* which was Chu Hsi's in the stone-classics instead of Tsao Ch'i's[6] of the Han dynasty as used in the *Shih San Ching Chu Su*, and in the commentary of the Hsiao Ching, which was that of Emperor Shih Tsu of the Ch'ing dynasty, instead of that of Ts'ung Chen of the Ming dynasty. The following are the names of the Thirteen Classics and their commentaries or versions:

Names of the Classics	No. of vols.	Commentaries or versions
Chou I	10	Wang Pi of Wei (魏)[7] and Han K'ang-po of Chin's commentaries (晋)[8]
Shang Shu	13	K'ung An-Kuo's Version (漢)[9]
Mao Shih	20	Mao Heng's version[10] Cheng Hsuan's commentary (漢)[11]
Chou Li	12	Cheng Hsuan's commentary[12]
I Li	17	Cheng Hsuan's commentary[13]
Li Chi	20	Cheng Hsuan's commentary[14]
Tso's Commentary on Ch'un Ch'iu	30	Tu Yu's commentary (晋)[15]
Kung-yang's Com. on Ch'un Ch'iu	12	Ho Hsiu's commentary (漢)[16]
Ku-liang's Com. on Ch'un Ch'iu	12	Fan Ning's commentary (晋)[17]
Lun Yu	10	Ho Yen's commentary (魏)[18]
Hsiao Ching	1	Emperor Shih Tsu's commentary[19]
Erh Ya	3	Kuo Po's commentary (晋)[20]
Mencius	7	Chu Hsi's commentary (宋)[21]

h. Ssu Shu, Wu Ching or the 'Four Books' and 'Five Classics'

This was a classification made by the Sung philosophers, especially Chu Hsi (A.D. 1130-1200), and has been popularly used since then.

The Ssu Shu or the "Four Books" are:

The Analects
Mencius
Ta Hsueh or *The Great Learning*
Chung Yung or *The Doctrine of the Mean*

The Wu Ching or the "Five Classics" are:

The Book of Changes
The Book of History
The Book of Poetry
The Spring and Autumn Annals
    Li Chi or *The Book of Rites*

(It does not, like *Chou Li*, treat of mere matters peculiar to one dynasty, but matters important in all time; not like *I Li*, of usages belonging to one or more of the official classes, but of those that concern all men. Thus *Li Chi* has taken a higher position than *I Li* and *Chou Li*.)

B. Controversies Between the Modern Text School and the Ancient Text School

When Confucianism gained complete ascendency over all other rival schools in the reign of Emperor Wu (140-86 B.C.) of the Han dynasty, the Five Classics became the official texts of learning. T'ai Hsueh or the Grand College was established and Po Shih or professors were selected to teach the classics. The texts were in Li Shu or "clerkly style", which was the prevailing style of calligraphy at that time. But the term Chin-wen or text in "modern characters" did not arise until the finding of the Ku-wen classics, or classics of "ancient" or "archaic script", by Prince Hsien of Ho-chien, Prince Kung of Lu and others. They were said to be the original texts which had fortunately escaped the great "burning" of Ch'in (213 B.C.). The classics of the archaic script thus found were *Chou Kuan* or *The Official System of Chou, Shang Shu* or *The Book of History, I Li*[22] or *The Lost Rites, Li Chi* or *The Book of Rites, Mao Shih* or *Mao's Edition of The Book of Poetry, Tso Chuan* or *Tso's Commentary on Spring and Autumn Annals, Lun Yu* or *The Analects, Hsiao Ching* or *The Book of Filial Piety,* and *Mencius, Lao-tzu,* etc.

Liu Hsin (c. 53 B.C.-A.D. 18), who was elected by Emperor Ai (6-2 B.C.) to succeed his father Liu Hsiang, the Court Consultant, to collate the classics and their commentaries, works of all schools of philosophy, poetry and rhymed prose, was the first man who sought official recognition of the Ancient Texts by urging the establishment of chairs for instruction of *Shang Shu, Chou Li, Tso Chuan* and *Mao Shih* in the Grand College. A fierce opposition at once arose from the classical scholars led by Kung Shen,[23] King-sun Lu[24] and Shih Tan[25] who accused Liu Hsin of "having changed confusedly the old text, and wronged and slandered those who had been elected by former emperors." Finally Liu Hsin was forced to resign from his position because of "the reviling of all scholars and the threat of murder." This was the beginning of the controversy. When Wang Mang, the usurper, assumed the imperial title Hsin Huang Ti or "Emperor of the Hsin Dynasty" in A.D. 8, Liu Hsin, being the friend of the usurper, was made prime minister of the new emperor, and classics of the ancient text were very much encouraged. But the characters of the archaic script were different from the characters commonly used, and were known only by a few. So under imperial patronage schools were established to teach the ancient text, and official positions were awarded to good scholars of the ancient script. Thousands of students, according to *Han Shu*, came from different parts of the country to receive the new education. Thus the "Ancient Text School" was firmly established, and the scholars of the modern text, for the sake of self protection, united to form what is called the "Modern Text School", and so the controversy continued. The more prominent leaders of the Modern Text School were Fan Sheng,[26] Li Yu,[27] Ho Hsiu,[28] Lin Shih,[29] Chang Hsing,[30] and others; and those of the Ancient Text School were Ch'en Yuan,[31] Chia K'uei,[32] Ma Yung,[33] Hsu Shen,[34] Lu Chih,[35] Cheng Hsuan,[36] and others. The modern Chinese scholar Liao Chi-p'ing says: "The Modern Text School came from the dynasties of Chou and Ch'in, while the Ancient Text School was established during the Later Han period (22 B.C.-A.D. 220); it is wrong to say both these schools existed together since Ch'in and Han."

The Ancient Texts around which most of the controversies were centred were *Chou Li, Mao's Edition of the Book of Poetry, Tso's Commentary on the Spring and Autumn Annals*, and *Kung-yang's Edition of the Ancient Text of the Book of History*. All these "ancient texts" were accepted officially by the chairs of instruction in the Grand College in the reign of Emperor P'ing[37] (A.D. 1-5). But the "modern texts" having a much longer history were still generally regarded as more orthodox and were accepted by most of the scholars in the Later Han period. Great classical scholars of the

Modern Text School like Chang Hsing,[38] Ch'ai Yuan,[39] and Lou Wang,[40] are recorded to have had about ten thousand students each. The texts of the Stone Classics put up in A.D. 183 were all from the Modern Text School. At the end of the Han dynasty there came Cheng Hsuan,[41] (A.D. 127-200), one of the greatest classical scholars in Chinese history. He was versed both in the Modern and the Ancient Texts, but he followed chiefly the Ancient Text in his famous commentaries on the classics, though occasionally he used also the Modern Text to comment on the Ancient Text. With him ended the first period of the controversy in favor of the Ancient Text School. K'ang Yu-wei, the leader of the Modern Text School of modern times, says, "The flame of the counterfeit Ancient Text was already high at the time of Chia (Ch'i) and Ma (Yung), but the reason why the Ancient Text was established and usurped the throne of the Modern Text can be attributed entirely to one person, Cheng K'ang-ch'eng (Cheng Hsuan)." After that the Modern Text School entered into an eclipse which lasted about sixteen centuries.

In the middle of the Ch'ing dynasty (A.D. 1644-1911), there was a marked resurrection of the Modern Text School. Some of its able leaders were Liu Feng-lu[42] (1776-1829), P'i Hsi-jui[43] (1850-1908), Kung Tzu-chen[44] (1792-1841), Wei Yuan[45] (1794-1856), Liao P'ing[46] (1852-1932), Ts'ui Shih[47] (1740-1816) and K'ang Yu-wei[48] (1858-1927). Among these leaders K'ang Yu-wei was the greatest, whose two epoch-making works, *Hsin-hsueh-wei-ching-k'ao*, or *Research on the False Classics of the School of Hsin*, and *K'ung-tzu-to-ku-kai-chih-k'ao* or *A Study of Confucius' Effort to Revolutionize the System of Chou by Attributing His System to the Ancient System*, have still a tremendous influence among present-day scholars. These leaders met the same opposition and difficulties as the leaders of the Ancient Text School during the Han dynasty. K'ang Yu-wei, for example, was many times imprisoned, and his work *Research on the False Classics of the School of Hsin* was burnt and prohibited three times by the Manchu government, in the years 1894, 1998, and 1900. The greatest leader of the modern Ancient Text School was Chang T'ai-yen (1869-1936), who led the more conservative classical scholars and challenged for a "pen-war" against the growing revolutionary school. (See *Ku Shih Pien*, Vol. 1, Introduction)

At present, both of these schools have many adherents, but most of the more careful scholars, though in favour of the Modern Text School, especially the works of its able exponent K'ung Yu-wei, are dissatisfied with both of these schools. Some of them have called themselves adherents of a third school which is gradually building up, namely, the Hsin Ku Shih P'ai or the New School of Ancient History. But since no definite forms or common principles or beliefs have yet been fixed or agreed upon, the writer is content to limit himself by calling them Modern Higher Critics of China, in so far as their criticisms on the Confucian Classics are taken into consideration.

The controversies between these two schools, either in ancient or in modern China, are too complicated and also beyond the scope of this thesis to discuss in detail. It is sufficient to state briefly two important points in the controversies which have a more direct bearing upon Confucius, namely, the differences with regard to the texts of the Confucian Classics, and the important interpretations of these Classics in relation to Confucius.

(A) Controversies About the Texts of the Classics

1. About the Written Characters Used in the Classical Texts

One of the chief points of the controversy between the two schools is that of the styles of written characters used in classical texts. The texts of the classics of the Modern Text School were written in "modern characters" called Li Shu or "clerkly style", the prevailing script in the Han time, while the texts of the Ancient Text School were written in "ancient characters" which were supposed to be widely used in the Chou and Ch'in periods. The scholars of the Ancient Text School criticized the texts used by the scholars of the Modern Text School as the later production of the early Han scholars, because they were written with modern characters; but their texts, which they claimed were written with the ancient characters presumably used at the time of Confucius, and fortunately escaped the Ch'in holocaust, were accidentally found in the wall of Confucius' house, and were the genuine ones compiled and transmitted by Confucius himself or his immediate disciples. The scholars of the Modern School, on the other hand, condemned the characters used in the archaic script of the Ancient Text School as being the forgery of the Han scholars and particularly of Liu Hsin. And so the controversy arose. Hsu Shen[49] (A.D. 30-124), one of the greatest leaders of the Ancient Text School, said in defence of "ancient characters" that many bronze vessels had been found with the inscription of "ancient characters" on them very similar to those of the ancient classical texts. The following is a quotation from the preface to his famous book *Shou Wen Chieh Tzu*[50] or *Treatise on Literature and on the Explanation of Characters*:

"The Texts of the Wall are those which were found by Prince Kung of Lu when he destroyed the wall of the house of Confucius. They consist of *Li Chi, Shang Shu, Ch'un Ch'iu* and *Hsiao Ching*. Besides, Chang Ts'ang,[51] the Marquis of Pei-p'ing,[52] offered *Tso's Commentary on Ch'un Ch'iu*. Frequently, in the mountains and rivers of the counties and states, Ting[53] and I[54] have been found with inscriptions of ancient characters similar to those of the ancient text. Although it is not possible to see in clear detail the characters of the remote past, still they can roughly be identified. Nevertheless, people in the world have greatly opposed and slandered the ancient characters, saying, that those who love curiosity have purposely and cunningly changed the correct words, forged the unknown characters, put them in the wall, and thus changed and confused the customary practices, so that they can show themselves in the world. . . ."

In answer to this argument K'ang Yu-wei in his *Hsin Hsueh Wei Ching K'ao* or *Research on the False Classics of the School of Hsin* said that all those bronze vessels with inscriptions of "ancient characters", as mentioned by Hsu Shen, were nothing but forgeries. They were made purposely by Liu Hsin and "were buried in the suburbs or country places and then dug out, or they were hidden in the mountains or valleys to deceive people of later generations". He argued convincingly that the texts of the classics with the "modern characters" of the Modern Text School were the same as those used in the pre-Ch'in time. The Ch'in Fires did not destroy all the classics as the scholars of the Ancient Text School thought they did, except *I Ching*, a book of divination, and those hidden in the wall of Confucius' house and later on discovered by Prince Kung of Lu and Prince Hsien of Ho-chien. He pointed out from Ssu-ma Ch'ien's *Shih Chi* or *The Historical Records* that the books of the Po Shih or professors of the Ch'in dynasty were not burnt. Some of the professors who taught in the Han dynasty were those who were professors of the Ch'in dynasty, and the texts of the classics which they taught were no doubt the same as those of the Ch'in or pre-Ch'in period. He also attributed the success of the "ancient character" to Hsu Shen whose *Shuo Wen Chien Tzu*, as mentioned above, has had a tremendous influence on Chinese writing.

It was chiefly from the differences of the characters of the classical texts that the names Modern Text School and Ancient School were derived.

2. About the Contents of the Classics

Not only did the characters of the classical texts form the centre of controversy, but also the contents of the classics. The contents of the classics of the two schools differed widely not only in some of the phrases, sections or chapters, and commentaries of some of the classics, but also in whole books of certain classics. In each school there were also different kinds of versions and commentaries of the classics which were recognized at court in one period or another. So there were various schools with their recensions of and commentaries on the classics of both the Modern Text School and the Ancient Text School, and all of them claimed to be more faithful to the teaching of their common master, Confucius.

It is impossible here to deal in detail with this most complicated though important problem in the study of Confucius. The following is a brief summary of the more important schools with their recensions of or commentaries on the classics of both the Modern Text and Ancient Text Schools as given in *Shih Chi, Han Shu*, and *Ching Tien Shih Wen* or *The Commentary on the Literature of the Classics*, commonly regarded as the three most authoritative historical records concerning the classics. As *The Historical Records* was written before the existence of the Ancient Text Schools, what is recorded there can, in general, be regarded as representing the views of the Modern Text School. That part of *Han Shu* on *I Wen Chi* or *The Records of Literature*, was directly based on Chi Lüeh[55] or Seven Summaries of Liu Shin, founder of the Ancient Text School. So, in general, it may be considered as representing the Ancient Text School in its early stage of development. *Ching Tien Shih Wen* was written in the T'ang dynasty when the controversy in the Han period was over, in favour of the Ancient Text School, so it can be taken as representing the general point of view of the later stage of development of the Ancient Text School.

As the controversy was centred around the following seven classics, namely, *Shih, Shu, I, Li, Ch'un Ch'iu, Lun Yu* and *Hsiao Ching*, the Seven Classics are to be discussed separately as follows:

a. *Shih* or *The Book of Poetry*

(a) Modern Text School

There were three schools with their respective recensions of and commentaries on *The Book of Poetry* as mentioned in *The Historical Records*.

First, the Lu[56] school. The Lu Shih or the Lu version of *The Book of Poetry* was first taught at the capital by Shen Kung,[57] who was appointed Po Shih or Professor by Wen Ti[58] (Emperor Wen, 179-157 B.C.), and who resigned in 162 and returned to teach in Lu, his native place.

Second, the Han[59] school. It was likewise recognized at court, where its chief exponent was Han Ying[60] whose doctrine was popular in Yen[61] and Chao,[62] and who also was appointed Po Shih by Emperor Wen.

Third, the Chi[63] school. It was headed by Yuan Ku-sheng[64] who was appointed Professor of *The Book of Poetry* by the Emperor Ching[65] (156-141 B.C.).

These three schools of *The Book of Poetry*, among which that of Han differed sharply from the others, were all taught at the capital from this time.

(b) Ancient Text School

According to *Han Shu* and *Ching T'ien Shih Wen*, there was a fourth school of *The Book of Poetry* which was not mentioned in *The Historical Records*, namely, the Mao version of *The Book of Poetry* which was supposed to be edited with commentary by Mao Kung,[66] and this was upheld by the Ancient Text School.

According to *Han Shu*, Mao Kung was a native of Chao[67] and was appointed Professor of *The Book of Poetry* at the Court of Prince *Hsien* or Ho Chien (155-130 B.C.). His version of *The Book of Poetry*, with the Commentary, was recognized at court in the time of P'ing Ti[68] (A.D. 1-5) through his fourth generation disciple, Ch'en Chieh.[69]

Ching Tien Shih Wen went further and quoted the saying of Hsu Cheng[70] that the Younger Mao Kung[71] or Mao Ts'ang[72] was the fifth generation disciple of Tzu Hsia,[73] the immediate disciple of Confucius. Thus it links up the Mao edition of *The Book of Poetry* right to Confucius. Again it quoted from "some say"[74] that the Elder Mao Kung[75] was the fourth (or sixth) generation disciple of Tzu Hsia,[76] and that Hsun Ch'ing,[77] the famous Confucian scholar in the period of the Warring States, was also one of the transmitters of the Mao Version.

After the Han dynasty the Mao edition of *The Book of Poetry* gained complete ascendency over the other three recensions, and the *Ching T'ien Shih Wen* gives the reason for that: "In the later Han, Cheng Chung[78] and Chia K'uei[79] transmitted the Mao edition of *The Book of Poetry,* Ma Jung[80] wrote commentaries on it, and Cheng Hsuan[81] wrote notes on it, explaining the meaning of the Mao edition and criticizing the other three schools, therefore the other three schools became extinct."

The differences between the classical text of *The Book of Poetry* of the Modern Text School and that of the Ancient Text School is very slight, though they differ considerably in the commentaries. According to the Modern Text School there are only 305 poems in the classical text of *The Book of Poetry*, but that in the Ancient Text School the names of six more have been added, making the total 311 poems. The names of the additional poems are: Nan Kai,[82] Pei Hua,[83] Hua Shu,[84] Yu Keng,[85] Ch'ung Ch'iu[86] and Yu I.[87] But these six additional chapters have only the names left, and the contents, according to the Ancient Text School, have been completely lost.

b. *Shu Ching* or *The Book of History*

(1) The Modern Text School

Both *Shih Chi* and *Han Shu* recorded that Fu Sheng[88] of Chi Nan,[89] a Po Shih or Professor of the Ch'in dynasty, was the first man who taught *The Book of History* in the Han dynasty. His teaching was passed on to two of his disciples, Ou-yang Sheng[90] and Chang Sheng.[91] Chang Sheng's teaching was passed on to Hsia Hou Sheng,[92] commonly known as the Elder Hsia Hou,[93] and Hsia Hou Chien,[94] the Younger Hsia Hou.[95] So before P'ing Ti or Emperor P'ing (A.D. 1-5), only *The Historical Records* of the Modern Text School were taught, and they were divided into two schools with two different versions and their respective commentaries on *The Book of History*, namely, the Ou-yang School and the Elder and Younger Hsia Hou School. The number of volumes of the versions and commentaries of these two schools as recorded in *Han Shu* is as follows: *Ta Hsiao Hsia Hou Chang Chu*[96] or the *Version of the Elder and Younger Hsia Hou with Commentaries* or *Chie Ku*,[97] each 29 volumes; *Ou-yang Ching*[98] or *Ou-yang Classic*, 32 volumes; and *Ou-yang Chang Chu*[99] or Ou-yang version (literally, chapters and sentences) 31 volumes. The reason for the difference in the number of volumes can be clearly seen in the following list of the names of all chapters of the text of *Shu Ching*, recognized by the scholars of the Modern Text School.

	Versions and Commentaries of Ta and Hsiao Hsia Hou each 29 volumes	Ou-yang Classics 32 volumes	Ou-yang Version 31 volumes
Yao Tien	1	1	1
Kao Yao Mo	2	2	2
Yu Kung	3	3	3
Kan Shih	4	4	4

T'ang Shih	5	5	5
Pan Keng		6	6
	6	7	7
		8	8
Kao Tsung T'ung Jih	7	9	9
Hsi Po K'an Chi	8	10	10
Wei Tzu	9	11	11
T'ai Shih	10	12	12
Mu Shih	11	13	13
Heng Fan	12	14	14
Chin T'eng	13	15	15
Ta Kao	14	16	16
K'ang Kao	15	17	17
Chiu Kao	16	18	18
Tzu Ts'ai	17	19	19
Shao Kao	18	20	20
Lo Kao	19	21	21
To Shih	20	22	22
Wu I	21	23	23
Chun Shih	22	24	24
To Fang	23	25	25
Li Cheng	24	26	26
Ku Ming	25	27	27
Hsien Shih	26	28	28
Fu Hsing	27	29	29
Wen Hou Chih Ming	28	30	30
Ch'in Shih	29	31	31
Shu Hsu		32	

The original version as taught by Fu Sheng contained only 28 volumes. Tai Shih[100] was first discovered by a girl in Ho Nei[101] and was added to *Shu Ching* during the time of Hsun Ti or Emperor Hsun (73-49 B.C.). *Shu Tsu* or The Preface was also added later.

(2) The Ancient Text School

The *Shu Ching* of the Ancient Text School was attributed to K'ung An Kuo[102] and was called *K'ung Shih Ku Wen Shang Shu*.[103]

It contains 16 more volumes than that of the Modern Text School, according to *Han Shu*. But sometimes the volume of *Chiu Kung*[104] has been divided into nine volumes, so it is sometimes said the "ancient text" contains 24 volumes more than the "Modern text". If the volume with a hundred chapters of the preface is added it becomes 25 volumes, as mentioned in *Ching Tien Shih Wen*. The names of the new additional volumes are as follows: *Shun Tien*,[105] *Lei Tso*,[106] *Chiu Kung*[107] (sometimes divided into nine volumes), *Ta Yu Mo*,[108] *Chi Chi*,[109] *Wu Tzu Chih Ko*,[110] *Yin Cheng*,[111] *T'ang Kao*,[112] *Han Yu Te*,[113] *Tien Pao*,[114] *I Hsun*,[115] *Szu Ming*,[116] *Yuan Ming*,[117] *Wu Ch'eng*,[118] *Lu Ao*,[119] and *Ch'iung Ming*.[120]

All these new additional volumes have been accounted forgeries by the scholars of the Modern Text School. But according to *Ching Tien Shih Wen*, the general belief of the scholars of the Ancient Text School is that *"Ko Wen Shang Shu* or *Shang Shu* of the Ancient Text was hidden away by K'ung Hui[121] (the descendent of Confucius). When Prince K'ung of Lu destroyed the wall of the old house of Confucius it was discovered with Li,[122] Lun Yu,[123] and Hsiao Ching.[124] They were all written with Kuo Tou[125] or "tadpole characters". Po Shih or Professor K'ung An Kuo, in comparing that with the text taught by Fu Sheng,[126] found it written in *Li Ku*[127] or the ancient "clerkly style" and thus added 25 volumes to the text as passed down by Fu Sheng. . . . An Kuo again received the Imperial Order to write commentaries on *Ko Wen Shang Shu*, but owing to the instigation of witches (referring to the scholars of the Modern Text School) the way of the classics was blocked and they (the "ancient text" and the commentaries) could not be presented to the emperor, and were stored up in private families. . . ." Not until the time of Emperor P'ing (A.D. 1-5) was *Ko Wen Shang Shu* formally recognized at court and taught in the Grand College.

c. *I Ching* or *The Book of Changes*

(a) The Modern Text School

There were six different schools interpreting *I* or *The Book of Changes* of the Modern Text School in the early Han period.

(1) The T'ien Ho[128] version of *I*. Both *Shih Chi* (*The Historical Records*) and *Han Shu* mentioned that the T'ien Ho of Ch'i was the

sixth generation disciple of Shang Chu[129] of Lu, who had received the learning of *I* directly from Confucius.

(2) The Yang Ho version of *I*.[130] Shih Chi mentions that T'ien Ho passed *I* to Wang T'ung,[131] who in turn passed it down to Yang Ho, a great exponent of the traditional teaching.

(3) The Shih version of *I*.[132] Shih Ch'ou,[133] editor of this version, was one of the disciples of T'ien Wang Sun,[134] who had learnt *I* under Ting Kuan,[135] one of the students of T'ien Ho who, as mentioned above, was the seventh generation disciple of Confucius. (See *Han Shu*)

(4) The Meng version of *I*[136] was edited by Meng Hsi[137] who was also one of the students of T'ien Wang Sun. (See *Han Shu*)

(5) The Liang Ch'iu version of I.[138] Liang Ch'iu was another student of T'ien Wang Sun. (See *Han Shu*)

(6) The Ching Shih version of *I*[139] was edited by Ching Fang,[140] a disciple of Chiao Yang Shao,[141] who had studied under Meng Hsi, but gave a somewhat different interpretation of the learning from his master. (See *Han Shu*)

(b) The Ancient Text School

(1) The Fei Shih version of *I*.[142] This was edited by Fei Chih[143] who, according to *Ching Tien Shih Wen*, "passed the study to Wang Huang,[144] and is called Fei Shih I.[145] Owing to the characters being written in the 'ancient' script, it is also called the 'ancient text' of *I*[146] . . . ."

(2) The Kao Shih version of *I*.[147] This was edited by Kao Hsiang,[148] who was a contemporary of Fei Chih, and his study was supposed to have originated from Ting Kuan, a disciple of T'ien Ho. He gave a sort of mystical interpretation of *I*. (See both *Han Shu* and *Ching Tien Shih Wen*)

Although there are different interpretations and commentaries regarding *I*, yet the classical texts used by different schools are very much the same. For example, *Ching Tien Shih Wen* mentions: "Liu Hsiang[149] (79-8 B.C.) compared the *I* of the 'ancient text' with those of Shih,[150] Meng,[151] and Liang Ch'iu,[152] and found out some of them had left out 'Wu Ch'iu[153] and 'Hui Wu'[154] phrases, but the Fei Shih[155] version of *I* was found to be the same as the 'ancient text'." So

According to *Ching Tien Shih Wen* the difference between the variant texts only involved the two phrases.

All the six versions of the Modern Text School as mentioned above were officially recognized at court in one period or another in the Han dynasty, but none of the Ancient Text School secured official recognition. (See *Ching Tien Shih Wen*)

d. *Li* or *Rituals*

(a) The Modern Text School

There were five schools with their versions of *Li* in the early Han period, and in the later Han period three more schools with their versions of *Li* of the Ancient Text School were added.

(1) The Kao T'ang Sheng Version of *Li*[156]

Shih Chi mentions that "*Li* came down from the time of Confucius, but its classical text (ching)[157] was not formed at that time. After the burning of books under Ch'in, many books were scattered and lost. At present there is only Kao T'ang Cheng's *Shih Li*[158] or *The Ritual of Nobility*." So according to Ssu-ma Ch'ien, the author of *Shih Chi*, *Shih Li* as taught by Kao T'ang Sheng at the beginning of the Han dynasty actually came down from the time of Confucius. *Han Shu* mentions that there were 17 chapters in *Shih Li*, and *Ching Tien Shih Wen* identified the 17 chapters with the present-day *I Li*,[159] or *The Rites*.

(2) The Hsu Sheng version of *Li*[160]

Shih Chi records, "Hsu Sheng of Lu was good in manners. In the time of Wen Ti,[161] or Emperor Wen (179-155 B.C.), he was appointed to the official post of Li Kuan Tai Fu,[162] owing to his good manners. He had many disciples, and hereafter, those who taught Li with special regard to good manners were said to have obtained it from Hsu Sheng." (See also *Han Shu* and *Ching Tien Shih Wen*)

(3) The Hou Ts'ang version of *Li*[163]

Both *Han Shu* and *Ching Tien Shih Wen* mention that Hou Ts'ang edited *Hou Shih Ch'u T'ai Chi*[164] with tens of thousands of words about *Li*. At the time of Emperor Hsuan (73-49 B.C.), he was the most prominent exponent of *Li*.

(4) The Ta Tai version of *Li*[165]

This was the version of *Li* edited by Tai Te,[166] known as the Elder

Tai or Ta Tai.[167]

(5) The Hsiao Tai version of *Li*[168]

This was edited by Tai Sheng,[169] known as the Younger Tai or Hsiao Tai.[170]

Both Tai Sheng and Tai Te were the students of Hou Ts'ang. (See both *Han Shu* and *Ching Tien Shih Wen*)

(b) The Ancient Text School

(1) Chou *Li* or *The Official System of Chou*

Ching Tien Shih Wen quoted from *Cheng Li*u *I Lun*[171] or *The Treatise of the Six Arts* by Cheng Hsun that 56 chapters of *Li Ching*[172] or *Li Classics*, 131 chapters of *Li Chi*[173] or *The Book of Rites*, and six chapters of *Chou Li*, of the "ancient text", were found in the wall of Confucius' house. It quoted again from "some say",[174] that "when Prince Hsien of Ho-chien opened the way for the offering of ancient books, a certain woman, Li Shih,[175] offered five chapters of *Chou Kuan*[176] or *The Officers of Chou*, which was the name given to *Chou Li* in Han times. The chapter of Shih Kuan[177] or The Officer of Affairs had become lost and could not be found, though a reward of one thousand Chin,[178] or gold, was offered, so the chapter of *K'ao Kung Chi*[179] was substituted for it. The six chapters of *Chou Li* of the "ancient text" were recognized at court by Wang Mang, the "Usurper" (A.D. 9-20).

(2) *I Li*[180] or *The Lost Li*

Ching Tien Shih Wen says: "Among the 56 chapters of *Ku Li Ching* or *The Li Classic of the Ancient Text*[181] (found from the wall of Confucius' house), 17 chapters were handed down by Hou Ts'ang,[182] (*Han Shu* says that 17 chapters were passed down by Kao T'ang Sheng), and the remaining 39 chapters . . . were called *I Li*. . . ."

(3) *Li Chi* or *The Book of Rites*

Ching Tien Shih Wen says clearly and authoritatively about the history of the present *Li Chi*, and it is worthwhile to quote a passage therefrom. "*Li Chi* was originally compiled by Confucius' disciples. Later on some parts of the text were added and some parts were left out by the later T'ung Ju[183] or learned Confucianists. Therefore, *Chung Jung* or *The Doctrine of the Mean* was written by Tzu Ssu

(Ch'i),[184] the chapter on Tzu I[185] was written by Kung-sun Ni Tzu.[186] Cheng Hsun said, 'The chapter on Yueh Ling[187] was edited by Professors of the Han period'. It is mentioned in the Preface to *Chou Li Lun*[188] or *The Treatise of the Chou Li* written by Ch'en Shao[189] that 'It was Tai Te[190] who cut down the 204 chapters of *Ku Li*[191] or *The Ancient Li* into 85 chapters, and called them *Ta Tai Li* or *The Elder Tai Record of Li*.[192] Tai Sheng[193] cut down *The Elder Tai Record of Li* into 49 chapters,·and called them *Hsiao Tai Li* or *The Younger Tai Record of Li*.[194] In the later Han period, Ma Jung[195] and Lu Chih[196] compared the differences and similarities of the different schools, and put the results of their study under the names of the chapters of Tai Sheng. After cutting out the complicated and duplicate parts, and adding in what had been left out or neglected, they offered the result to the world, and that is the present text of *Li Chi*. Cheng Hsun also commented according to the text of Lu and Ma.' "

So according to this statement, *Li Chi*, in its present form, though based on the ancient records, is primarily the work of the Later Han scholars, especially Ma Jung, Lu Shih and Cheng Hsun. It had undergone a great many revisions before it came to its present form.

At present all versions of *Li* have been lost or neglected or combined, except the three: *Chou Li*, *I Li* and *Li Chi*, commonly known as *San Li* or *Three Li*.[197]

e. *Ch'un Ch'iu* or *The Spring and Autumn Annals*, with its Commentaries

There are three commentaries on *The Spring and Autumn Annals*: the Kung-yang Commentary, the Ku-liang Commentary of the Modern Text School, and the Tso Commentary of the Ancient Text School. This has been the most controversial classics, with commentaries from the two schools. The scholars of the Modern Text School in the Ch'ing dynasty sometimes called themselves the Kung-yang Hsueh P'ai[198] or the Kung-yang Literary Party, because one of their chief aims was to dethrone Tso's Commentary in the literary world, and resurrect the study of the Kung-yang Commentary of the Ch'un Ch'iu. With this came the revival of the Modern Text School in the middle of the Ch'ing dynasty.

(1) *Kung-yang Ch'un Ch'iu*[199]

There were three different versions of *Kung-yang Ch'un Ch'iu*, respectively mentioned in *Shih Chi, Han Shu,* and *Ching Tien Shih Wen.*

First, the Hu Mu Sheng version of the Kung-yang Commentary.[200] Hu Mu Sheng was elected Po Shih or Professor of the Kung-yang Ch'un Ch'iu during the reign of Emperor Ching.[201] (156-141 B.C.)

Second, the Tung Chung-hsu version of *Ch'un Ch'iu.*[202] Tung Chung-hsu (b. 106 B.C.) was elected Professor of the Kung-yang *Ch'un Ch'iu* at the same time as Hu Mu Sheng.

Third, the Yen Yen version[203] of *Ch'un Ch'iu.* This was edited by Yen P'an-tsu[204] and Yen An-lo,[205] the third-generation disciple of Tung Chung-hsu.

(2) *Ku-liang Ch'un Ch'iu*[206]

Shih Chi mentions that Chiang Sheng[207] of Chia Ch'iu[208] worked on *Ku-liang Ch'un Ch'iu,* but *Han Shu* and *Ching Tien Shih Wen* go further and say that Chiang Sheng learnt *Ku-liang Ch'un Ch'iu* and *Shih* from Shen Kung of Lu. This school was recognized at court during the reign of Emperor Hsuan.[209] (73-49 B.C.)

(3) *Tso Chuan*[210]

In *Shih Chi* there is no record of *Tso Chuan,* or *Tso Commentary,* of *The Spring and Autumn Annals. Han Shu* mentions that the first man who worked on *Tso Chuan* was Chang Ts'ang.[211] But according to *Ching Tien Shih Wen,* representing the traditional belief, *Tso Chuan* was first edited by Tso Ch'iu-ming, the immediate disciple of Confucius, who lived seven generations before Chang Ts'ang. Hsun Ch'ing,[212] a famous Confucian scholars in the period of the Warring States, was one of the transmitters, not only of the Mao edition of the *The Book of Poetry* but also of *Tso Chuan.* It was officially recognized at court during the reign of Emperor P'ing (A.D. 1-5).

f. *Lun Yu* or *The Confucian Analects*

(a) The Modern Text School

The formation of *Lun Yu* was later than any of the above classics. In the time of Emperor Hsuan (73-49 B.C.), there existed already two recensions of *Lun Yu,* namely *Lu Lun* or *The Lu Version of the Analects*[213] and *Ch'i Lun*[214] or *The Ch'i Version of the Analects.* In *Lu Lun* there are only twenty books which is the present form, but in *Ch'i Lun* there are twenty-two books. The contents, however, are not very much different. There are, in fact, more chapters in the 20 books of *Lu Lun* than in the 22 books of *Ch'i Lun.*

(b) The Ancient Text School

Among the classics of the "archaic script" as found in the wall of the house of Confucius, *Lun Yu* was one of them. *Lun Yu* thus found was called *Ku Wen Lun Yu*[215] or *The Lun Yu of the "Ancient Text".* *Ku Wen Lun Yu* is almost exactly the same as *Lu Lun* except that the last book of *Lu Lun,* "Yao Yueh"[216] has been divided into two books, "Yao Yueh" and "Tzu Chang".[217] So instead of 20 books *Ku Wen Lun Yu* has 21 books. There is already one book, that is book 19, called "Tzu Chang", so *Ku Wen Lun Yu* has two books of the same name, "Tzu Chang".

g. *Hsiao Ching* or the *Book of Filial Piety*

This is supposed to be a record of conversation between Confucius and his disciple Tseng Tzu[218] about the problems of filial piety.

(a) Modern Text School

There are eighteen chapters in *Hsiao Ching* of the Modern Text School, which is said to be the version of Yen Chih[219] of Ho Chien. "When Ch'in burnt the books, Yen Chih of Ho Chien hid the book. At the beginning of the Han dynasty, Yen Chih's son Yen Chen presented it to Prince Hsien of Ho Chien, who in turn presented it to the imperial court. Chang Sun Shih,[220] Chiang Weng,[221] Hou Ts'ang,[222] I Feng,[223] and Chang Yu[224] were all famous for their knowledge of this book.

(b) The Ancient Text School

There are twenty-two chapters in the Ancient Text, which has been written in different versions:

First, the K'ung's version.[225] It was hidden in the wall of the house of Confucius by K'ung Fu,[226] and was later discovered by Prince Kung of Lu. This version, according to *Ching Tien Shih Wen,* was lost during the chaos of Liang (502-557 A.D.).

Second, the Liu Hsuan version.[227]

In the time of Emperor Wen[228] of the Sui dynasty (581–618 A.D.), the K'ung version was discovered by Liu Hsuan, but at that time it was generally believed to be the forgery of Liu Hsuan.

Third, the Japanese version, edited by T'ai Chai Shun[229] and incorporated in *The Collection of the Chih Po Chu Chai.*[230]

There is, in fact, very slight difference between the Modern Text and the Ancient Text. The difference of the four chapters between the two texts comes in the following way: the chapter of Kuang Yang Ming[231] of the Modern Text is divided into two chapters in the Ancient Text. The chapter of Shu Jen[232] is also divided into two in the Ancient Text, and the chapter of Sheng Chih[233] is divided into three chapters. So in the Ancient Text there are four chapters more than in the Modern Text, but the contents of the two texts are very much the same.

(B) The Interpretation of the Classics

It is difficult to say exactly how the two schools differ in the interpretation of the classics, because, as a matter of fact, no great scholars have exactly the same interpretations. It is, therefore, safe to speak in a general way of certain characteristics particular to each school.

In *The Analects* Confucius called himself "a transmitter and not an originator". But the scholars of the Modern Text School have interpreted this as being the self-depreciatory expression of Confucius, who, in fact, was primarily a great originator rather than transmitter. Originally all Six Classics—*Shih, Shu, Li, Yueh, I,* and *Ch'un Ch'iu*—were the works of Confucius. He wrote them for the exposition of his social and political ideas. Although there were many ancient materials incorporated in his works, yet, to use K'ang Yu-wei's words, "his hidden meaning and profound sense" lie elsewhere. In following this line of thought, Mr. Kang named one of his famous books *A Study of Confucius' Effort to Revolutionize the System of Chou by Attributing His System to the Ancient System.*

On the other hand, the scholars of the Ancient Text School have taken literally what Confucius said about himself, and regarded him primarily as a transmitter rather than an originator. They have maintained that originally the classics all formed part of the official literature, which Confucius merely transmitted but did not make. This is what Chang Tai-yen, the modern leader of the Ancient Text School, holds as he puts in the prominent place one of the beliefs of the Ancient Text School, that "the classics are all histories", preserved, studied, and transmitted by Confucius. Those histories of ancient Chinese institutions and traditions have been supposed to have come down primarily from the so-called "sage-kings" like Yao,[234] Shun,[235] Yu,[236] T'ang,[237] Wen,[238] and Wu,[239] and Chou Kung,[240] the Duke of Chou.

The difference of the interpretations can best be illustrated by the order of the Six Classics as arranged by the scholars of the two schools. *Ching Tien Shih Wen* gives some of the reasons why a certain order has been adopted. The following order of arrangement of the Six Classics has been generally accepted by scholars of both schools.

a. The Modern Text School
(a) *Shih* or *The Book of Poetry*
(b) *Shu* or *The Book of History*
(c) *Li* or *The Book of Rites*
(d) *Yueh* or *The Book of Music*
(e) *I* or *The Book of Changes*
(f) *Ch'un Ch'iu* or *The Spring and Autumn Annals*
b. The Ancient Text School
(a) *I* or *The Book of Changes*
(b) *Shu* or *The Book of History*
(c) *Shih* or *The Book of Poetry*
(d) *Li* or *The Book of Rites*
(e) *Yueh* or *The Book of Music*
(f) *Ch'un Ch'iu* or *The Spring and Autumn Annals*

As scholars of the Modern Text School regard Confucius as the author of the classics, he is supposed to have arranged his own works in a sort of psychological order, from simple to complex, as a great teacher would do. *Shih, Shu, Li* and *Yueh* constitute the general course of study, while *I* and *Ch'un Ch'iu* are more of a technical nature, and constitute a higher course of study. *Shih* and *Shu* are used for reading or symbolic education: *Li* and *Yueh* are for practice or moral education; *I* and *Ch'un Ch'iu* represent the philosophy of Confucius. They contain his social and political theories and cannot be understood by ordinary students. They are the technical learning and belong to a higher form of education. That is why they are put at the end of the whole course of study.

As the scholars of the Ancient Text School regard Confucius as a transmitter of the ancient Chinese culture, the classics are supposed to have been arranged according to the historical sequence, or the dates of their appearance. The Diagrams of *I Ching* are supposed to have first been drawn by Fu Hsi[241] traditionally c.2852 B.C., the earliest person to contribute material towards the formation of the classics, so *I Ching* comes first in the list of the six classics. The earliest record in *Shu Ching* is about Yao, traditionally c.2356 B.C., so *Shu Ching* is put next to *I Ching*. The earliest record of *Shih* is concerning Shang, about 1766-1122 B.C., so *The Book of Poetry* is ranked in the third place. *Li* and *Yueh* are supposed to be the works of Chou Kung, and so are put after *Shih* and before *Ch'un Ch'iu*, which is supposed to have been the history of Lu, but somewhat "expunged and rectified" by Confucius.

The following two quotations from two leading modern scholars of the Modern Text School bear out very clearly the chief difference between the two schools in their interpretation of the classics in relation to Confucius.

Kang Yu-wei says: "According to the old saying *Shih, Shu, Li, Yueh,* and *I* were all the works of Chou Kung, and Confucius was only in the position of expunging and approving. . . . But the six classics were all the works of Confucius, and this was believed to be so before the Han dynasty." (See *K'ung Tzu Kai Chih K'ao*)

Liao P'ing[242] says in his *Chih Sheng Pien*:[243] "The six classics are the works of one man, Confucius. Schooling is the specially established policy of the 'uncrowned king'. This is why he is called the Crown of a Hundred Kings in Tao (the Way), and the Ideal Teacher among the Thousand Generations. Before Liu Hsin this was all believed to be so, so in the *I Shu*[244] it is recorded that the six classics have all come down from Confucius. Later on, as a reason for attacking the Po Shih[245] or Professors, Chou Kung was brought in to challenge Confucius. So *Li* and *Yueh* were attributed to Chou Kung, *Shih* and *Shu* were ascribed to the ancient kings and emperors, *Ch'un Ch'iu* was written in accordance with the works of the historians, and *I* had only the commentary of the Formers Sage. By distributing one man's work to the emperors, kings, and Chou Kung, the Liu I[246] or the Six Disciplinary Arts (classics) are merely like selected prose and selected poetry. Sometimes even the belief in the work of 'expunging and rectifying' was criticized, and then Confucius became a very common man who did not establish anything . . . but was merely like an old teaching scholar who selected many textbooks and had many disciples. . . ."

C. Some Views of the Modern Higher Critics with Regard to the Relation of Confucius to the Classics

(A) The Backgrounds of the Modern Higher Critics

1. The General Sceptical Spirit of the Modern Age

The present period is one of the most unique periods in Chinese history. The bondage of thought to the past has been done away with following the removal of the absolute monarchy of the Ch'ing dynasty. The rule of the Confucian classicalism over the intellectual world of China, which lasted as long as some two millennia, has collapsed with the inauguration of the Republic of China. It is no longer true that the general condition now is like it was in the past, as represented by the saying of Liu Chih Chi[247] of the T'ang dynasty, that "restrained by traditions and laws, restricted by the teachings of masters, many people have refrained from speaking, though they have been conscious in their hearts, of the fallacy (of the traditional classical beliefs)". There is practically absolute freedom of thought and criticism with regard to the time-honoured classics. The contact with Western civilization has had a revolutionary effect upon the general attitude of Chinese thinkers towards their nation's cultural heritage. There is what is known as the "New Thought Movement" in China to-day, and an important phase of that movement is an insistent demand for a scientific re-evaluation of the national heritage, based upon the critical and historical study of the ancient materials. "Re-organization of the National Heritage"[248] has become a popular slogan in Chinese intellectual circles. The modern higher critics of the Confucian classics are but the product of the general critical spirit of the present age.

2. The Modern Archaeological Discoveries

These discoveries include the inscribed oracle-bones of the Shang dynasty first brought to light in Honan in 1899, the bronze vessels of the Shang and Chou dynasties, and the Tun Huang[249] manuscripts which had been walled up for protection from the Tangutans in a cave temple at Tun Huang about 1000 A.D. The library of these manuscripts was discovered by accident in 1900, and there have been other discoveries such as pottery, stone tablets, inscribed sculpture, and other objects. Many of these materials have been carefully studied, and have shed much light on the classics and on other ancient Chinese historical records. Many modern Chinese archaeologists like Wang Kuo-wei,[250] Ma Heng,[251] Jung Keng,[252] and others have written many articles and studies in the discussion of the ancient Chinese histories and classics, based on concrete investigations of these new discoveries. (See *Ku Shih Pien* or *Symposium on Ancient Chinese History*, Vols. 1-6)

3. Higher Critics of the Earlier Periods

The sceptical spirit which is so prominent a note in to-day's cultural transformation is by no means unknown to Chinese history, for almost every period has seen a few bold spirits who revolted against the traditional beliefs. Their expressed doubts of antiquity have been taken as a foundation by the modern higher critics for building up their theories. For example, Ku Chieh-kang wrote in his autobiography in the first volume of *Ku Shih Pien*, "Long before my time, there had existed an unbroken line of critical scholars who had attacked spurious elements in Chinese literature. . . . Knowing now the importance of their insight, we can build on the inheritance which they left us." The following are some of the outstanding higher critics of the past with some of their characteristic scepticisms.

(a) Mencius (372-289 B.C.). He doubted the authenticity of certain parts of *The Book of History*. For example he says: "It would be better to be without *The Book of History* than to give entire credit to it. In the Wu Ch'eng or the 'Completion of the war', I select two or three passages only which I believe." (*Mencius*, Bk. 7, Pt. 2, Chap.

3, Vers. 1-2)

(b) Han Fei-tzu (died 233 B.C.).[253] Two of his characteristic sayings are sufficient to show his critical spirit: "Confucius and Mo-tzu all talked about Yao and Shun, but were different in their recommendation and rejection. They both claimed to be true to Yao and Shun, but since Yao and Shun cannot come to life again who could possibly decide the sincerity between Confucianism and Mohism? (Ch. on Hsien Hsueh)[254]

"Those who talk about antiquity with a view to setting up false theories are relying on external power to·further their private aims, and so neglect the interests of the kingdom." (Ch. on Wu Tu)[255]

(c) Wang Ch'ung (A.D. 27-97).[256] He severely criticizes those who "trust in delusive books, taking everything indited on bamboo and silk for the records of wise and sage men, and as absolutely true." (Forke's translation of *Lun Heng*, Vol. 2, p. 240) In his *Lun Heng* he has such chapter-headings as "Falsehood in Books", "Literary Exaggerations", "Criticism of Confucius", "Censures on *Mencius*", etc.

(d) Liu Chih Chi[257] (A.D. 661-721). He doubted the authenticity of *Ch'ung Ch'iu* and *Shang Shu*, and pointed out certain fallacies concerning the ancient histories as recorded in *Lun Yu* and *Mencius*. He has such chapter-headings as "Ho Ching"[258] or "Doubts Concerning the Classics", "I Ku"[259] or "Doubts Concerning Antiquity". (See *Shih T'ung*[260] or *Comprehensive Study of History*)

(e) Ou-yang Hsiu[261] (A.D. 1017-1072). He was sceptical about any relation of Confucius to *The Book of Changes*, and was certain that Confucius did not write certain appendices of the "Ten Appendices" or Shih I[262] to *The Book of Changes*, such as, Hsi Tzu[263] or the Great Appendix, Wen Yen[264] or remarks on the first two Kua, or diagrams, Shuo Kua[265] or remarks on some of the Kua, and Tsa Kua[266] or Miscellaneous Remarks. He had doubts also about the historicity of the material in the Tao, Ku-liang, and Kung-yang Commentaries on *The Spring and Autumn Annals*, and the authenticity of *Chou Li*.

(f) Chu Hsi[267] (A.D. 1130-1200). He was one of the first to doubt the authenticity of the Ancient Text of *The Book of History* (*Yu*

Lei,[268] p. 67), *The Book of Filial Piety* (*Wen Chi*,[269] p. 66), and parts of *Li Chi* (*Yu Lei*, p. 86). He held that *The Book of Changes* was primarily a book of divination (*Yu Lei*, p.66), and that the Preface to *The Book of History* (*Wen Chi*, p. 71), and the K'ung An-kuo version[270] of *The Book of History* were forgeries. (*Wen Chi*, p. 71)

(g) Yeh Shih[271] (1150-1223). He doubted, among others, the following traditionally accepted views: that the Duke of Chou compiled *Chou Li*, that Confucius edited *The Book of History*, or revised *The Book of Poetry*, or that *The Spring and Autumn Annals* harbour profound and recondite meanings. (See his *Shih Hsueh Chi Yen*)[272]

(h) Wang Po[273] (1197-1274). He wrote *Shu I*[274] or *Doubts Concerning the Book of History*, and *Shih I*[275] or *Doubts Concerning the Book of Poetry*. In them he discarded *The Small Preface to the Book of Poetry* written by Wei Hung[276] (first century A.D.), holding that the meaning of *The Book of Poetry* must be found in the text itself and not in commentaries. He also suspected the authenticity of the "ancient text" classics.

(i) Yen Jo-chu[277] (1636-1704). He was the first to demonstrate by the most critical methods, after a lifetime of study, the forgery of the "ancient text" of *The Book of History* in his epoch-making essay "Shang Shu Ku Wen Shu Cheng",[278] thus finally accomplishing the overthrow of a work that had been accepted for a millennium as an unimpeachable classics.

(j) Yao Chi-heng[279] (1647-1715). He wrote *Ku Ching Wei Shu K'ao* or *The Investigation of Forgeries of Ancient and Modern Times*. This is the most complete exposition of forged literature up to the close of the 18th century. It analyzes solely on the basis of authenticity some ninety works in every department of literature.

(k) Ts'ui Tung-pi[280] (1740-1816). He was the first to point out that the model-emperor lore was built up in successive strata so that the more remote from a given event, the more detailed becomes the information about that event. This theory has been very much exemplified by Ku Chieh Kang in his famous hypothesis of "the stratified fabrication of *Ancient Chinese History*"[281] (*Ku Shih Pien*, Vol. 1, p. 97). He also criticized the authenticity of *Shih*

Hsu[282] or *The Introduction to the Book of Poetry*, and the *I Li* or *The Rites*. (See *Tung Pi I Shu*, or *The Bequeathed Works of Tsui Tung-pi*)[283]

(1) Kang Yu-wei[284] (1858-1927). He was the champion of the modern Modern Text School and has had great influence on modern higher critics. (See Ku Chieh-kang's preface to the first volume of *Ku Shih Pien*) His criticism was that all the classics of the "ancient text" were the forgeries of Liu Hsin, and he gave his views in the six chapters of his epoch-making work, *Hsin Hsueh Wei Ching K'ao*. The following is a brief summary of this work:

a. There was no "ancient text" in the Former or Western Han dynasty. The classics of the "ancient text" were all the forgery of Liu Hsin.

b. Ch'in Shih Huang, or the First Emperor of Ch'in, did not destroy the six classics of the Po Shih or Professors. So the classics used by the 14 professors of the Former Han dynasty were all complete copies.

c. The style of the written characters used during the time of Confucius was the same as that in the Ch'in and Han periods. There is no such thing as the "ancient" or "modern" characters.

d. Liu Hsin wanted to cover up the traces of his forgery, so when he succeeded his father in collating the ancient books, he modified at will all of them in order to suit his purpose.

e. The motive of Liu Hsin's forgery was to help Wang Mang to usurp the throne, so he upheld Chou Kung, who, like Wang Mang, had acted for some time as the Prince Regent, and neglected the inner meaning and profound sense" of the works of Confucius.

(B) The Views of the Modern Higher Critics

The present critical study of the Confucian classics has been characterized by the historical approach, re-dating all classical writings according to their proper setting. This new approach in the present era in China can be said to have been inaugurated by Dr. Hu Shih, who, in writing his *Development of the Logical Method in Ancient China* in 1917, intended it, as he said in the preface, to be an "historical study" different in many respects from what he called the "traditional scholarship". He is, in fact, the first Chinese who ever used the term "higher criticism" and applied it to the Confucian classics. "In determining the authenticity of our source-material", he says, "we have already had to resort to what has been called 'Higher Criticism'." (Preface to *Development of the Logical Method in Ancient China*). So there is some reason why people should sometimes call him the first modern Chinese higher critic. He has been the leader not only in the famous literary revolution, but in the reorganization of Chinese culture in the fields of history, literature, and philosophy, including the Confucian classics. But in criticizing the Confucian classics, and other ancient Chinese literature such as that of Lao-tzu, many of his followers and students have gone much further and become more radical than he.

In order to study the views of the modern higher critics, it is best to refer to the six volumes of *Ku Shih Pien* or *Symposium on Ancient Chinese History*, published in 1926, 1930, 1931, 1933, 1935, and 1938 respectively. The fourth and sixth volumes were published by Lo Ken-tse[285] and the rest by Ku Chieh-kang, a former student of H'u Shih, who once characterized this book as "a revolutionary book in the field of Chinese historical scholarship." (*Ku Shih Pien*, Vol. 2, p. 334) It contains monographs and letters by most of the leading modern higher critics or the leaders of the "New Culture Movement", Hsin-wen-hua-yun-tung,[286] including Hu Shih,[287] Ku Chieh-kang,[288] Ch'ien Hsuan-t'ung,[289] Fung Yu-lan,[290] Lo Ken-tse,[291] Chou Yu-t'ung,[292] Chien Mu,[293] Fu Shih-nien,[294] Kuo Mo-jo,[295] Chang Yin-ling,[296] Wei Chien Kung,[297] Mei Ssu P'ing,[298] Yu Hok Nien, and others. Although many of them differ somewhat in the details about the authenticity of the classics, yet in general most of them agree that the name Confucius is to be dissociated from almost all of the classics.

It is impossible here to give all the views of the modern higher critics, but some of the more famous ones will suffice for the present purpose.

(a) Hu Shih. In the *Development of the Logical Method in Ancient China* he maintains that the following books are the works of

Confucius:

a. *The Book of Poetry*. It contains "the popular songs and poems that have been edited and preserved to us by Confucius" (p.3). He regards it as the most authentic material that has come down from ancient China. "Of the so-called 'Five Classics' of Confucianism," he says, "I have accepted only *The Book of Poetry*." (Preface to the *Development of the Logical Method in Ancient China*)

b. Several Appendices or Shih I "Ten Wings"[300] to *The Book of Changes*. "It is impossible for a modern student to attribute all the ten appendices to Confucius. It seems safe to hold that 1, 2, 3, and 4 were written by Confucius himself", and the rest, though not likely to be written by Confucius, contain many genuine views of the Master. (*Ibid.*, p. 31)

c. *The Spring and Autumn Annals*. He maintains that Confucius "completed a history of his own state known as *The Spring and Autumn Annals*" (*Ibid.*, p. 21), thereby he exemplifies his theory of the "rectification of names". But he also says, "The work as we possess it to-day is probably not entirely the original text. In its present form, it contains numerous inconsistencies with regard to its ethical judgments. Such inconsistencies are probably due to later modification." (*Ibid.*, p. 51)

(b) Feng Yu-lan.[301] In 1923 when he wrote "A Comparative Study of Life Ideals", he believed that Confucius, having thoroughly read *The Book of Changes*, transmitted it to his disciples and wrote the ten appendices to it. "Before Confucius", he says, "this book was used for divination. It did not receive its meaning and significance until Confucius added to it the 'Ten Wings', or the ten appendices". (p. 159) Four years later, in his article "The Place of Confucius in Chinese History"[302] published in *The Yenching Journal*, or Yenching Hsueh Po,[303] Vol. 2, 1927, he discarded his former position and concluded that Confucius had nothing to do with any of the classics, including the appendices to *The Book of Changes*. He compared the idea of Heaven as recorded in *The Analects*, a personal or "purposeful God",[304] or "the Heaven that rules,[305]" with that of Heaven as recorded in *The Book of Changes*, including the appendices, as an impersonal "Cosmic Force"[306] or a "Moral

Heaven".[307] He then came to the conclusion that "If we recognize the words in *The Analects* as spoken by Confucius and also recognize the *Diagrams of the I*[308] as the work of Confucius, we are involving Confucius in the position of inconsistency." (*Ku Shih Pien*, Vol. 2, p. 200) Since *The Analects* is generally accepted as the most authentic record of the teachings of Confucius, *The Book of Changes* cannot possibly be the work of Confucius. In the same article he also disagrees with Hu Shih's view that Confucius wrote *The Spring and Autumn Annals* in order to exemplify his theory of the rectification of names; on the contrary, he argued, Confucius only deduced his theory of the rectification of names from the existing histories of his time, especially the history of his own State of Lu, known as *Ch'un Ch'iu*, or *The Spring and Autumn Annals*. He did not write it nor did he "produce or expunge and rectify any of the 'Six Classics'."

(c) Ku Chieh-kang. He also maintains that Confucius has nothing to do with the Classics. He assumes that, historically the Six Classics had already existed at the time of Confucius, and the idea that Confucius wrote or expunged and rectified them came gradually in much later periods; also the Six Classics themselves show many inferior or alien elements which are not worthy of the name of the great Master as depicted in *The Analects*. The following quotation from one of his essays in the first volume of *Ku Shih Pien* well illustrates his point of view.

"The Six Classics", he says, "were the few books which were prevalent in the Chou dynasty. There is not a single word about the 'expurgating and rectifying work' in *The Analects*; until Mencius (372-289 B.C.), he (Confucius) was said to have written *Ch'un Ch'iu* or *The Spring and Autumn Annals*; until *Shih Chi* or *The Historical Records* (compiled by Ssu-ma Ch'ien, 140-80 B.C.), he was said to have appraised *I* or *The Book of Changes* (written the ten appendices), prefaced Shu or *The Book of History*, and expunged *Shih* or *The Book of Poetry*; until *Shang Shu Wei*[309] or *The Apocrypha of the Book of History* (c. the Later Han Period A.D. 25-221), he was said to have expunged *Shu* or *The Book of History*; until the scholars of the Modern Text School of the Ch'ing dynasty (A.D. 1644-1911), he was said to have written *I Ching* or *The Book of Changes* and the *I Li* or *The Rites*. In short, they regarded the imperfect classics as expunged by Confucius, and the perfect ones as written by Confucius. But, in fact, if we see *Ho Ching*[310] or *Doubts Concerning the Classics* written by Liu Chih-chi[311] (A.D. 661-721), we know that if *The Spring and Autumn Annals* had really been written by Confucius, is it not that it would have been far from 'making the traitors and thieves afraid?' If we see the criticisms of Wan Shih-tung[312] about *The Book of History* and *The Book of Poetry* of the 'modern text', we know that if the two books had actually been expunged by Confucius, he would really have been one who praised the cruel rulers and promoted adultery and disorder. If we see *I Chiao*[313] or *The Teaching of the Book of Changes* and *I Li* or *The Rites* by Chang Hsueh-ch'eng,[314] we know that if they had been written by Confucius he would also have been one who usurped the title of kings. The saying that all the six classics were the codes of Chou Kung has already been discredited by the Modern Text School, and now the notion that the six classics were all the works of Confucius can also be discarded." (*Ku Shih Pien*, Vol. 1, p. 42)

(d) Ch'ien Hsuan-tung,[315] professor in Hsing Hua university, Peiping, known as Mr. Doubter of the Ancient.[316] The following are some quotations from one of the essays incorporated in the first volume of *Ku Shih Pien*.

a. "Confucius had nothing to do with the expurgating, editing or writing of the 'Six Classics'."

b. "*Shih, Shu, Li, I* and *Ch'ung Ch'iu* are five volumes of books which have no relation with one another (actually there has never been such a book as *The Book of Music*)."

c. "*The Book of Poetry* is the oldest Grand Collection",[317] and it was already in existence before the time of Confucius.

d. "*The Book of History* seems to be a collection of government documents during the 'Three Dynasties' and should be looked upon as a history. But I am rather suspicious of its being compiled into a book. Neither the 28 chapters of the Modern Text nor the 100 chapters of the Ancient Text are credible."

e. "*I Li* is a spurious book carelessly copied during the period of

Warring States (491-249 B.C.); *Chou Li* is a forgery by Liu Hsin (*c.* 53 B.C.-A.D. 18); nine-tenths of the two *Tai Li* were written by philosophers during the Han dynasty (206 B.C.-A.D. 220)."

f. "Originally there never was *The Book of Music*; it came into being from the Ancient Text School".

g. "*The Book of Changes* is the worst production among the six classics". That Confucius ever saw this book is to be seriously doubted. The Ten Appendices were written after the time of Confucius.

h. "*The Spring and Autumn Annals* was called a 'mutilated court record'[318] by Wang An-shih (A.D. 1021-1086) though (some say he did not use that epithet); and a 'mercantile day-to-day account'[319] by Liang Ch'i-ch'ao (1873-1928 A.D.). These are all adequate criticisms." It never was even read seriously by Confucius.

i. The "Three Commentaries" are three independent works, and "have nothing to do with *The Spring and Autumn Annals*". (See *Ku Shih Pien*, Vol. 1, pp. 67-82)

(e) Chou Yu-t'ung.[320] He entirely accepts Professor Ch'ien's points of view and concludes that "the five classics are five volumes of independent and variously combined books, and have not the slightest relation with Confucius." (*Ku Shih Pien*, Vol. 2, pp. 257-270)

(f) Lo Ken-tse,[321] the editor of the fourth and sixth volumes of *Ku Shih Pien*. He assumes that "there had not been private schools' writings before the period of the Warring States", thus he deprives Confucius of the authorship of any of the classics. (*Ku Shih Pien*, Vol. 4, pp. 8-68)

In short, the modern higher critics, in general, in maintaining that Confucius had nothing to do with the classics, differ widely from both the Modern Text and the Ancient Text Schools, which, though disagreeing with each other in many respects, have at least agreed that Confucius, in any event, was closely connected with the Classics. The Modern School maintains that Confucius was the originator of the classics, the Ancient Text School only recognizes that he was their transmitter but not originator, while the modern higher critics repudiate both these views and hold that Confucius was neither an originator nor a transmitter of these classics, and that he had nothing whatever to do with them.

D. The Conclusions of the Present Writer

Only the original "six classics", namely, *Shih Ching, Shu Ching, I Ching, I Li, Yueh Ching*, and *Ch'un Ch'iu* can be called Ching or Classics. *Yueh Ching* was lost about the time of the Han dynasty, so there are now only "Five Classics". The rest, including *Chou Li, Li Chi*, the "three commentaries" to *Ch'un Ch'iu*, the "Four Books", *Hisao Ching*, and *Erh Ya* are merely commentaries or treatises written by Confucius' disciples or later Confucian scholars in the periods of the Warring States and the Han dynasty. They are, however, all valuable materials for the study of Confucianism and have moulded, to a large extent, the thought-pattern of the Chinese people for over two thousand years.

All the six classics had already existed, in one form or another, before the time of Confucius. For example, *Kuo Yu*[322] informs us that a crown prince of Ch'u, son of King Chuang[323] of Ch'u[324] (613-591 B.C.), was given instruction in such works as the "poetry", "rites", "music", "spring and autumn", and "old records" (Ch'u Yu[325] 1.1.). Both *Kuo Yu* and *Tso Chuan* record numerous conversations between important personages, in which *Shih* or poetry, and *Shu* or history are frequently mentioned; while *Li* or *Rites* were used in diplomatic relations, and the *I* or *Changes* were used in divination. Those ancient materials were specially well preserved in Confucius' own native state, the State of Lu. For instance, in *Tso Chuan* it says that in the 29th year of Duke Hsiang[326] (544 B.C.), Chi Cha[327] of the State of Wu[328] came to the State of Lu where he learnt "the *Shih* or poetry and *Yueh* or music of different states". Also in the second year of Chao[329] (540 B.C.), Han Hsuan Tzu[330] of Chin[331] came to Lu and saw the books of the Grand Historian.[332] There he saw *Hsiang* or *Diagrams* of *I* or *Changes*, and the *Ch'un Ch'iu* of Lu, and said: "All the canons of Chou have been in Lu, and I now know the virtues of Chou Kung and the reason why Chou could rule over the empire." So the Ancient Text School is no doubt right in saying that Confucius was a great transmitter of the ancient Chinese cultural heritage, the "Six Classics", sometimes called the "Six Arts".[333]

Nevertheless, being a great teacher, Confucius did not merely transmit the ancient materials which had been handed down, but he also selected, expurgated and rectified the old materials in order to exemplify his own ideas. Through the extensive reading of the existing materials he could deduce from them certain moral and social principles which he thought were badly needed in his time and then in teaching or illustrating these principles to his disciples he drew freely from the ancient materials, and turned them into something new. So the ancient "six classics" soon after being selected, expurgated and rectified by Confucius became the special heritage of the Confucian school. For example, he deduced his principle of the "rectification of names" from the existing histories of his time, especially the history of his own State of Lu, called *Ch'un Ch'iu*, and then applied the principles in his teaching of the history course. In doing so, he would naturally select, expurgate and rectify the original history materials in order to exemplify his principles. So both Dr. Hu Shih and Dr. Feng Yu-lan are right when the former holds that Confucius did compile *Ch'un Ch'iu* for the purpose of exemplifying his principle of the rectification of names, and the latter maintains that Confucius did not compile the book in order to exemplify his principle, but rather deduced it from the *Ch'un Ch'iu* of Lu. What Confucius actually wrote was of course not the *Ch'un Ch'iu* of Lu but the *Ch'un Ch'iu* which was based primarily on the *Ch'un Ch'iu* of Lu but much expurgated and rectified in order to exemplify his own points of view. This is what Mencius had in mind when he said that Confucius took the *I*[334] or principles from the current histories of the various states of his time, like the *Sheng*[335] of Chin, *Tao-wu* of Ch'u,[336] and the *Ch'un Ch'iu* of Lu (*Mencius*, Bk. 4, pt. 2, Chap. 21); and what Ssu-ma Ch'ien meant when he wrote, "Confucius wrote *Ch'un Ch'iu* on the basis of the existing histories. . . . He wrote from the point of view of Lu, but tried to show proper respect to the Chou Emperors, harking back to the Shang dynasty and showing the changes in the systems of the Three Dynasties. He adopted a most concise style, but injected into it a profound meaning." (*Shih Chi*, "The life of Confucius") In the same way he dealt with many other old materials of the other classics. (See Chapters 5 and 6) In teaching his students, he very likely had prepared some form of lecture-notes, as any good teacher would do, based in most cases on the existing materials, but carefully selected, rectified or commented upon. These notes, either from the pen of Confucius himself or from that of his disciples who had taken them down from the master, were later on either incorporated with the original classics or edited separately, and have become the "six classics" peculiar to the Confucian School.

Lo Ken-tse,[337] in his article "Before the Period of the Warring States There Had Not Been Private Schools' Writings",[338] points out clearly that most of the quotations of *Shih* or Poetry, and *Shu* or History in the classics of the Mohist School,[339] a rival school of Confucianism in the period of the Warring States, are found to be very different from those in the present *Shih Ching* or *The Book of Poetry* and *Shu Ching* or *The Book of History* of the Confucian school; while those quotations of *Shih* and *Shu* in the writings of the Confucian scholars of the same period, like Mencius and Hsun-tzu, are very much the same as those in the present *Shih Ching* or *Shu Ching*. It seems very probable that many of both the Confucian classics and the Mohist classics were all drawn from the existing literature, specially the "Six Classics" or "Six Arts",[340] of the ancients, but each school selected, revised and rectified only those portions which supported or exemplified its principles. This is, as has been widely and traditionally believed, what Confucius actually did. (See *Ku Shih Pien*, Vol. 4, pp. 8-68) Any modern higher critics (e.g. Chang Shou Lin[341] in his article, "Shih Ching Was Not Expurgated or Edited by Confucius", *Ku Shih Pien*, Vol. 3; Ch'ien Hsun-t'ung, *Ku Shih Pien*, Vol. 1, p. 74) thought, for example, that the poems had nothing to do with Confucius, because Confucius only talked about the poems numbering three hundred in his time as they do at present, and nearly all the eighteen poems quoted by Confucius in *The Analects* are to be found in the present *The Book of Poetry*; there is no trace of his work of expurgating or rectifying. They have failed to see that the thirteen quotations of the poems in the Mohist School as Lo Ken-tse shows us, are nearly all different in some respects from the three hundred odd poems of the Confucian School.

In short, Confucius was not only a transmitter but also an originator of the "six classics" to which he was closely related. As an ideal teacher, he drew new meanings from the old materials and gave new interpretations of the same, in order to meet the need of his age, both that of society and that of individuals. He was both a reformer and a conserver, originating reforms through conserving, and transmitting the best of the ancient. This will be seen more fully in the later chapters.

It is almost certain that there are many faked materials and many mistakes in the Confucian classics as we now have them; they are not exactly the same as those which came from Confucius. The difficulty of writing before the invention of printing, the friability of the materials, usually bamboos, on which the classics were written, the opposition of rulers and scholars of the Mohist and Legalistic schools to Confucianism between the period of the Warring States (481-221 B.C.) and the reign of Wu Ti of the Han dynasty (140-85 B.C.), and especially during the reign of the First Emperor of the Ch'in dynasty (255-206 B.C.), and the selfish motives of scholars in misinterpreting and writing spurious classics for personal power or profit, all this has caused the distortion of many a part of the present classics, including their commentaries and treatises. But many of the modern higher critics have gone too far in denying the authenticity of nearly all of the classics. Dr. Hu Shih, one of the leaders of the critical study of ancient literature, has recently realized the danger and mistake of many purely subjective and irresponsible criticisms of long cherished beliefs, so in 1937, for example, he warned his fellow critics, "The sceptical attitude is to be encouraged, but more to be encouraged is the capacity for suspension of judgment, pending the appearance of sufficient evidence." (Hu Shih: "A criticism of Some Recent Methods Used in Dating Lao-tzu, *Harvard Journal of Asiatic Studies*, Vol. 2, nos. 3 and 4, p. 373, Dec. 1937)

The following are quotations from an article "The New Evidence of Ancient History",[342] by Wang Kuo Wei, (A.D. 1877-1927), one of the greatest modern Chinese archaeologists and Confucian scholars, a conclusion, based on his long and laborious archaeological researches and critical study of ancient Chinese literature.

(1) "*Shang Shu* or *The Book of History*. The chapters in *The Book of Yu and Hsia*[343] like Yao Tien,[344] Kao Yao Mu,[345] Yu Kung,[346] Kan Shih,[347] the chapter on T'ang Shih[348] in *The Book of Shang*[349] are all more plainly and clearly written in their literature and were probably re-edited in later periods; but at least they were the productions of the early Chou people. As regards the chapters in *The Book of Shang*, P'an Keng,[350] Kao Ts'ung T'ung Jih,[351] Hsi Po K'an Chi,[352] Wei Tzu,[353] and the chapters in *The Book of Chou*,[354] Mu Shih,[355] Hung Fang,[356] Chin T'eng,[357] Ta Kao,[358] K'ang Kao,[359] Chiu Kao,[360] Tzu Ts'ai,[361] Shao Kao,[362] Lo Kao,[363] To Shih,[364] Wu I,[365] Chun Shih,[366] To Fang,[367] Li Cheng,[368] Ku Ming,[369] K'ang Wang Chih Kao,[370] Lu Hsing,[371] Wen Hou Chih Ming,[372] Fei Shih,[373] and Chin Shih,[374] were all the works of their times."

(2) "*Shih* or *The Book of Poetry*. The poems were productions from the early Chou to the early part of the Spring and Autumn period. The five chapters of Shang Shun[375] were probably also the works of the Sung people[376] at the time of Tsung Chou."[377]

(3) "*I* or *The Book of Changes*. The Kua Tzu[378] and Yao Tzu[379] were the productions of the early Chou. The Ten Wings[380] have been traditionally believed to be the work of Confucius, at least they were the narrations of the seventy disciples of Confucius."

(4) "*Ch'un Ch'iu* or *The Spring and Autumn Annals*. It is the history of the State of Lu, revised by Confucius."

(5) "Tso's commentary and *Kuo Yu*[381] were productions of the period between the latter part of the Spring and Autumn period and the early part of Chan Kuo or the Warring States. They appeared in the world at the beginning of the Han dynasty."

Scholars, so far, have never entirely agreed with one another as to the nature of the classics and their relation to Confucius; some have taken more conservative views, and some have taken more radical ones. At any rate, it is safe to conclude that the relation of Confucius to the classics is, more or less, the same as the relation of any great teacher to his teaching materials, his lecture notes, and his selections of the literature of his time. But just how far the present-day classics are true to the original, as handed down by Confucius, we can by no means exactly know, and we have to wait for further archaeological discoveries or the appearance of other adequate evidences. It is also beyond the purpose of the present essay to deal particularly with problems of textual criticism, and it must suffice to point out some divergent views with regard to the relation of Confucius to the classics, and show that after all Confucius was a great teacher, both a transmitter and an originator of the classics or the literary records of the history, institution, and traditions of the ancient Chinese.

CHAPTER IV

THE AIM OF THE TEACHING OF CONFUCIUS

OUTLINE

A. According to the immediate disciples of Confucius, as recorded in *The Analects*

(A) Individual aim:

1. The highest stage of the ideal individual life—Sage (Sheng Jen or the Holy One)

2. The intermediate stage of a practical ideal life—Superior Man (Chun-tzu)

(1) Subjective aim—self-cultivation

(a) Moral aim:
    a. love; b. righteousness; c. optimism; d. simplicity, frugality, and self-satisfaction; e. obedience to the will of God; f. sociability and friendliness; g. peacefulness and quietness; h. carefulness in speech and earnestness in action; i. Propriety (Li), humility, and sincerity

(b) Intellectual aim

(c) Physical aim

(2) Objective aim—"to give peace to others"

(B) Social aim:

1. The first stage of the ideal society: "Small tranquility" (Hsiao K'ang), or the stage of "Lu" ("Ch'i, by one change, would come to Lu")
    Reasons for the idealization of the past
    Some characteristics of this stage of social development

2. The second and the highest stage of the ideal society: "Great Harmony" (Ta T'ung), or the stage of "Tao" ("Lu, by one change, would come to Tao")
    Some characteristics of this stage of social development

B. According to Mencius and His school of Conficianism

(A) Individual aim: a Sage, or a Superior Man

1. Moral aim:
(a) Love (Jen)
(b) Righteousness (*I*)
(c) Propriety (*Li*)
(d) Sincerity (Sheng)
(e) The doctrine of the Mean
(f) Sociability and friendliness
(g) Optimism
(h) Loyalty, fidelity, etc.
2. Intellectual aim
3. Physical aim
(B) Social aim:
    "The government of Love" (Jen Cheng)
1. Political factors
2. Social factors
3. Economic factors

C. According to Hsun-tzu and his school of Confucianism
(A) Individual aim:
    Three grades of virtue and wisdom:
(1) Scholar (Shih)
(2) Superior Man (Chun-tzu)
(3) Sage (Sheng Jen)
(B) Social aim:
    The government of Li (rules of proper conduct)

D. Conclusion

A. According to *The Analects*

The aim of the teaching of Confucius was, to state it very briefly, to bring about social reforms through educating individuals of society; to put forth an ideal social order through cultivating ideal ways of life and full development of the personality of the individual. He believed in the importance of the individual to ensure the progress or reform of society. So he spent much of his life-time in travelling from one state to another, receiving different classes of people to be his disciples, and teaching them, according to their capacities and environment, the way to live an ideal life. He has been supposed to be the first or at least the greatest advocate of his time of popular education. "In education", he said, "there should be no distinctions of class" (*The Analects*, 15,38), and he never refused to teach anyone who came to him for learning, even if they had but a very small amount for fees. (*The Analects*, 7,7) The children, too, who came from disreputable villages and were looked down upon by his disciples, were warmly received by the Master. (*The Analects*, 7,28; 47,14). He put the importance of education on the same level as that of population and wealth, and regarded these as the three essentials of any nation. (*The Analects*, 13,9)

On the other hand, he was also fully aware of the importance of social institutions to ensure the stability and safety of individuals. Society must adjust itself to the individual in order to escape stagnation, and the individual must also adjust himself to society in order to become human, and he cannot live or develop himself as a human without the help of society. So Confucius did not teach people, as the pessimists of his time did, to flee from the world and to become irresponsible hermits or political nihilists. What was needed, he thought, was to work in society to bring about social reforms through education. Once he was heard to say, with a sigh, "It is impossible to associate with birds and beasts. If I associate not with these people, with mankind, with whom shall I associate? If right principles prevailed through the world, there would be no use for me to change its states." (*The Analects*, 18,4)

The two favourite subjects in the teaching of Confucius, as recorded in *The Analects*, are love (*Jen*), and the rules of proper conduct (*Li*). *Li* may mean propriety, ceremony or rite in its narrower sense; in its broader sense it may mean the rules of proper conduct in general. Such rules of proper conduct (*Li*) are really a sort of unwritten law and regulations recognized by society to govern the thought and action of every individual in society. They are the most important social product to ensure the solidarity of society. Love (*Jen*) is another favourite theme of the teaching of Confucius. It presupposes and ensures the importance and uniqueness of every individual. The full development of the personality of the individual is very much emphasized in the teaching of Confucius.

Both social solidarity and individual development were thus emphasized by Confucius. "Some one addressed Confucius, saying, 'Sir, why are you not engaged in the government?' The Master said, 'What does *Shu Ching* say of filial piety? You are filial, you discharge your brotherly duties. These qualities are displayed in government.' This then also constitutes the exercise of government. Why must there be that 'to make one be in the government?' " (*The Analects*, 2,21) According to Confucius, to cultivate the individual is the same as being in the government; there is no necessary gap between the individual and society. They are not antagonistic, in the mind of Confucius, but rather correlated and complementary to each other.

The problem still remains. What are the ideal social order, and the ideal way of the individual life, in the mind of Confucius, that constitute the aim of his teaching? For the sake of clearness, the following two headings are given for separate discussion, namely, the social aim of the teaching of Confucius, and the individual aim of his teaching, though as a matter of fact, as shown above, these two are fundamentally correlated and complementary to each other.

(A) Individual Aim—the Ideal Life of the Individual

In *The Analects*, it is recorded that, according to Confucius, there are, generally speaking, two stages of the ideal life of an individual; —the highest stage of the ideal life, called Sheng Jen[1] or Sage; and the intermediate stage, a stage of practical human ideals, called Chun-tzu,[2] or Superior Man.

1. The Highest Stage of the Ideal Life—Sheng Jen, or Sage

The highest stage of the ideal life was called Sheng Jen,[3] as used by Confucius in *The Analects*. The term Sheng Jen has been commonly translated into English as a "sage", but literally it should be translated as the "holy man" or the "Holy One". As to the conception of Confucius, as recorded in *The Analects*, with regard to Sheng Jen, the term "Holy One" would perhaps be the better translation. But since the same term, commonly used in the writings of later scholars, is, in general, more or less synonymous with the English word sage, the writer retains here the English term of the common usage, and employs capital letters to make it more distinctive.

Confucius did not teach very much about this stage of ideal life, because he knew that it would be too far a way from the grasp of his disciples, and too much beyond their common practical and intellectual experiences. Nevertheless, he did mention certain important characteristics of such a life, as a breath of idealism to inspire people to press forward even more towards something higher and better.

One of the chief characteristics of the Sage is that he is able to confer benefits on all the people of the world, assist them in all difficulties, and "afford universal relief"; he is, in a sense, a "Saviour of the World". In the mind of Confucius there never had been a Sage before him, even Yao[4] and Shun,[5] the ancient model sovereigns who were honoured as Sage-kings by later Confucian writers, fell short of such a standard. The following quotation bears this out very clearly:

"Tzu-kung said, 'Suppose the case of a man extensively conferring benefits on the people and able to afford universal relief, what would you say of him? Might he be called perfectly virtuous (*Jen*)?'[6] The Master said, 'Why speak only of perfect virtue (*Jen*) in connexion with him? Must he not have the qualities of a Sage? Even Yao and Shun were still solicitous about this." (*The Analects*, 6, 26, 1)

It is important to be noted here that, unlike the later Confucian scholars, and contrary to the conception of nearly all the modern Chinese or Western scholars on Chinese studies, Confucius, in *The Analects*, did not think that any of the great personalities of the past, not even the "Sage-kings", had achieved the highest standard of life which he conceived. He looked to the high ideal in the future and not entirely in the past. Like his ideal personality, was his ideal society, which is not in the "golden past" but rather in the unrealized future, and is a question which will be discussed later. In another incident, mentioned in *The Analects*, Confucius was heard to say to Tzu-lu,[7] one of his favourite disciples:

"He cultivates himself so as to give peace to all the people: even Yao and Shun (the ideal personalities of his time) were still solicitous about this." (*The Analects*, 14, 45)

It is no wonder that such a person who could give peace to all the people in the world, and extensively assist them in all difficulties, had never been seen by Confucius, who once said in despair, "A Sage it is not mine to see!" (*The Analects*, 7,25) Though he was later canonized as a sage, yet he spoke very frankly and honestly in his life-time that "The Sage and the man of perfect virtue, how dare I rank myself with them?" (*The Analects*, 7,32) He was satisfied to see people who could live a practical ideal life, an inferior stage to the highest standard of life. Such people he called Chun-tzu,[8] or Superior Man. About such personalities: he taught a great deal in *The Analects*, and to such a group he was anxious that he might belong himself. "The Master said, 'A Sage it is not mine to see; could I see a Superior Man, that would satisfy me.' " (*The Analects*, 7,25,1)

Indeed, a Sage would have transcended the achievements of any living being which had so far existed. He was thought as being in the same category as the Divine Being of whom the Superior Man should always stand in awe. (*The Analects*, 16,8,1) He is, in short, the ideal of the ideal human life, and the highest standard for human beings.

2. **The Intermediate Stage Between a Common Man and a Sage, a Stage of Practical Human Ideal Life—Chun-tzu,[9] or the Superior Man**

The terms Chun-tzu, like many other Chinese terms, has no satisfactory English equivalent. The fundamental meaning of Chun[10] is "prince" or "ruler", Tzu[11] is "viscount" or "baron", and the whole term Chun-tzu originally indicated in general those people with official power or rank. Again, those men who had official power or rank were at the same time also believed to be virtuous men. Virtue and power or rank generally went together. But to Confucius the term Chun-tzu assumed a very different meaning; it signified only those who had virtues, no matter whether they had any official power or rank or not. He might not be the first one who changed the original meaning of the term, but he was no doubt responsible for many of the new meanings which have been connected with it. For its later and broader meaning used by Confucius, the English terms "Princely Man", "Kingly Man", and "Superior Man" have been suggested. The word "gentleman", in its best usage, approaches, but only to a degree, the significance of the Chinese term. On the whole, perhaps the translation "Superior Man" best suits the term which Confucius discussed with his disciples. In *The Analects*, Confucius deals extensively with the qualities of the Superior Man. The term "Chun-tzu" is recorded over 30 times in *The Analects*, and over 60 of the references are supposed to have been spoken by Confucius. From this, one can realize somewhat the importance which Confucius attached to the qualities of the Superior Man. What are the qualities which characterize the Superior Man?

"Tzu-lu asked what constituted the Superior Man. The Master said, 'The cultivation of himself in reverential carefulness'. 'And is this all?' said Tzu-lu. 'He cultivates himself so as to give peace to others', was the reply. 'And is this all?' again asked Tzu-lu. The Master said, 'He cultivates himself so as to give peace to all the people: even Yao and Shun were still solicitous about this.' " (*The Analects*, 14,45)

According to the above saying, the Superior Man should, subjectively, cultivate his own self in reverential carefulness, and objectively, he should give peace to others. What are the aims of the self-cultivation of the Superior Man, and his objective aims of giving peace to others? The following is a brief outline of these aims.

(1) Subjective—to cultivate one's self

"The Master said, 'The Way of the Superior Man has three essentials, to which I have not attained: he has love (*Jen*) without anxiety, wisdom without perplexity, and courage without fear'. Tzu-kung said, 'Master, that is what you yourself say'." (*The Analects*, 14,30)

So in cultivating himself, the Superior Man would be careful in all the moral, intellectual and physical aspects of his training. But in the teaching of Confucius the moral aim was always predominant. The following are some quotations from *The Analects*, to illustrate the three-fold self-cultivation of the Superior Man.

(a) Moral aim

a. Love or Benevolence (*Jen*[12])

"If a Superior Man abandons *Jen*, how can he fulfil the requirements of that name? The Superior Man does not, even for the space of a single meal, act contrary to *Jen*. In moments of haste, he cleaves to it. In seasons of danger, he cleaves to it." (*The Analects*, 4,5,2-3)

b. Righteousness (*I*)[13]

"The Superior Man, in the world, does not set his mind either for anything or against anything; what is righteous (*I*) he will follow." (*The Analects*, 4,10)

"The mind of the Superior Man is conversant with righteousness (*I*); the mind of the mean man is conversant with gain." (*The Analects*, 4,16)

"Tzu-lu said, 'Does the Superior Man esteem valour?' The Master said, 'The Superior Man holds righteousness (*I*) to be of highest importance. A man in his superior position, having valour without righteousness, will be guilty of insubordination; one of the lower people, having valour without righteousness (*I*), will commit robbery." (*The Analects*, 17,23)

"The Superior Man in everything considers righteousness (*I*) to be essential." (*The Analects*, 15,17)

c. Optimistic

"The Superior Man is satisfied and composed; the mean man is always full of distress." (*The Analects*, 7,36)

"Ssu-ma Niu asked about the Superior Man. The Master said, 'The Superior Man has neither anxiety nor fear.' 'Being without anxiety or fear!' said Niu;—'does this constitute what we call the Superior Man?' The Master said, 'When internal examination discovers nothing wrong, what is there to be anxious about, what is there to fear?' " (*The Analects*, 12,4)

d. Simple, frugal and virtuous in his living; not covetous of securing money or power

"The Master said, 'He who aims to be a Superior Man in his food does not seek to gratify his appetite, nor in his dwelling-place does he seek the appliances of ease.' " (*The Analects*, 1,14) ·

"The Master said, 'The Superior Man thinks of virtue; the small man thinks of comfort. The Superior Man thinks of the sanctions of law; the small man thinks of favours which he may receive.' " (*The Analects*, 4,11)

"The object of the Superior Man is truth. Food is not his object. ... The Superior Man is anxious lest he should not get truth (*Tao*); he is not anxious lest poverty should come upon him." (*The Analects*, 15,31)

e. Recognising and obeying the ordinances of Heaven (*T'ien Ming*[14]) or the will of God

"The Master said, 'Without recognising the ordinances of Heaven, it is impossible to be a Superior Man.' " (*The Analects*, 20,3,1)

"The Superior Man stands in awe of the ordinances of Heaven. ... The mean man does not know the ordinances of Heaven, and consequently does not stand in awe of them." (*The Analects*, 16,8)

"The Master said, 'At fifty, I knew the ordinances of Heaven.' " (*The Analects*, 2,4,4)

f. Sociable and friendly

"The Superior Man is dignified, but does not wrangle. He is sociable, but not a partisan." (*The Analects*, 15,21)

"Let the Superior Man never fail reverentially to order his own conduct, and let him be respectful to others and observant of propriety:—then all within the four seas will be his brothers. What has the Superior Man to do with being distressed because he has no brothers?" (*The Analects*, 12,5,4)

g. Peaceful and quiet

"The Master said, 'The Superior Man has no contentions.' " (*The Analects*, 3,7)

"The Superior Man is dignified, but does not wrangle." (*The Analects*, 15,21)

"The Master said, 'Is he not a Superior Man, who feels no discomposure though men may take no note of him?' " (*The Analects*, 1,1,3)

h. Careful and slow in speech, earnest and quick in action

"The Superior Man wished to be slow in his words and earnest in his conduct." (*The Analects*, 4,24)

"The Superior Man is earnest in what he is doing, and careful in his speech." (*The Analects*, 1,14)

"The Superior Man is modest in his speech, but exceeds in his actions." (*The Analects*, 14,29)

i. Observant of propriety (*Li*[15]), humble and sincere

"The Master said, 'The Superior Man in everything considers righteousness to be essential. He performs it according to the rules of propriety.[16] He brings it forth in humility. He completes it with sincerity. This indeed is a Superior Man.' " (*The Analects*, 15,17)

"The Superior Man hates those who have valour merely, and are unobservant of propriety." (*The Analects*, 17,4,1)

"The Master said, 'The Superior Man has a dignified ease without pride. The mean man has pride without a dignified ease.' " (*The Analects*, 13,25)

"Let his words be sincere and truthful, and his actions honourable and careful;—such conduct may be practised among the rude tribes of the South or the North. If his words be not sincere and truthful, and his actions not honourable and careful, will he, with such conduct, be appreciated, even in his neighborhood?" (*The Analects*, 15,5,2)

"Hold faithfulness and sincerity as first principles. Have no friends not equal to yourself. When you have faults, do not fear to abandon them." (*The Analects*, 1,8,2-4)

"The Superior Man, extensively studying all learning, and keeping himself under the restraint of the rules of propriety, may this likewise not overstep what is right." (*The Analects*, 6,25)

"Respectfulness, without *Li*, becomes laborious bustle; carefulness, without *Li*, becomes timidity; boldness, without *Li*, becomes insubordination; straightforwardness, without *Li*, becomes rudeness." (*The Analects*, 6,2,1)

(b) Intellectual aim of the Superior Man

a. Study extensively, but always be kept under the restraint of virtue. Knowledge without virtue is undesirable.

"The Master said, 'The Superior Man, extensively studying all learning, and keeping himself under the restraint of the rules of propriety (*Li*),[17] may thus likewise not overstep what is right.' " (*The Analects*, 6,25)

"Where the natural qualities are in excess of accomplishments, we have rusticity; where the accomplishments are in excess of the natural qualities, we have the manners of a clerk (who is learned but insincere). When the accomplishments and natural qualities are equally blended, we then have the Superior Man." (*The Analects*, 6,16)

"If a Superior Man be not careful (in his manner or virtue), he will not call forth any veneration, and his learning will not be solid." (*The Analects*, 1,8,1)

b. To love learning by living a simple life, practising earnestly what he has learned, and constantly seeking for good teachers from whom his learning could be rectified.

"He who aims to be a Superior Man in his food does not seek to gratify his appetite, nor in his dwelling-place does he seek the appliances of ease; he is earnest in what he is doing, and careful in his speech; he frequents the company of men of principle that he may be rectified:—such a person may be said indeed to love to learn." (*The Analects*, 1,14)

c. The purpose of learning is for self-cultivation, and not for the praise of others; for practical conduct, and not for empty talk, —learning by doing.

"What the Superior Man seeks, is in himself. What the mean man seeks, is in others." (*The Analects*, 15,20)

"In ancient times, men learned with a view to their own improvement. Nowadays, men learn with a view to the approbation of others." (*The Analects*, 14,25)

"The Superior Man is distressed by his want of ability. He is not distressed by men's not knowing him." (*The Analects*, 15,18)

"Is he not a Superior Man, who feels no discomposure though men may take no note of him?" (*The Analects*, 1,1,3)

"Tzu-kung asked what constituted the Superior Man. The Master said, 'He acts before he speaks, and afterwards speaks according to his actions.' " (*The Analects*, 2,13)

"The Superior Man is modest in his speech, but exceeds in his actions." (*The Analects*, 14,29)

"The Master said, 'I would prefer not speaking'. Tzu-kung said, 'If you, Master, do not speak, what shall we, your disciples, have to record?' The Master said, 'Does Heaven speak? The four seasons pursue their courses, and all things are continually being produced, but does Heaven say anything?' " (*The Analects*, 17,13)

d. The aim of learning is to seek the Truth (*Tao*).[18] If the Truth be found, the Superior Man would be satisfied, no matter in what condition he was placed.

"The Superior Man learns, in order to reach to the Truth." (*The Analects*, 19,7)

"The object of the Superior Man is Truth. Food is not his object. There is ploughing;—even in that there is sometimes want. So with learning;—emolument may be found in it. The Superior Man is anxious lest he should not get Truth; he is not anxious lest poverty should come upon him." (*The Analects*, 15,31)

"If a man in the morning hears the Truth, he may die in the evening without regret." (*The Analects*, 4,8)

e. Nine subjects of thought to the Superior Man:—various instances of the way in which he cultivates himself.

"The Superior Man has nine things which are subjects with him of thoughtful consideration. In regard to the use of his eyes, he is anxious to see clearly. In regard to the use of his ears, he is anxious to hear distinctly. In regard to his countenance, he is anxious that it should be benign. In regard to his demeanour, he is anxious that it should be respectful. In regard to his speech, he is anxious that it should be sincere. In regard to his doing of business, he is anxious that it should be reverently careful. In regard to what he doubts about, he is anxious to question others. When he is angry, he thinks of the difficulties (his anger may involve him in). When he sees gain to be got, he thinks of righteousness." (*The Analects*, 16,13)

f. Strange Doctrines are not to be studied; always progress upward, not downward.

"The study of strange doctrines is injurious indeed!" (*The Analects*, 2,16)

"The progress of the Superior Man is upwards; the progress of the mean man is downwards." (*The Analects*, 14,24)

In short, the intellectual aim of the Superior Man is to attain the Truth (*Tao*[19] or the Way). (This will be discussed more fully in chapter five, the substance of the teaching of Confucius). In order to attain the Truth, the Superior Man should study extensively, and love the true learning. He should earnestly put his learning into practice, and be sincere to himself and others. He should not speak more than he is able to fulfil, and he should also be ready to be rectified by good teachers, and be constrained by virtues. His aim should not be diverted by any difficult condition of life, but he should ever progress upwards toward the Truth, always be careful in what he sees, hears, speaks, and acts, in his countenance and demeanour, and in the moment when in doubt, anger, or facing opportunities for gain. (Further discussion on the methods of learning will be found in Chapter Six, the Methods of the Teaching of Confucius).

(c) Physical aim of the Superior Man

Confucius did not deal much with the physical aspect of the Superior Man in *The Analects*. He lived in a time of inter-state chaos, when every state was engaged in fighting, and physical strength or valour was universally honoured, so it was not necessary for Confucius to lay stress on the physical aspect in his teachings. What he was interested in, on the physical side, was rather the negative restriction and discouragement of excessive boldness and over-emphasis on sheer physical valour.

"Tzu-lu said, (to Confucius), 'If you had the conduct of the armies of a great state, whom would you have to act with you?' The Master said, 'I would not have him to act with me, who will unarmed attack a tiger, or cross a river without a boat, dying without any regret. My associate must be the man who proceeds to action full of solicitude, who is fond of adjusting his plans, and then carries them into execution.' " (*The Analects*, 7,10,2-3)

This does not mean that Confucius looked down upon physical valour. He ranked it with wisdom and virtue as the three most important requirements of a Superior Man. (*The Analects*, 14,30; 9,23) What he emphasized was that physical boldness, strength or valour, must go together with knowledge and virtue—love (*Jen*), propriety (*Li*) or righteousness (*I*).

"There is the love of boldness without the love of learning;—the beclouding here leads to insubordination." (*The Analects*, 17,8,3)

"Men of love (*Jen*) are sure to be bold." (*The Analects*, 14,5)

The determined scholar and the man of virtue (*Jen*) will not seek to live at the expense of injuring their virtue (love—*Jen*). They will even sacrifice their lives to preserve their virtue (*Jen*) complete." (*The Analects*, 15,8)

"Physical valour without propriety (*Li*) is to be hated". (*The Analects*, 17,24,1)

"The man who is valorous and is dissatisfied with poverty, will proceed to insubordination." (*The Analects*, 8,10)

"Tzu-lu said, 'Does the Superior Man esteem valour?' The Master said, 'The Superior Man holds righteousness (*I*) to be of the highest importance. A Superior Man, having valour without righteousness, will be guilty of insubordination; a small man, having valour without righteousness, will commit robbery.' " (*The Analects*, 17,23.)

Although the teaching of Confucius on the physical aim of the Superior Man was chiefly concerned with the moral and intellectual restrictions on sheer physical valour and boldness, yet he did, on some occasions, encourage archery, horse-riding, charioteering, and other healthy exercises. For example, he allowed no other contentious striving except archery. "The Superior Man has no contentions", he said, "If it be said he cannot avoid them, shall this be in archery?" (*The Analects*, 3,7) He himself seems to have constantly practiced the arts of archery (*The Analects*, 7,26; 3,16), and charioteering. (*The Analects*, 9,2,2; 10,17) Physical health, according to Confucius, should be greatly taken care of, at least for the sake of one's parents, who "are anxious lest their children should be sick." (*The Analects*, 2,6) So good health is essential in the Confucian primary virtue of Filial Piety. The Superior Man, then, should be careful in his daily living,—eating, drinking, sleeping, etc. (*The Analects*, 10,8); he should not "be overcome of wine" (*The Analects*, 9,15), and should constantly guard against lust, quarrelsomeness and covetousness.

"There are three things which the Superior Man guards against. In youth, when the physical powers are not yet settled, he guards against lust. When he is strong and the physical powers are full of vigour, he guards against quarrelsomeness. When he is old, and the animal powers are decayed, he guards against covetousness." (*The Analects*, 16,7)

(2) Subjective—"to give peace to others"

The subjective aim of the Superior Man, as outlined above, was to cultivate himself physically, intellectually, and morally; the objective aim was, according to Confucius, "To give peace to others" (*The Analects*, 14,45), so that after his death his name would be mentioned.

"The Master said, 'The Superior Man is sick at the thought that his name would not be mentioned after his death.' " (*The Analects*, 15,19)

Not that the Superior Man cares about fame, but fame is the invariable concomitant of merit. He cannot have been the Superior Man, if he be not remembered by the people of his kind or meritorious deeds. So a Superior Man would love all people and regard them as his own brothers.

"When the Superior Man has learned the Truth (*Tao*), he loves men." (*The Analects*, 17,4,3)

"Let the Superior Man never fail reverentially to order his own conduct, and let him be respectful to others and observant of propriety (*Li*)—then all within the four seas will be his brothers. What has the Superior Man to do with being distressed because he has no brothers?" (*The Analects*, 12,5,4)

As to the definite methods and ideals which the Superior Man would adopt for helping the people, these will be discussed fully in the next section—the social aim of the teaching of Confucius.

The Superior Man, Chun-tzu, was sometimes called *Shih*, or "Scholar" by Confucius in *The Analects*. Some scholars have suggested that *Shih* was the third class of personality in the mind of Confucius, next to *Chun-tzu*. This is definitely so in the writings of Hsun-tzu, who has three grades of virtue and wisdom, which will be discussed later. From the few quotations about *Shih* given in *The Analects*, one cannot see clearly the distinction between *Shih* and *Chun-tzu* in their attributes. They seem to have been used as synonymous terms to indicate the practical ideal life of an individual, next to the absolute ideal life, *Sheng Jen*, the Sage or the "Holy One" of the Chinese. The following are the qualities of a *Shih* or Scholar.

(a) He aims at the Truth (*Tao*), and is indifferent to poverty or any other hard environment.

"A Scholars, whose mind is set on the Truth (*Tao*), and who is ashamed of bad clothes and bad food, is not fit to be discoursed with." (*The Analects*, 4,9)

"The Scholar who cherished the love of comfort is not fit to be deemed a scholar." (*The Analects*, 14,3)

(b) He has breadth of mind and vigorous endurance.

"The philosopher Tseng[20] said, 'The Scholar may not be without breadth of mind and vigorous endurance. His burden is heavy and his course is long." (*The Analects*, 8,7)

(c) He is natural, straightforward, righteous, observant, and humble.

"Tzu-chang[21] asked, 'What must the Scholar (*Shih*) be, who may be said to be distinguished?' The Master said. . . . 'Now the man of distinction is natural and straightforward, and loves righteousness. He examines people's words, and looks at their countenances. He is anxious to humble himself to others. Such a man will be distinguished in the country; he will be distinguished in his clan." (*The Analects*, 12,20)

(d) Three classes of Scholars: those who perform the duties of their states, conscientiously and successfully, those who are filial and fraternal, and those who are sincere in speech and persistent in action.

"Tzu-kung[22] asked, saying, 'What qualities must a man possess to entitle him to be called a Scholar (*Shih*)?' The Master said, 'He who in his conduct of himself maintains a sense of shame and when sent to any quarter will not disgrace his prince's commission, deserves to be called a Scholar'. Tzu-kung pursued, 'I venture to ask who may be placed in the next lower rank?' and he was told, 'He whom the circle of his relatives pronounce to be filial, whom his fellow-villagers and neighbours pronounce to be fraternal.' Again the disciple asked, 'I venture to ask about the class still next in order.' The Master said, 'They are determined to be sincere in what they say, and to carry out what they do. They are obstinate little men. Yet perhaps they may make the next class.' " (*The Analects*, 13,20,1-3)

(e) He is courageous, righteous, reverential and sympathetic.

"Tzu-chang said, 'The Scholar, seeing threatening danger, is prepared to sacrifice his life. When the opportunity of gain is presented to him, he thinks of righteousness. In sacrificing, his thoughts are reverential. In mourning, his thoughts are about the grief which he should feel. Such a man commands our approbation indeed." (*The Analects*, 19,1)

(f) He is earnest, urgent and bland.

"Tzu-lu asked, saying, 'What qualities must a man possess to entitle him to be called a Scholar (*Shih*)?' The Master said, 'He must be thus,—earnest, urgent, and bland:—among his friends, earnest and urgent; among his brethren, bland'. (*The Analects*, 13,28)

From the above quotations, one can easily see that the qualities of the Scholar are almost the same as those of the Superior Man. They seem to indicate that, according to Confucius, a Superior Man should also be a Scholar, and a Scholar should have the qualities of a Superior Man. So in the present study, the writer is not separating the two as two different classes of people, but treating them as the same class in the ideal life taught by Confucius in *The Analects*.

(B) Social Aim—the Ideal Social Orders

Like the two stages of the ideal individual life in the teachings of Confucius in *The Analects*, there are also two stages of the ideal social order.

"The Master said, 'Ch'i,[23] by one change, would come to Lu,[24] Lu, by one change, would come to Tao.'[25] " (*The Analects*, 6,22)

The State of Ch'i was the first and the greatest of the Five Leaders (Wu Pa),[26] who dominated China, one after another, during the Spring and Autumn period. It is taken here to represent the general condition of the social order of all the states during the time of Confucius, when, as *Mencius* described, "The world faced decay and principles of right government faded away. Perverse speaking and oppressive deeds became rife. There were instances of ministers who murdered their sovereigns, and of sons who murdered their fathers." (*Mencius*, 3,2,9)

Lu, here, cannot be taken as meaning the state of Lu during the time of Confucius, because it was just as corrupt as other states, if not more so. The government of that state fell into the hands of three most powerful families, and the whole political and social orders were in the most chaotic condition; there were many cases of regicides, parricides, assassinations, murders, and usurpations for the sake of wealth or power or pleasure. (See *The Political and Social Backgrounds of the Teaching of Confucius,* and *The Life of Confucius,* Chapter 2) By Lu here is meant the original ideal state of Lu, when Chou Kung (the Duke of Chou) was its Feudal Lord. (*Mencius* 4,2,8,6) After he died, his descendant, Lu Kung (the Duke of Lu) received many of the precious cultural objects from King Ch'eng, the descendant of King Wu, the conqueror of the Shang dynasty, "thus the brilliant virtue of Chou Kung might be made illustrious." (See *Tso Chuan,* under the 4th year of Duke Ting of Lu, 506 B.C.) Down to the time of Confucius, the State of Lu still preserved some of the oldest cultural heritage handed down from Chou Kung, such as the music of Chou, the symbols of *I,* the rites and historical records of the early Chou, etc. To Confucius, Chou Kung was an ideal ruler, and the social order regulated by him was regarded as an ideal social order. He spoke about Chou Kung as an ideal person of ability and goodness (*The Analects,* 8,11), and he would feel badly when the vision of the Duke grew dim in his mind. Once he lamented over his own decadence, saying, "Alas! Extreme is my decay. For a long time, I have not dreamed, as I was wont to do, that I saw Chou Kung". (*The Analects,* 7,5) He wanted to perpetuate the Chou culture, as transmitted through Chou Kung. He said, "If there were one willing to employ me, might I not create an Eastern Chou?" (*The Analects,* 17,5) Again, he said, "Chou had the advantage of viewing the two past dynasties. How complete and elegant are its regulations! I follow Chou." (*The Analects,* 3,14) In short, by Lu was meant the best traditional social order, as handed down through the remote past, and culminated in Chou Kung, the over-lord of the State of Lu.

Confucius did not always idealize the past, as most modern scholars think he did. It is true that he usually talked about the good things in the past, especially during the times of the recognized ideal rulers,—Yao,[27] Shun,[28] Yu,[29] T'ang,[30] Wen,[31] Wu,[32] and Chou Kung.[33] The chief reasons for this may be summarized as follows:

(1) As the above paragraph mentioned, there were plenty of traditional writings about the morality and social orders during the

times of the ancient ideal rulers, and they were definitely much higher and better than those which were prevalent during the time of Confucius. So Confucius was anxious to transmit them, particularly those moral standards and social orders which had come down through the early Chou rulers especially Chou Kung. But he was by no means a blind transmitter, for he carefully selected, expurgated, rectified, and gave new meanings to the transmitted materials. He was a creator through being a transmitter. (See Chaps. 3 and 5) He did not entirely idealize the past, but rather used his own present judgment to pick up freely the past human experiences which would be suited to meet the present social and individual needs.

(2) People generally have the habit of idealizing the good old times, so in order to make his teaching more authoritative and effective, Confucius had sometimes to borrow the authority of the ancient ideal rulers. (See Kang Yu-wei's *K'ung-tzu T'oa Ku Kai Chih K'ao*[34] A Study of Confucius' Effort to Revolutionize the System of Chou by Attributing His System to the Ancient System) He might not have done that purposely, because there were enough traditional materials and popular beliefs for him to work out many of his own theories as having a basis in the teachings of the ancient ideal rulers, traditionally believed and recorded. Indeed, in the long run, people would never believe in him so firmly, if there were entirely no ground for him to attribute a certain part, at least, of his system to the ancient system. This method of borrowing the authority of ancient ideal rulers to illustrate one's own viewpoints was widely and sometimes abusively practised by the philosophers of the succeeding periods, such as Mo-tzu, Mencius, Chuang-tzu and Hsun-tzu. (See Lo Ken-tze,[35] *Wan Chou Chu Tzu Fan Ku K'ao*[36] "A Study of the Efforts of the Philosophers of the Late Chou Period in Revolt Against the Ancient Systems", *Ku Shih Pien*, Vol. 6, pp.1-49)

(3) Confucius said, "If anything is to be praised, it must first be proved". This saying was quoted from an unknown source, and interpreted by Pan Ku, the author of *Han Shu, The Official History of the Han Dynasty*, to mean that the practices of the ancient ideal

rulers had proved to be very successful, therefore, Confucius determined to carry them out in his own days. (See *Han Shu*, "I Wen Chih").[37] Not only the borrowing of the great names of the past would carry with it the prestige and authority of his teachings, but also with that, Confucius thought that he would be able to show to the world that after all his teachings were not too theoretical, they were practical and workable, and had been attained, to a large extent with great success, by the ancient ideal rulers.

So much for the reasons why Confucius did sometimes idealize the past. Nevertheless, he did not stop here with past ideal systems of social orders. He went a step further,—"Lu, by one change, would come to Tao." The third and the highest stage of the social progress would be realized, according to the teaching of Confucius in *The Analects*, when the great *Tao* prevails. With the vision of the highest stage of social evolution before him, Confucius could criticize the shortcomings of the past ideal rulers. It is chiefly through the neglect of the third stage of social progress, that many difficulties of the teachings of Confucius have arisen. For example, it is difficult to reconcile his teaching on the graded or conditional love ("Recompense injury with justice, and recompense kindness with kindness" *The Analects* 14,36,3) with the unconditional and universal love ("To over-flow in love to all people" *The Analects*, 1,16; "To afford universal relief" *The Analects*, 6,28); or the distinction between the ideal social order of the Superior Man and that of the Holy One, or Sage; if the conception of the two stages, not one, of the ideal social orders of Confucius, is neglected.

The characteristics of the two stages of social ideals, the stage of practical ideals which had been realized in the past when the social order like that of the ideal state of Lu prevailed, and the stage of ultimate ideal in the future when the Great *Tao* will prevail in the world, are very well summarized in the passage on *Ta T'ung*, or "Great Harmony", and *Hsiao K'ang* or "Small Tranquility", in *Li Chi, The Book of Rites*. Nearly all modern scholars believe that the passage was a forgery, and that instead of being spoken by Confucius, it was written by the scholars in the Han dynasty. The opinion of the present writer is that the present form or the wordings of the present passage must have been written by later scholars, possibly in the Han dynasty, but it is an excellent summary of the general spirit and teaching of Confucius as recorded in *The Analects*. The possibly later appearance of the present form of the passage does not destroy the genuineness of its substance and its general spirit. It gives a very good summary of the two stages of the ideal social orders, as taught by Confucius.

"Confucius said, 'the prevalence of the Great *Tao* and the beauty of the Three Dynasties are beyond my reach, but are within my ambition and purpose.

'When the Great *Tao* prevails, the world belongs to all. The people elect men of talents, virtue and ability (for rulers). They advocate sincerity, and cultivate friendship. Thus men do not regard as their parents only their own parents, nor treat as their children only their own children. A competent provision is made for the aged until their death, and employment of the able bodied, and a means of education for the young. The widowers, widows, orphans, childless men, and those who are disabled by disease are all efficiently maintained. Each man has his mate and each woman her home. Goods, though not to be wasted, are not necessarily kept privately. Disliking idleness, the people work, but not alone with a view to their own advantage. In this way selfish schemes are repressed and find no way to arise. Robbers, thieves, and rebels do not exist. Hence the outer door remains open and is not shut. This is the stage of Great Harmony. ·

'But at present the Great *Tao* is hidden. The world belongs to families. Each one regards as his parents only his own parents, and treats as his children only his own children. The wealth of each and his labour are only for his self-interest. Great men imagine it is the rule that their estates should descend in their own families. Their object is to make the walls of their cities and suburbs strong; and their ditches and moats secure. Propriety (*Li*) and justice (*I*) are regarded as the threads by which they seek to maintain in its correctness the relation between the rulers and the minister; in its generous regard the relation between father and son; in its harmony the relation between elder and younger; and in a community of sentiment the relation between husband and wife; and in accordance with them they regulate consumption, distribute land and dwellings, distinguish the men of military ability and cunning, and achieve their work with a view to their own advantage. Thus selfish schemes and enterprises are constantly taking their rise, and war inevitably ensues.

'In this course of propriety and justice, Yu, T'ang, Wen, Wu, Ch'eng Wang, and the Duke of Chou, are the best examples of good government. Of these six Superior Men, every one was attentive to propriety (*Li*), thus to secure the display of justice (*I*), the realization of sincerity (*Ch'eng*),[38] the exhibition of errors, the exemplification of love (*Jen*),[39] and the discussion of courtesy (*Jang*),[40] showing the people all the constant virtues. If any ruler, having power and position, would not allow this course, he shall be driven away by the multitude who regard him as a public enemy. This is the stage of Small Tranquility (*Hsiao K'ang*).'"[41] (*Li Chi*, Chap. on *Li Yung*)[42]

(4) The first stage of the ideal society—the stage of *Hsiao K'ang*[43] or "small tranquility"

The general social and political order of this stage of social progress, as described in the above classical statement, was similar to that which existed during the time of Confucius. The family was the basis of social and political organization. "Selfish schemes and enterprises were constantly taking their rise," in acquiring private property, and in protecting and expanding one's own state. Consequently, military heroes and cunning diplomats were worshipped, and war between different states was inevitably forthcoming.

In order to preserve possible tranquility, and practical ideals, the government of the ancient ideal rulers, such as Yu, T'ang, Wen, Wu, Ch'eng Wang, and Chou Kung, was elevated. These ideal rulers were all called *Chun-tzu*, Superior Man, the first stage of the ideal personality, and their kingdoms represented the ideal Kingdom of the Superior Man, the first stage of the ideal social order. In that Kingdom of the Superior Man, the following practical ideals were emphasized.

(a) Moral characters, such as, *Li* (propriety, courtesy, rites, or the rules of proper conduct), *I* (justice, or righteousness), *Hsin* (sincerity, faithfulness, or confidence), and *Jen* (love, benevolence, or perfect virtue), are to be observed by all people, especially *Li*, to which "every one (of the ideal rulers) was attentive". *Li*, as a matter of fact, is taken as the guiding principle or virtue of this stage of social progress.

(b) The doctrine of the "rectification of names" (*Cheng-ming*) between the relations of rulers and ministers, fathers and sons, elder and younger brothers, husbands and wives, and other social groups, such as employers and employees, land-owners and agricultural serfs, etc., is emphasized. That is to say, there must be maintained a right relationship between the people according to their proper ranks or situations in the feudal social system. Such right relationship is generally called *Li*, the rules of proper conduct. The conception of love (*Jen*), according to the doctrine of the rectification of names, is differentiated in accordance with the different classes of people. When "each one regards as his parents only his own parents, and treats as his children only his own children", the doctrine of universal and undifferentiated love would be impossible.

(c) The government according to virtue is put into practice.

(d) Education, especially moral education, is advocated, in order to "show the people all the constant virtues" and to "exhibit errors".

(e) People are regarded as having the final and highest authority. If they are treated with injustice by the rulers, they have the right to revolt and drive them away as public enemies. So the theories of political democracy are applied in the monarchical form of government with the Superior Men as the kings.

All these ideals are the constant themes of the teaching of Confucius in *The Analects*, and the following are some of them;

(a) Moral characters (See Chap. 5)

a. *Li*, (propriety, courtesy, rites, rules of proper conduct)

"The management of a state demands the rules of proper

conduct (*Li*)". (*The Analects*, 11,25,10)

"Is a prince able to govern his kingdom with the complaisance proper to *Li*, what difficulty will he have? If he cannot govern it with that complaisance, what has he to do with *Li*?" (*The Analects*, 4,13)

"Look not at what is contrary to *Li*; listen not to what is contrary to *Li*: speak not what is contrary to *Li*; make no movement which is contrary to *Li*." (*The Analects*, 12,1,2)

"Respectfulness, without *Li*, becomes laborious bustle; carefulness, without *Li*, becomes timidity; boldness without *Li*, becomes insubordination; straightforwardness, without *Li*, becomes rudeness". (*The Analects*, 8,2,1)

b. *I* (justice, or righteousness)

"Tzu-lu said, 'Does the Superior Man esteem valour?' The Master said, 'The Superior Man holds *I* to be of highest importance. A Superior Man, having valour without *I*, will be guilty of insubordination; a small man, having valour without *I*, will commit robbery.' " (*The Analects*, 17,23)

"To see what is *I* and not to do it is want of courage" (*The Analects*, 2,24,2)

c. *Jen* (love, benevolence, perfect virtue, etc.)

"Now the man of *Jen*, wishing to be established himself, seeks also to establish others; wishing to be enlightened himself, he seeks also to enlighten others." (*The Analects*, 6,28,2)

"Tzu-chang asked Confucius about *Jen*. Confucius said, 'To be able to practice five things everywhere under heaven constitutes *Jen*.' He begged to ask what they were, and was told, 'Gravity, generosity, sincerity, earnestness, and kindness. If you are generous, you will win all. If you are grave, you will not be treated with disrespect. If you are sincere, people will repose trust in you. If you are earnest, you will accomplish much. If you are kind, this will enable you to employ the services of others.' " (*The Analects*, 17,6)

(b) The doctrine of rectification (See also Chapter 5)

One day, Tzu-lu, a disciple of Confucius, asked his master what he should do first if employed in the government. Confucius replied that, "What is necessary is to rectify names. . . . If names be not correct, language will not be in accordance with the truth of things. If language be not in accordance with the truth of things, business cannot be carried on with success. When business cannot be carried on with success, propriety (*Li*) and music (*Yueh*) will not flourish. When propriety and music do not flourish, justice and law will disappear. When justice and law disappear, people do not know how to move hand or foot (they will suffer from anarchism)." (*The Analects*, 13,3)

"Duke Ching of Ch'i asked Confucius about government. Confucius replied, 'There is government, when the prince is prince, and the minister is minister; when the father is father and the son is son.' 'Good', said the Duke; 'If, indeed, the prince be not prince, the minister not minister, the father not father, and the son not son, although I have my revenue, can I enjoy it?' " (*The Analects*, 12,11)

(c) Government of virtue

"The Master said, 'He who exercises government by means of his virtue may be compared to the north polar star, which keeps its place and all the stars turn towards it.' " (*The Analects*, 2,1)

(d) Education

"When the Master went to Wei, Yen Yu acted as driver of his carriage. The Master observed, 'How numerous are the people!' Yu said, 'Since they are so numerous, what more shall be done for them?' 'Enrich them', was the reply. 'And when they have been enriched, what more shall be done?' The Master said, 'Teach them'!" (*The Analects*, 13,9)

"The Master said, 'If the people be led by laws, and uniformity sought to be given them by punishment, they will try to avoid the punishment, but have no sense of shame. If they be led by virtue, and uniformity sought to be given them by the rules of proper conduct (*Li*), they will have the sense of shame, and moreover will become good.' " (*The Analects*, 2,3)

"The Master said, 'Let a good man teach the people seven years, and they may then likewise be employed in war'." (*The Analects*,

13,29)

(e) Rights of the people

The rights of the common people should be honoured and protected, because this is the duty of the rulers as steward of Heaven, and it is the best policy to secure peace and power.

a. Political stewardship

"Yao said, 'Oh! you, Shun, the Heaven-determined order of succession now rests in your person. Sincerely hold fast the due Mean. If there shall be distress and want within the four seas, the Heavenly revenue will come to a perpetual end.' " (*The Analects*, 20,1)

In other words, rulers are appointed by Heaven as His stewards, whose duties are to work for the welfare of the people. Their authority as rulers of the people would be taken away from them, as soon as the people suffered from their misgovernment. In this case, the theory of revolution is justified.

Once, one of the disciples of Confucius helped the ruler to usurp and extort from the people, Confucius then encouraged the people "to beat the drum and assail" the usurpers. (*The Analects*, 11,16) This theory of political stewardship, and the justification of revolution was very well exemplified by Mencius. (See *Mencius*, 1,2,3)

b. The best policy of the government to gain peace and power

"Tzu-kung asked about government. The Master said, 'The requisites of government are that there be sufficiency of food, sufficiency of military equipment, and the confidence of the people in their ruler.' Tzu-kung said, 'If it cannot be helped, and one of these must be dispensed with, which of the three should be foregone first?' 'The military equipment', said the Master. Tzu-kung again asked, 'If it cannot be helped, and one of the remaining two must be dispensed with, which of them should be foregone?' Master answered, 'Part with the food. From of old, death has been the lot of all men; but if the people have no faith in their rulers, there is no standing for the state'." (*The Analects*, 12,7)

"If remoter people are not submissive, all the influences of civil culture and virtue are to be cultivated to attract them to be so; and when they have been so attracted, they must be made contented and tranquil." (*The Analects*, 16,1,11)

But how to secure the trust of the people, and make them contented and tranquil?

"The Master said, 'To rule a country of a thousand chariots, there must be reverent attention to business, and sincerity; economy in expenditure, and love for men; and the employment of the people at the proper seasons'." (*The Analects*, 1,5)

In other words, these five factors—respect for people's business, sincerity, economy in government, love of the people, and proper taxation, are the means of securing the confidence of the people, attracting the people from other countries and making them contented and tranquil. So to honour the rights of the people is the best policy not only to maintain peace inside the country, but also to extend power over other countries, through what may be called benevolent imperialism.

In short, the ideal government of this stage of social progress is the government of *Li* under the rule of Superior Man, among them the ancient ideal rulers—Yao, Shun, Yu, T'ang, Wen, Wu, and Chou-kung being the best examples. The chief trouble of the social order of his time was, according to Confucius, the general neglect of *Li*, the rules of proper conduct, especially among rulers of the different states.

"Baron Chi Kang asked Confucius about the government. Confucius replied, 'To govern means to rectify. If you lead on the people with correctness, who will dare not to be correct?' " (*The Analects*, 12,17)

"Duke Ting asked how a prince should employ his ministers, and how ministers should serve their prince. Confucius replied, 'A prince should employ his ministers according to *Li*; ministers should serve their prince with faithfulness'." (*The Analects*, 3,19)

(2) The second and highest stage of the ideal society—the stage of *Ta T'ung*,[44] or "Great Harmony"

According to the above classical statement the state of Great Harmony will be realized "when the great *Tao* prevails". In *The Analects*, Confucius says, "Ch'i, by one change, would come to Lu, Lu, by one change, would come to *Tao*". (*The Analects*, 6,22) So when the great *Tao* prevails, that is, when the state of Great Harmony is realized, we shall have the highest stage of social evolution.

Analyzing the above statement in *Li Chi, The Book of Rites*, the following factors will be found in the ideal state of Great Harmony:

(a) Political factors:

a. The whole world forms one political organization, belonging to all, and working for the common good of the people. Both socialistic and individualistic characters reach their highest point.

b. Men of virtue and talents are elected to manage government affairs.

c. The chief business of the government is educative: to advocate faithfulness and sincerity, and to cultivate friendship and universal love.

(b) Social factors:

Love permeates human society; every one loves all others, just as naturally as he loves his own parents or his children or himself. Everybody, regardless of age, sex, or different conditions of life, is properly taken care of by society under a perfect system.

a. For the aged, a competent provision is made until their death.

b. For the able bodied, a competent provision of employment is made.

c. For the young, a competent provision of education is made available.

d. For the helpless, such as widows, widowers, orphans, childless men, the sick and the disabled, a competent provision of sufficient maintenance is made.

e. For men and women, a competent provision of proper and happy marriage is arranged for.

(c) Economic factors:

a. No private property

b. No idle class

c. No private inheritance

Everyone works, not for himself alone but for the good of the general public.

(d) Results:

There is complete absence of selfish scheming, immorality and crime, consequently, there is no need for law, punishment and police. "Hence the outer door remains open, and is not shut". This is a stage of extreme social harmony and perpetual peace.

In short, the whole system of this highest stage of social progress is entirely worked out on the basis of universal and undifferentiated love—everybody loves everybody else as his own parent or his child or himself. It is a stage of the highest moral excellence and social communism—everybody works to the utmost, and obtains all that he needs. It is a state of perfect social equality, harmony, and peace, resulting from the fullest and highest development of human nature—the nature of love.

This ideal stage of Great Harmony, as described above, represents also the general spirit of the teaching of Confucius in *The Analects*, with regard to the highest social order. His most important teachings in *The Analects*, are those on *Li*, the rules of proper conduct, and *Jen*, love. His teachings on love were numerous and varied in degrees of universality, according to the situations and problems that were brought before him. Sometimes, he spoke about love *(Jen)* as something very easy to be achieved, and something very essential towards becoming a Superior Man.

"The Master said, 'Is *Jen*[45] a thing remote? I wish to be *Jen*,[46] and lo! *Jen*[47] is at hand.' " (*The Analects*, 7,29)

"Is any one able for one day to apply his strength to *Jen*? I have not seen the case in which his strength would be insufficient." (*The Analects*, 4,6,2)

"If a Superior Man abandons *Jen*, how can he fulfil the requirements of that name? The Superior Man does not, even for the space of a single meal, act contrary to *Jen*. In moments of haste, he cleaves to it. In seasons of danger, he cleaves to it." (*The Analects*, 4,5,2-3)

On the other hand, he sometimes claimed that *Jen* was something which was difficult to be achieved, so difficult, indeed, that neither he himself, nor any of the ancient ideal rulers had attained it. It was closely connected with *Sheng Jen*, the Holy One or Sage, the highest stage of individual development.

"Tzu-kung said, 'Suppose the case of a man extensively conferring benefits on the people, and able to afford universal relief, what would you say of him? Might he be called *Jen?*' The Master said, 'Why speak only of *Jen* in connexion with him? Must he not have the qualities of a Sage *(Sheng)*? Even Yao and Shun were still solicitous about this.' " *(The Analects,* 6,28,1-2)

"The Master said, 'The Sheng *(Sage)* and Jen *(Love)*; how dare I rank myself with them?' " *(The Analects,* 7,23)

"The subjects of which the Master seldom spoke were—profitableness, and the appointments of Heaven *(Ming)*,[48] and Love *(Jen)*". *(The Analects,* 9,1)

Love *(Jen)* was a favourite theme of the teachings of Confucius, as recorded in *The Analects*. It is the love in its highest sense of "affording universal relief" and "conferring extensive benefits to the people" that Confucius seldom spoke about, because it was too far beyond the grasp of the people of his time. It belongs to and is the chief characteristic of the highest social order—the state of Great Harmony.

As to the detailed factors of the stage of Great Harmony, we can find many equivalent sayings by Confucius from *The Analects*.

(a) Political factors

a. The whole world forms one political organization, and the rights of the people are respected to the fullest extent.

The rule of the ancient ideal kings, according to the traditional belief at the time of Confucius, extended all over the world, and only Heaven alone could correspond to them in greatness.

"The Master said, 'How majestic was the manner in which Shun and Yu held possession of all under Heaven, as if it were nothing to them.' " *(The Analects,* 8,18)

"The Master said, 'Great indeed was Yao as a sovereign! How majestic was he! It is only Heaven that is grand, and only Yao corresponded to it.' " *(The Analects,* 8,19)

Confucius believed in unitary sovereignty. Everywhere he and his disciples emphasized the oneness of political authority over all the world, as the ancient ideal rulers did, because it was essential to the promotion of political unity so badly needed in his day. But even the great ancient ideal rulers, according to Confucius in *The*

Analects, fell short of the highest standard of the stage of Great Harmony, when all the people in the world would get peace (14,25), extensive benefits would be conferred on the people, and universal relief would be afforded (6,28). Only in the highest and most perfect social order can the rights and welfare of all the people in the world be fully and equally respected and achieved.

b. Men of virtue and talents are elected to run the government. All the ancient ideal rulers were believed to have been elected because of their talents and virtue.

"Advance the upright and set aside the crooked, then the people will submit. Advance the crooked and set aside the upright, then the people will not submit." (*The Analects*, 2,19; 12,22,3)

"Elect to office men of virtue and talents". (*The Analects*, 13,2,1)

c. Education, especially moral education, is the chief function of the government.

"Some one addressed Confucius, saying, 'Sir, why are you not engaged in the government?' The Master said, 'What does Shu Ching say of filial piety?' 'You are filial, you discharge your brotherly duties. These qualities are displayed in government.' This then also constitutes the function of government. Why must there be that—making one be in the government?' " (*The Analects*, 2,21)

"Advance the good to teach the incompetent. (*The Analects*, 2,20)

Population, livelihood and education are the three essentials of a nation. (*The Analects*, 13,9)

(b) Social factors

a. Universal and undifferentiated love binds everybody together in a perfect and harmonious social order.

"The man of love (*Jen*), wishing to be established himself, seeks also to establish others; wishing to be enlightened himself, he seeks also to enlighten others." (*The Analects*, 6,28,2)

"All within the Four Seas are brothers." (*The Analects*, 12,5,4)

"Do not to others what you would not want done to yourself." (*The Analects*, 15,23; *Chung Yung*, 13,3)

b. Every kind of people is properly taken care of by society under a perfect system.

"Tzu-lu said (to Confucius), 'I should like, sir, to hear your wishes.' The Master said, 'They are:

In regard to the aged, to give them rest;
In regard to friends, to show them sincerity;
In regard to the young, to treat them tenderly.' "
    (*The Analects*, 5,25,4)

"Give peace to all people." (*The Analects*, 14,25)

"Extensively confer benefits on the people, and afford universal relief." (*The Analects*, 6,28,1)

(c) Economic factors

Once a disciple of Confucius inquired of him the fundamental principles of government. In reply he gave five good principles of government, three of which were all concerned with economic measures.

"First, to benefit the people without wasting the resources of the country." In telling how this principle could be carried out, Confucius suggested, "Follow what is of profit to the people and profit them."

"Secondly, to encourage labour without cause for complaint." In telling how this principle could be carried out, he suggested, "When the government demands labour from the people in proper manner and for their own good, who will repine?"

"Thirdly, to desire the enjoyments of life without being covetous." In telling how this principle could be carried out, he suggested: "When your desires are set on Love (*Jen*), and you secure it, you will never be liable to be covetous." (*The Analects*, 20,2,1-3)

In other words, if the desires of everybody are set on loving everybody else, all economic problems could be solved; there would be no conflicts between the employer and the employee, the tax-gatherer and the tax-payer, or between the government and the people; there would be no such problems as unemployment, unequal distribution of wealth, private property or self-gratification.

B. According to Mencius and His School

Mencius and his school emphasized the psychological aspect of the teaching of Confucius, and esteemed Love (*Jen*) as the highest standard for individual conduct and social organization.

"Mencius said, 'That whereby the Superior Man is distinguished from other man is what he preserves in his heart; namely, love (*Jen*) and propriety (*Li*). The man of love loves others; the man of propriety shows respect to others. He who loves others is constantly loved by them; he who respects others is constantly respected by them.' " (*Mencius*, 4,2,28, 1-3)

Here *Li* or propriety is really only one aspect of *Jen* or love; a man of love would naturally respect others and be respected by them. The word *Jen* (Love) appears 155 times, and *Ai* (which also means love) 37 times in The Works of Mencius. Love was the central theme of Mencius and his school in exemplifying the teaching of Confucius. Mencius quoted the saying of Confucius' that "there are but two courses, which can be pursued, that of love (*Jen*) and its opposite (*Pu Jen*)."[49] (*Mencius*, 4,1,2,3)

(A) Individual Aim—the Ideal Life of an Individual

The individual was regarded as the root of all social organizations, so the cultivation of the ideal individual life was taken as the chief aim of the teachings of Mencius and his school of Confucianism. Mencius says:

"People have this common saying,—'The kingdom under Heaven, the state, the family.' The root of the kingdom is in the state. The root of the state is in the family. The root of the family is in the person of its head.' " (*Mencius*, 4,1,5)

"Of charges which is the greatest? The charge of one's-self is the greatest. . . . There are many charges, but the charge of one's-self is the root of all others." (*Mencius*, 4,1,19, 1-2)

The author of *The Doctrine of the Mean* (*Chung Yung*) says: "The Superior Man must not neglect the cultivation of his own self. . . . Knowing how to cultivate his own self, he knows how to serve his people. Knowing how to serve his people, he knows how to serve the kingdom under Heaven with all its states and families." (*Chung Yung*, 20,7)

According to Mencius and his school, there seems to have been no distinction between the two stages of the ideal life of an individual, as taught by Confucius in *The Analects*. Both the Superior Man (Chun-tzu) and the Sage (*Sheng Jen*) seem to have been used interchangeably to indicate the same ideal personality.

(1) Both the Superior Man and the Sage have the same nature —the transforming power of a spiritual nature.

"Wherever the Superior Man (*Chun-tzu*) passes through, transformation follows; wherever he abides, his influence is of a spiritual nature. It flows abroad, above, and beneath, like that of Heaven and Earth." (*Mencius*, 7,1,13,3)

"When the great man exercises a transforming influence, he is what is called a Sage (*Sheng-jen*). When a Sage is beyond our knowledge, he is what is called a "spiritual being" (*Shen*).[50]

(2) A Sage, according to Mencius, need not be perfect as the Sage of Confucius in *The Analects*. If a man has a certain special characteristic which surpasses others, and has a good transforming influence over them, he would be called a Sage by Mencius. "Po-i was narrow-minded and Hui of Liu-hsia was wanting in self-respect. The Superior Man will not follow either narrow-mindedness, or the want of self-respect." (*Mencius*, 2,1,9,3) Nevertheless, both Po-i and Hui of Liu-hsia were called Sages by Mencius, simply because they had certain outstanding characteristics surpassing other people, and with those special characteristics they exercised certain transforming influences over later generations.

"Mencius said, 'A Sage is the teacher of a hundred generations: —this is true of Po-i and Hui of Liu-hsia. Therefore, when men now hear the character of Po-i, the corrupt become pure, and the weak acquire determination. When they hear the character of Hui of Liu-hsia, the mean become generous, and the niggardly become liberal.' " (*Mencius*, 7,2,15)

"Mencius said, 'Po-i among the sages was the pure one; I-yin was the one most inclined to take office; Hui of Liu-hsia was the accommodating one; and Confucius was the sage standard or type of all time.' "(*Mencius*, 5,2,1,5)

Again, Tzu-chang and Tzu-hsia, who, according to Confucius, lacked the important quality of being a Superior Man, were called Sages by Mencius.

"The Master (Confucius) said, 'Shih (Tzu-chang) goes beyond the due mean, and Shang (Tzu-hsia) does not come up to it. . . . To go beyond is as wrong as to fall short.' " (*The Analects*, 11,15)

"Confucius said, 'The Superior Man embodies the course of the Mean; the mean man acts contrary to the course of the Mean.' " (*Chung Yung* or *The Doctrine of the Mean*, 2,1)

"Tzu-hsia, Tzu-yu, and Tzu-chang, had each one member of the Sage. Yen-niu, the disciple Min, and Yen Yuan, had all the members, but in small proportions." (*Mencius*, 2,1,2,20)

Moreover, the standard of a Sage is not something which cannot be attained by the common people; it is within reach of every individual if he wills to reach it.

"All things which are the same in kind are like to one another; why should we doubt in regard to man, as if he were a solitary exception to this? The Sage and we are the same in kind. The sages only apprehended before me that of which my mind approves along with other men." (*Mencius*, 6,1,7,3 and 8)

"The officer Ch'u said to Mencius, 'Master, the king sent persons to spy out whether you were really different from other men.' Mencius said, 'How should I be different from other men! Yao and Shun (Ancient Sages) were just the same as other men.' " (*Mencius*, 4,2,32)

"Chiao of Tsao asked Mencius, saying, 'It is said, "All men may be Yao and Shun":—is it so?' Mencius replied, 'It is.' " (*Mencius*, 6,2,2,1)

(3) Confucius was satisfied with being a Superior Man, but "A Sage", said he, "is what I cannot rise to." (*Mencius*, 2,1,2,19; see also *The Analects*, 7,33; 7,25) He was honoured by Mencius as being the greatest of the Sages that had ever been born. He was the embodiment of all ancient ideal personalities, and the culmination of all saintly characters.

"Kung-sun Ch'au said, 'Comparing Po-i and I-yin (two recognized Sages) with Confucius, are they to be placed in the same rank?' Mencius replied, 'No. Since there were living men until now, there never was another Confucius.' " (*Mencius*, 2,1,2,23)

"Tsai Wo said, 'According to my view of our Master, he was far superior to Yao and Shun (the acknowledged ancient Sage-kings).' " (*Mencius*, 2,1,2,26)

"In Confucius we have what is called a complete concert", the fulfilment of ancient virtues. (*Mencius*, 5,2,1,6)

In short, the standard of a Sage, according to Mencius, is much lower than that of a Sage as recorded in *The Analects*. He and the Superior Man are both on the same level, representing the best personalities in the past, but not the ideal ones to be realized in the future.

The following are some of the characteristics of the ideal individual life, which Mencius and his disciples sought to cultivate in themselves and others as true followers of Confucius, their common revered master.

"The Master (Confucius) said, 'Knowledge, love (*Jen*), and energy, these three, are the virtues universally binding. . . . To be fond of learning is to be near to knowledge. To practice with vigour is to be near to love (*Jen*). To possess the feeling of shame is to be near to energy. He who knows these three things, knows how to cultivate his own characters. Knowing how to cultivate his own character he knows how to govern other men. Knowing how to govern other men, he knows how to govern the kingdom under the Heaven, with all its states and families.' " (*Chung Yung, The Doctrine of the Mean*, 20,8-11)

Just like the teachings in *The Analects*, the cultivation of the ideal life of an individual involves all the three aspects of human life

—moral, intellectual and physical. Like Confucius in *The Analects*, the moral aspect was also predominantly emphasized by Mencius and his school of Confucianism.

1. Moral Aim

(a) Love (*Jen*). "To practice with vigour is to be near to love." Love is the most important characteristic of an ideal personality, and is the central theme of the teachings of Mencius and his school. It is the most honorable dignity conferred by Heaven, and is the most abiding virtue of man.

"Confucius said, 'It is love (*Jen*) which constitutes the excellence of a neighbourhood. If a man, in selecting a residence, do not fix on one where love (*Jen*) prevails, how can he be wise?' Now Love (*Jen*) is the most honourable dignity conferred by Heaven, and the quiet home in which man should dwell. Since no one can hinder us from being so, if yet we have no love (*Jen*);—this is being not wise.' " (*Mencius*, 2,1,7,2)

The aim for all the life and teachings of the ancient Sages or Superior Men was, according to Mencius, the virtue of love, though they might have different courses to reach that aim.

"The courses pursued by those three worthies (Po-i, I-yin and Hui of Liu-hsia) were different, but their aim was one. And what was their one aim? We must answer—'Love' (*Jen*). And so it is simply after this that Superior Men strive. Why must they all pursue the same course?" (*Mencius*, 6,2,6,2)

There were three grades of love (*Jen*) taught by Mencius, namely, *Ai*[51], *Jen*[52], *Ch'ing*[53], which may be translated as "Kind", "Benevolent", and "Affectionate", respectively.

"Mencius said, 'In regard to inferior creatures, the Superior Man is kind (*Ai*) to them, but not benevolent (*Jen*). In regard to people generally, he is benevolent to them, but not affectionate (*Chi'in*). He is affectionate to his parents, and benevolent to people generally. He is benevolent to people generally, and kind to creatures." (*Mencius*, 7,1,45)

He criticized very severely Micius' principle of universal and equal love, saying, 'Micius' principle is—'to love all equally', which does not acknowledge the peculiar affection due to a father. But to acknowledge neither king nor father is to be in the state of a beast". (*Mencius*, 3,2,9,9)

According to Mencius, the love of parents and brothers is innate in human nature. To love other people and inferior creatures is but the extension of the natural love of one's parents and brothers, and other members of the family.

"Children carried in the arms all know to love their parents, and when they are grown a little, they all know to love their elder brothers. Filial affection for parents is the working of love (*Jen*). Respect for elders is the work of righteousness (*I*). There is no other reason for those feelings;—they belong to all under heaven." (*Mencius*, 7,1,15, 2-3)

"Treat with the reverence due to age the elders in your own family, so that the elders in the families of others shall be similarly treated; treat with the kindness due to youth the young in your own family, so that the young in the families of others shall be similarly treated:—do this, and all under the heaven (the kingdom) may be made to go round in your palm. It is said in *The Book of Poetry*, 'His example affected his wife. It reached to his brothers, and the family of the state was governed by it.'—The language shows how King Wen simply took his kindly heart, and exercised it towards those parties. Therefore the extension of the kindly heart by a prince will suffice for the love and protection of all within the four seas, and if he does not extend it, he will not be able to protect his wife and children. The way in which the ancient came greatly to surpass other men, was no other than this: —simply that they knew well how to extend to others what they themselves did." (*Mencius*, 1,1,7,12)

First thing should be done first, so the love of the members of one's family should be considered first, and should be regarded as the root of all virtues.

"Mencius said, 'The substance of love (*Jen*) is this,—the service of one's parents. The substance of righteousness (*I*) is this,—the obeying of one's elder brothers.' " (*Mencius*, 4,1,27,1)

"The course of Yao and Shun (the acknowledged sage-kings) was simply that of filial piety and fraternal duty." (*Mencius*, 6,2,2,4)

"Mencius said, 'Of services, which is the greatest? The service of parents is the greatest.' " (*Mencius*, 4,1,19,1)

(b) Righteousness (*I*)

There are 24 instances in the Works of Mencius that love (*Jen*) and righteousness (*I*) are considered together in the teachings of Mencius. Love (*Jen*) to Mencius is allied more to the deep-rooted nature of man, and constitutes the motive of all good human conduct. Righteousness (*I*) to him is one of the most important expressions of love (*Jen*) in right human actions.

"Love (*Jen*) is the tranquil habitation of man, and righteousness (*I*) is the straight path. Alas for them, who leave the tranquil dwelling empty and do not reside in it, and who abandon the right path and do not pursue it!" (*Mencius*, 4,1, 10,2)

"Love (*Jen*) is man's mind and righteousness (*I*) is man's path. How lamentable is it to neglect the path and not pursue it, to lose his mind and not know to seek it again." (*Mencius*, 6,1,11)

"All men have some things which they cannot bear;—extend that feeling to what they can bear, and love (*Jen*) will be the result. All men have some things which they will not do;—extend that feeling to the things which they do, and righteousness (*I*) will be the result." (*Mencius*, 7,2,31,1)

"I like life, and I also like righteousness. If I cannot keep the two together, I will let life go and choose righteousness." (*Mencius*, 6,1,10,1)

(c) Propriety (*Li*)

Propriety (*Li*) is another important expression of love (*Jen*) in action.

"Righteousness (*I*) is the way, and propriety (*Li*) is the door, but it is only the Superior Man who can follow this way, and go out and in by this door." (*Mencius*, 5,6,7,8)

"The substance of propriety (*Li*) is this,—the ordering and adorning those two things (the service of one's parents, and the obeying of one's elder brothers—the family love)." (*Mencius*, 4,1,27)

(d) Sincerity (*Ch'eng*)

Sincerity is the way of Heaven. To think how to be sincere is the way of man. Never has there been one possessed of complete sincerity, who did not move others. Never has there been one who had not sincerity who was able to move others." (*Mencius*, 4,1,12,2-3)

"It is only the individual possessed of the most entire sincerity that can exist under heaven, who can adjust the great invariable relations of mankind, establish the great fundamental virtues of humanity, and know the transforming and nurturing operations of Heaven and Earth;—shall this individual have any being or anything beyond himself on which he depends?" (*Chung Yung*, 32,1)

(e) To act according to the *Doctrine of the Mean*. (*Chung Yung*)

"Those who keep the mean, train up those who do not." (*Mencius*, 4,2,7)

"Mencius said, 'Confucius did not do excessive things.' " (Mencius, 4,2,10)

"Confucius said, 'The Superior Man embodies the course of the Mean; the mean man acts contrary to the course of the Mean.' " (*Chung Yung*, 2,1,)

"The Master (Confucius) said, 'Perfect is the virtue which is according to the Mean! Rare have they long been among the people, who could practice it!' " (*Chung Yung*, 3)

(f) To be sociable and friendly towards all good people

"The scholars whose virtue is most distinguished in a village shall make friends of all the virtuous scholars in the village. The scholars whose virtue is most distinguished throughout the state shall make friends of all the virtuous scholars of that state. The scholars whose virtue is most distinguished throughout the kingdom shall make friends of all the virtuous scholars of the kingdom." (*Mencius*, 5,2,8,1)

"Friendship should be maintained without any presumption on the ground of one's superior age, or station, or the circumstances of his relatives. Friendship with a man is friendship with his virtue, and does not admit of assumptions of superiority." (*Mencius*, 5,2,3,1)

(g) To be optimistic in all circumstances

"The Superior Man does not murmur against Heaven, nor

grudge against men." (*Mencius*, 2,2,13,1)

"In a high position, the Superior Man does not treat with contempt his inferiors. In a low situation, he does not court the favour of his superiors. He rectifies himself, and seeks for nothing from others, so that he has no dissatisfactions. He does not murmur against Heaven, nor grumble against men." (*Chung Yung*, 14,3)

Misery or suffering is but a way in which Heaven prepares men for great services. "Thus, when Heaven is about to confer a great office on any man, it first exercises his mind with suffering, and his sinews and bones with toil. It exposes his body to hunger, and subjects him to extreme poverty. It confounds his undertakings. By all these methods it stimulates his mind, hardens his nature, and supplies his incompetencies. . . . Life springs from sorrow and calamity, and death from ease and pleasure." (*Mencius*, 6,2,15, 2 and 5)

(h) Loyalty, fidelity and other virtues

"Love (*Jen*), righteousness (*I*), loyalty (*Chung*), and fidelity (Hsin), with unwearied joy in these virtues; these constitute the nobility of Heaven." (*Mencius*, 6,1,16,1)

2. Inntellectual Aim

To be fond of learning is to be near to wisdom.

Wisdom, together with Love (*Jen*), righteousness (*I*) and propriety (*Li*), form four most important principles of mankind. "Men have these four principles just as they have their four limbs." (*Mencius*, 2,1,6,5-6)

"The Master said, 'There was Shun:—He indeed was greatly wise! Shun loved to question others, and to study their words, though they might be shallow. He concealed what was bad in them, and displayed what was good. He took hold of their two extremes, determined the Mean, and employed it in his government of the people. It was by this that he was Shun!' " (*Chung Yung*, 6)

Knowledge or wisdom can be obtained in the following ways:

(a) In the investigation or careful study of natural phenomena. It is significant that the rule which Mencius lays down is quite in harmony with that of modern science.

"What I dislike in your wise men is their boring out their

conclusions. If those wise men would only act as Yu did when he conveyed away the waters, there would be nothing to dislike in their wisdom. The manner in which Yu conveyed away the waters was by doing what gave him no trouble. If your wise men would also do that which gave them no trouble, their knowledge would also be great. There is heaven so high; there are the stars so distant. If we have investigated their phenomena, we may, while sitting in our places, go back to the solstice of a thousand years ago." (*Mencius*, 4,2,26, 2-3)

(b) In the diligent study of past human cultural experience.

"The Duke of Chou desired to unite in himself the virtues of those kings, those founders of the three dynasties, that he might display in his practice the four things which they did. If he saw anything in them not suited to his time, he looked up and thought about it, from daytime into the night, and when he was fortunate enough to master the difficulty, he sat waiting for the morning." (*Mencius*, 4,2,20,5)

(c) In questioning others and studying carefully their answers.

"There was Shun:—He indeed was greatly wise! Shun loved to question others, and to study their words, though they might be shallow." (*Chung Yung*, 6)

"There are five ways in which the Superior Man effects his teaching. . . . There are some whose questions he answers. . . ." (*Mencius*, 7,1,40)

(d) In self-examination of self-seeking. This is, according to Mencius, the most important method of gaining wisdom. To him, everybody is born good with different faculties of knowing and with admirable virtues. (See *Mencius*, 6,1,6,7) He believed that was the teaching of Confucius. He said:

> *"It is said in The Book of Poetry,*
> *'Heaven in producing mankind,*
> *Gave them their various faculties and*
> *   relations with their specific laws.*
> *These are the invariable rules of*
> *   nature for all to hold,*

And all love this admirable virtue.

Confucius said, 'The maker of this ode knew indeed the principle of our nature.' " (*Mencius*, 6,1,6,8)

Although man is born good and wise, yet later on through experience bad habits are formed, and the original good and wise nature becomes obscured or lost. So the aim of education should be to bring back or to unfold the original good and wise nature.

"Mencius said, 'All things are already complete in us. There is no greater delight. than to be conscious of sincerity on self-examination.' " (*Mencius*, 7,1,4, 1-2)

"Mencius said, 'When we get by our seeking and lose by our neglecting;—in that case seeking is of use of getting, and the things sought for are those which are in ourselves.' " (*Mencius*, 7,1,3,1)

"Mencius said, 'Love (*Jen*) is man's mind, and righteousness (*I*) is man's path. How lamentable is it to neglect the path and not pursue it, to lose this mind and not know to seek it again! When men's fowls and dogs are lost, they know to seek for them again, but they lose their mind, and do not know to seek for it. The great end of learning is nothing else but to seek for the lost mind.' " (*Mencius*, 6,1,11)

(e) Knowledge or wisdom must go together with morality. Without morality knowledge would be undesirable or perilous. As a matter of fact, knowledge is generally meant to be moral knowledge. Wisdom without virtue would cease to be wise at all.

"The substance of wisdom is this,—the knowing those two things (the service of one's parents, and the obeying one's elder brothers) and not departing from them." (*Mencius*, 4,1,27,2)

"Love (*Jen*) is the most honourable dignity conferred by Heaven, and the quiet home in which man should dwell. Since no one can hinder us from being so, if yet we have no love;—this is being not wise." (*Mencius*, 2,1,7,2)

"P'an-ch'eng Kuo having obtained an official situation in Ch'i, Mencius said, 'He is a dead man, the P'an-ch'eng Kuo!' P'an-ch'eng Kuo being put to death, the disciples asked, saying, 'How did you know, Master, that he would meet with death?' Mencius replied,

'He was a man, who had a little ability, but had not learned the great doctrines of the Superior Man.—He was just qualified to bring death upon himself, but for nothing more." (*Mencius*, 7,2,29)

(f) In studying extensively and carefully with the object of getting to the substance and essence of things.

"Mencius said, 'In learning extensively and discussing minutely what is learned, the object of the Superior Man is that he may be able to go back and set forth in brief what is essential."

3. Physical Aim

"To possess the feeling of shame is to be near to energy."

Like Confucius, Mencius did not lay stress upon the physical aspect of the ideal personality. Physical valour or energy was already universally praised and encouraged during his period of the Warring States. Again like Confucius, he endeavoured to modify the purely physical valour with moral character, and esteemed moral life as more important and valuable than physical life.

"Mencius said, 'I like fish and I also like bear's paws. If I cannot have the two together, I will let the fish go, and take the bear's paws. So, I like life, and I also like righteousness (*I*). If I cannot keep the two together, I will let life go and choose righteousness. I like life indeed, but there is that which I like more than life and therefore, I will not seek to possess it by any improper ways. I dislike death indeed, but there is that which I dislike more than death, and therefore there are occasions when I will not avoid danger.' " (*Mencius*, 6,1,10, 1-2)

Mencius discouraged what is called "small valour", the purely physical energy or strength, and encouraged the valour which would bring about moral results or the welfare of other people. He once advised King Hsuan of Ch'i, saying,

"I beg your majesty not to love small valour. If a man brandishes his sword, looks fiercely, and says, 'How dare he withstand me?' —this is the valour of a common man, who can be the opponent only of a single individual. I beg your majesty to greaten it." He then encouraged the prince to imitate King Wen who used his valour "to give repose to all the people of the kingdom." (*Mencius*, 1,2,3,5-8)

In conclusion, *Chung Yung* or the *Doctrine of the Mean* gives a very full summary of the chief characteristics of the ideal individual personality, so far discussed, as being the teaching of Mencius and his school of Confucianism. All the moral, intellectual, and physical aspects are emphasized.

"It is only he, possessed of all sagely qualities that can exist under heaven, who shows himself quick in apprehension, clear in discernment, of far-reaching intelligence, and all-embracing knowledge, fitted to exercise rule; magnanimous, generous, benign, and mild, fitted to exercise forbearance; impulsive, energetic, firm, and enduring, fitted to maintain a firm hold; self-adjusted, grave, never swerving from the Mean, and correct, fitted to command reverence; accomplished, distinctive, concentrative, and searching, fitted to exercise discrimination. All-embracing is he and vast, deep and active as a fountain, sending forth in their due season his virtues." (*Mencius*, 31,1-2)

(B) Social Aim—the Ideal Social Organization

The social aim of the teaching of Mencius was to bring about what he frequently called *Jen Cheng*,[54] or "government of love." (See *Mencius*, 1,1,5,3; 1,1,7,18; 1,2,11,3; 1,2,12,3; 2,1,1,10; 2,1,1,13; 3,1,3,13; etc.) He emphasized love (*Jen*) as the chief characteristic of an ideal individual, and so he regarded love (*Jen*) as the most essential characteristic of his ideal social order. He believed that "the man of love has no enemy" (*Mencius*, 1,1,5,6), and 'if the prince of a state loves love (*Jen*), he will have no opponent in all the kingdom under heaven'. (*Mencius*, 4,1,7,5) His argument for this is clear and simple, that, if a ruler loves the people, the people will also love him in return and will not oppose him or fight against him; thus he will easily become the ruler of the whole world. Peace and happiness will, consequently, appear under the leadership of the kind-hearted ruler in the single united kingdom of the world, and the ideal social order will, then, be realized. If a ruler can truly carry out the government of love, he said, "then the people in the neighbouring kingdoms will look up to him as a parent. From the first birth of mankind till now, never has any one led children to attack their parent, and succeeded in his design. Thus, such a ruler will not have an enemy in all the kingdom, and he who has no enemy in the kingdom is the minister of Heaven. Never has there been a ruler in such a case who did not attain to the royal dignity." (*Mencius*, 2,1,5,6)

Such an ideal social organization was not a mere theory, an impractical one as it appeared to the rulers of his time, for it was, according to Mencius, a historically accomplished event. It had been put into practice with great success during the early rulers of the so-called "Three Golden Dynasties", Hsia, Shang, and Chou. So the social order under the reign of those ancient ideal kings or rulers was taken by Mencius to be the model for his social theory of the government of love.

"Mencius said, 'it was by love (*Jen*) that the three dynasties gained the kingdom under heaven, and by lack of love (Pu *Jen*) that they lost it." (*Mencius*, 4,1,3,1)

"The principles of Yao and Shun, without the government of love, could not secure the tranquil order of the kingdom under heaven." (*Mencius*, 4,1,1,1)

Mencius was especially interested in Yao and Shun, and he claimed that the aim of his social teaching was to realize once again in his society the doctrines taught and practiced by those two ancient Sage-kings. He says:

"I do not dare to set forth before the king any but the ways of Yao and Shun." (*Mencius*, 2,2,2,4)

"When Duke Wen of T'ang was crown-prince, having to go to Ch'u, he went by way of Sung, and visited Mencius. Mencius discoursed to him how the nature of man is good, and when speaking, always made laudatory reference to Yao and Shun." (*Mencius*, 3,1,1,1-2)

He sometimes called his ideal government of love (*Jen Cheng*), the "Kingly government" (*Wang Cheng*[55]) or "Sage government" (*Sheng-jen chih Cheng*[56]). (See *Mencius*, 3,2,5,1; 3,1,4,2) His ideal social organization, he claimed, was the social order of the ancient

Sage-kings.

The following are some important factors which characterize the ideal social organization as taught by Mencius and his school:

1. **Political Factors:**

(a) Form of Government. Mencius seems to prefer, to put it in the modern term, a constitutional form of monarchical government, with a Sage-king, like Yao or Shun, as the political head. Like Yao and Shun again, who were supposed to have ruled over the whole world, the Sage-king has the whole world as his empire. The method of bringing about the world-empire is not by military conquest—to conquer other states by external force, but by kind political policies, to win the hearts of the people by the acts of love.

"If any state were practising kingly government, all within the four seas would be lifting up their heads, and looking for its prince, wishing to have him for their sovereign." (*Mencius*, 3,2,5,7)

"When one by force subdues men, they do not submit to him in heart. They submit, because their strength is not adequate to resist. When one subdues men by virtue, in their hearts' core they are pleased, and sincerely submit, as was the case with the seventy disciples in their submission to Confucius. What is said in *The Book of Poetry*, 'From the west, from the east, from the south, from the north, there was not one thought of refusing submission', is an illustration of this." (*Mencius*, 2,1,3,2)

"There is a way to get the empire:—get the people, and the empire is got. There is a way to get the people:—get their hearts, and the people are got. There is a way to get their hearts:—it is simply to collect for them what they like, and not to lay on them what they dislike. The people turn to love (*Jen*) as water flows downwards, and as wild beasts fly to the wilderness." (*Mencius*, 4,1,9,1)

(b) Rulers of the world-empire

· The most important characteristic of the political policy of the Sage-king and his ministers is love. "Only the men of love ought to be in high stations. When a man destitute of love is in a high position, he thereby disseminates his wickedness among all below him." (*Mencius*, 4,1,1,7) They treat their people as their children, and their people look up to them as their parents. (See *Mencius*, 1,1,4,5; 1,2,7,6; 3,1,3,7; etc.) They are moral leaders of their people as well as their political leaders, and their people obey their orders and act according to what is right, not so much because of their fear of punishment, but rather because of their moral influence.

"Mencius said, 'If the sovereign be loving, all will be loving. If the sovereign be righteous, all will be righteous.' " (*Mencius*, 4,2,5; 4,1,20)

"Confucius said . . . , 'The relation between the Superior Men and the inferior men is like that between the wind and grass. The grass must bend, when the wind blows upon it.' " (*Mencius*, 3,1,2,4)

The rulers love their people and act as their moral leaders not only because this is the best political policy,—"If you put in practice a government of love (*Jen Cheng*), this people will love you and all above them, and will die for their officers",—but also because they regard themselves as the ministers of God to carry out His loving will to His people. The rulers are sometimes called "*T'ien Li*"[57] or "Ministers of Heaven". (*Mencius*, 2,1,5,6) "Wan Chang said, 'Was it the case that Yao gave the empire to Shun?' Mencius said, 'No. The emperor cannot give the empire to another.' 'Yes; —but Shun had the empire. Who gave it to him?' 'Heaven gave it to him' was the answer." (*Mencius*, 5,1,5,1-2)

Mencius said, "*The Book of History* says, 'Heaven having produced the inferior people below, appointed for them rulers and teachers with the purpose that they should be assisting to God, and therefore distinguished them throughout the four quarters of the land. Whoever are offenders, and whoever are innocent, here am I to deal with them. How dare any under heaven give indulgence to their refractory wills?'" (*Mencius*, 1,2,3,7; see also *Shu Ching*, 5,1, sect. 1,7)

Indeed, the rulers, being the assistants of God, should be moral leaders. As soon as they cease to be moral leaders, they would lose their characteristic of being political leaders, and revolution would be justifiable. (*Mencius*, 1,2,8,3)

(c) Rights of the people
a. People are sacred to God and are the most important element

in a country. They are all children of God. Their will is God's will; their voice is God's voice.

> "It is said in The Book of Poetry
> 'Heaven gives birth to mankind,
> And endows them with various faculties
> and relations with their specific laws.
> These are the invariable rules of nature for all to hold,
> And all love this admirable virtue.' "

(*Mencius*, 6,1,6,8; Shi-Ching, 3,3,6,1)

"Heaven sees according as my people see; Heaven hears according as my people hear." (*Mencius*, 5,1,5,8) (*Shu-ching*, 4,1,2,7)

Mencius said, 'The people are the most important element in a nation; the spirits of the land and grain are the next; the sovereign is the lightest." (*Mencius*, 7,2,14,1)

b. People are given the right to elect and discharge their officers, and to decide in the case of capital punishment.

"When all those about you say,—'This is a man of talents and worth', you may not for that believe it. When your great officers all say,—'This is a man of talents and virtue,' neither may you for that believe it. When all the people say,—'This is a man of talents and virtue', then examine into the case, and when you find that the man is such, employ him. When all those about you say,—'This man won't do,' don't listen to them. When all your great officers say,—'This man won't do,' don't listen to them. When the people all say,—'This man won't do,' then examine into the case, and when you find that the man won't do, send him away. When all those about you say,—'This man deserves death,' don't listen to them. When all your great officers say,—'This man deserves death,' don't listen to them. When the people all say,—'This man deserves death,' then inquire into the case, and when you see that the man deserves death, put him to death. In accordance with this we have the saying, 'The people killed him'. You must act in this way in order to be the parent of the people." (*Mencius*, 1,2,7, 4-6)

c. People have the right to revolt against their sovereign if he acts contrary to the principles of love and righteousness.

"King Hsuan of Ch'i asked, saying, 'Was it so, that T'ang banished Chieh, and that King Wu smote Chou?' Mencius replied, 'It is so in the records'. The king said, 'May a minister then put his sovereign to death?' Mencius said, 'He who outrages the love (*Jen*) proper to his nature, is called a robber; he who outrages righteousness (*I*), is called a ruffian. The robber and ruffian we call a mere fellow. I have heard of the cutting off of the fellow Chou, but I have not heard of the putting a sovereign to death, in his case.' " (*Mencius*, 1,2,8)

2. Social Factors

(a) Careful attention is paid to education.

"Let careful attention be paid to education in schools, inculcating in it especially the filial and fraternal duties." (*Mencius*, 1,1,3,4; 1,1,7,24)

"Establish Hsiang, Hsu Hsueh, and Hsiao,—all those educational institutions,—for the instruction of the people. The name Hsiang indicates nourishing as its object; Hsiao indicates teaching; and Hsu indicates archery. By the Hsia dynasty, the name Hsiao was used; by the Yin dynasty, that of Hsu; and by the Chou, that of Hsiang. As to the Hsueh, they belonged to the three dynasties, and by that name. The object of them all is to illustrate the human relations. When those are thus illustrated by superiors, kindly feeling will prevail among the inferior people below." (*Mencius*, 3,1,3,10)

(b) Everybody is properly taken care of by society.

a. The aged

"Persons not kept warm nor supplied with food are said to be starved and famished, but among the people of King Wen (one of the ideal ancient Sage-kings), there were no aged who were starved or famished." (*Mencius*, 7,1,22,3)

b. The helpless, miserable and solitary

"There were the old and wifeless, or widowers; the old and husbandless, or widows; the old and childless, or solitaries; the young and fatherless, or orphans:—these four classes are the most destitute of the people, and have none to whom they can tell their wants, and King Wen, in the institution of his government with its loving action, made them the first objects of his regard, as it is said in *The Book of Poetry*, 'The rich may get through. But alas! for the miserable and solitary!' " (*Mencius*, 1,2,5,3)

c. The sick, and the mutual care and protection of one another in the same district

"In the fields of a district, those who belong to the same nine squares render all friendly offices to one another in their going out and coming in, aid one another in keeping watch and ward, and sustain one another in sickness. Thus the people are brought to live in affection and harmony." (*Mencius*, 3,1,3,18)

d. Boys and girls happily married

"At that time (of King Wen), in the seclusion of the house, there were no dissatisfied women, and abroad, there were no unmarried men." (*Mencius*, 1,2,5,5)

3. Economic Factors

(a) The livelihood of the people is well regulated, so as to make sure that all the people in the world-kingdom have enough to live on in bad years as well as in plenteous ones. To solve the problem of livelihood is, according to Mencius, one of the most important factors of his ideal social order, the government of love. It is the pre-requisite of all moral, social and political reforms.

"An intelligent ruler will regulate the livelihood of the people, so as to make sure that, above, they shall have sufficient wherewith to serve their parents, and below, sufficient wherewith to support their wives and children; that in good years they shall always be abundantly satisfied, and that in bad years they shall escape the danger of perishing. After this he may urge them, and they will proceed to what is good, for in this case the people will follow after that with ease." (*Mencius*, 1,1,7,21)

"The way of the people is this:—if they have a certain livelihood, they will have a fixed heart. If they have not a certain livelihood, they have not a fixed heart, and if they have not a fixed heart, there is nothing which they will not do in the way of self-abandonment, of moral deflection, of depravity, and of wild license. When they have thus been involved in crime, to follow them up and punish them:—this is to entrap the people. How can such a thing as entrapping the people be done under the rule of a man of love?"

(*Mencius*, 3,1,3,3)

(b) Production is encouraged, taxes and levies are made light, and moral characters of those people are cultivated.

"If your majesty will indeed dispense a government of love to the people, being sparing in the use of punishments and fines, and making the taxes and levies light, so causing that the fields shall be ploughed deep, and the weeding of them be carefully attended to, and that the strong-bodied, during their days of leisure, shall cultivate their filial piety, fraternal respectfulness, sincerity, and truthfulness, serving thereby, at home, their fathers and elder brothers, and abroad, their elders and superiors;—you will then have a people who can be employed, with sticks which they have prepared, to oppose the strong mail and sharp weapons of Chin and Ch'u." (*Mencius*, 1,1,5,3)

(c) The *Ching-t'ien* system is perfected and successfully carried out. It is fundamentally an economic system with the purpose of nationalization and equitable distribution of land, according to the size and needs of individual families. In ancient China the land was divided in the form of a *ching* or "well",[58] with nine squares of land in each *Ching*. Since the shape of the field was like the word *ching*,[59] the whole system, which is based on such land divisions, is called *Ching-t'ien*, literally "well-field", system. This system actually operated in different forms with various degrees of success in different parts of China, before the time of Confucius. As time went by, this system became much abused, and was gradually abolished or neglected. Mencius was a great advocate of such a system, and gave a clear account of it in the following brief section, which was what he understood to be the ancient scheme of *Ching-t'ien* system, as practiced under the ideal rule of the Sage-kings.

"A square *Li* covers nine squares of land, which nine squares contain nine hundred *Mow*. The central square is the public field, and eight families, each having its private hundred *Mow*, cultivate in common the public field. And not till the public work is finished, may they presume to attend to their private affairs." (*Mencius*, 3,1,3,19)

C. According to Hsun-tzu and His School

Hsun-tzu and his school of Confucianism put more emphasis upon the social aspect of the teaching of Confucius, and esteemed Li,[60] "the rules of proper conduct", as the highest individual and social ideal. It is a cosmological principle from which all social and individual rules of conduct are derived. It was first understood by ancient Sages who devised the rules for their social order by imitating those of the natural order, and the rules which they set down were recognized by Hsun-tzu and his school as the rules of proper conduct (Li) which should be carefully followed by every individual or by society as a whole. The aim of education, then, according to this school of Confucianism, is just to illustrate that "illustrious virtue", derived from nature and set down by the ancient Sages as social and individual rules of proper conduct (Li), and to renovate the people with those rules (Li) until the highest excellence is reached.

"Li is that whereby Heaven and Earth unite, whereby the sun and moon are bright, whereby the four seasons are ordered, whereby the stars move in the courses, whereby rivers flow, whereby all things prosper, whereby love and hatred are tempered, whereby joy and anger keep their proper place. It causes the lower orders to obey, and the upper orders to be illustrious; through a myriad changes it prevents going astray. But if one departs from it, he will be destroyed. Is not Li the greatest of all principles? When it is established grandly, it becomes the centre of all, and the whole world will not be able to subtract from or add to it. Its source and aim accord with one another. Its end and beginning reach each other. It is most beautiful, but preserves the distinctions. It can be most closely scrutinized, and will be found to be explicable. When the country follows it, there is good government and prosperity;

when it is not followed there is anarchy and calamity. He who follows it is safe; he who does not follow it is in danger. He who follows it will be preserved; he who does not follow it will be destroyed." (*The Works of Hsun-tzu*, Book 19, on the rules of proper conduct, pp. 223-224, translated by H. H. Dubs)

"The code of proper conduct (*Li*) has three sources; Heaven and Earth gave birth to it—this is a source; our ancestors made it fit the situation—this is a source; the princes and teachers formed it—this is a source." (*ibid.*, p. 219)

"The *Sage* gathers together ideas and thoughts, and becomes skilled by his acquired training, so as to bring forth *Li* and *Yi*, and originates laws and regulations." (Book 23, p. 305)

"The principle of the Great Learning is to illustrate illustrious virtue; to renovate the people; and to rest in the highest excellence." (*The Great Learning*, "The text of Confucius", verse 1)

The word *Li* appears 183 times in the works of Hsun-tzu as translated by H. H. Dubs. Closely connected with *Li* is *Yi* or *I*,[61] "class rights", "social rights" or justice, that is, the rights proper to each social class or people, and that word appears 144 times. There are 75 times when *Li* and *Yi* are mentioned together. *Jen* (Love), the highest individual and social virtue, and most frequently mentioned in the Works of Mencius, only appears 55 times in the Works of Hsun-tzu. This will give some idea of how the social aspect of the teaching of Confucius was emphasized by Hsun-tzu and his school. Education becomes simply a process of helping the individual to adjust himself to the existing social order, with its rules of proper conduct (*Li*), including the social rights which are proper to each class of people (*Yi*).

(A) Individual Aim—the Ideal Life of an Individual

Hsun-tzu has three grades of virtue and wisdom: Scholar (Shih),[62] Superior Man (Chun-tzu),[63] and Sage (Sheng Jen).[64] The following are some quotations from the Works of Hsun-tzu, translated by H. H. Dubs, which show some of the characteristics of these three grades of personality.

"He who loves to follow the Way (*Tao*)[65] and carries it out is a Scholar. He who has a firm purpose and treads the Way is a Superior Man. He who is inexhaustibly wise and illustrious in virtue is the Sage." (Bk. 2, p. 51)

"The common people's standard of virtue is that goodness consists in following custom, that the great good of life is possessions and wealth, and that supporting one's parents is to have already reached the right Way (*Tao*). When a person's character is formed according to rule and his will is firm; when he does not allow his selfish desires to confuse what he has learned—when a man is like this, he can be called a strong *Scholar*. When a person's character is formed according to rule and his will is firm; when he likes to correct himself according to what he has learned, so as to force and to beautify his emotional nature; when his speech is for the most part correct, though he does not know everything; when his actions are for the most part correct, though not without effort; when his knowledge and reflection is for the most part correct, though not completely so; when on the one hand he is able to magnify those whom he exalts, and on the other hand he is able to instruct those who have not already attained to his achievements—when a man is like that, he can be called a solid *Superior Man*. When a person can adjust himself to the principles of all the kings like distinguishing white from black; when he can respond to the changed situation of the moment like counting 'one, two'; when he can carry out the rules of proper conduct (*Li*) and treat people according to ceremony, but yet be at ease in it like using his four limbs; when he can compel the occasion to show his genius for producing achievements, like commanding the four seasons; when the goodness of his just government harmonizes his people so that though they be hundreds or tens of thousands in number he yet binds them together like one man—when a man is like that, he may be called a *Sage*." (Bk. 8, pp. 102-103)

"To have the wisdom of having everything, but not the manner of an impetuous braggart; to be doubly good and generous, but without the air of boasting of his virtue; when his teachings are carried out, the country is upright; when his teachings are not carried out, he is still wise in the Way (*Tao*) but retires into private life—this is the dialectic of the *Sage*. The ode says:

Amiable and courtly,
Pure as a sceptre of mace or jade,
Of honourable reputation and great hopes,
My joyous young prince,
You are the bond of the empire—

this expresses what I mean. He has the moderation that comes from politeness; he obeys the principles of the elder and younger; he does not speak of what is shunned or forbidden; he does not utter imprecations; he speaks from a loving heart; he listens with a receptive mind; he disputes in a fair spirit; he is unmoved by the criticism or praise of the multitude; he does not pervert the ears and eyes of the onlooker; he does not corrupt the power of people of rank; he does not take pleasure in repeating the speech of the depraved (heretics); hence he is able to dwell in the right Way (*Tao*) and not err; he may be oppressed but cannot be forced to act wrongly; it may bring gain, but he will not depart from the right; he respects fairness and uprightness and despises vulgar striving—this is the dialectic of the *Scholar* or *Superior Man*. The ode says:

'The long night is endless;·
My ever-flowing thoughts are nimble;
They do not dis-esteem the ancients;
They do not vary from the rules of proper
*   conduct (Li) and class rights (Yi);*
What care I for people's talk?' (a lost ode)

This expresses what I mean." (Bk. 22, pp. 291-292)

"There are those who have the knowledge of the *Sage*; there are those who have the knowledge of the Scholar or Superior Man; there are those who have the knowledge of the small-minded man, and there are those who have the knowledge of the menial. To be able to speak much, polished and in order, to discuss a matter for a whole day; through a thousand turns and changes, altogether to be discussing only one subject—this is the wisdom of the *Sage*. To speak little, but to the point and sparingly, coherently, and according to rule, as if a thread ordered the speech—this is the wisdom of the *Scholar* or *Superior Man....*" (Bk. 23, p. 315)

"I desire to be mean and yet noble, stupid yet wise, poor yet right. Can I bring that about? It is only accomplished by study. That student who carries it (study) out is called *Scholar*. He who exerts himself and longs for it is a *Superior Man*. He who is versed in it is a *Sage*." (Bk. 8, p. 99) "What should one study? How should one begin? The art begins by reciting the Classics and ends in learning the rules of proper conduct (*Li*)." (Bk. 1, p. 36)

"To strive for the right Way (Tao) is the duty of every *Scholar*; to become of a class with this is to be almost a *Superior Man*. He who knows this right Way is the *Sage*." (Bk. 21, p. 277)

"The Scholar takes the right Way (*Tao*) of the Sage-kings as the judgments of an authority; he takes the government of the Sage-kings as his laws." (Bk. 21, p. 276)

"A man who practises hoeing and ploughing becomes a farmer; if he practices chopping and shaving wood, he becomes an artisan; if he practices trafficking in goods, he becomes a merchant; if he practices the rules of proper conduct (*Li*) and social rights (*Yi*), he becomes a Superior Man." (Bk. 8, pp. 115-116)

"To grasp the spirit of the right Way (*Tao*) firmly is to be a Sage." (Bk. 8, p. 104)

"If the common man on the street cultivates goodness and wholly completes its cultivation, he will be called a Sage. First he must seek and then only will he obtain; he must do it, and then only will he reach perfection; he must cultivate it, and then only can he rise; he must complete its cultivation, and then only can he be a Sage. For the Sage is the man who has cultivated himself. (Bk. 8, p. 115)

From the above quotations, one can easily see that the ideal individual life, according to Hsun-tzu and his school, is divided into different grades of development. It begins by being a scholar, and ends in becoming a Sage. That is what he meant when he said,

"The purpose of study begins with making the Scholar, and ends in making the Sage." (Bk. 1, p. 36) Those different grades are different only in the degrees of attaining the right Way (*Tao*) or the rules of proper conduct (*Li*), as brought forth by the ancient Sage-kings. "The Sage-kings brought forth the rules of proper conduct (*Li*) and rights (*Yi*)." (Bk. 23, p. 303) Generally speaking, a Scholar is one who determines to learn and follow the right Way (*Tao*) or the rules of proper conduct (*Li*); the Superior Man is one whose knowledge, desire and action "are for the most part correct, though not without effort", in other words, he is for the most part following the right Way (*Tao*) or the rules of proper conduct (*Li*) in his thought, will and deeds; a Sage is one whose cultivation in knowledge, desire and action is completely in accordance with the right Way (*Tao*) or the rules of proper conduct (*Li*), so that he can easily "adjust himself to the principles of all the Kings (Sage-kings) like distinguishing white from black." The highest grade of personality, which education is aimed at, is, then, the Sage, who can freely "adjust" himself to the existing social ideals, or the best social traditions and regulations as handed down from the ancient Sage-kings. In short, "*Li* is the utmost of human morality. . . . He who resolutely studies *Li* becomes a Sage." (Bk. 19, p. 225)

(B) Social Aim—the Ideal Social Order

Hsun-tzu, like most other Confucianists and other contemporary philosophers of rival schools, such as, the followers of Micius, believed that the ideal social order had been realized in the past, under the rules of Sage-kings, such as Yao, Shun, Yu, T'ang, Wen, Wu, and Duke Chou. Hsun-tzu, however, unlike most of his contemporaries, taught that we should follow the government of the later Sage-kings, that is, Kings Wen and Wu, and Duke Chou, and not the government of the earlier Sage-kings, with whose doctrines, Micius, particularly, had argued that his teachings accorded. He did not mean that the earlier Sage-kings were not good enough to be followed. His reason of following the later Sage-kings was simply that there was a better record of the government of the later kings than that of the earlier ones. Since the later kings had carried out the ways of the earlier kings and had left behind them clear records of their ways of government, why then, Hsun-tzu, argued, we should "give up the later kings and follow those of the extremely ancient kings"? The ways which were followed by the sage-kings are the right Ways (*Tao*), and rules, both social and individual, which they brought forth are the rules of proper conduct (*Li*). The social order in which those Sage-ways (*Tao*) or Sage-rules (*Li*) are observed, is deemed to be the ideal social order.

"The rules of proper conduct (*Li*) are the greatest thing in government and in making social distinctions; they are the foundation of strength and security; they are the way of being majestic; they are the focus of honour. Kings and dukes gained the empire by following them. By not following them, they lost their territory. Hence strong armour and trained armies were insufficient to gain virtue; high city walls and deep moats were insufficient to make those rules feared. If they followed this principle (*Tao*) they were successful; if they did not follow this principle (*Tao*), then they failed." (Bk. 19, p. 216)

"The rules for proper conduct (*Li*) are not greater than the Sage-kings. But there were many Sage-kings; which one shall I follow? When rules of nice conduct are preserved too long, they are lost. There are officers to preserve the arts and rules of proper conduct (*Li*); but if preserved to a great age, they are relaxed. Hence it is said: if you wish to see the footprints of the Sage-kings, then look where they are most clear; that is to say, at the later kings. These later kings were the princes of the whole country. To give up the later kings and follow those of the extremely ancient times is like giving up one's own prince and serving another's prince. Hence it is said: if you wish to know a thousand years, then consider to-day; if you wish to understand ten or a hundred thousand, then examine one and two: if you wish to know the ancient times, then examine the Way (*Tao*) of the Chou dynasty; if you wish to know the way of the Chou dynasty, then examine its men, what princes it honours. Hence it is said: by the present you can understand the past; by one you can understand a myriad;

by the subtle you can understand the clear—this saying expresses what I mean. . . . Previous to the Five Emperors (preceding Yao) there is no record; not that there were no worthy men, but because of the length of time intervening. Of the period of the Five Emperors there is no record of their government, not because they did not have a good government, but because of the length of time intervening. Of Yu and T'ang (The first rulers of the Hsia and Shang dynasties respectively) there is a record of their government, but it is not as good as that of the Chou dynasty to investigate; not because there is no good government, but because of the length of time intervening. The longer things have been handed down, the more in outline they are; the more recent they are, the more detailed they are." (Bk. 5, pp. 72-75)

What is the ideal social order which prevailed under the rule of the Sage-kings? What is the characteristic of the government which was run according to the rules of proper conduct (*Li*)? The chief characteristic of the government of *Li* is that the ideal of a harmonious social order is achieved through the application, in minute details, of the doctrine of rectification. Everybody in society is ranked in a consistent order of superiority and inferiority, and is expected to carry out his social duties according to the rules of conduct which are proper for him (*Li*), and to act what is right according to his own social status (*Yi*). Men are not born equal in natural capacity or in mental and physical abilities, they are meant to serve in different occupations or unequal positions which are all necessary for society. So if everybody acts honestly according to his own social status or class rights, then there will be no tension or conflict between ruler and ruled, father and son, husband and wife, elder and younger brothers, friend and friend, employer and employee, etc., and the state of "great equableness", as Hsun-tzu calls it, will be realized. Men are born with various selfish desires, Hsun-tzu argued, if there were no third element, the standard of right and wrong, brought in to check improper desires, there would be bound to occur conflicts between the opposing classes of people, the "lower and higher". So *Li*, the rules of proper conduct, make distinction between the different classes of people, and enable them to live and work harmoniously for the common good of society. That is why Hsun-tzu said, "the rules of proper conduct (*Li*) are the greatest thing in government", and only when those rules prevail in the world, can the ideal social order be achieved.

"To be honourable as the emperor, to be so wealthy as to own the country—this is what men's passions alike desire. But if men's desires are given rein, then their authority could not be endured, and things would not be sufficient to satisfy them. Hence the ancient kings invented the rules of proper conduct (*Li*) and class rights (*Yi*) for men in order to divide them; causing them to have the classes of noble and base, the disparity between the aged and young, and the distinction between the wise and stupid, the able and the powerless; all to cause men to assume their duties and each one to get his proper position; then only can the amount and grade of their emoluments be made fitting to their position. This is the way of living in society and having harmony and unity. For when the man of love is in control, the farmers by their strength will be expert at the fields; the merchants by their knowledge of values will be expert at using wealth; all kinds of artisans by their skill will be expert at using tools; none of those above the grade of Office and Prefect up to the Duke and Marquis will fail to fulfill the duties of their office according to love, generosity, wisdom and power—then this will be called Great Equableness. Then whether a man's emolument is the whole empire, he will not think it too much for himself; or whether he is gate-keeper, receiver of guests keeper of the gate-bar, or night watchman, he will not think it too little for himself. Hence it is said: Irregular but uniform, oppressive but favourable, unlike but like—these are the human relationships." (Bk. 4, pp. 65-66)

"Heaven and Earth are the source of life. The rules of proper conduct (*Li*) and class rights (*Yi*) are the source of good government; the Superior Man is the source of the rules of proper conduct (*Li*) and class rights (*Yi*). To carry them out, to practice them, to study them much, and to love them greatly is the source of being a Superior Man. . . . That the prince should be treated as prince, the minister should be treated as minister, the father should be treated as father, the son as son, the older brother as older brother, the younger brother as younger brother, is following the same principle. That the farmer should be treated as farmer, the scholar as scholar, the labourer as labourer, and the merchant as merchant, is the same principle." (Bk. 9, pp. 134-126)

"The rules of proper conduct (*Li*) furnish the means of determining the observance towards relatives, near and remote; of settling points which may cause suspicion or doubt; of distinguishing where there should be agreement and difference; and of making clear what is right and what is wrong. . . . Duty, virtue, love, and righteousness cannot be fully carried out without the rules of proper conduct (*Li*); nor can the means of education and rectification be perfected; nor can the quarrels and lawsuits be settled; nor can the duties between ruler and ruled, high and low, father and son, elder and younger brothers, be determined; nor can students for office and other learners in serving their masters have an attachment for them; nor can majesty and dignity be shown in assigning the different places at court, in the government of the armies, and in discharging the duties of office so as to secure the operation of the laws." (*Li Chi, The Book of Rites*, bk. 25,10)

"If the classes are equal, there will not be enough for everybody; when everyone's powers are equal, there is no unity in the state; when everyone is equal, there is no one to employ the people on public services. As soon as there was heaven and earth, there was the distinction of above and below; when the first wise king arose, the country he occupied had the division of classes. For two nobles cannot serve each other; two commoners cannot employ each other—this is a law of nature. Were people's power and position equal, and their likes and dislikes the same, there would not be sufficient goods to satisfy everybody, and hence there would inevitably be strife. If there were strife, there would inevitably result general disorder; if general disorder, then general poverty. The ancient kings hated any disorder, and hence established the rules of proper conduct (*Li*) and class rights (*Yi*) to divide the people, to cause them to have the classes of poor and rich, of noble and inferior, so that everyone would be under someone's control —this is the fundamental thing in caring for the whole country. The History says: 'They are only uniform in that they are not uniform'—this expresses what I mean." (Bk. 9, pp. 123-4)

Like Mencius, Hsun-tzu also preached about the importance of love (*Jen*) in the government. He characterized a righteous king as one who possesses love, justice, and majesty: "His love (*Jen*) fills the empire, his justice (*Yi*) permeates the land, and his majesty pervades the country." (Book 9, p. 130) Again he says:

"For the superior there is nothing as good as loving his inferior and ruling according to the rules of proper conduct (*Li*). The relation of the superior and inferior should be that of protecting infants. . . . In this respect all the kings were alike, and it is the central and indispensable thing in the rules of proper conduct (*Li*) and laws." (Book 11, p. 154)

Unlike Mencius, however, who preached that love (*Jen*) is innate in original human nature, and is the most important characteristic for both the ideal individual and the ideal social order, Hsun-tzu taught that human nature is evil, and all good conduct, including love, comes from the rules of proper conduct (*Li*), taught by the Sage-kings. He says, for example, "All rules of proper conduct (*Li*) and social rights (*Yi*) come from the acquired training of the Sage, no from man's original nature." (Book 23, p. 305) Love is only one of many rules of proper conduct (*Li*), though it is one of the most important rules, "the central and indispensable thing in the rules of proper conduct (*Li*)" concerning kings and rulers. In other words, love, to Mencius, comes from human nature, the depth of the human heart; while to Hsun-tzu, it is merely the following of the rules of proper conduct (*Li*), taught by Sage-kings, as one of the best policies that should be taken by any wise king and ruler.

"Of the things that are in Heaven there are none brighter than the sun and moon; of the things that are on earth, there are none brighter than water and fire; of goods there are none brighter than pearls and jade; of the things that are human there are none brighter than the rules of proper conduct (*Li*) and social rights (*Yi*)". (Book 17, p. 182)

D. Conclusion

In short, it may be concluded that Confucius as recorded in *The Analects*, that is, according to his immediate disciples, puts emphasis upon the full development of both the individual and the society, or the creative and collective man, as the aim of his teaching. He advocated the doctrine of the Mean,—the individual should not go too far so as to neglect the welfare and development of society, nor should society go too far so as to neglect the welfare and development of the individual. Both, however, should be allowed to be developed to their fullest extent, until the ideal state of "great harmony" (*Ta T'ung*) between the individual and society is realized.

Confucius, in *The Analects*, has two stages of both individual and social developments, namely, the practical ideals and the theoretical ideals of both the individual personalities and the social orders. The practical ideals were achieved in the "golden age" of the past, while the theoretical ideals are still to be realized in the future. In the stage of the practical ideals of society and the individual, both love (*Jen*) and the rules of proper conduct (*Li*) are to be emphasized, but both of them are graded according to the different classes of people. Only in the stage of the theoretical ideals of both the individual and society will the universal and undifferentiated love prevail.

Both Mencius and Hsun-tzu and their schools of Confucianism, emphasize only the practical ideals of their common master, Confucius. They all idealize the ancient Sage-kings and their governments. They may have done so for the reason of making their teachings more authoritative, and effective, as many of the modern Chinese scholars have suggested. Nevertheless, it is beyond any doubt that during their time there must have been many traditional historical records, that give the characters of the ancient Sage-kings and their governments, which were definitely superior to the general conditions of their times.

Mencius, on the other hand, develops more the individual aspect of the teaching of Confucius. Man's original nature is conferred by God and so is entirely good and should be fully developed. If any society or government acts contrary to the individual nature, it should be done away with. Men are the children of God who "hears as my people hear, and sees as my people see"; everybody is unique and sacred in the sight of God, and his nature or conscience is the chief standard of right or wrong. Since human nature is good, the method of education is simply to unfold it or to "seek for the lost mind", that is, the original nature which is lost or covered up with bad habits through the contact with the outside world or other people. "What Heaven has conferred is called the Nature; an accordance with this nature is called the Way (*Tao*); the cultivation of this Way is called Education." (*Chung-yung*, 1,1) Human nature is among the "Nature" which Heaven has conferred, and love (*Jen*) is the most important characteristic of the human nature. Mencius says: "Love (*Jen*) is man's mind. . . . The great aim of learning is nothing else but to seek for the lost mind", that is love. (*Mencius*, 6,1,11)

Hsun-tzu, on the other hand, emphasizes more the social aspect of the teaching of Confucius. He regarded human nature as fundamentally evil, and the good comes only from the work of teaching of ancient sages. He denies there is any spiritual principle in the universe that gives Mencius the chief basis for his theory of the goodness of human nature, and attributes the so-called works of the spirits to the unknown causes and effects of the nature. He says:

"The fixed stars make their round; the sun and moon alternately shine; the four seasons come in succession; the Yin and Yang go through their great mutations; the wind and rain widely affect things; all things acquire their germinating principle, and are brought into existence; each gets its nourishing principle and develops to its completed state. We do not see the cause of the occurrences, but we do see their effects—this is what is meant by the influence of the spirits. The results of all these changes are known, but we do not know the invisible source—that is, what is meant by the work of Heaven. Only the sage does; not seek to know Heaven." (*The Works of Hsun-tzu*, translated by Homer H. Dubs, Bk. 7, p. 175)

Only the sages or Superior Men know the courses of nature, the Heaven and Earth, and give us the rules of proper conduct (*Li*), so "The Superior Man forms a triad with Heaven and Earth" (*ibid.*, Ch. 9, p. 135) The *Tao*, or the right Way, to Hsun-tzu, is not "an accordance with the nature" which is conferred by Heaven. "The Way (*Tao*) is not primarily the Way to Heaven; it is not the Way (*Tao*) of Earth; it is the way (*Tao*) man acts, the way (*Tao*) the Superior Man acts." (*ibid.*, Bk. 8, p. 96) It is primarily ethical rather than metaphysical. Education, which is "the cultivation of the Way (*Tao*)" of nature conferred by Heaven, according to Mencius' school of interpretation, becomes to Hsun-tzu and his school, the cultivation of the rules of proper conduct (*Li*) as taught chiefly by ancient Sage-kings. Those rules (*Li*) become the highest source of the standard of action. Since human nature is evil, the function of education is to control and change the human nature through the indoctrination of the social good, that is, the rules of proper conduct (*Li*). "What should one study? How should one begin?" Hsun-tzu asks, and he answers, "The art begins by reciting the Classics and ends in learning the rules of proper conduct (*Li*). . . . Study advances to *Li*, and stops there. This is what is meant by the extreme of virtue." (*The Works of Hsun-tzu*, Bk. 1, pp. 36-37)

Mencius says: "It is simply after love (*Jen*) that the Superior Man strives." (*Mencius*, 6,2,6,2)

Hsun-tzu says: "Study advances to the rules of proper conduct (*Li*) and stops there. This is what is meant by the extreme of virtue." (*Hsun-tzu*, Bk. 1, p. 37)

Confucius says: "If a man is without love (*Jen*), what has he to do with the rules of proper conduct (*Li*)?" (*The Analects*, 3,3)

"To subdue one's self and return to *Li*, is love (*Jen*)." (*The Analects*, 12,1,1,)

CHAPTER V

THE SUBSTANCE OF THE TEACHING OF CONFUCIUS

OUTLINE

A. Moral Teaching

(A) According to the immediate disciples of Confucius

1. Love (*Jen*)

(a) Love the greatest of all virtues

(b) The meaning of love

a) Different degrees and manifestations of love

    a. *Ai*; b. *Hao*; c. *Ch'in*; d. *Jen* (social love); e. *Jen* (ethical love); f. *Jen* (religious love)

b) Both motive and action of love emphasized

c) Love expressed in both positive and negative forms ·

(c) The methods of acquiring love

2. The rules of proper conduct (*Li*)

(a) *Li* as social regulations

a) Necessary for everybody to know and obey *Li*

b) Necessary for the government to act according to *Li*

c) Better and more effective as compared with laws and punishments

d) *Li* as the chief factor in the Doctrine of Rectification

(b) *Li* as the expression of personal feeling or desire

a) Sincerity as the foundation of *Li*

b) Individual freedom respected in observing *Li*

    a. Personal economy as a criterion

    b. Personal conscience as a criterion

    c Personal natural ease or comfort as a criterion

3. Filial Piety (*Hsiao*)

(a) As the root of moving force of all virtues

(b) The ways of being filial to one's parents

a) To serve parents according to *Li* when they are alive

    a. To obey one's parents

    b. To "nourish the will" of one's parent

c. Reverence as the basis of filial piety
b) To serve parents according to *Li* when they are dead
  a. Burial rituals
  b. Three years mourning
  c. Ancestor-worship
  d. To carry out the will of the departed ancestors
(c) The place of filial piety in modern society
4. The Doctrine of the Mean (*Chung-yung*)
(a) According to Aristotle
(b) As the perfect virtue
(c) As the purpose of the teaching of Confucius
(d) The character of Confucius as a typical example
(e) The ancient origin of the Doctrine of the Mean
(B) According to Mencius and his school of Confucianism
1. Love
(a) The origin of love—the ethical Heaven or God
(b) The way of securing love—self-development
a) Passively, through self-examination
b) Actively, through "nourishing the mind"
(c) The expression of love
a) In family relationships
  a. Yang Chu—self-love
  b. Mo-tzu—universal love
  c. Mencius—relational love
b) In political applications—Love versus War
2. The rules of proper conduct (*Li*)
3. Filial Piety
4. The Doctrine of the Mean
(C) According to Hsun-tzu and his school of Confucianism
1. The rules of proper conduct (*Li*)
(a) The importance of *Li*
a) *Li* is a cosmological principle, the greatest of all principles
b) *Li* is the utmost of human morality
c) The aim of all learning
d) The greatest thing in government
e) The standard of all human actions

(b) The functions of *Li*
a) To regulate human desire
b) To carry out the Doctrine of Rectification
c) To beautify and refine the expression of human emotions
(c) The sources of *Li*
2. Love
(a) The place of love in Hsun-tzu's teaching
(b) Love in the government
(c) Love and the problem of war
(d) Love subordinate to *Li*
3. Filial Piety
4. The Doctrine of the Mean
(D) Conclusion of the moral teaching of Confucius

B. Intellectual Teaching
(A) According to his immediate disciples
1. Poetry
(a) The use of poetry at the time of Confucius
(b) The teaching of Confucius on poetry
a) The values of poetry
    a. Social value
    b. Moral value
    c. Intellectual value
b) The ways of using poetry
2. History
3. The rules of proper conduct (*Li*)
4. Music
(a) Confucius' interest in music
(b) Confucius' conception on music
a) To promote the music of *Ya* and banish the music of
    Cheng
b) The rectification of music
(c) The musical instruments possibly used by Confucius
(B) According to Mencius and Hsun-tzu
1. According to Mencius
2. According to Hsun-tzu

C. Religious Teaching of Confucius

(A) According to *The Analects* and other Classics

1. Confucius not a teacher of religion but a religious person
2. The doctrine of God
3. The doctrine of man
(a) Man is the creature of God
(b) Original nature of man
(c) The duty of man
(d) The destiny of man
4. The communication between God and man
(a) The revelation of God to man
a) Through natural phenomena
b) Through the moral nature of man
c) Through rulers and teachers
d) Through the spirits of God
(b) Human attempt to enter into communication with God, or His spirits
a) Through prayer
b) Through sacrifices (*Chi*)
    a. The meaning of *Chi*
    b. Twofold sacrifice
    c. Sacrifice as oblations rather than propitiation
    d. Reverence as the most important attitude in sacrifice
c) Through divination and magic
(B) According to Mencius and Hsun-tzu and their schools
1. According to Mencius and his school
2. According to Hsun-tzu and his school
(a) The idea of God
(b) Religious ceremonies
a) Prayer and divination
b) Funeral rites
c) Sacrifices

D. Conclusion

The substance of the teaching of Confucius can be grouped under three headings, namely, moral, intellectual, and religious. Confucius was mainly interested in the moral life of men. The intellectual aim of his teaching was in general subordinate to his moral aim, and his religious teaching was chiefly that of the traditional beliefs on which he had very few comments. Both intellectual knowledge and religious beliefs were, according to him, useless and not worth teaching if they could not contribute towards the betterment of the practical moral life of the individual. Confucius was primarily a moral teacher.

A. Moral Teaching

The moral teachings of Confucius can be said to have been centred around the four main topics,—Jen,[1] Li,[2] Hsiao,[3] and Chung Yung.[4]

The word Jen[5] has been variously translated into English. Lin Yu-tang translated it as "true-manhood", and sometimes as "kindness". Hu Han-min translated it as "the moral sense" in most cases. James Legge's translation given in The Chinese Classics gives different translations to the same Chinese word Jen. Sometimes he translates it as "perfect virtue", sometimes as "virtuous", sometimes "goodness", sometimes "benevolence", sometimes "love" and sometimes "principle". Nearly all modern scholars on Chinese studies have followed the same way of giving different renderings of the word Jen. The difficulty of translating this term is admitted, but it seems preferable to use only one English term for the one Chinese term of Jen, and that term is "love". The following are the reasons:

In the first place, to give different translations of the word Jen

247

simply means that different interpretations of the word are given, and these different meanings are supposed to have been in the mind of the original writer. *Jen* may in different places have different meanings, but certainly the translator has no authority to decide that one rendering belongs here and another there. Any rendering of this sort is bound to be arbitrary. Moreover, with *Jen* rendered in different terms, it becomes disintegrated and thus loses its original content and force. For example, in *The Analects* the word *Jen* is mentioned 108 times; yet it would be difficult for an ordinary English reader, who does not read Chinese, to be impressed by the prominence of *Jen* in the teaching of Confucius in *The Analects*, when it has been translated in so many different terms and phrases. So in order to do justice to the original author and to be consistent, the same term will be used throughout the translations for this important character *Jen*; or if the same term is not used in certain particular cases, reasons will be given for the exception to the rule.

In the second place, the English word Love is nearest to the Chinese word *Jen*. It is the highest virtue of Christian people, and it is also the highest virtue in the Confucian teaching. *Jen*, like Love, has various shades and intensities of meaning. James Hastings, in his *Dictionary of the Bible*, gives five different meanings of the English word Love which are discriminated in the original Greek language. He says: "The Greek language distinguished (1) Sexual Love, 'erōs'; (2) Family Love, natural affection, 'storgē'; (3) Social Love, friendship, 'philia' (4) sometimes, in a broader ethical sense, 'philanthropia', humanity, kindness. The LXX translators though not consistent in their usage, enlisted (5) 'agapē' to denote Religious Love, the love of God to man, or man to God, or of man to man under God's covenant—i.e. Love suffused with Religion." The Chinese word *Jen* has all these five meanings. Although *Jen*, in the sense of Religious Love, is not frequently used in the teaching of Confucius, yet it is a central theme in the teaching of Micius, a contemporary and once a disciple of Confucius. *Jen*, in the sense of Sex Love, is also very seldom used in the Confucian literature, but there is no doubt that *Jen* in its larger sense will often include

Sex Love. In Chinese writing, the character *Jen* is composed of "two" and "person",[6] signifying the relationship between man and man, man and woman, or between the human person and the divine.

The word *Li*[7] has also been variously translated. Hu Han-min translated it as "moral and religious institutions (of the Three Dynasties)", and sometimes as "the laws of usuages of social life" (see *The Conduct of Life*—John Murray, London). Lin Yu-tang thought that the word *Li* "cannot be rendered by an English word. In a narrow sense, it means 'ritual', 'propriety'; in a generalized sense, it simply means "good manner'; in its highest philosophic sense, it means an ideal social order with everything in its place, and particularly a rationalized feudal order, which was breaking down in Confucius' days. (*The Wisdom of Confucius*, p. 13) James Legge also translated the word *Li* by different English terms. He sometimes translated it as "rules of Propriety", sometimes as "what is proper", sometimes as "regulations" sometimes "ceremonies", and sometimes "rituals". H. H. Dubs translated it as "the rules of proper conduct" throughout his whole translation of *Works of Hsun-tze*. The present writer thinks that the Chinese moral concept of the term *Li* like that of *Jen* has really no exact equivalent in English, yet he is willing to accept Dubs' translation, "the rules of proper conduct", as the best and the most approximate translation. It is both expressive and comprehensive; it expresses and includes pretty well all the important characteristics of the term *Li*. *Li* may be the rules of proper conduct of "propriety" or "good manners", in "ceremonies", "rites", moral and religious institutions", "social life", or in a "rationalized feudal order". Moreover, Dubs is consistent in using the same term for *Li*, and his transliteration of the Chinese term in brackets placed after the translation is very suggestive.

Hsiao[8] is generally translated as "filial piety" or "filiality". It is one of the fundamental doctrines taught by Confucius and his followers.

Chung Yung[9] is another Chinese term which has been variously translated. Hu Han-min in his *The Conduct of Life* translated it as the "universal moral order", or sometimes as "to find the central clue in our moral being which unites us to the universal order". Lin Yu-tang translated the title of the book of *Chung-Yung* as *Central Harmony*. But usually it has been translated by James Legge and others as "The Doctrine of the Mean" or "Golden Mean". The present writer holds that there is a close resemblance between "The Doctrine of the Mean" of virtue taught by Aristotle and the *Chung-Yung* taught by Confucius, so it is appropriate to use the same term for the teaching of Confucius and that of Aristotle, namely, "The Doctrine of the Mean" or the "Golden Mean". The ideas of the "central harmony", or the "universal moral order", or "to find the central clue in our moral being which unties us to the universal order" should be looked upon as more of the later development of the doctrine of the Golden Mean, especially in Mencius' school of Confucianism.

(A) According to the Immediate Disciples of Confucius

1. Love (*Jen*)
(a) Love is the greatest of all virtues

One of the greatest contributions of Confucius is to hold the virtue of Love (*Jen*) in the highest esteem. The word *Jen* is very seldom mentioned in the literature before or during the time of Confucius. It occurs only five times in *The Book of History* (*Shu-ching*), twice in *The Book of Poetry* (*Shi-ching*), and 39 times in *Tso Chuan* during the whole Spring and Autumn Period. The most prominent virtue during the Spring and Autumn Period is *Li* which occurs 489 times in *Tso Chuan* alone. It is largely through the effort of Confucius that Love (*Jen*) has become the chief virtue in Chinese ethics. It occurs 108 times in *The Analects*, and is regarded there as the most important characteristic of a Superior Man, the ideal personality of Confucianism. "If a Superior Man abandon love (*Jen*), how can he fulfil the requirements of that name? The Superior Man does not, even for the space of a single meal, act contrary to love (*Jen*). In moments of haste, he cleaves to it. In seasons of danger, he cleaves to it." (*The Analects*, 4, 5, 2-3)

Love (*Jen*), wisdom (*Chih*)[10] and courage (*Yung*)[11] are taken to be the most important three-fold Way (*Tao*) of a Superior Man, and the three *Ta Teh*,[12] that is, the "virtues that are universally binding".

"The Master said, 'The Way (*Tao*) of the Superior Man is three-fold, but I am not equal to it. Loving (*Jen*), he is free from anxiety; wise (*Chi*), he is free from perplexities; courageous (*Yung*), he is free from fear.' Tzu Kung said, 'Master, that is what you yourself say.' " (*The Analects*, 14, 30)

"The Master said, 'The man of wisdom is free from perplexities; the man of love (*Jen*) from anxiety; and the man of courage (*Yung*) from fear.' " (*The Analects*, 9,28)

"The Master said. . . . 'Wisdom (*Chi*), Love (*Jen*), and Courage (*Yung*), these three, are the virtues universally binding (*Ta Teh*). . . . To be fond of learning is to be near to wisdom (*Chi*). To practice with vigour is to be near to love (*Jen*). To possess the feeling of shame is to be near to courage (*Yung*). He who knows these three things, knows how to cultivate his own character.' " (*Chung-Yung*, 20, 8-11)

Among these three universally binding virtues, love (*Jen*) is considered to be the greatest. Love is greater than wisdom:

"The Master said, 'When a man's wisdom (Chi) is sufficient to attain, and his love (*Jen*) is not sufficient to enable him to hold, whatever he may have gained, he will lose again.' " (*The Analects*, 15, 32, 1)

Love (*Jen*) is also greater than Courage (*Yung*):

"The Master said, 'Men of Love (*Jen*) are sure to be courageous (*Yung*), but those who are courageous (*Yung*) may not always be men of love (*Jen*).' " (*The Analects*, 14, 5)

To put it in the Biblical language, Confucius would say: "And now abideth Wisdom, Courage and Love, these three; but the greatest of these is Love."

Cheng Ming-tao (A.D. 1032-1085), one of the greatest Confucian scholars in the Sung dynasty, gave a very good description of love (*Jen*) in his essay *The Knowledge of Love* (*Jen*) (*Shih Jen*),[13] in which he said, "The learner must first understand love (*Jen*), for love (*Jen*) is a feeling of kinship with all creation. Justice (*I*), the rules of proper conduct (*Li*), knowledge (*Chih*), and faithfulness (*Hsin*) are all manifestations of love. Once let this principle be grasped, all that is needed is that it be held in reverence and integrity."[14]

(b) The meaning of Love (*Jen*)

While the meanings of the word Love (*Jen*) as spoken by Confucius, and recorded and interpreted by his immediate disciples in *The Analects* are different, they may be summed up in some such definition as this: Love (*Jen*) is an earnest desire and beneficent action, both active and passive, for the well-being of the one loved. Three things involved in the above statement are to be considered separately, namely, a) that there are different degrees and manifestations of love, according to the circumstances and relations of the one loved; b) that both motive and action of love are emphasized; and c) that love expresses itself in both negative and positive terms.

a) Different degrees and manifestations of Love

These are recognized in *The Analects* and other Confucian or non-Confucian literature of early China, according to the circumstances and relations of life, e.g., the expression of love as between the members of a family, friends or other people in society, and between the spirit and man in religious beliefs and practices. As is mentioned above, practically all the Greek terms, such as, erōs, storge, philia, philanthropia, and agapē, are used to distinguish the various shades and intensities of the Christian conception of love as recorded in the Bible, under the English term Love, and that these are also involved in the Chinese term *Jen* (love). Besides *Jen*, there are other Chinese terms which have the meaning of love in different degrees or intensities as used in the Confucian Classics, and can all be included, in one sense or another, in the term *Jen* (love).

a. *Ai*.[15] This is as general a term as *Jen*, and also implies the various degrees of love. *Jen* is commonly used as a noun and much less frequently used as a verb. The reverse seems to be the case with *Ai*. "Fan Ch'ih asked about Love (*Jen*). The Master said, 'It is

to love (*Ai*) all men.' " (*The Analects*, 12, 22, 1) "Mencius said. . . .
'The man of love (*Jen*) Loves. (*Ai*) others.' " (*Mencius*, 4, 2, 28, 2) "It
is only the man of love (*Jen*) who can love (*Ai*) or who can hate
others." (*The Great Learning, Ta Hsueh*, 10,15,) There are some
important expressions of the term *Ai* (love) in ancient Chinese
literature such as the following:

Fan Ai.[16] This term means comprehensive or overflowing love,
and sometimes universal love. This term was originally used by
Confucius in *The Analects*. "The Master said, 'A youth . . . should
comprehensively love (*Fan Ai*) all people, and cultivate natural
affection of Love (*Jen*).' " (*The Analects*, 1, 6)

Chien Ai.[17] This means equal, indiscriminating or universal love.
This term was frequently used by Micius (Mo-tzu)[18] in contrast to
the general Confucian idea of love of his time that was partial to
some and graded in its attitude to others. "Mencius said, 'Micius
loves all equally (*Chien Ai*). If by rubbing smooth his whole body
from the crown to the heel, he could have benefited the empire,
he would have done it.' " (*Mencius*, 7, 1, 26, 2)

Po Ai.[19] It means universal love. This term appeared for the first
time in the writings of the philosopher, statesman and poet Han
Yu[20] (A.D. 768-824), and since then it has generally been accepted
as the orthodox interpretation of the Confucian teaching on love.
Wang Yang Ming (A.D. 1472-1528), one of the greatest Confucian
scholars, for example, though he rejected Micius' idea of Equal Love
(*Chien Ai*), accepted Han Yu's interpretation as orthodox. (See
Philosophy of Wang Yang Ming, Henke, p. 376) Han Yu identified
Universal Love (*Po Ai*) with Love (*Jen*), and said, "Universal Love
(*Po Ai*) is called Love (*Jen*), putting it into rightful practice is called
Righteousness (*I*).[21] The channel of Love and Righteousness is
called *Tao*".[22] (*Han Yu*, "Yuan Tao").[23] What Han Yu did was simply
to take the highest mark of the teachings of Confucius and Mencius
about love (*Jen*), and put it in a concise and expressive terms, *Po
Ai*. The word Po[24] was used by Confucius in *The Analects* in
connection with love, "Universally (*Po*) conferring benefits on the
people" (*The Analects*, 7, 28, 1) Mencius also said, "The man of love
(*Jen*) has nothing which he does not love (*Ai*), but what he

considers of the greatest importance is to cultivate an earnest affection (Ch'in)[25] for the virtuous." (*Mencius*, 7, 1, 46, 1) In the present usage, the two words *Jen*[26] and *Ai*[27] usually go together to denote the general meaning of love.

b. *Hao*.[28] When used as an adjective, it means "good"; when used as a verb, it means "love", such as, "to love virtue", *Hao Teh*[29] (*The Analects*, 15,12), "to love learning" *Hao Hsueh* (*The Analects*, 1,14), "to love the rules of proper conduct", *Hao Li* (*The Analects*, 1,15,1). It is sometimes used to mean "sexual love" like the Greek term "erōs", *Hao Se*[30] "love of beauty" or "sexual love" (see *The Analects*, 15,12; *Mencius*, 1,2,5,5), *Hao Ho*[31] "loving union". "Loving union (*Hao Ho*) with wife and children is like the music of lutes." (*The Book of Poetry*, 2,1,4,7; *The Doctrine of the Mean*, 15,2) The Chinese word *Hao*[32] is composed of two words "Girl" (Nu)[33] and "Boy" (Tzu).[34] It suggests the love between the boy and the girl, "erōs". Such love is sometimes regarded as the starting point of the right Way (Tao) or Love (*Jen*) which characterizes the Superior Man. "The Way (Tao) of the Superior Man may be found, in its simple elements, in the intercourse of men and women; but in its utmost reaches, it shines brightly through heaven and earth." (*The Doctrine of the Mean* 12, 4)

c. *Ch'in*.[35] It generally means family love, natural affection, or in Greek "storge". It constitutes one of the most important meanings of love (*Jen*) as taught by Confucius and his followers:

"Filial piety and fraternal submission!—are they not the root of love (*Jen*)?" (*The Analects*, 1, 2, 2)

"Love (*Jen*) is the characteristic element of humanity, and the great exercise of it is in loving (Ch'in) parents" (*The Doctrine of the Mean*, 20,5)

"What he considers precious is the love (*Jen*) due to his parents." (*The Great Learning*, 10,13)

"To love (*Ch'in*) one's parents is love (*Jen*)". (*Mencius*, 7,1,15,3)

d. *Jen*.[36] *Jen* in the sense of social love, friendship, or "philia" in Greek, constitutes another important meaning of love (*Jen*) in general.

"The Master said, 'It is love (*Jen*) which constitutes the excellence of a neighbourhood. If a man in selecting a residence do not fix on one where love (*Jen*) prevails, how can he be wise?' " (*The Analects*, 4,1)

"The Superior Man on grounds of culture meets with his friends, and by their friendship helps his love (*Jen*)." (*The Analects*, 12,24,)

e. *Jen* in the broader ethical sense of humanity, kindness, or "philanthropia". This also constitutes one of the most important meanings of love (*Jen*) in general.

"Now the man of love (*Jen*), wishing to be established himself, seeks also to establish others; wishing to be developed himself, he seeks also to develop others." (*The Analects*, 6,28,2) "Chung Kung asked about love (*Jen*). The Master said, '. . . not to do to others as you would not wish done to yourself.' " (*The Analects*, 12,2; 15,23)

"Love (*Jen*) is the characteristic element of humanity." (*The Doctrine of the Mean*, 20,5; *Mencius*, 7,2,16)

f. *Jen* in the sense of religious love, "agape"

"Now, love (*Jen*) is the most honourable dignity conferred by Heaven, and the quiet home in which man should dwell." (*Mencius*, 2,1,7,2)

The love (*Jen*) which Confucius and his followers emphasized most was the family, social, and ethical love. They did not deal so much with religious love as did the Mohist school, a great rival school of Confucianism of the period of the Warring States. "The subjects of which the Master seldom spoke were—profitableness, and also the appointments of Heaven, and love (*Jen*)" (*The Analects*, 9,1) The love (*Jen*) which Confucius seldom spoke about was the equal, indiscriminate, or universal love based upon the religious faith of the Fatherhood of God and the Brotherhood of man. This does not mean that Confucius never spoke about love (*Jen*) in the sense of "agape", or "love suffused with religion". The traditional materials which he selected as the text-books to teach his disciples have many instances which speak about the Fatherhood of God:

"Oh vast and distant Heaven, who art called our parent." (*The Book of Poetry*, 2,5,4,1)

"Heaven gives birth to mankind." (*The Book of Poetry*, 3,3,1,1,; 3,3,6,1; *Mencius*, 6,1,6,8)

Micius, founder of the school of Mohism, who based his doctrine of the equal or universal love (*Chien Ai*) upon his religious belief of the "Will of Heaven", was once an immediate disciple of Confucius. "Micius studied the works of the Confucians, and learnt the methods of Confucius" (*Huai Nan Tzu*).[37] Tzu Hsia, one of the most brilliant disciples of Confucius, might have deduced his famous conclusion about the brotherhood of man from the teaching of his Master or from the textbooks which he used in his school days about the Fatherhood of God. "Tzu Hsia said, 'There is the following saying which I have heard:—"Death and life have their determined appointment; riches and honours depend upon Heaven." Let the Superior Man never fail to be reverent, and let him be respectful to others and observant of the rules of proper conduct (*Li*):—then all within the four seas will be his brothers. What has the Superior Man to do with being distressed because he has no brothers?' " (*The Analects*, 12,5) Mencius, though he did not dwell much upon the doctrine of the Fatherhood of God, did frequently point the origin of love (*Jen*) to God. He said, "Love (*Jen*) is the most honourable dignity conferred by Heaven". (*Mencius*, 2,1,7,2) Human nature, he maintains, is good, and predominantly love, because it derives from God. "Love (*Jen*) is man's mind." (*Mencius*, 6,1,11,1) "Love (*Jen*), righteousness (*I*), rules of proper conduct (*Li*), wisdom (*Chih*), are not infused into us from without. We are certainly furnished with them. . . . It is said in *The Book of Poetry*, 'Heaven gives birth to mankind, and endowed them with their various faculties and relations with their specific laws. These are the invariable rules of nature for all to hold, and all love this admirable virtue.' Confucius said, 'The maker of this Ode knew indeed the principle (*Tao*) of our nature.' " (*Mencius*, 6,1,6) "He who has exhausted all his mental constitution knows his nature. Knowing his nature, he knows Heaven." (*Mencius*, 7,1,1,1)

Much of the teaching of Confucius and his followers about love (*Jen*) is based upon the doctrine of filial piety. "Filial piety and fraternal submission!—are they not the root of love (*Jen*)?" (*The Analects*, 1,2,2) "The master said, '. . . The great exercise of love (*Jen*) is in loving parents.' " (*The Doctrine of the Mean*, 20,5) The love of one's parents, according to the teaching of Confucius and his followers, goes beyond the natural affection as expressed by the Greek term, "storgē". It contains much of the meaning of the religious love, "agapē." (See sections on Confucius' teachings on filial piety and religion)

In Short, Confucius, was essentially a practical teacher. Though he had two stages, the practical and the theoretical, of the ideal individual life and the ideal social order, he dwelt primarily on the practical ideals of individual life and social order. This explains the reason why he did not teach much about religious problems, including religious love.

b) Both the motive and action of love emphasized

"Yen Yuan asked about love (*Jen*). The Master said, 'To subdue one's self and respond to the rules of proper conduct (*Li*) is Love (*Jen*).' " (*The Analects*, 12,1,1)

To subdue one's self is to overcome one's selfish desires and to cultivate good attitudes to react against one's environment. This is essential to all true acts of love (*Jen*). But if the motive or attitude of one's action is good and the consequence resulting from such action is bad, it also falls short of the standard of true love (*Jen*). One's action should follow not only one's own motive, but also the social standard of right and wrong, or the rules of proper conduct (*Li*). So both the individual motive and the social consequence resulting from his action are emphasized.

a. The motive of love (*Jen*)

"The Master said, 'Such was Hui that for three months there would be nothing in his mind contrary to love (*Jen*). The others attain to this on some days or in some months, but nothing more.' " (*The Analects*, 6,5)

"Meng Wu Po asked about Tzu Lu, whether he was love (*Jen*). The Master said, 'I do not know.' He asked again, when the Master replied, 'In a kingdom of a thousand chariots, Yu might be employed to manage the military levies, but I do not know whether he be love (*Jen*).' 'And what do you say of Ch'iu?' The Master replied, 'In a city of a thousand families, or a clan of a hundred chariots Ch'iu might be employed as governor, but I do not know whether he is love (*Jen*).' 'What do you say of Ch'ih?' The Master replied 'With his sash girt and standing in a court, Ch'ih might be employed to converse with the visitors and guests, but I do not know whether he is love (*Jen*).' " (*The Analects*, 5,7)

Some one said, 'Yung is love (*Jen*), but he is not ready with his tongue.' The Master said, 'What is the good of being ready with the tongue? They who encounter men with smartnesses of speech for the most part procure themselves hatred. I know not whether he be love (*Jen*), but why should he show readiness of the tongue?' " (*The Analects*, 5,4)

"Tzu Chang asked, saying, 'The minister Tzu Wen thrice took office, and manifested no joy in his countenance. Thrice he retired from office, and manifested no displeasure. He made it a point to inform the new minister of the way in which he had conducted the government;—what do you say of him?' The Master replied, 'He was loyal.' 'Was he love (*Jen*)?' 'I do not know. How can he be pronounced love?' " (*The Analects*, 5,18)

From the above quotations, it may be seen closely that to be love-minded is very difficult, according to Confucius. His most favourite disciple, Yen Hui could have only three months when there was nothing in his mind contrary to love (*Jen*). The motive of love (*Jen*) in the minds of all the other prominent disciples of his, like Yu (Ch'i Lu),[38] Ch'iu (Jan Yu),[39] Ch'ih (Kung Hsi Hua),[40] and Yung (Chung Kung)[41] was all questioned by Confucius. The way of achieving the motive of love (*Jen*) was "to subdue one's self". This was interpreted by the scholars of the Sung Dynasty to mean the exercise of ascetic practices similar to that of the Buddhist monks. But Confucius, as clearly recorded by his immediate disciples, disapproved of the conceptions of achieving love (*Jen*) through ascetic practices. Once Confucius was asked, "When the love of superiority, boasting, resentments, and covetousness are repressed, may this be deemed love (*Jen*)?. The Master said, 'This may be regarded as the achievement of what is difficult. But I do not know that it is to be deemed love (*Jen*).' " (*The Analects*, 14,2) The social consequence resulting from the action of love according to the rules of proper conduct (*Li*) is needed to make up the perfect love (*Jen*).

b. The action of love (*Jen*)

Although it is very rare to have a perfect motive of love (*Jen*) in one's mind, yet it is not so difficult to practice love (*Jen*) if one only wills.

"The Master said, 'I have not seen a person who loved love (*Jen*), or one who hated what was not love (*Pu Jen*). He who loved love (*Jen*), would esteem nothing above it. He who hated what is not love (*Pu Jen*), would practice love (*Jen*) in such a way that he would not allow anything that is not love (*Pu Jen*) to approach his person. Is any one able for one day to apply his strength to love (*Jen*)? I have not seen the case in which his strength would be insufficient. Should there possibly be any such case, I have not seen it.' " (*The Analects*, 4,6)

"The Master said, 'If the will be set on Love (*Jen*), there will be no practice of wickedness.' " (*The Analects*, 4,4)

"The Master said, 'Is love (*Jen*) a thing remote? I wish to have love (*Jen*), and lo! love (*Jen*) is at hand.' " (*The Analects*, 7,29)

It was chiefly looked upon from the expression of love in conduct rather than from the motive in the mind, as when Confucius said: "If a Superior Man abandon love (*Jen*), how can he fulfil the requirements of that name? The Superior Man does not even for the space of a single meal *act* contrary to love (*Jen*). In the moments of haste, he cleaves to it. In seasons of danger, he cleaves to it." (*The Analects*, 4,5,2-3)

It was also judged from the beneficent consequences following the action of Kuan Chung, that he was highly praised by Confucius as being a man of love (*Jen*). The following conversation between Confucius and his disciples about the love (*Jen*) of Kuan Chung, gives an excellent example of how Confucius did sometimes, at least, use the pragmatic test in his evaluation and verification of truth and virtue.

"Tzu-lu said, 'Duke Huan caused his brother Chiu to be killed, when Shao Hu died with his master, but Kuan Chung did not die. May I say that he was wanting in love (*Jen*)?' The Master said, 'Duke Huan assembled all the princes together, and that not with weapons of war and chariots:—it was all through the influence of Kuan Chung. Whose love (*Jen*) was like this? Whose love (*Jen*) was like this?'

"Tzu-kung said, 'Kuan Chung, I apprehend, was wanting in love (*Jen*). When Duke Huan caused his brother Chiu to be killed, Kuan Chung was not able to die with him. Moreover, he became prime minister to Huan.' The Master said, 'Kuan Chung acted as prime minister to Duke Huan, made him leader of all the princes, and united and rectified the whole kingdom. Down to the present, the people enjoy the gifts which he conferred. But for Kuan Chung, we should now be wearing our hair unbound, and the lappets of our coats buttoning on the left side. Will you require from him the small fidelity of common men and common women, who would commit suicide in a stream or ditch, no one knowing anything about them?' " (*The Analects*, 14,17-18)

When Confucius talked about love (*Jen*), it should always be remembered, there were these two distinct meanings,—one referring primarily to the motive in the mind, and the other to the action in society. Again, by being essentially a practical teacher, Confucius, though fully aware of the importance of the motive of love (*Jen*), inclined more towards the teaching on the action or the expression of love (*Jen*), rather than the teaching on the methods or problems of how to cultivate one's mind. That is why he taught very little about human nature or mind, and much about human conduct or his relation with the social environment.

c). Love (*Jen*) expressed in both positive and negative forms

Love (*Jen*) in action is expressed both in positive and in negative forms by Confucius in *The Analects* and in other Classics.

a. Positive

"The Master said. . . . 'The man of love (*Jen*), wishing to be established himself, seeks also to establish others; wishing to be developed himself, he seeks also to develop others.' " (*The Analects*, 6,28,2)

"Fan Ch'ih asked about love (*Jen*). The Master said, 'It is to love (*Ai*) all men.' " (*The Analects*, 12,22,1)

"The Master said. . . 'In the way of the Superior Man there are four things . . .,—To serve my father, as I would require my son to serve me . . .; to serve my prince, as I would require my minister to serve me . . .; to serve my elder brother, as I would require my younger brother to serve me . . .; to set the example in behaving to a friend, as I would require him to behave to me. . . .' " (*The Doctrine of the Mean*, 13,4)

  b. Negative

"Chun Kung asked about love (*Jen*). The Master said, . . . 'Not to do to others as you would not wish done to yourself. . . .' " (*The Analects*, 12,2)

"Tzu Kung asked, saying, 'Is there one word which may serve as a rule of practice for all one's life?' The Master said, 'Is not Like-mindedness such a word? What you do not want done to yourself, do not do to others.' " (*The Analects*, 15,23)

"The Master said. . . 'Loyalty (*Chung*), and Like-mindedness (*Shu*) are not far from the Way (*Tao*). What you do not like when done to yourself, do not do to others.' " (*The Doctrine of the Mean*, 13,3)

"What a man dislikes in his superiors, let him not display in the treatment of his inferiors; what he dislikes in his inferiors, let him not display in the service of his superiors; what he hates in those who are before him, let him not therewith precede those who are behind him; what he hates in those who are behind him let him not therewith follow those who are before him; what he hates to receive on the right, let him not bestow on the left; what he hates to receive on the left, let him not bestow on the right:—this is what is called 'The principle with which, as with a measuring-square, to regulate one's conduct.' " (*The Great Learning*, 10,2)

Tseng Sheng, one of the most prominent disciples of Confucius, summarized the moral teachings of Confucius in two words, namely, *Chung*[42] or "loyalty", and *Shu*[43] or "like-mindedness."

"The Master said, 'Sheng, my doctrine is that of an all- pervading unity.' The disciple Tseng replied, 'Yes'. The Master went out, and the other disciples asked, saying, 'What do his words mean?' Tseng said, 'The doctrine (*Tao*) of our master is *Chung* and *Shu*,—this and nothing more.' " (*The Analects*, 4,15)

Dr. Legge commented on the two words *Chung* and *Shu* as

follows: " 忠 and 恕 , which seem to be two things, are both formed from 心 , 'the heart', 忠 being compounded of 中 , 'middle', 'centre', and 心 , and 恕 , of 如 'as', and 心 . The 'centre heart' = I, the ego; and the 'as heart' = the I in sympathy with others. 忠 (*Chung*) is duty-doing, on a consideration, or from the impulse, of one's own self; 恕 (*Shu*) is duty-doing, on the principle of reciprocity (like-mindedness)."

Instead of using the term "duty-doing", Chung can be taken as to mean love (*Jen*) "on a consideration, or from the impulse, of one's own self"; and *Shu*, the love (*Jen*) on the principle of like-mindedness, namely, "do not do to others what you would not want done to yourself." Chucius[44] (A.D. 1130-1200), the greatest Confucian scholar in the Sung dynasty, commented on the same two words, saying, "To devote one's self is called *Chung*, to extend one's own self is called Shu".[45] *Chung* is more the expression of the positive aspect of love (*Jen*) and always leads to some positive action. "The Master said, . . . 'Can there be *Chung* (generally translated as loyalty) which does not lead to the instruction of its object?' " (*The Analects*, 14,8) *Shu* is more the expression of the negative aspect of love (*Jen*), "to extend one's own self", "in sympathy with others". As a matter of fact, the practical result of both the positive and negative statements differ little in significance. They are but two forms of the same Golden Rule. Suppose a man sees a boy about to fall into a well, to use Mencius' illustration, according to the negative statement, if he does not help the boy from falling into the well he is doing something to the boy that he would not want done to himself. Both the positive and negative statements require that the man should put himself in the boy's place or put the boy in his own place and then decide what should be done. The negative statement is perhaps to put the emphasis more on putting the other man in your place than putting yourself in his place, but the result is the same.

Both of these two forms of statements are, however, liable to be abused, if they are wrongly interpreted: the negative statement might lead to inaction, and the positive one to aggression. It is good that Confucius should have these two forms of the action of love clearly stated:—to seek to establish or develop others as you would wish to be established or developed yourself; but the sacredness and rights of the personalities of others should be fully appreciated, putting others in your own place and not doing to them what you would not want done to yourself. It has been repeatedly mentioned that the Confucian teaching of the Golden Rule is inferior to that of the Christian teaching. (See, for example, Dr. Paul Monroe's *The Text-book in the History of Education*, Chap. 2, p. 20) Professor William Hung of Yenching University, Peiping, China, once spoke plainly and somewhat impatiently, about this problem. He said:

"Chinese scholars are not willing to recognize what hair-splitting theologians often speak of as the superiority of the positive Christian Golden Rule over the Golden Rule of Confucius expressed in a negative form. It takes the vigorous and overwhelmingly impetuous temperament of western people to follow either the Golden Rule of Christian missionary pioneers, 'Whatever ye would that men should do to you do ye even so to them', interpreted in the sense of Cromwell's words, 'not what you wish but what is good for them" or the Golden Rule of the fictitious David Harum, 'Do unto the other fellow the way he'd like to do unto you, and do it first', which unfortunately is not less widely practised than the Christian Golden Rule. The modern West has developed in its people an attitude of aggressive mercilessness towards nature which they attack and conquer at will and which seems to influence even their attitude towards one another. Are they really conscious of the fact that the other man is on the same plane of existence and with an equality that deserves recognition? Or, in the world of competition, of promotion, of efficiency and of production and consumption on a large scale, do they sometimes forget the inherent worth and dignity of the other man, patronizing him or exploiting him or using him as a mere part of a machine?" (W.H. Stuart, *The Use of Material from China's Spiritual Inheritance in the Christian Education of Chinese Youth*, pp. 105-106)

(c) The methods of acquiring love (*Jen*)

The methods of acquiring the virtue of love (*Jen*), according to

Confucius, as understood by his immediate disciples, are not primarily through intuition, as most of the famous scholars of the Sung and Ming dynasties understood and interpreted. The following quotations from *The Analects* show clearly that the methods of acquiring love (*Jen*) are primarily through human experience, especially through the intellectual and social experiences.

a) Through extensive learning

"Tzu Hsia said, 'There are learning extensively, and having a firm and sincere aim; inquiring with earnestness, and reflecting with self-application:—love (*Jen*) is in such a course.' " (*The Analects*, 19,6)

"The Master said, 'There is the love (*Ai*) of love (*Jen*) without the love (*Ai*) of learning;—the beclouding here leads to a foolish simplicity.' " (*The Analects*, 17,8,3)

b) Through the help of good friends

"The philosopher Tseng said, 'The Superior Man on grounds of culture meets with his friends, and by their friendship helps love (*Jen*).' " (*The Analects*, 12,24)

"The Master said, 'It is love (*Jen*) which constitutes the excellence of a neighbourhood.' " (*The Analects*, 4,1)

c) Through carefulness in daily life and manner

"Fan Ch'ih asked about love (*Jen*). The Master said 'It is, in retirement, to be sedately grave; in management of business, to be reverently attentive; in intercourse with others, to be strictly sincere.' " (*The Analects*, 13,19)

"Chung Kung asked about love (*Jen*). The Master said, 'It is, when you go abroad, to behave to every one as if you were receiving a great guest; to employ the people as if you were assisting at a great sacrifice. . . .' " (*The Analects*, 12,2)

d) Through carefulness in speech

"Ssu-ma Niu asked about love (*Jen*). The Master said, 'The man of love (*Jen*) is cautious and slow in his speech.' 'Cautious and slow in his speech!' said Niu,—'is this what is meant by love (*Jen*)?' The Master said, 'When a man feels the difficulty of doing, can he be other than cautious and slow in speaking?' " (*The Analects*, 12,3)

"The Master said, 'Fine words and an insinuating appearance are seldom associated with love *(Jen).*' " *(The Analects,* 1,3)

e) Through obeying the rules of proper conduct *(Li)*

"Yen Yuan asked about love *(Jen).* The Master said, 'To subdue one's self and return to the rules of proper conduct *(Li)* is love *(Jen).* . . .' Yen Yuan said, 'I beg to ask the steps of that process.' The Master replied, 'Look not at what is contrary to *Li;* listen not to what is contrary to *Li;* speak not what is contrary to *Li;* make no movement which is contrary to *Li.*' " *(The Analects,* 12,1)

f) Through personal desire and determination

"The Master said, 'Is love *(Jen)* a thing remote? I wish to have love *(Jen),* and lo! love is at hand.' " *(The Analects,* 7,29)

"The Master said, 'If the will be set on love *(Jen),* there will be no practice of wickedness.' " *(The Analects,* 6,4)

g) Through courage and self-sacrifice

"Men of love *(Jen)* are sure to be courageous." *(The Analects,* 14,5)

"The Master said, 'The determined scholar and the man of love *(Jen)* will not seek to live at the expense of injuring their love *(Jen).* They will even sacrifice their lives to preserve their love *(Jen)* complete.' " *(The Analects,* 15,8)

h) Through loving all people, especially one's parents and elder brothers

"Fan Ch'ih asked about love *(Jen).* The Master said, 'It is to love all men.' " *(The Analects,* 12,22,1)

"Filial piety and fraternal submission!—are they not the root of love *(Jen)*?" *(The Analects,* 1,2,2)

i) Through subduing one's self

"Yen Yuan asked about love *(Jen).* The Master said, 'To subdue one's self and respond to the rules of proper conduct *(Li),* is love. . . .' " *(The Analects,* 12,1)

"Confucius said, 'There are three things which the Superior Man guards against. In youth, when the physical powers are not yet settled, he guards against lust. When he is strong and physical powers are full of vigour, he guards against quarrelsomeness. When he is old, and the animal powers are decayed, he guards against covetousness.' " *(The Analects,* 16,8)

j) Through performing good deeds for the benefit of others

"Tzu Chang asked Confucius about love (*Jen*). Confucius said, 'To be able to practice five things everywhere under heaven constitutes love (*Jen*).' He begged to ask what they were, and was told, 'Reverence, generosity, sincerity, earnestness, and kindness. . . .'" (*The Analects*, 17,6)

"The Master said. . . . 'Now the man of love (*Jen*), wishing to be established himself, seeks also to establish others; wishing to be enlightened himself, he seeks also to enlighten others. (*The Analects*, 6,28,2)

Mencius, however, in advocating his theory that human nature is good, held that "love (*Jen*) is man's mind". (*Mencius*, 6,1,11,1) "All things are already complete within us," he said. "There is no greater delight than to find sincerity (*Ch'eng*) when one examines oneself". (*Mencius*, 7,1,4) This method of seeking love (*Jen*) within oneself through self-examination was very much exemplified by the idealistic philosophers of the Sung and Ming dynasties, especially the followers of Lu Chiu-yuan (A.D. 1139-1192) and Wang Yang-ming (A.D. 1473-1529). They believed that all men originally possess an "intuitive knowledge" (*liang chih*),[46] if they only examined their own selves and followed that knowledge, they would always act according to love (*Jen*) and never fall into error under any circumstances. Confucius, however, never preached that doctrine himself. He maintained that love (*Jen*) is something that needs effort to acquire through various human experiences.

2. The rules of Proper Conduct (*Li*)

Li was another favourite subject taught by Confucius. This word (*Li*) appears seventy-one times in *The Analects*. In the Spring and Autumn Period of 241 years, *Li* was practically the supreme standard of judgment for all political, social and individual affairs. It appears, as mentioned above, 489 times in *Tso Chuan* alone. The following are some quotations from *Tso Chuan*, to show some of the conceptions of leading men at the time of Confucius, with regard to *Li*, the rules of proper conduct.

In the 21st year of Duke Hsiang 552 B.C., Shu Hsiang[47] said, "The rules of proper conduct (*Li*) are the vehicles of government. . . .

		Book subtotal		£7.95
		VAT	0	
		Cassette Subtotal		
		VAT	17.5	
		SUB TOTAL		£7.95
		P & P		£0.85
		VAT for P&P	17.5	£0.15
		GRAND TOTAL (£)		**£8.95**
		Including VAT Total		**£0.15**

England No. 1934628   Registered office as above

OK CO. (UK) LTD

ational Book Trading Corporation
Britannia Way, London NW10 7PA, UK
Fax: **(020) 84530709**
com visit www.cypressbooks.com

OICE

Deliver To:

CREDIT TERM 30 days
SUPPLIER NO.
PAGE   1/1

TITLE	REMARK	PRICE	DISC(%)	
cher	completed	7.95	0	£7.95

When *Li* is dishonoured, government is lost."

In the 4th year of Duke Chao, 538 B.C., Chiao Chu[48] said to the Duke of Ch'u, "I have heard that with the different states the thing which regulates their preference and adhesion is the *Li* which is observed by them. Your lordship has now got it for the first time, and must be careful with your *Li*."

In the 5th year of Duke Chao, 537 B.C., Shu Ch'i[49] distinguished between *I* or deportment,[50] and *Li*. About *Li*, he said, "*Li* is that by which a ruler maintains his state, carries out his governmental orders, and does not lose his people. . . . The beginning and end of *Li* should be these matters." So when a state is badly governed, like that of Lu, its ruler cannot be called one who "knows *Li*".

In the 6th year of Duke Chao, 536 B.C., Shu Hsiang[51] expressed his preference of *Li* to the written laws of punishment, saying: "When a people know what the exact laws are, they do not stand in awe of their superiors. They also come to have a contentious spirit, and make their appeal to the express words, hoping peradventure to be successful in their argument. They can no longer be managed. . . . *The Book of Poetry* (4,1 Ode 7) says,

'*I imitate, follow, and observe the virtue of King Wen,*
And daily there is tranquility in all the regions';

and again (3,1, Ode 1,7),

'*Take your pattern from King Wen,*
And the myriad states will repose confidence in you.'

In such a condition, what need is there for any code? When once the people know the grounds for contention, they will cast *Li* away, and make their appeal to your descriptions. They will be contending about a matter as small as the point of an awl or a knife. Disorderly litigations will multiply, and bribes will walk abroad. Cheng will go to ruin, it is feared, in the succeeding age."

In the 7th year of Duke Chao, 534 B.C., Meng Hsi Tzu[52] said, "A knowledge of *Li* is the stem of a man. Without it, it is impossible for him to stand firm."

In the 15th year of Duke Chao, 527 B.C., Shu Hsiang said, "When a death that should be mourned for three years has occurred, even the noblest (Son of Heaven) should, according to *Li*, complete the mourning for it. . . . *Li* is the king's great canons (*Ta Ching*)".[53]

In the 25th year of Duke Chao, 517 B.C., Chao Tzu[54] said, "Without *Li*, he is sure to come to ruin."

In the 25th year of Duke Chao, 517 B.C., Tzu Ta Shu[55] had an interview with Chao Chien Tzu,[56] and was asked about the *Li* of bowing, yielding precedence, and moving from one position to another. "These", said Tzu Ta Shu, "are matters of deportment (*I*),[57] and not of *Li*." "Allow me to ask", said Chien Tzu, "What we are to understand by *Li*." The reply was, "I have heard our late great officer, Tzu Chan[58] say, '*Li* constitute the warp of Heaven, the principle of Earth, and the conduct of the people.' Heaven and Earth have their regular ways, and men take these for their pattern, imitating the brilliant bodies of Heaven, and according with the natural diversities of the Earth. . . ."

In the 26th year of Duke Chao, 516 B.C., An P'ing Chung[59] said to the Marquis of Ch'i: "By *Li*, the boundaries of a family cannot extend to all the state. Sons must not change the business of their fathers—husbandry, some mechanical art, or trade; scholars must not be negligent; officers must not be insolent; great officers must not take to themselves the privileges of the ruler." "Good," said the Marquis, "I am not able to attain to this; but henceforth I know how a state can be governed by the rules of proper conduct (*Li*)." "Long have those rules possessed such a virtue," was the reply. "Their rise was contemporaneous with that of Heaven and Earth. That the ruler order and the subject obey, the father be kind and the son dutiful, the elder brother loving and the younger respectful, the husband be harmonious and the wife gentle, the mother-in-law be kind and the daughter-in-law obedient; these are things in *Li*. That the ruler in ordering order nothing against the right, and the subject obey with any duplicity; that the father be kind and at the same time be able to teach, and the son be filial and at the same time be able to learn; the elder brother, while loving, be friendly, and the young docile, while respectful; that the husband be righteous, while harmonious, and the wife correct, while gentle;

that the mother-in-law be condescending, while kind, and the daughter-in-law be winning, while obedient; these are excellent things in *Li*." "Good," said the Marquis, "Henceforth I have heard the highest style of *Li*." An Tzu replied, "It was what the ancient kings received from Heaven and Earth for the government of the people, and therefore they ranked it in the highest place."

In the 15th year of Duke Ting, 495 B.C., Tzu Kung[60] said, "*Li* embodies the principle of death or life, existence or destruction, and can be brought about through one's turning right or left, proceeding or receding, looking down or looking up."

Confucius was living in the period when *Li* was still holding its supreme authority over all political, social and individual problems. He had been born and brought up in the State of Lu where the *Li* of the early Chou period was most carefully preserved and practiced. When he was a child, it was recorded in *Shih Chi* that "he used to play at making sacrificial offerings and performing the ceremonies." ("The Life of Confucius")[61] At fifteen years of age, when his "mind was set on learning", he began to study very extensively the *Li* of different dynasties, for example, of Hsia, Shang and Chou. He said, "The Yin (Shang) Dynasty following the *Li* of Hsia: wherein it took from or added to them may be known. Chou has followed the *Li* of Yin: wherein it took from or added to them may be known." (*The Analects*, 2,23) He was famous in his days as the man who "knew *Li*.[62] (*Tso Chuan* under the 10th year of Duke Ting; *The Analects*, 3,15) With his environment, his natural inclination, and his learning, it is only natural that he should have dwelt so much on *Li*. Being versed in the *Li* of his days, its development, its merits and defects, he was able not only to transmit to his disciples the best of the *Li* that existed during his time, but also to give new meaning, and interpretations of the real significance of many of the traditionally accepted rules of proper conduct (*Li*). Traditionally, *Li* was generally regarded as the restraint placed by the rules of society upon the individual. Confucius recognized the importance of such restraint in his days, and chiefly on that, he built up his famous doctrine the Rectification of Names. But the greatest contribution which Confucius gave to *Li* was his new emphasis which he placed upon the personal aspect and value of his teaching on *Li*. Both social and individual aspects were equally emphasized.

(a) *Li* as social regulations

a) Necessary for everybody to know and obey *Li* as social regulations

He agreed perfectly with Meng Hsi Tzu, as recorded in *Tso Chuan*, that "a knowledge of *Li* is the stem of a man. Without it, it is impossible for him to stand firm."

"The Master said, "Without a knowledge of *Li*, it is impossible for a man to stand firm.' " (*The Analects*, 20,2; 16,13,3)

"The Master said, 'Respectfulness, without *Li*, becomes laborious bustle; carefulness, without *Li*, becomes timidity; boldness, without *Li*, becomes insubordination; straightforwardness, without *Li*, becomes rudeness.' " (*The Analects*, 8,2,1)

One of the important functions of *Li* was, according to Confucius, the restraint placed by social regulations, or the rules of proper conduct recognized by society, upon the individual. So Yen Yuan, the most favoured disciple of Confucius, said in admiration of the teaching of his master, ". . . He enlarged my mind with learning, and taught me the restraints of *Li*. . . ." (*The Analects*, 9,10)

"The Master said, 'By extensively studying all learning, and keeping himself under the restraint of *Li*, one may thus likewise not err from what is right.' " (*The Analects*, 12,15)

"The Master said, 'The Superior Man, extensively studying all learning, and keeping himself under the restraint of *Li*, may thus likewise not overstep what is right.' " (*The Analects*, 6,25)

"The Master said, 'Look not at what is contrary to *Li*; listen not to what is contrary to *Li*; speak not what is contrary to *Li*; make no movement which is contrary to *Li*.' " (*The Analects*, 12,1,2)

b) Necessary for the government to act according to *Li*

Confucius agreed entirely with Shu Hsiang, as recorded in *Tso Chuan*, when he said, "*Li* is the vehicles of government. . . . When *Li* is dishonoured, government is lost."

"The Master said, 'The management of a state demands *Li*.' " (*The Analects*, 11,25,10)

"The Master said, 'Is a prince able to govern his kingdom with the complaisance proper to *Li*, what difficulty will he have? If he cannot govern it with that complaisance, what has he to do with *Li*?' " (*The Analects*, 4,13)

c) Better and more effective as compared with laws and punishments

Confucius had full sympathy again with Shu Hsiang regarding *Li* as being much better and more effective social regulations than laws and punishments. In 536 B.C. Shu Hsiang said, "When a people know what the exact laws are, they do not stand in awe of their superiors. They also come to have a contentious spirit. . . ." A few years later Confucius spoke in much the same tone:

"If the people be led by laws, and uniformity sought to be given them by punishments, they will try to avoid the punishment, but have no sense of shame. If they be led by virtue, and uniformity sought to be given them by *Li*, they will have the sense of shame and moreover will become good." (*The Analects*, 2,3)

d) *Li* as the chief factor in the doctrine of the Rectification of Names

Confucius regarded the Rectification of Names as the first thing he would do if he had the chance of administering the government. It was most essential in any successful government.

"Tzu Lu said, 'The ruler of Wei had been waiting for you, in order with you to administer the government. What will you consider the first thing to be done?' The Master replied, 'What is necessary is to rectify names. . . . If names be not correct, language is not in accordance with the truth of things. If language be not in accordance with the truth of things, business cannot be carried on with success. When business cannot be carried on with success *Li* and Music will not flourish. When *Li* and Music do not flourish, punishments will not be properly awarded. When punishments are not properly awarded, the people do not know how to move hand or foot.' " (*The Analects*, 13,3)

By the Rectification of Names, he meant that everything should be in its proper order, and every man should be true to his name and act accordingly. For example, a son should act as a son, a father as a father, a king as a king, and a minister as a minister. So when Duke Ching of Ch'i asked Confucius about government, Confucius answered:

"There is government, when the prince is prince, and the minister is minister; when the father is father, and the son is son." (*The Analects*, 12,11)

This doctrine of rectification was fully worked out in *The Spring and Autumn Annals*, which was supposed to be written, or at least edited, by Confucius.

The rules of proper conduct, which regulate every person according to his name, are called *Li*. Supposing the proper conduct of a father is to be kind to his son, and that of the son is to be filial to his father, if the father is not kind, and the son not filial, they would be counted by Confucius as not acting according to *Li* or the rules of proper conduct.

This idea of rectification of names through *Li* was by no means originated by Confucius. An P'ing Chung, in 516 B.C., as mentioned above, gave a very clear statement concerning the same doctrine, as recorded in *Tso Chuan* under the 26th year of Duke Chao. As a matter of fact, the whole feudal system was largely maintained through *Li*. When *Li* was disregarded, the whole feudal system collapsed.

(b) *Li* as the expression of personal feeling or desire

As above mentioned, the greatest contribution of Confucius with regard to *Li* was his emphasis put upon the value of personality, at a time when the restraints, placed by the regulations of society upon the individual were so overwhelming that individual personality, in general, was crushed or sadly neglected. So Confucius, in dealing with the problem of *Li*, not only transmitted the best of the traditional idea of the social values of *Li*, but also gave new meanings to *Li* by laying stress upon the value of personality, —that individual freedom should be respected, and that the sincerity of individual desires should be taken as the foundation of *Li*.

a) Sincerity as the foundation of *Li*

The following conversation between Confucius and his disciple Tzu Hsia, as recorded in *The Analects*, gives a clear account of the subordination of *Li* to the sincere genuineness of human nature. The beauty of *Li* is only secondary to the natural beauty of human character.

Tzu Hsia asked, "What is the meaning of:

> *'Her cunning smiles,*
> *Her dimples light,*
> *Her lovely eyes,*
> *So clear and bright,*
> *All unadorned,*
> *The background white.'?* (*Shih Ching*, 1,5,3)"

"Colouring," said the Master, "is second to the plain ground." "Then *Li* is a subsequent thing," said Tzu Hsia. "Shang (Tzu Hsia)," said the Master, "thou hast hit my meaning! Now I can talk poetry with thee." (*The Analects*, 3,8)

Confucius here means that aesthetics and ethics are one, both presupposing a plain background. A man must first have a plain beautiful nature of sincere genuineness before he may practise *Li*, just as a beautiful woman must first have a "cunning smile" and "lovely eyes", before she may make use of any artificial adornment. If not, *Li* would be a false and empty form, and as such not worthy of being prized, but actually ugly and cheapening. Therefore Confucius said, "If a man be without love (Jen), what has he to do with *Li*?" (*The Analects*, 3,3) And it was the same reason why Confucius esteemed the personal feeling of reverence or sincerity as the most essential in the rules of proper conduct (*Li*), such as, in sacrificing, mourning, etc.

"The Master said, '. . . *Li* performed without reverence; mourning conducted without sorrow;—wherewith should I contemplate such ways?' " (*The Analects*, 3,26)

". . . In sacrificing, his thoughts are reverential. In mourning, his thoughts are about the grief which he should feel. Such a man commands our approbation indeed." (*The Analects*, 19,1)

"Tzu Yu said, 'Mourning should be carried on with grief, and should stop with it.' " (*The Analects*, 19,14)

"Lin Fang asked what was the first thing to be attended to in *Li*.

The Master said, 'A great question indeed! . . . In the ceremonies of mourning, it is better that there be deep sorrow than a minute attention to observances.' " (*The Analects*, 3,4)

b) Individual freedom respected in observing *Li*

When Confucius laid stress upon what the foundation of *Li* was, the sincerity of individual nature or feeling, he was emphasizing the independence and freedom of the individual. *Li* existed primarily for man and not man for *Li*. Personal economy, conscience, and the natural poise of every individual should be taken as some of the criteria of practising the rules of proper conduct (*Li*).

a. Personal economy as a criterion of practicing *Li*

"Lin Fang asked what was the first thing to be attended to in *Li*. The Master said, 'A great question indeed! In *Li* it is better to be sparing than extravagant. In the ceremonies of mourning, it is better that there be deep sorrow than a minute attention to observances.' " (*The Analects*, 3,4)

"The Master said, 'The linen cap is that prescribed by the rules of proper conduct (*Li*), but now a silk one is worn. It is economical, and I follow the common practice.' " (*The Analects*, 9,3)

When Yen Yuan, the favourite disciple of Confucius, died, the other disciples wished to give him a great funeral, but Confucius disapproved of the idea, because he thought that would cost too much money. (*The Analects*, 11,10)

b. Personal conscience as a criterion of carrying out *Li*

"Tsai Wo asked about the three years' mourning for parents, saying that one year was long enough. . . . The Master said, 'If you were, after a year, to eat good rice, and wear embroidered clothes would you feel at ease (in your conscience)?' 'I should,' replied Wo. The Master said, 'If you can feel at ease, do it. But a Superior Man, during the whole period of mourning, does not enjoy pleasant food which he may eat, nor derive pleasure from music which he may hear. He also does not feel at ease, if he is comfortably lodged. Therefore he does not do what you propose. But now you feel at ease (in your conscience) you may do it.' " (*The Analects*, 17,21)

c. Personal natural poise or comfort as a criterion of practising *Li*

"In practising the rules of proper conduct (*Li*), a natural poise (or comfort) is to be prized. In the ways prescribed by the ancient kings, this is the excellent quality, and in things small and great we follow them. Yet it is not to be observed in all cases. If one, knowing how much poise should be prized, manifests it, without regulating it by *Li*, this likewise is not to be done." (*The Analects,* 1,12)

In short, *Li* was not regarded as some lifeless rules, which imposed restrictions upon the individual irrespective of his condition and freedom, but rather they were conditioned by his economic conditions, his conscience, and his comfort. Indeed, what better safe-guards could a man have against the autocratic oppression of social regulations, or customs, upon his individual freedom or independence, than such principles which Confucius laid down, as, "If you can feel at ease do it"; "In *Li*, it is better to be sparing than extravagant"; "It is better that there be deep sorrow (sincerity) than a minute attention to observances."

The individual aspect of the teaching of Confucius on *Li* was emphasized by Mencius, while the social or traditional aspect of his teaching was very much exemplified by Hsun-tzu.

3. Filial Piety, *Hsiao*[64]

"Oh my father, who begot me!
Oh my mother, who nourished me!
Ye indulged me, ye fed me,
Ye helped me up, ye supported me,
Ye looked after me, ye never left me,
Out and in ye bore me in your arms.
If I would return your kindness,
It is like great Heaven, illimitable."
(*The Book of Poetry,* 2,5,8,4)

Chinese people, from the very beginning of their history, have manifested a deep sense of filial piety. Confucius was a great transmitter and interpreter of this important traditional virtue.

(a) Filial piety as the root of moving force of all virtues

Filial piety has a very much wider significance in Chinese ethics than it has in that of other peoples. It is the root of all virtues, and serves as the moving force for action in accordance with moral standards. It permeates all virtues, and gives life and strength for their translation into actions. It breeds a sense of family honour and love, very near to that of genuine religious belief. As a matter of fact, the Chinese word for teaching or religion (*Chiao*)[64] is derived from the word for filial piety,[65] being written with the character for filial piety plus a causative radical.[66] So the whole word,[67] *Chiao*, according to its component derivatives, simply means "to make filial", and that is the word for religion. It shares with religion much of the emotional feeling or passion which, as Matthew Arnold puts it, would "light up morality", and give warmth to cold moral concepts. If a man really loves his parents, no matter whether they are dead or still alive, he would, according to Confucius and his followers, be a dutiful member in his family, and a good citizen in society, for thereby the name of his parents would be honoured. On the contrary, the man who fails to carry out his obligations as a son, a husband, a father, and a member of society thereby dishonours his parents and thus commits a breach of filial piety. "The Master said, 'Those who love their parents dare not show hatred to others. Those who respect their parents, dare not show rudeness to others.' " (*The Book of Filial Piety*, Chap. on T'ien Tzu)[68] "The philosopher Yu said, 'They are few who, being filial and fraternal, are fond of offending against their superiors. There have been none, who, not liking to offend against their superiors, have been fond of stirring up confusion.' " (*The Analects*, 1,2,1) In this sense Confucius could say to Tseng Tzu, his disciple:

"Filial piety is the root of virtue, and the origin of culture. Sit down again, and let me tell you. The body and hair and skin are received from the parents, and may not be injured: this is the beginning of filial piety. To establish oneself and walk according to the right Way (*Tao*), in order to glorify one's parents: this is the culmination of filial piety. Filial piety begins with serving one's parents, leads to serving one's king, and ends in establishing oneself. . . ." (*The Book of Filial Piety*, Chap. 1, K'ai Tsung Ming I)[69]

Filial piety is the root of love (Jen)—the greatest and all-embracing virtue:

"The Superior Man bends his attention to what is radical. That being established, all practical courses naturally grow up. Filial piety and fraternal submission!—are they not the root of love (*Jen*)?" (*The Analects*, 1,2,2)

Indeed, a filial son would, to put it in Biblical terms, "love his neighbour as himself."

a) Love of oneself

A son is unfilial if through vice, neglects, or other avoidable cause he falls into ill-health or meets with bodily disaster; because his body, having been received from his parents, must, out of respect for them, be treated with the utmost care.

"The body and hair and skin are received from the parents and may not be injured." (*The Book of Filial Piety, Hsiao Ching*)[70]

"Meng Wu Po asked what filial piety was. The Master said, 'Parents are anxious lest their children should be sick.' " (*The Analects*, 2,6)

"Tseng Tzu being ill, he called to him the disciples of his school, and said, 'Uncover my feet, uncover my hands. It is said in *The Book of Poetry*, "We should be apprehensive and cautious, as if on the brink of a deep gulf, as if treading on thin ice", and so have I been. Now and hereafter, I know my escape from all injury to my person. O ye, my little children.' " (*The Analects*, 8,3)

b) Love of others

A son is unfilial if he commits a crime or if he does not love others through his beneficial deeds, because, by rendering himself liable to legal penalty, he had brought disgrace upon his parents, or by not performing any good deed in society, he has not glorified the names of his parents through his loving actions.

"To develop oneself and walk according to the right Way (*Tao*), in order to glorify one's parents: this is the culmination of filial piety." (*The Book of Filial Piety*, Chap. 1)

"Some one addressed Confucius, saying, 'Sir, why are you not engaged in the government?' The Master said, 'What does *Shu Ching* say of filial piety?'—"You are filial, you discharge your brotherly duties. These qualities are displayed in government." This then also constitutes the function of government. Why must there be that—to make one be in the government?' " (*The Analects*, 2,21)

"They are few who being filial and fraternal are fond of offending against their superiors." (*The Analects*, 1,2)

Mr. Yung-chi Hoe, a modern contemporary Chinese sociologist, sums up the virtue of filial piety in the following words:

"Filial piety is the alpha and omega of his (Confucius) ethics. It includes and logically presupposes every other virtue under heaven. Thus, honesty, justice, courage, self-control, modesty and loyalty, all come under the single rubric of devotion to parents." (*China Critic*, Vol. 3, No. 43)

(b) The ways of being filial to one's parents

"As Fan Ch'ih was driving him, the Master told him, saying, 'Meng Sun asked me what filial piety was, and I answered him, —"not being disobedient." ' Fan Chih said, 'What did you mean?' The Master replied, 'That parents, when alive, should be served according to *Li*; that, when dead, they should be buried according to *Li*; and that they should be sacrificed to according to *Li*.' " (the Analects 2, 5, 2-3; *Mencius*, 3,1,2,2)

"The Master said, '...Serve the dead as you serve the living; serve the departed as you serve those present....' " (*The Doctrine of the Mean*, 19,5)

The ways of being filial to one's parents, according to the above quotations, can be summarized under two headings, namely, to serve them according to *Li* when they are alive, and to serve them according to *Li* when they are dead.

a) To serve parents according to *Li* when they are alive

How should one serve one's parents according to *Li* when they are alive? The answer is, to state it briefly, to obey them and "nourish their will".

a. To obey one's parents

"Meng I Tzu asked what filial piety was. The Master said, 'It is not being disobedient.' " (*The Analects*, 2,5,1)

To obey does not mean to obey undoncitionally or to yield unreasonably. Chucius, commented on the above statement by Confucius, saying, " 'not being disobedient' means not to act contrary to reason". There is a place for reasoning in the act of obedience to one's parents. "The Master said, 'In serving his parents, a son may remonstrate with them, but gently; when he sees that they do not incline to follow his advice, he shows an increased degree of reverence, but does not abandon his purpose; and should they punish him, he does not allow himself to murmur.' " (*The Analects*, 4,18) If to obey means to yield unconditionally, then there would be no place for remonstrance. What Confucius meant by "not being disobedient" is that, if it is right to obey the will of one's parents, then obey them, if it is not right, then remonstrate with them gently. The record of Elder Tai on *Li* says:

"If the conduct of your parents is in accordance with the right Way (*Tao*), then obey them. If their conduct is not in accordance with the right Way (*Tao*), then remonstrate with them. If they do not accept the remonstrance, then act upon their will as if it were your own will. To obey them without remonstrance is unfilial; to remonstrate with them without obeying them is also unfilial." (*Ta Tai Li*, chap. entitled "Serving one's parents")[71]

If the parents do not follow the advice of their sons, according to Elder Tai, the sons should give in and obey the will of their parents. But they should remonstrate again and again, until their parents are converted, like Shun did to his obstinate father. That is what Elder Tai meant when he said, "To remonstrate gently without being tired out."[72] (*Ta Tai Li*, chap. entitled "To establish filial piety")[73] Chucius, in commenting upon the three unfilial things mentioned by Mencius (*Mencius*, 4,1,26,1), said, "To obey unreasonably and flatteringly, thereby to involve one's parents in unrighteousness is unfilial." So to displease one's parents temporarily by remonstrance is better than to please them by flattering assent, if the final result would be good to the parents. This is why Confucius gave the advice to the son that "when he sees that his parents do not incline to follow his advice, he should show an increased degree of reverence, but should not abandon his purpose" until his parents are converted.

Hence family depotism, with all the evils resulting from it, such as the belief that "if a father wants his son to die, the son cannot do otherwise but go to die", is really a later development of

Confucianism, especially in the Han period, and is not in accordance with the spirit of Confucius himself and his earlier disciples.

　　b. To nourish the will of one's parents

　　The phrase "to nourish the will"[74] comes from Mencius, in comparison with his physical nourishment—"nourishing the mouth and body" ( ).[75]

　　"Mencius said,' . . . Tseng Tzu, in nourishing Tseng Shih, was always sure to have wine and flesh provided. And when they were being removed, he would ask respectfully to whom he should give what was left. If his father asked whether there was anything left, he was sure to say, "There is". After the death of Tseng Shih, when Tseng Yuan came to nourish Tseng Tzu, he was always sure to have wine and flesh provided. But when the things were being removed, he did not ask to whom he should give what was left, and if his father asked whether there was anything left he would answer "No";—intending to bring them in again. This was what is called—"nourishing the mouth and body". We may call Tseng Tzu's practice—"nourishing the will". To serve one's parents as Tseng Tzu served his may be accepted as filial piety.' " (Mencius, 4,1,19,3-4)

　　By "nourishing the will" of one's parents, one should act in accordance with their will; negatively, one should not let them worry; positively, one should "establish oneself and walk according to the right Way (Tao), in order to glorify one's parents".

　　A son should not worry his parents, such as:

　　Parents are anxious lest their children should be sick." (The Analects, 2,6)

　　"While his parents are alive, the son may not go abroad to a distance. If he does go abroad, he must have a fixed place to which he goes." (The Analects, 4,19)

　　A son should be faithful to his parents and glorify their names.

　　"To establish oneself and walk according to the right Way (Tao) in order to glorify one's parents: this is the culmination of filial piety.

　　"The Master said, 'While a man's father is alive, look at the bent of his will; when his father is dead, look at his conduct. If for three years he does not alter from the way of his father, he may be called filial.' " (*The Analects*, 1,11)

c. Reverence as the basis of filial piety

To obey one's parents and nourish their will would amount to nothing, if they are not done with reverence or sincerity. Here again the motive of one's action is emphasized.

"Tzu Yu asked what filial piety was. The Master said, 'The filial piety of nowadays means the support of one's parents. But dogs and horses likewise are able to do something in the way of support; —without reverence, what is there to distinguish the one support given from the other?' " (*The Analects*, 2,7)

"Tzu Hsia asked what filial piety was. The Master said, 'The difficulty is with the countenance. If, when their elders have any troublesome affairs, the young take the toil of them, and if, when the young have wine and food, they set them before their elders, is this to be considered filial piety?' " (*The Analects*, 2,8)

Here Confucius shows very clearly the difference between his teaching about filial piety and the traditional teaching of his days. "The filial piety of nowadays means the support of one's parents", but he said, to support one's parents, or give them labour and wine and food, is meaningless if it is not done with reverence or sincerity, which will certainly appear in one's countenance. Reverence is the thing which distinguishes the filial piety of a man from that of a lower animal, such as a dog or a horse. It is the basis of the filial piety of human beings.

b) To serve one's parents according to *Li* when they are dead

Confucius said when one's parents are dead, "they should be buried according to *Li*, and be sacrificed to according to *Li*" (*The Analects*, 2,5,3); and they should be served as if they were still alive. (*The Doctrine of the Mean*, 19,5)

a. Burial rituals

There were detailed regulations concerning burial rituals as handed down from the remote past in Chinese history. They were often carried out with great pomp and extravagance. Confucianism was sometimes criticized, as early as the fourth century B.C., for its "burial rituals being too extravagant and tending to impoverish the people." (See *Huai Nan Tzu*, Chap. 21) But the great principle which Confucius laid down was, "it is better to be sparing than extravagant . . . it is better that there should be deep sorrow than a minute attention to observances." (*The Analects*, 3,4) So the extravagance of Confucian burial rituals should be attributed more to the long traditional practices before and during the time of Confucius, rather than to the actual teaching of Confucius.

b. Three years mourning

The practice of the three years mourning for the death of one's parents also dated back to very ancient Chinese history. For example, it is recorded in *The Book of History* that when King Yao (traditionally 2357-2358 B.C.) died, "People mourned for him three years, as if for the death of their own parents." (*Shu Ching*, "Shun Tien")[76] *Tso Chuan*, under the 15th year of Duke Chao, 527 B.C., records this saying of Shu Hsiang, "When a death that should be mourned for three years has occurred, even the noblest (the king) should, according to *Li*, complete the mourning for it." Confucianism was again severely attacked, especially by Micius and his followers, that its "unnecessarily long period of mourning (three years) was injurious both to the vitality of men and the normal conduct of business". (*Huai Nan Tzu*, Chap. 21) The same problem was brought up by one of the disciples of Confucius, and the attitude of Confucius towards that case was very striking, and, in a sense, revolutionary. He did not stick to the much-honoured ancient practices but rather left the whole matter to the individual conscience for decision. If one felt that his conscience did not blame him, then the mourning for three years could be shortened even to but one year. The following is the important conversation between Confucius and this disciple, which makes clear the nature of mourning and the attitude of Confucius thereto:

"Tsai Wo asked about the three year's mourning for parents, saying that one year was long enough. 'If the Superior Man,' said he 'abstains for three years from the observances of *Li*, *Li* will be quite lost. If for three years he abstains from music, music will be ruined. Within a year the old grain is exhausted, and the new grain has sprung up, and, in procuring fire by friction, we go through all the changes of wood for that purpose. After a complete year, the mourning may stop.' The Master said, 'If you were, after a year, to eat good rice, and wear embroidered clothes, would you feel at ease?' 'I should', replied Wo. The Master said, 'If you can feel at ease, do it. But a Superior Man, during the whole period of mourning, does not enjoy pleasant food which he may eat, nor derive pleasure from music which he may hear. He also does not feel at ease, if he is comfortably lodged. Therefore he does not do what you propose. But now you feel at ease and may do it.' " (*The Analects*, 17,21)

c. Ancestor worship

Ancestor worship has a very long history in the development of Chinese culture. In the Shang and early Chou period, both the Supreme Being and the spirits of departed ancestors were worshipped. The spirits of ancestors were supposed to be agents of God to carry out the divine will, and to interfere actively in the affairs of their descendants. To Confucius and other Chinese thinkers, both ancient and modern, ancestorworship has a practical or utilitarian as well as a religious or spiritual aspect, and is consciously and deliberately maintained as a method whereby a Chinese family not only shows its reverence or respect for its departed forefathers, but also maintains the continuity of its traditions, strengthens its ties with its scattered members and collateral branches, and safeguards the material interests of its descendants. This will be discussed more fully in the section on the religious teaching of Confucius. It suffices to mention here that Confucius was much interested in such a cult of ancestors, and he advised that it should be carefully carried on according to the prescribed rules of proper conduct (*Li*). (*The Analects*, 2,5,3) Again the most important thing in such worship was, according to Confucius, not the external "minute attention to observances", but rather the internal or mental mood of reverence.

"He sacrificed to the dead, as if they were present. He sacrificed to the spirits, as if the spirits were present. The Master said, 'I consider my not being present at the sacrifice, as if I did not sacrifice.' " (*The Analects*, 3,12)

"The Master said . . . '. . . Respect spiritual beings, but keep aloof from them. . . .' " (*The Analects*, 6,20)

"In sacrificing, the thoughts of the scholar are reverential. In mourning, his thoughts are about the grief which he should feel." (*The Analects*, 19,1)

d. To carry out the will of departed ancestors

"The Master said, '. . . Now filial piety is seen in the skilful carrying out of the wishes of our forefathers, and the skilful carrying forward of their undertakings. . . .' " (*The Doctrine of the Mean*, 19,2)

(c) The place of filial piety in modern society

This all-embracing virtue, filial piety, which had been greatly honoured in all ages, before the Republican Revolution of 1911, has now been seriously questioned and criticized. Most of the criticisms may be grouped under the following headings: a) There has been a traditional association between filial piety and loyalty to a sovereign; b) the doctrine of filial piety has had much to do with family autocracy and all its evil results; and c) It tends to make the family absorb much of the loyalty and devotion that should be given to larger groups, social and national. Much of the criticism is, no doubt, true to facts, for the virtue of filial piety has been very often very much distorted and abused. But if we go back to the original teaching of Confucius, or to that of his immediate disciples, we find that many of the evils which have been attributed to the mask of filial piety may be eliminated. Liang Ch'i-ch'ao, an outstanding modern Chinese thinker, and a Confucian scholar, thinks that the logical result of the doctrine of filial piety should be that "all mankind is but one large family", and if rightly understood, such a doctrine should be a strong moving force towards the realization of the universal brotherhood of man. He says:

"The family group underlies the whole fabric of society. Each smaller group is gathered up into a larger group, so that all trace their relationship to the prime ancestor. . . . Therefore, *Tso Chuan* says, 'The way of men is to love one's relatives. Because of love for relatives, ancestors are honoured; honour for ancestors brings respect for distant relatives; respect for distant relatives brings a sense of kinship.' This family concept constitutes the fundamental basis of political organisation. When this conception is further strengthened by religious ideals, its effect is the more vigorous. . . . The logical result of such concepts is the recognition that all mankind is but one large family." (*History of Chinese Political Thought,* pp. 153-155)

Bertrand Russell's remarks on the place of biological instincts, such as that of family love, are noteworthy:

"The harm that is done at present by biological groupings is undeniable, but I do not think the social problem can be solved by ignoring the instincts which produce those groupings. . . . Nationalism also perhaps has its place, though clearly armies and navies are an undesirable expression of it, and its proper sphere is cultural rather than political. Human beings can be greatly changed by institutions and education, but if they are changed in such a way as to thwart fundamental instincts, the result is a loss of vigour." (*Sceptical Essays,* London:1928, pp. 230-1)

Dr. J. Wilson says:

"A long experience proves that the family life is invaluable, and that, so far from being inconsistent with individual liberty or antagonistic to society, it more than anything else provides the conditions under which freedom is developed, and the strong foundations of a social state are securely laid." He warns those who "maintain that domestic unity is opposed to social unity" of the fate of Rome. "Rome in her best days", he says, "held the family life sacred; but when she violated that life, dissolute morals sapped her very foundations, and did far more than the armies of her enemies in causing the fall of the Empire. The teachings of history cannot be safely or wisely neglected. They indubitably prove that the family is essential to the State, and also to the unity of the human race." (*The Hibbert Journan,* Jan. 1923, p. 308)

Dr. Harper here refuses flatly to accept the idea that family life is "inconsistent with individual liberty or antagonistic to society", which, as pointed out above, has been the chief criticism of the Chinese family system, given by modern Chinese scholars. But the healthy family life must be maintained by right feelings of filial piety expressed by each member of the family. In one of the letters of Charles Lamb to Coleridge, we find the following words:

"Oh, my friend, cultivate the filial feelings; and let no one think himself relieved from the kind charities of relationship: these shall give him peace at the last; these are the best foundation for every species of benevolence." These words might have been written by Confucius, some twenty centuries before Charles Lamb.

4. The Doctrine of the Mean, *Chung Yung*[77]

The doctrine of *Chung Yung*, taught by Confucius and his followers, as above mentioned, has a great resemblance to the doctrine of the Mean as taught by Aristotle.

(a) The doctrine of the Mean according to Aristotle

Aristotle gives a list of principal virtues, which includes temperance, valour, generosity, and magnanimity. Each of these principal virtues stands as a Mean between two opposite vices, one being an excess and the other a deficiency. For example:

Courage is the due mean between cowardice and rashness;

Temperance is the due mean between insensibility and greed;

Liberality is the due mean between avarice and prodigality;

Modesty is the due mean between impudence and bashfulness;

Sincerity is the due mean between self-disparagement and boastfulness;

Good temper is the due mean between surliness and obsequiousness;

Just resentment is the due mean between callousness and spitefulness;

Magnanimity is the due mean between meanness of mind and pomposity.

(b) The Mean as a perfect virtue

Confucius regarded the Mean (*Chung Yung*) as the perfect virtue, and the chief trouble of his time was, according to him, that the virtue of the Mean was not properly observed.

"The Master said, 'Perfect is the virtue which is according to the Mean! Rare for a long time has been its practice among the people.' " (*The Analects*, 6,27)

"The Master said, 'Perfect is the virtue which is according to the Mean! Rare have they long been among the people, who could practice it!' " (*The Doctrine of the Mean, Chung Yung*, Chap. 3)

"The Master said, I know how it is that the path of the Mean is not walked in:—The clever go beyond it, and the stupid do not come up to it. I know how it is that the path of the Mean is not understood:—The worthy go beyond it, and the worthless do not come up to it.' " (*The Doctrine of the Mean, Chung Yung*, Chap. 4,1)

Those who overshoot their mark are just as wrong as those who fall short of it. Only those who hold the Mean are supposed to be right.

"Tzu Kung asked which of the two, Shih or Shang, was the superior. The Master said, 'Shih goes beyond the due Mean, and Shang does not come up to it.' 'Then,' said Tzu Kung, 'the superiority is with Shih, I suppose.' The Master said, 'To go beyond is as wrong as to fall short.' " (*The Analects*, 11,15)

(c) To keep to the Mean as the purpose of the teaching of Confucius

Much of the effort of Confucius in teaching his disciples was spent to keep them in the Mean. When they were too retiring and slow, he would urge them forward, and when they went too far he would keep them back. The following quotation is a good illustrations for this:

"Tzu Lu asked whether he should immediately carry into practice what he heard. The Master said, 'There are your father and elder brothers to be consulted;—why should act on that principle of immediately carrying into practice what you hear?' Jan Yu asked the same, whether he should immediately carry into practice what he heard, and the Master answered, 'Immediately carry into practice what you hear.' Kung-hsi Hua said, 'Yu asked whether he should carry immediately into practice what he hears, and you said, "There are your father and elder brothers to be consulted." Ch'iu asked whether he should immediately carry into practice what he heard, and you said, "Carry it immediately into practice". I, Ch'ih, am perplexed, and venture to ask you for an explanation.' The Master said, Ch'iu is retiring and slow; therefore, I urge him forward. Yu has more than his own share of energy; therefore, I kept him back.' " (*The Analects*, 11,21)

The chief purpose of the teaching of Confucius was, as a matter of fact, to keep to the doctrine of the Mean. All his teachings, as so far considered, were consistent with that doctrine. For example, in regard to the aim of his teaching, he did not take the extreme theories of an entirely social or an entirely individualistic aim. In his teachings on love (*Jen*), or the rules of proper conduct (*Li*), or filial piety (*Hsiao*), he emphasized both social and individual, motive and consequence, mind and action, or the acquired experiences and the innate tendencies. The chief characteristic of a Superior Man is not to be entirely concerned with the acquired form, or with the innate natural substance, but it is the "Harmony of both the acquired form and the natural substance" (*The Analects*, 6,16) "A Superior Man of the world," said Confucius, "does not insist on doing anything or abstaining from anything; he stops at what is right and proper (the Mean)." (*The Analects*, 4,10) The five excellent things of a Superior Man, as Confucius outlined them in the last book of *The Analects*, are all virtues of moderation, or the Mean:

"Tzu Chang said, 'What are meant by the five excellent things?' The Master said, 'When a Superior Man (Chung-tzu) is beneficent without great expenditure; when he lays tasks on the people without their repining; when he pursues what he desires without being covetous; when he maintains a dignified ease without being proud; when he is majestic without being fierce.' " (*The Analects*, 20,2,1)

(d) The character of Confucius as a typical example of the man who holds the doctrine of the Mean

Mencius said, "Chung (Confucius) did not do excessive things". (*Mencius*, 4,2,10)

Confucius said about himself that "with me there is no inflexible may or may not", and he acknowledged his own behaviour as different from the extremely inflexible characters of some famous ancient saints whom he mentioned. (*The Analects*, 18,8)

He never went to extremes. The four things which he was known as being entirely free from were that "he had no foregone conclusions, no arbitrary pre-determinations, no obstinacy, and no egoism". (*The Analects*, 9,4) His general manner was "mild, and yet dignified; majestic, and yet not fierce; respectful, and yet easy." (*The Analects*, 8,37)

In other words, in Confucius we have a typical example of a balanced life. Never would he be allowed to be led astray from his due course by any extreme desire or passion. He would rather be led by common sense or what is sometimes called the "play safe" policy, than by any attractive ideologies or unprofitable adventures. There were, for example, two extreme theories common in his days. On the one extreme, there was the theory which believed in absolute governmental control and interference, represented, for instance, by Kuan Chung, Tzu Ch'an and others, and later on developed into the extreme right Legalist School. On the other extreme, there were people who believed in what is called the laissez-faire policy, despising any external interference of individual matters. They were represented, for example, by Lao-tzu, or those hermits mentioned in the 18th chapter of *The Analects*, such as, Chieh Yu, Chang Chu, Chieh Ni and others, and were later on developed into the extreme left Taoist School. Confucius, being a man of moderate temperament, always adhered to the Mean. He emphasized the importance of both social control and individual freedom. He paid attention, for example, to the social rules of proper conduct (*Li*) in different ceremonies, rituals, etc., yet at the same time he laid stress on the importance of individual elements, such as, individual conscience, personal economic condition, reverence, sincerity, etc. The keeping of the doctrine of the Mean which so characterized the teaching and behaviour of Confucius, had an important influence upon the success of the Confucian School as against other more extreme rival schools, and consequently upon the general mental make-up of all Confucian Chinese, both of individuals, and of the nation as a whole.

(e) The ancient origin of the doctrine of the Mean

The doctrine of the Mean is one of the most ancient cultural heritages of the Chinese people. It is supposed to have originated in the very remote past of Chinese history, but it was much emphasized and exemplified by Confucius and his followers. All the ancient so-called Sage-kings, as recorded in the Confucian Classics, such as Yao, Shun, Yu, T'ang, Wen and Wu took the doctrine of the Mean as one of their chief political and social policies.

a) Yao

When king Yao handed on his governmental duties to his successor, King Shun, he advised him to hold fast the Golden Mean, saying,

"Oh! You, Shun, the Heaven-determined order of succession now rests in your person. Sincerely hold fast the due Mean. . . ." (*The Analects*, 20,1,1)

b) Shun

"Shun also used the same language (as Yao, as quoted above) in giving charge to Yu." (*The Analects*, 20,1,2)

"The Master said, 'There was Shun:—He indeed was greatly wise! . . . He took hold of their two extremes, determined the Mean, and employed it in his government of the people. It was by this that he was Shun.' " (*The Doctrine of the Mean*, Chap. 6)

c) Yu

He got the charge from Shun to "hold fast the due Mean." (*The Analects*, 20,1,2)

Confucius praised very much the character of Yu, saying, "I can find no flaw in the character of Yu", because he was not too simple nor too extravagant, and in his private or personal life he was generally very simple, but on public occasions he "displayed the utmost elegance" so as to ensure the dignity of his own person, and make those occasions more beautiful and inspiring. (*The Analects*, 8,21)

d) T'ang

"T'ang held fast the Mean, and employed men of talents and virtue without regard to where they came from." (*Mencius*, 4,2,20,2)

e) Wen and Wu

"To push on without relaxation: that Wen and Wu could not do. To relax without pushing on and then relax alternately: that was the way of Wen and Wu."

That is to say, they did not fall into the errors of insistent expansion or indolent relaxation, but steered safely between the two.

So Confucius was really a true heir of this long traditional heritage, the doctrine of the Mean. It was later on very much emphasized by Mencius and his school of Confucianism, so we have now the book of *The Doctrine of the Mean, Chung-Yung*, as one of the "Four Books" of Confucianism.

(B) Teaching According to Mencius and His School of Confucianism

1. Love (Jen)

One of the greatest contributions of Mencius to Confucianism is his transmission and exemplification of Confucius' teaching on love (*Jen*). It is chiefly through his effort in reiterating and systematising the doctrine of love (*Jen*), which was newly brought into prominence by Confucius, that it has become the generally accepted central doctrine of Confucianism throughout the ages. The new light which Mencius brought forward with regard to love can be grouped under three headings, namely, the origin of love, the way of securing love, and the application of love.

(a) The origin of love—the ethical Heaven or God

Although Confucius did not give a very clear statement about the origin of love or human nature in general, yet he did, according to Mencius, give certain suggestions about the ultimate origin of our moral nature. Mencius says:

"It is said in *The Book of Poetry*:
'Heaven, in giving birth to the multitudes of the people.
To every faculty and relationship annexed its law.
The people possess this normal nature,
And they (consequently) love its normal virtue.'

Confucius said, 'The maker of this song knew indeed the principle of our nature.' " (*Mencius*, 6,1,6,8)

Human moral nature, according to this song and approved by

Confucius comes directly from the ethical Heaven. Mencius and his school accepted this idea, so they say, "What Heaven has conferred is called nature", (*Chung Yung* 1,1) if "one knows one's nature, one knows Heaven." (*Mencius*, 1,1,1) As Heaven is ethical, what Heaven has conferred must also be ethical, love (*Jen*) the greatest of all virtues, which is deep-rooted in human nature, must have its origin in Heaven. That is why Mencius says, "Love (*Jen*) is the most honourable dignity conferred by Heaven (*Mencius*, 2,1,7,2)

(b) The way of securing love—through self-development

Although love has its origin in Heaven, yet it has been incarnate in human nature. thus if a man "knows his nature, he knows Heaven", and if he wants to secure love, all that he needs to do is to turn to his own mind and develop it, for "love", Mencius says, "is man's mind". (*Mencius*, 6,1,11,1) The mind can be developed passively through self-examination, and actively through "nourishment".

a) Passively, through self-examination

Human nature is originally good, but through contact with evil environment the original good mind may be influenced and becomes bad. Mencius says:

"In good years the children of the people are most of them good, while in bad years the most of them abandon themselves to evil. It is not owing to their natural powers conferred by Heaven that they are thus different. The abandonment is owing to the circumstances through which they allow their minds to be ensnared and drowned in evil." (*Mencius*, 6,1,7,1)

Through self-examination, Mencius opined that one is able to find the "lost mind", which has been "ensnared and drowned in evil", and restore it to its original state. "Seek and you will get it, neglect and you will lose it. . . . There is no greater delight than to be conscious of sincerity on self-examination" (*Mencius*, 7,1,3-4)

b) Actively, through nourishing the mind (Yang Hsin)[78]

When one has found one's "lost mind" through self-examination, one should constantly nourish or strengthen it so that it will not be lost again. "To nourish the heart", Mencius says, "there is nothing better than to make the desires few." (*Mencius*,

7,2,25) Mencius sometimes distinguished clearly between the human nature, which is entirely good, and the animal nature, which frequently leads man astray. He sometimes called human nature, mind (*hsin*),[79] reason (*Li*),[80] love (*Jen*), "nobler part" or the "part of man which is great" (Ta T'i);[81] the animal nature he sometimes called the "inferior part" or the "part of man which is small (*Hsiao T'i*),[82] which man has in common with the lower animals, such as the senses of hearing and seeing.

"Kung Tu Tzu said, 'All are equally men, but some are great men, and some are little men. How is this?' Mencius replied, 'Those who follow that part of man which is great (*Ta T'i*) are great men; those who follow that part of man which is small (*Hsiao T'i*) are small men. (Kung Tu Tzu) pursued, 'All are equally men, but some follow that part of man which is great, and some follow that part which is small. How is this?' Mencius answered, 'The senses of hearing and seeing do not think, and are obscured by (external) things. When a thing comes into contact with another (i.e. with one of our senses), it simply leads it away (from the right path). To the mind belongs the office of thinking. By thinking it gets (the right view of things); by neglecting to think, it fails to do this. This (i.e. the mind) is what Heaven has given to us. Let a man first establish firmly the nobler part of his constitution, and the inferior part will not be able to take it from him. It is simply this which makes the great man.' " (*Mencius*, 6,1,15)

The desires of men are connected with the inferior part of their constitution, for example, the senses which are easily to be obscured and led astray by things of the outside world. So "to make the desires few" means to weaken the "inferior part of man's constitution", and the best way to weaken the "inferior part" is to let him "first firmly establish the nobler part of his constitution". In other words, if a man wants to "make the desires few", the best way is to develop fully first his nobler or human nature, that is, the mind. "Mencius said, 'He who exercises his mind to the utmost (*Chin Hsin*)[83] knows his nature. Knowing his nature, he knows Heaven.' " (*Mencius*, 7,1,1,1) By exercising one's mind to the utmost is the best to make the desires few, by making the desires few is the best to nourish the mind.

In short, the way of securing love (*Jen*) is by self-development through self-examination, and the nourishing of the mind through "making the desires few" by "exercising the mind to the utmost."

"Mencius said, 'All things are already complete in us. There is no greater delight than to be conscious of sincerity on self-examination. If one acts with a vigorous effort at the law of reciprocity, when he seeks for (the realization of) love (*Jen*) nothing can be closer than his approximation to it.' " (*Mencius*, 7,1,4)

Mencius, in emphasizing the psychological aspect of Confucius' teaching of love (*Jen*), had a tendency towards the mystic interpretation of the origin, the nature, and the way of securing love. Therefore most of the famous idealist or mystic Confucian scholars of later times, especially those of the Sung and Ming dynasties, have based the authority of their philosophies generally on the teaching of Mencius.

(c) The expression of love

Mencius did not stop with the idealistic tendency of his theory of love, as outlined above, but he had some very practical teachings of the expression of love in family relationships and political applications. In general he succeeded very well in putting the central teaching of Confucius on love in a more systematic and explicit form and language.

a) In family relationships

Mencius was the great champion of the theory of relational love as against the two great rival theories of his time, the theory of self-love as presented by Yang Chu, and that of universal love as presented by Mo Ti. Mencius spoke about his age that "the doctrines held by the world, if they do not approach those of Yang, approach those of Mo." (*Mencius*, 3,2,9,9) So Mencius thought that his chief responsibility was "to oppose Yang and Mo." (*Mencius*, 3,2,9,14) So in order to understand Mencius interpretation of the expression of love, we must know something of those theories as held by his rival schools, and see how Mencius as an orthodox Confucian interpreter differed from both of them.

"Mencius said, 'The principle of Yang Tzu was—' each one for himself. Though he might have benefited the whole empire by plucking out a single hair, he would not have done it. Mo-tzu loves all equally. If by rubbing smooth his whole body from the crown to the heel, he could have benefited the empire, he would have done it.' " (*Mencius*, 7,1,26,1-2)

"Mencius said, . . . 'Yang's principle is—each one for himself (*Wei wo*),[84] which does not acknowledge (the claims of) the sovereign. Mo's principle is—to love all equally (or, universal love, *chien ai*),[85] which does not acknowledge (the peculiar affection due to) a father. But to acknowledge neither king nor father is to be in the state of a beast.' " (*Mencius*, 3,2,9,9)

"Universal love, exaltation of the worthy, assistance to the spirits and anti-fatalism: these were what Mo-tzu established and they were condemned by Yang Tzu. Completeness of living (*Ch'uan Sheng*),[86] preservation of what is genuine, and not allowing outside things to entangle one's person: these were what Yang Tzu established, and they were condemned by Mencius." (*Huai-nan-tzu*, chapter 13, p. 155)

a. Yang Chu[87]—Self-love

The chief doctrine of Yang Chu, as the above quotations show, is "every one for himself", a complete self-love. Han Fei Tzu wrote also about the behaviour of one of the followers of Yang Chu, saying:

"Here is a man. His policy is not to enter a city which is in danger, nor to remain in the army, and for the great profit of the world he would not give one hair of his shank. Rulers inevitably follow and pay him courtesy. They value his knowledge and exalt his conduct, because he is a scholar who has slight regard for mere things and holds life as something important." (*Han Fei Tzu*, chapter 50)

Both Mencius and Han Fei Tzu mentioned the extreme teaching of Yang Chu about self-love that even if he were to be given the world as a return for pulling out one of his hairs, he would not do so. This is because the world is something external, whereas the hair is part of his own person and life. Since he had 'slight regard for mere things and held life as something important' and he always strove after 'completeness of living, preservation of what is genuine, and not allowing outside things to entangle his person', it is only logical for him to conclude that the world, though large, may be neglected, whereas the hair, though small, should be looked upon as important.

b. Mo Ti (Micius)[88]—Universal love

The chief doctrine of Micius, according to the above quotations from *Mencius* and *Huai-nan-tzu*, is 'universal love' (*Chien Ai*). One of his most important arguments for the doctrine of universal love is that we should take the Will of Heaven (*Tien Chih*[89]) as the standard of our action, and the Will of Heaven is that we should have universal love, or love all people equally and impartially. Heaven shows His universal love, he argued, through His manifestation in the world, His virtuous, just and impartial actions, such as, "the certain reward to the good and punishment to the evil from the virtuous (Heaven), the acceptance of 'sacrifices from all' without discrimination." The following are some quotations from *The Ethical and Political Works of Motse*, translated from the original Chinese text by Dr. Yi-pao Mei, 1929.

"Motse (Micius) established the will of Heaven as his standard, just as the wheelwright uses his compasses and the carpenter uses his square as their standards. The wheelwright with his compasses and the carpenter with his square can judge the circularity and the squareness of objects. Similarly, with the will of Heaven as the standard, Motse can tell that the gentlemen of the world are far from righteousness." (p. 156)

"Those gentlemen of the world who desire to do righteousness have only to obey the will of Heaven. To obey the will of Heaven is to be universal (in love) and to oppose the will of Heaven is to be partial (in love)." (p. 155)

"What is the will of Heaven that is to be obeyed? It is to love all the people in the world universally. How do we know it is to love all the people in the world universally? Because (Heaven) accepts sacrifices from all. . . . Accepting sacrifice from all, Heaven must love them all. . . ." (p. 153)

"Heaven loves the people dearly, Heaven loves the people inclusively. And this can be known. How do we know Heaven loves the people? Because of the certain reward of the good and punishment to the evil from the virtuous (Heaven). How do we know the virtuous (Heaven) certainly rewards the good and punishes the evil? I know this from the (examples of) the sage-kings of the Three Dynasties. . . ." (p. 154)

c. Mencius—Relational love

As a true Confucianist, Mencius took the position of the Golden Mean between Yang Chu's self-love and Micius' universal love, and emphasized what may be called Rational Love or family love. He started from the common experience of man as man. It is not true that man as man has only self-love, 'each one for himself', as Yang Chu held. He has some innate social instincts, which Mencius called the "four beginnings" (*Szu Tuan*),[90] of love (*Jen*), righteousness (*I*), rules of proper conduct (*Li*), and wisdom (*Chih*). (*Mencius*, 2,1,6) They are born with every individual and are not something acquired from without. Mencius said, "*Jen*, *I*, *Li* and *Chih* are not infused into us from without. We are certainly furnished with them." (*Mencius*, 6,1,6,7) Again, he said, "What belongs by his nature to the Superior Man are *Jen*, *I*, *Li* and *Chih*. These are rooted in his heart; their growth and manifestation are a mild harmony appearing in the countenance, a rich fullness in the back, and the character imparted to the four limbs. Those limbs understand (to arrange themselves), without being told." (*Mencius*, 7,1,21,4)

Again, it is also not true, Mencius argued, that man as man has universal love, or can love all people equally and impartially, as Micius held. Those native social tendencies or the 'beginnings' only manifest themselves naturally in the family relationships. Mencius says, "Yao and Shun were what they were by nature", (*Mencius*, 7,2,32,1) and "the course of Yao and Shun, was simply that of filial piety and fraternal duty." (*Mencius*, 6,2,2,4) So the relational love and duties should be the beginning and end of all virtues and conducts.

"Mencius said, 'The substance of love is this,—the service of one's parents. The substance of righteousness is this,—the obeying one's elder brothers. The substance of wisdom is this,—the know-ing those two things, and not departing from them. The substance of the rules of proper conduct (*Li*) is this,—the ordering and adorning those two things. The substance of music is this,—the rejoicing in those two things.' " (*Mencius*, 4,1,27) Again: "The Sage is the apogee of human relationships." (*Mencius*, 4,1,2,1)

The fundamental cause of the error of the teaching of Micius about his universal love, according to Mencius, is his misunder-standing of the "root" of human nature. Mencius said:

"Heaven gives birth to creatures in such a way that they have one root, and yi (a disciple of Micius) makes them to have two roots. This is the cause (of his error)." (*Mencius*, 3,1,4,3)

By the "one root" Mencius meant the parents, to whom there-fore should be given a peculiar affection. Micius, saying that other men should be loved as much, and in the same way as parents, made two roots. Therefore the chief criticism which Mencius gave to Micius' doctrine of universal love is that Micius "does not acknowledge (the peculiar affection due to) a father."

To Mencius then the expression of love cannot and should not be equal to everybody. There should be different degrees and intensities of love, according to the nature of man, towards differ-ent people and things, but the highest and the greatest love should be given to one's parents.

"Mencius said, 'Of services which is the greatest? The service of parents is the greatest.' " (*Mencius*, 4,1,19,1)

"Mencius said, 'In regard to (inferior) creatures, the Superior Man is kind (*Ai*[91]) to them, but not loving (*Jen*). In regard to people generally, he is loving to them, but not affectionate (*Ch'in*).[92] He is affectionate to his parents, and lovingly disposed to people (gener-ally). He is lovingly disposed to people (generally), and kind to creatures.' " (*Mencius*, 7,1,45)

It is only natural that one should love one's parents most, because in them lies the only 'root' of love as well as all other mental and physical qualities that constitute man as man; man is born by his parents, but this does not mean that love should be limited to one's parents or to one's family only. Mencius paid much·

attention to the doctrine of the "extension of kindness" (*Tui En*)[93] from the members of the family to the people in general, or the development of the individual social instincts from the individual self to the members in the family, and from the family to the world at large.

"Treat with the reverence due to age the elders in your own family, so that the elders in the families of others shall be similarly treated; treat with the kindness due to youth the young in your own family, so that the young in the families of others shall be similarly treated:—do this, and the world may be made to go round in your palm. It is said in *The Book of Poetry*, 'His example affected his wife. It reached to his brothers, and his family of the state was governed by it.' The language shows how (King Wen) simply took this (kindly) heart, and exercised it towards those parties. Therefore the extension of kindness (by a prince) will suffice for the love and protection of all within the four seas, and if he do not extend it, he will not be able to protect his wife and children. The way in which the ancients came greatly to surpass other men was no other than this:—simply that they knew well how to extend to others what they themselves did." (*Mencius*, 1,17,12)

"Since all men have these four beginnings in themselves, let them know to give them all their development and completion, and the issue will be like that of fire which has begun to burn, or that of a spring which has begun to find vent. Let them have their complete development, and they will suffice to love and protect all within the four seas. Let them be denied that development, and they will not suffice for a man to serve his parents with." (*Mencius*, 2,1,6,7)

By extending one's love from the family to the state, one would naturally love also the sovereign of the state and honour his claims. This is what Yu Tzu meant when he said, "They are few who, being filial and fraternal, are fond of offending against their superiors. There have been none, who, not liking to offend against their superiors, have been fond of stirring up confusion." (*The Analects*, 1,2,1) Therefore the chief criticism which Mencius gave to Yang Chu's doctrine of self-love was that Yang Chu 'does not acknowledge (the claims of) the sovereign.'

In short, by emphasizing the relational love as against the self-love of Yang Chu and the universal love of Mo Ti, Mencius was treating man as man in his present state with certain specific natural tendencies. The doctrines of Yang and Mo might sound plausible but, Mencius said, they did not treat man as man, instead, they regarded man as 'in the state of a beast.'

Confucius, in certain cases as recorded by his immediate disciples, also prized more the genuine expression of one's human nature, that is, the nature of man as man in his present stage of development, than any high-sounding theories or principles that are not in accordance with the genuine human nature.

"The duke of Sheh informed Confucius, saying, 'Among us here there are those who may be styled upright in their conduct. If their father have stolen a sheep, they will bear witness to the fact.' Confucius said, 'Among us, in our part of the country, those who are upright are different from this. The father conceals the misconduct of the son, and the son conceals the misconduct of the father. Uprightness is to be found in this.' " (*The Analects*, 13,18)

"Some one said, 'What do you say concerning the principle that injury should be recompensed with kindness?' The Master said, 'With what then will you recompense kindness? Recompense injury with justice, and recompense kindness with kindness.' " (*The Analects*, 14,26)

What Confucius spoke here only dealt with the practical situation of life (not his ideal stage of life). Mencius only put this practical idea of Confucius concerning the natural expression of love into a more clear and systematic form and language, in order to refute the widely accepted theories of his rival schools.

b) In political applications—love versus war

Mencius was a strong advocate of the "government of love" (*Jen Cheng*),[94] and great opponent of using the method of war to end wars. This is the general spirit of the whole *Book of Mencius*, and the sayings are so many, and some of them have already been mentioned in Chapter 4, under the heading of the social ideal of Mencius and his school, that it will suffice just to give some of the quotations here.

"The principles of Yao and Shun, without a government of love (*Jen Cheng*), could not secure the tranquil order of the empire." (*Mencius*, 4,1,1,1)

"If you will put in practice a government of love, this people will love you and all above them, and will die for their officers." (*Mencius*, 1,2,12,3)

"If a ruler will put in practice a government of love, no power will be able to prevent his becoming emperor." (*Mencius*, 2,1,1,10)

"At the present time, in a country of ten thousand chariots, let the government of love be put in practice, and the people will be delighted with it, as if they were relieved from hanging by the heels. With half the merit of the ancients, double their achievements is sure to be realized. It is only at this time that such could be the case." (*Mencius*, 2,1,1,13)

The chief policy of the 'government of love' is to rule the people and gain control over the world with the method of love, instead of killing or fighting. So in advocating the policy of love for governmental control, Mencius condemned severely the use of the method of killing people or war, in order to gain peace or power.

"He who has no pleasure in killing men can unite (the world)." (*Mencius*, 1,1,6,4)

"When contentions about territory are the ground on which they fight, they slaughter men till the fields are filled with men. When some struggle for a city is the ground on which they fight, they slaughter men till the city is filled with them. This is what is called 'leading on the land to devour human flesh .' Death is not enough for such a crime. Therefore, those who are skilful to fight should suffer the highest punishment." (*Mencius*, 4,1,14,2-3)

"There are men who say—'I am skilful at marshalling troops. I am skilful at conducting a battle!—They are great criminals. If the sovereign of a state loves love (*Jen*), he will have no enemy in the world." (*Mencius*, 7,2,4,1-2)

"In the 'Spring and Autumn' there are no righteous wars. Instances indeed there are of one war better than another. 'Correction' is when the supreme authority punishes its subjects by force of arms. Hostile states do not correct one another." (*Mencius,* 7,2,2) "From this time forth I know the heavy consequences of killing a man's near relations. When a man kills another's father, that other will kill his father; when a man kills another's elder brother, that other will kill his elder brother. So he does not himself indeed do the act, but there is only an interval (between him and it)." (*Mencius,* 7,2,7)

Confucius, in upholding the importance of love, also condemned the method of killing or fighting in order to gain peace and power.

"Chi K'ang Tzu asked Confucius about government, saying, 'What do you say to killing the unprincipled for the good of the principled?' Confucius replied, 'Sir, in carrying out your government, why should you use killing at all? Let your (evinced) desires be for what is good, and the people will be good.' " (*The Analects,* 12,19)

" 'If good men were to govern a country (in succession) for a hundred years, they would be able to transform the violently bad, and dispense with capital punishment.' True indeed is this saying!" (*The Analects,* 13,11)

"Duke Ling of Wei asked Confucius about tactics. Confucius replied, 'I have heard about sacrificial vessels, but I have not learned military matters.' On this, he took his departure the next day." (*The Analects,* 15,1,1)

"The head of the Chi family was going to attack Chuan-yu. Jan Yu and Chi-lu had an interview with Confucius, and said, 'Our chief, Chi, is going to commence operations against Chuan-yu.' Confucius said, 'Ch'iu, is it not you who are in fault here? . . . If remoter people are not submissive, all the influences of civil culture and virtue are to be cultivated to attract them to be so; and when they have been so attracted, they must be made contented and tranquil. Now here are you, Yu and Ch'iu , assisting your chief. Remoter people are not submissive, and (with your help) he cannot attract them to him. In his own territory there are divisions and downfalls, leavings and separations, and, (with your help), he cannot preserve it. And yet he is planning these hostile movements within the state. I am afraid that the sorrow of the Chi-sun (family) will not be on account of Chuan-yu, but will be found within the screen of their own court.' " (*The Analects*, 16,1)

Mencius also cited the same case about the military operations of the Chi family, as mentioned above in *The Analects*, and concluded:

"Looking at the subject from this case, (we perceive that) when a prince was not practising the government of love (*Jen Cheng*), all (his ministers) who enriched him were rejected by Confucius." (*Mencius*, 4,1,14,1-2)

But neither Confucius nor Mencius was a pacifist, in the sense of one who opposes all kinds of war. They did not oppose military preparation nor fighting for self-protection.

"Duke Wen of Teng asked Mencius, saying, 'Teng is a small kingdom, and lies between Ch'i and Ch'u. Shall I serve Ch'i? or shall I serve Ch'u?' Mencius replied, 'This plan (which you propose) is beyond me. If you will have me counsel you, there is one thing (I can suggest). Dig deeper your moats; build higher your walls; guard them along with your people. (In case of attack), be prepared to die (in your defense), and have the people so that they will not leave you;—this is a proper course.' " (*Mencius*, 1,2,13)

Here Mencius is very clearly shown to be one who opposed a policy of non-resistance. Get ready your arms, and guard your country to your last man and last drop of blood in case of being attacked: this is the advice of Mencius, and 'this', he said, 'is a proper course'. Confucius also advised the rulers of his days to teach people first before they are actually employed in war. "The Master said, 'Let a good man teach the people seven years, and they may then likewise be employed in war. . . To lead an uninstructed people to war is to throw them away.' " (*The Analects*, 13,29-30)

What Confucius and Mencius aimed at was to show to the world that killing or fighting is not the best method of winning other people or one's own people. Love is the greatest power in the world to enable the ruler to gain control over his own people and all the people of the world. They all preached a sort of benevolent imperialism.

"If the prince of a state loves love(*Jen*), he will have no opponent in all the empire." (*Mencius*, 4,1,7,5)

"The man of love has no enemy." (*Mencius*, 1,1,5,6)

"Love (*Jen*) subdues its opposite just as water subdues fire." (*Mencius*, 6,1,18,1)

The reason for the power of love as an instrument to conquer other people is simply this, "If a ruler can truly practise these five things (the policies in a government of love), then the people in the neighbouring kingdoms will look up to him as a parent. From the first birth of mankind till now, never has any one led children to attack their parent, and succeeded in his design." (*Mencius*, 2,1,5,6) Again: "If you put in practice a government of love, this people will love you and all above them, and will die for their officers." (*Mencius*, 1,2,12,3) That is the same reason why Confucius suggested:

"If remoter people are not submissive, all the influences of civil culture and virtue are to be cultivated to attract them to be so; and when they have been so attracted, they must be made contented and tranquil." (*The Analects*, 16,1,11)

Mencius distinguished between two kinds of rulers, the Dictators, *Pa*,[95] and the Kingly-rulers, *Wang*.[96] The Dictators were those who ruled simply by force and cunning, and were represented by the "five leaders", *Wu Pa*;[97] whereas the Kingly-rulers were those who ruled by love and virtue, and were represented by the Sage-kings. Mencius condemned all the wars raised by those dictators, saying, "In the 'Spring and Autumn' there are no righteous wars." (*Mencius*, 7,2,2,1) He had no sympathy with their government, saying, "(Love and righteousness) were natural to Yao and Shun. T'ang and Wu made them their own. The five dictators (Wu Pa) feigned them." (*Mencius*, 7,1,30,1) The Sage-kings did sometimes go to war, but they did so only from the motive of love, to deliver the people from their despotic rulers. So the people of the conquered countries were pleased at being conquered and released from tyranny. Mencius mentions again and again the incident recorded in *The Book of History* of one of the military expeditions of T'ang, the Sage-king.

"As soon as T'ang began his work of executing justice, he commenced with Ko. The whole empire had confidence in him. When he pursued his work in the east, the rude tribes on the west murmured. So did those on the north, when he was engaged in the south. Their cry was—Why does he make us last? (Thus), the looking of the people to him, was like the looking in a time of great drought to the clouds and rainbows. The frequenters of the markets stopped not. The husband-men made no change (in their operations). While he punished their rulers, he consoled the people. (His progress) was like the falling of opportune rain, and the people were delighted. It is said (again) in *The Book of History*, 'We have waited for our prince (long); the prince's coming will be our reviving!' " (*Mencius*, 1,2,11,2; 3,2,5,4; cp. *Shu Ching*, 4,2,6)

Thus war is justified, if it is carried out by the 'Kingly-ruler' whose policy is the 'government of love' (*Jen Cheng*), and he goes to war simply out of the motive of love, of 'executing justice', or delivering the people from the tyranny of despotic rulers. In such a case, the people of the conquered states, as a rule, would welcome the conquerors with delight. So the attitude or public opinion of the people, in general, may be taken as the chief criterion of whether a war is justified or not. Once when the State of Ch'i conquered the State of Yen, the prince of Ch'i asked Mencius whether he should take possession of Yen or not. Mencius replied:

"If the people of Yen will be pleased with your taking possession of it, then do so. Among the ancients there was (one) who acted on this principle, namely, King Wu. If the people of Yen will not be pleased with your taking possession of it, then do not do so. Among the ancients there was (one) who acted on this principle, namely King Wen." (*Mencius*, 1,2,10,3)

2. The Rules of Proper Conduct (*Li*)

Li was not the most important doctrine taught by Mencius and his school, still it is mentioned 65 times in *The Book of Mencius*. His chief emphasis was put on the psychological or individual aspect of *Li* as taught by Confucius. He firmly believed in the idea of Confucius that the rules of proper conduct (*Li*) are made for man and not man for the rules of proper conduct (*Li*). If these rules (*Li*) are at any time recognized by men to be wrong, they need no longer be acknowledged and may be revised. The following conversation between Mencius and King Hsuan of Ch'i bears out this idea very clearly:

"Mencius said to King Hsuan of Ch'i, 'When the prince regards his ministers as his hands and feet, his ministers regard their prince as their belly and heart; when he regards them as his dogs and horses, they regard him as any other man; when he regards them as the ground or as grass, they regard him as a robber and an enemy.' The king said, 'According to the rules of proper conduct (*Li*), a minister wears mourning when he has left the service of a prince. How must (a prince) behave that his (old ministers) may thus go into mourning?' Mencius replied, 'The admonitions (of a minister) having been followed, and his advice listened to, so that blessings have descended on the people, if for some cause he leaves (the country), the prince sends an escort to conduct him beyond the boundaries. He also anticipates (with recommendatory intimations) his arrival in the country to which he is proceeding. When he has been gone three years and does not return, (only) then at length does he take back his fields and residence. This treatment is what is called 'a thrice-repeated display of consideration'. When a prince acts thus, mourning will be worn on leaving his service. Nowadays, the remonstrances of a minister are not followed, and his advice is not listened to, so that no blessing descend on the people. When for any cause he leaves the country, the prince tries to seize him and hold him a prisoner. He also pushes him to extremity in the country to which he has gone, and on the very day of his departure, he takes back his fields and residence. This treatment shows him to be what we called 'a robber and an enemy'. What mourning can be worn for a robber and an enemy?' " (*Mencius*, 4,2,3)

Mencius here refused to recognize the old rules of proper conduct (*Li*) concerning a minister wearing mourning when he left the service of a prince, because the princes in his days did not act as princes; they were, as Mencius bravely put it, 'robbers and enemies' of the people and the ministers. The rules of proper conduct (*Li*) are made for man, and if they do not fit into his present state of circumstance, they can be neglected or revised. Again Mencius said:

"The rules of proper conduct (*Li*), which are not really proper (*Li*), and acts of righteousness *(I)*, which are not really righteous *(I)*, the great man does not do."

This also implies that the authority of the decisions made by the individual person are superior to what are customarily accepted as being the rules of proper conduct (*Li*) and righteousness *(I)*. Man is the measure of all things. His mind is the mind of God: "Heaven sees according as my people see; Heaven hears according as my people hear" (*Mencius*, 5,1,5,8; see *Shu Ching*, 4,1,2,7) He may even be justified in breaking one of the most important rules of proper conduct (*Li*), that of being loyal and submissive to his superiors, especially to the prince, by starting a revolution, if he is treated unjustly. (*Mencius*, 1,2,8)

3. Filial Piety (*Hsiao*)

Filial piety was regarded as the root of all virtues by Mencius as well as by his master Confucius. In it lies all the virtues of his ideal personality, that of the Sage-kings.

"Mencius said, 'The substance of love (*Jen*) is this,—the service of one's parents. The substance of righteousness *(I)* is this—the obeying one's elder brothers. The substance of wisdom (*Chih*) is this,—the knowing of those two things, and not departing from them. The substance of the rules of proper conduct (*Li*) is this, —the ordering and adorning those two things. The substance of music (Yueh) is this,—the rejoicing in those two things.' " (*Mencius*, 4,1,27)

"Mencius said. . . 'The course of Yao and Shun was simply that of filial piety and fraternal duty.' " (*Mencius*, 6,2,2,4)

"Mencius said, 'Of service which is the greatest? The service of parents is the greatest.' " (*Mencius*, 4,1,19,1)

As a true humanist, in the real sense of the term, Mencius always esteemed man as being the most important thing in the universe. So when he talked about filial piety, he said the most unfilial thing was to have no children.

"Mencius said, 'There are three things which are unfilial and to have no posterity is the greatest of them'." (*Mencius*, 4,1,26,1)

This brief saying of Mencius has widely been taken as an excuse for the existence of the polygamy system for these thousands of years in China. Perhaps it has also had a great deal to do with the present huge population of China. At any rate, as during the periods of the Spring and Autumn and the Warring States, constant warfare was going on, and the population was rapidly decreasing in every state, this teaching of Mencius about filial piety may be deemed wise and suitable for his time and circumstances.

Also on this virtue of filial piety Mencius largely depended when he taught his doctrine of relational love. (See the section on Love as taught by Mencius)

4. The Doctrine of the Mean (*Chung Yung*)[98]

As a true transmitter of the traditional doctrine of the Mean, Mencius said:

"The Superior Man draws the bow, but does not discharge the arrow. (The whole thing) seems to leap (before the learner). Such is his standing exactly in the middle of the right Way (*Tao*) Those who are able, follow him." (*Mencius*, 7,1,41,3)

"Those who keep the Mean, train up those who do not, and those who have abilities, train up those who have not, and hence men rejoice in having fathers and elder brothers who are possessed of virtue and talent. If they who keep the Mean spurn those who do not, and they who have abilities spurn those who have not, then the space between them—those so gifted and the ungifted—will not admit an inch." (*Mencius*, 4,2,7)

"Mencius said, 'Chung Ni (Confucius) did not do excessive things.' " (*Mencius*, 4,2,10)

This traditional doctrine of the Mean was greatly exemplified and systematized by Mencius' school of Confucianism as recorded in the book of *The Doctrine of the Mean (Chung Yung)*. It becomes not only the middle way of human thought and action, but also the cosmic principle from which the human nature derives. So it is the duty of man to observe the principle, that is, as Hu Han-min translated the term *Chung Yung*, "To find the central clue in our moral being which unites us to the universal order." The following is a passage from the book of *Chung Yung*, as translated by Lin Yu-tang:

"What is God-given is what we call human nature. To fulfil the law of our human nature is what we call the moral law (*Tao*). The cultivation of the moral law is what we call culture (*Chiao*). . . . When the passions, such as joy, anger, grief, and pleasure, have not awakened, that is our central self, or moral being (*Chung*). When these passions awaken and each and all attain due measure and degree, that is harmony, or the moral order (*Ho*). Our central self or moral being is the great basis of existence, and harmony or moral order is the universal law in the world. When our true central self and harmony are realized, the universe then becomes a cosmos and all things attain their full growth and development." (*Chung Yung*, Chap. 1, tr. by Lin Yu-tang in his *The Wisdom of Confucius*, p. 104)

In this quotation we see that according to Mencius and his school our human nature, given by God, constitutes our 'central self', which, as the *Book of Mencius* repeatedly shows, is entirely good. Evil comes in when the human nature or the central self does not express or develop itself fully and harmoniously according to the principle of universal order, which expresses itself in all its constituent parts fully and harmoniously. The universe cannot be a perfect cosmos if human nature, a part of the universal nature, is not full and harmoniously developed. So only when "our true central self and harmony are realized, the universe then becomes a cosmos and all things attain their full growth and development."

Here the school of Mencius strikes home on a very important principle of the universe, that is, nature does act according to the doctrine of the Mean or the 'central harmony' (*Chung Ho*).[99] The modern educational psychologists, for example, build up almost entirely their theory of the normal curve or bell-shape ⋔ distribution, upon the principle of the natural order, that everything in the universe, including man, tends always towards the central mean or 'central harmony'. Indeed the world would be a very different world, if Nature did not pull everything or everybody both physically and mentally, towards the Golden Mean. So it is scientifically true, and philosophically sound, that "Central self (including moral being) is the great basis of existence, and Harmony (including moral order) is the universal law in the world." Through the effort of Confucius, and the interpretation of Mencius and his school, the Doctrine of the Mean has become a deep-rooted doctrine in the very centre of the Chinese mind, and has influenced greatly the life and thought of the individual Chinese as well as the social and political policies of the country as a whole.

(C) According to Hsun-tzu and His School of Confucianism

1. The Rules of Proper Conduct (*Li*)

The greatest and the most fundamental teaching of Hsun-tzu and his school is about the rules of proper conduct (*Li*). Confucius, as mentioned above, emphasized both the importance of individual freedom, and the importance of the restraining mould that is imposed upon the individual from without by the socially recognized rules of proper conduct (*Li*). With Mencius, comparatively greater emphasis was placed upon individual freedom, but with Hsun-tzu, greater emphasis was placed upon external standards of authority. It was chiefly through the efforts of Hsun-tzu and his school of Confucianism that so much Confucian literature on *Li* has been written and preserved, and that the aspect of the teaching of Confucius about the importance of the socialization of individuals, by imposing upon them social institutions with their rules of proper conduct (*Li*), has been so well established and exemplified.

(a) The importance of *Li*

a) *Li* is a cosmological principle, the greatest of all principles.

"*Li* is that whereby Heaven and Earth unite, whereby the sun and moon are bright, whereby the four seasons are ordered, whereby the stars move in their courses, whereby rivers flow, whereby all things prosper, whereby love and hatred are tempered, whereby joy and anger keep their proper place. It causes the lower orders to obey, and the upper orders to be illustrious; through a myriad changes it prevents going astray. But if one departs from it, he will be destroyed. Is not *Li* the greatest of all principles?" (The Works of Hsun-tzu, translated by Homer H. Dubs, pp. 223-224)

b) *Li* is the utmost of human morality.

"For the plumb-line is the extreme of straightness; the balances are the extreme of equableness; the compass and square are the extreme of squareness and roundness; *Li* is the utmost of human morality." (Ibid, p. 225)

c) *Li* is the aim of all learning.

"Study advances to *Li*, and stops there. This is what is meant by the extreme of virtue." (ibid, p. 37)

"In study, what should one begin with? What end with? The art begins by reciting the classics, and ends in learning with *Li*." (p. 36)

d) *Li* is the greatest thing in government.

"*Li* is the greatest thing in government and in making social distinctions; it is the foundation of strength and security; it is the way of being majestic; it is the focus of honour. Kings and dukes gained the empire by following it. By not following it, they lost their territory. Hence strong armour and trained armies were insufficient to gain virtue; high city walls and deep moats were insufficient to make those rules feared. If they followed this principle they were successful; if they did not follow this principle, then they failed." (p. 216)

"When the country follows *Li*, there is good government and prosperity; when it is not followed there is anarchy and calamity. He who follows it is safe; he who does not follow it is in danger. He who follows it will be preserved; he who does not follow it will be destroyed." (p. 224)

e) *Li* should be the standard of all human actions.

"Man's emotions, purposes and ideas, when proceeding according to *Li*, will be orderly. If they do not proceed according to *Li*, they become wrong and confused, careless and negligent. Food and drink, clothing, dwelling places and movements, if in accordance with *Li*, will be proper and harmonious. If not in accordance with *Li*, they will meet with ruin and calamity. A person's appearance, his bearing, his advancing and retiring when he hastens or walks slowly, if according to *Li*, are refined. If not according to *Li*, he will be haughty, intractable, prejudiced and rude. Hence man without *Li* cannot exist; affairs without *Li* cannot be completed; government without *Li* cannot be peaceful." (pp. 44-45)

"To try to act according to the Odes and History without making *Li* your pattern, is like sounding a river with the fingers or using a spear to pound a millet or using an awl in eating from a pot—it will not succeed. For if a man exalts *Li*, although he may not be renowned, he will be a learned man of principle. If he does not exalt *Li*, although he should investigate and discuss, he would be a useless scholar. . . . For one must first reverence *Li*, and then only can he speak of the means of obtaining virtue; his speech must accord with *Li*, and then only can he speak of the principles of virtue; his demeanour must conform to *Li*, and then only can he speak of attaining to virtue." (pp. 38-39)

"The rules of proper conduct (*Li*) are the standards of all measurement of ministers and officers by their ruler; it includes all grades of men." (p. 118)

"In the beginning, the ancient kings founded their rule on love and justice; *Li* controlled their ingoings and outgoings, their entire path." (p. 38)

(b) The functions of *Li*

a) The most important function of *Li* is to regulate human desire. One of the fundamental conceptions of Hsun-tzu was that the original nature of man is evil. Man by nature is full of evil desire, and if it is followed, strife, hatred, lust, disorder, and all other evil things will be the result in society as well as in the individual. Hence *Li* is needed to regulate the evil desires which are innate in human nature.

"The nature of man is evil; his goodness is only acquired training. The original nature of man to-day is to seek for gain. If this desire is followed, strife and rapacity result, and courtesy dies. Man originally is envious and naturally hates others. If these tendencies are followed, injury and destruction follow; loyalty and faithfulness are destroyed. Man originally possesses the desires of the ear and eye; he likes praise and is lustful. If these are followed, impurity and disorder result, and *Li* and justice and etiquette are destroyed. Therefore to give rein to man's original nature, to follow man's feelings, inevitably result in strife and rapacity, together with violations of etiquette and confusion in the proper way of doing things, and a reversion to a state of violence. Therefore the civilizing influence of teachers and laws, the guidance of *Li* and justice are absolutely necessary." (p. 301)

"Whence does *Li* arise? Man by birth has desire. When desire is not satisfied, then he cannot be without a seeking for satisfaction. When this seeking for satisfaction is without measure or of limits, then there cannot but be contention. When there is contention, there will be disorder; when there is disorder, then there will be poverty. The former kings hated this confusion, hence they established *Li* and justice in order to set limits to this confusion, to educate, and nourish men's desires, to give opportunity for this seeking for satisfaction, in order that desires should never be extinguished by things, nor should things be used up by desire; that these two should support each other and should continue to exist. This is whence *Li* arise. Thus *Li* is to educate and nourish." (p. 313)

"Of all the methods of controlling the body and nourishing the mind, there is none more direct than *Li*. . . ." (p. 47)

"Straight wood does not need to undergo the action of the carpenter's rule in order to be straight; its nature is straight. Crooked wood does need to undergo the action of the carpenter's rule; it needs to be steamed and then only will it be straight, because its nature is crooked. Now the nature of man is evil; he needs to undergo the government of Sage-kings, the reforming action of *Li* and justice, then good government and order will issue, and actions will accord with virtue." (p. 309)

b) Another important function of *Li* is to carry out the doctrine of "rectification of names", or to divide the people in society according to their present status in that society. *Li* provides for expression of the feelings of good or bad fortune, sorrow or joy, shown in the features. Singing, jesting, weeping, and wailing are the expression of the feelings of good or bad fortune, sorrow or joy, shown in the voice. Meat, grain, wine, fish, pork, and congee, greens, beans, water, and broth are the expression of the feelings of good or bad fortune, sorrow or joy, shown in food and drink. Caps, crowns, embroidered garments, woven silk garments, and coarse mourning clothes, sackcloth badges, loose woven cloth, and straw sandals are the expression of feelings of good or bad fortune, sorrow or joy, shown in clothing. Large houses, deep temples, elevated beds, fine rush mats, low tables and mats, and thatched roofs, lean-to houses, firewood for chairs, clods for a pillow, are the expression of the feelings of good or bad fortune, sorrow or joy, shown in dwellings. These two kinds of feelings certainly have their origin in human life. If they are cut down or extended, enlarged or made shallow, added or diminished, thus made to fit the situation, completely expressed, glorified and beautified, to make the origin and aim, end and beginning all harmonize, so that they can become a pattern for all generations—these are the rules of proper conduct (*Li*)." (pp. 233-234)

"All *Li*, if for the service of the living, are to beautify joy; or if to send off the dead, they are to beautify sorrow; or if for sacrifice , they are to beautify reverence; or if they are military, they are to beautify majesty. In this all the Kings were alike, the ancient times and the present are the same. But we do not know whence they came. . . . Service of the living is beautifying their life; sending off the dead is beautifying their end; when the end and the previous life are both attended to, the way of the Sage is completed." (pp. 237-238)

. (c) The sources of *Li*

"*Li* has three sources; Heaven and Earth gave birth to it—this is a source; our ancestors made it fit the situation—this is a source; the princes and teachers formed it—this is a source. Without Heaven and Earth, how could it be born? Without our ancestors, how could it be produced? Without princes and teachers, how could it be given form? If one of these were lacking, men would be without peace. Hence *Li* on the one hand serves Heaven and on the other Earth; it honours our ancestors and magnifies the princes and teachers—this is how it serves the three sources of *Li*." (pp. 219-220)

Beside these three sources—Heaven and Earth, ancestors, and princes and teachers—there were two other sources frequently mentioned, namely, the Sage-kings and the Superior Man. The following are some of the quotations:

"The ancient Kings invented *Li* and justice for men in order to divide them." (p. 65)

"The Sage gathers together ideas and thoughts, and becomes skilled by his acquired training, so as to bring forth *Li* and justice, and originate laws and regulations. So *Li* justice, laws and regulations come from the acquired knowledge of the Sage, not from man's original nature." (p. 305)

"The former Kings hated this confusion, hence they established *Li* and justice in order to set limits to this confusion, to educate and nourish men's desires, to give opportunity for this seeking for satisfaction. . . ." (p. 213)

"Heaven and Earth are the source of life. *Li* and justice are the source of good government; the Superior Man is the source of *Li* and justice. To carry them out, to practice them, to study them much, and to love them greatly is the source of being a Superior Man. For Heaven and Earth give birth to the Superior Man; the Superior Man brings Heaven and Earth into order; the Superior Man forms a triad with Heaven and Earth; he is the controller of all things, the father and mother of the people. Without the Superior Man, Heaven and Earth are not ordered, *Li* and justice have no control." (p. 135)

Hsun-tzu's conception of the source of *Li* was very similar to that of Cheng Tzu Ch'an and his follower Tzu Ta Shu as recorded in *Tso-Chuan* under the 25th year of Duke Chao, 517 B.C. When Tzu Ta Shu was asked about the meaning of the *Li*, he said:

"I have heard our late great officer, Tzu Ch'an, say, '*Li* constitutes the warp of Heaven, and the principle of Earth, and the conduct of the people.' Heaven and Earth have their regular ways, and men

The best government, as the above few paragraphs show, is the government of love. It attracts others by virtue, and does not conquer them by force of arms. Hsun-tzu points out very clearly the folly of going to war, which leads only to one's own danger and destruction. His argument is simple and clear, and is worth quoting as follows:

"Against the man who uses force, the cities of others are guarded and the military officers of others are belligerent; but if I by my strength overcome them, then I must inevitably injure the people of others greatly. If I injure the people of another state greatly, then they will certainly hate me greatly. If they hate me greatly, then they will more and more seek to strive with me. If the cities of another state are guarded and its officers are belligerent, but I by my strength overcome them, then I must unavoidably injure my own people greatly. If I injure my people greatly, then they will certainly hate me greatly. If my people hate me greatly, then they will continually be less willing to strive for me. If the people of another state more and more seek to strive with me, and my own people are continually less willing to strive for me—this is the way that a strong ruler becomes weak. If territory comes to me but my people leave me—I shall have much trouble but little gain. If that which I need to guard is increased, yet that whereby it should be guarded be reduced—this is the way that a great country becomes small. Then the feudal nobles will certainly form alliances, nurse their hatred, and not forget their enmity. They will wait for the weakness of the ruler who is strong through force to show itself; they will take advantage of his defeat—this will be the time of danger for the ruler who is great through force." (pp. 127-128)

Like Confucius and Mencius again, Hsun-tzu did not condemn all kinds of war. They all believed that in their stage of social development when "the Great Way (*Tao*)" was far from prevailing in the world, war might sometimes be inevitable. According to Hsun-tzu, war can only be justified when it is carried out with the motive of love and justice, when it is waged with the purpose of stopping tyranny and getting rid of injury, like those revolutionary wars led by T'ang and Wu, and other ancient Sage-kings. The following quotation will show very clearly what he meant by war and justice.

"Chen-hsiao asked a question of the master, Hsun Ch'ing (Hsun-tzu), saying, 'When you discuss military affairs, you always speak of love and justice as the roots of action. The man of love loves others; the just man follows principle; then why do you speak of military actions? All that armies are good for is to contend and take things from others.' The master, Hsun Ch'ing, said, 'It is not as you think. This man of love (*Jen*) loves others. He loves others, hence he hates what injures others. This just man follows principle. He follows principle, hence he hates those that lead others astray. These armies are for the purpose of stopping tyranny and getting rid of injury, not to contend and take things from others. Hence when the armies of the man of love (*Jen*) remain in a place, it is like a god being there; when they have passed, civilization develops. It was like the falling of a timely rain; no one failed to rejoice —this was when Yao punished Huan-tou, or Shun punished the ruler of the Miao, or Yu punished the Minister of Works, or T'ang punished the lord of Hsia, or King Wen punished Ch'ung, or King Wu punished Chou; these four emperors and two kings all used love (*Jen*) and just (*Yi*) armies to gain the empire. Therefore those who were near were attached by their goodness; those who were far loved their justice. Their armies did not ensanguine their swords, yet distant regions came to submit to them; their virtue was so great that it reached to the four ends of the world.' " (pp. 167-169)

(d) Love subordinate to *Li*

To Hsun-tzu love is subordinate to *Li*. It is according to the rules of proper conduct (*Li*), for example, that the prince should love his people, and should refrain from using force to expand his territory, or to fight other countries merely out of selfish motives.

"For the superior there is nothing as good as loving his inferior and ruling according to *Li*. The relation of the superior to the inferior should be that of protecting infants. . . . In this respect all the Kings were alike, and it is the central and indispensable thing in the rules of proper conduct (*Li*) and laws." (p. 154)

Love, then, is only one thing or a part, though "the central and indispensable thing" or part in *Li,* which alone is the final criterion of government or of the conduct of a person.

"The principles of proper conduct (*Li*) have remained unchanged through the time of all the kings. They are sufficient to permeate the way of life. One king fell and another arose; that which conformed to these principles permeated them all. When these principles permeate a government, there can be no misgovernment or disorder. He who does not know how to make them permeate his actions does not know how to alter his actions to suit changing conditions. When they permeate the whole of a person's conduct, he can never fail. Ill-government and calamity is born on their lack; good government comes from exhausting their minutiae. . . . One who walks in the water tests its depth. If he does not test it rightly, then he is likely to fall into the water. The one who governs the people tests their virtue. If he does not test rightly there is likely to be disorder. What he tests by are the rules of proper conduct (*Li*). If there is no proper conduct (*Li*) the age is dark. When the age is dark there will be great disorder. For the right way of life is never unclear. Conduct relating to what is without and within the family circle is tested differently. Conduct which refers to these inner and outer circles has its uniform principles. Thus we can remove the causes which would make the people sink into trouble." (pp. 183-184)

In short, with the fundamental conception of the evil nature of man, love cannot come from human nature, as Mencius taught. Man by nature is full of selfish desires, and the following of the policy of love can only come from the observance of the rules of proper conduct (*Li*) as formulated by the ancient Sages or Superior Men. By following those rules of proper conduct, for example, those rules of loving other people, in the government "there can be no misgovernment or disorder"; by observing them in one's conduct, "one can never fail."

3. Filial Piety (*Hsiao*)

Hsun-tzu also preached the virtue of filial piety. But like in his teaching of love (*Jen*), he emphasized also the superiority of the rules of proper conduct (*Li*) over filial piety. Like the virtue of love, which does not come from human nature as Mencius taught, the virtue of filial piety does not derive from the nature of man. Man by nature, Hsun-tzu maintained, is unfilial, and his filiality comes from the observance of the rules of proper conduct, as formulated by the Ancient Sages or Kings.

"The son yielding precedence to his father, the younger brother yielding precedence to his older brother; the son working for his father, the younger brother working for his older brother—these two kinds of actions are contrary to original nature and antagonistic to natural feeling. Nevertheless, there is the doctrine of filial piety, the etiquette or the rules of proper conduct (*Li*) and justice. If a person follows his natural feelings, he has no courtesy; if he has courtesy, then it is antagonistic to his natural feelings." (p. 304)

"Heaven was not partial to Tsen, Ch'ien, and Hsiao Yi, nor did it neglect the common multitude. Then why are Tsen, Ch'ien, and Hsiao Yi alone truly and perfectly filial, and why do they alone have the name of special filiality? The reason is that they observed the rules of proper conduct (*Li*) and justice to the utmost extent. Heaven was not partial to the people of Ch'i and Lu, nor did it neglect the people of Ch'in. But the people of Ch'in are not as good in the righteous relation between father and son and in the proper reserve between husband and wife, as are the people of Ch'i and Lu in filial piety and reverential respect. Why is this? The reason is that the people of Ch'in follow their feelings and original nature, take pleasure in haughtiness, and are remiss in observing the rules of proper conduct (*Li*) and justice (*Yi*)." (pp. 311-312)

4. The Doctrine of the Mean

The Doctrine of the Mean is one of the fundamental teachings of Confucius, and has always been esteemed and observed by his followers. Hsun-tzu, as a great Confucian believer, advised strongly his disciples to follow the doctrine of the Golden Mean. But Hsun-tzu identified the Mean with *Li*. To act in according with *Li* was, according to him, the same as to act in according with the Mean.

"When that which the Way of life (*Tao*) stresses is the Golden

Mean, it can be followed; when it is an extreme, it should not be done; when it is evil, a person is greatly misled." (p. 184)

"The Way of the ancient Kings is the magnifying of love. Follow the Mean in acting it out. What is meant by the Mean? It is the rules of proper conduct (*Li*) and justice." (p. 93)

(D) Conclusion of the Moral Teaching of Confucius

Confucius was primarily a moral teacher. Love (*Jen*), the rules of proper conduct (*Li*), filial piety (*Hsiao*), and the doctrine of the Mean (*Chung Yung*) are the four main topics of the moral teaching of Confucius, according to his immediate disciples, Mencius and his school of Confucianism, and Hsun-tzu and his school of Confucianism.

In his teaching on love (*Jen*), he emphasized the sanctity and value of the individual, and the importance of his motive and will in moral conduct; yet at the same time he did not neglect the social aspect of love. The motive of love only, without the act of love towards others, is not true love. "The Master said, 'If the will be set on love (*Jen*), there will be no practice of wickedness.' " (*The Analects*, 4,4)

In his teaching on *Li*, he emphasized the value of the cultural heritage of society and the accepted rules of proper conduct. But he was fully aware of the evils that might result from the over-emphasis on *Li*; formalism, hypocrisy, or arbitrariness might be some of the evil results. Morality would become an external thing; to abide by customary regulations or accepted rules only would be regarded as moral, and the breach of them would be regarded as sinful. In order to safeguard one against such dangers, Confucius, on the one hand, emphasized the virtue of love (*Jen*), and, on the other hand, gave new interpretations on *Li*, by putting the individual motive, especially sincerity and reverence, as the foundation of *Li*. "The Master said, 'A man can enlarge the principles (*Tao*); those principles (*Tao*) do not enlarge the man.' " (*The Analects*, 15,28) This is the same as to say that *Li* is made for man and not man for *Li*. Man should be regarded as the end and never as a means only. *Li* in the sense of the external social restraint has its important place in the teaching of Confucius, but it should be regarded only as the means to bring to pass the welfare and enrichment of human life. There was no class of people that Confucius hated more than the smug hypocrites whom "their whole village styled good and careful" (*Mencius*, 7,2,37,10); Confucius scolded severely, saying, "You good careful people of the villages (*Hsieng-yuan*)[100] are the thieves of virtue." (*The Analects*, 17,13; *Mencius*, 7,2,37,8) He had no sympathy with those who cared only for the outward form or ceremony. In his teaching on *Li* both the outward form and the inward spirit were emphasized.

In his teaching on filial piety, he emphasized the extension of the emotional power that derives from the love of one's parents to the wider moral and social applications. Filial piety was, to Confucius, a strong moving force, very similar to that of the religious passion, that drives and attracts the individual "to establish himself and walk according to the Way (*Tao*), so that the names of his parents might be glorified."

In his teaching on the doctrine of the Mean, he emphasized a sort of balanced life, or a state of complacency in thought and in action. If the history of human civilization can be looked upon as the shifting emphasis between social heritage and individualism, the individual adaptation, discipline and freedom, then the Confucian doctrine of the Mean can be regarded as the doctrine of "synthesis" between the two extremes.

Mencius and his school put more emphasis on the individual aspect of the teaching of Confucius, so they took up the teaching of love (*Jen*) as their most important doctrine. They based their doctrines primarily on their basic conception of the goodness of human nature, so they stressed the individual's right and his free moral judgment.

Hsun-tzu and his school, on the other hand, emphasized more the social aspect of the teaching of Confucius, so they took up the teaching of the rules of proper conduct (*Li*) as their most important doctrine. They based their doctrines primarily on the conception of the evil nature of man, so they laid stress upon external standards and authority as the restraining mould to regulate the evil nature of the individual.

The chief political and social thoughts at the time of Confucius, as shown in the second chapter, "The Background to the Teaching of Confucius", were the patriarchal system of the pre-Chou period, and the well developed feudal system of the early Chou period. The most important virtue that ensured the success of the patriarchal system was the relational or family love, and that of the feudal system was the rules of proper conduct (*Li*). So it is only natural, that Mencius, who "when speaking always made laudatory reference to Yao and Shun", should put more emphasis upon the doctrine of love (*Jen*), especially that of the relational or family love; while Hsun-tzu, who took "later kings" as his ideal personalities, should dwell more on the doctrine of the rules of proper conduct (*Li*).

B. Intellectual Teaching

Confucius, as already pointed out, was primarily a moral teacher. He was chiefly interested in the moral conduct and the practical life of the people. His intellectual and religious teachings were, generally speaking, subordinated and secondary to his moral teaching. So it is not necessary here to go into a detailed discussion of these two phases of the teaching of Confucius. A general outline of each of them will be briefly given in the following.

(A) According to the Immediate Disciples of Confucius

One of the immediate disciples of Confucius recorded that "there were four things which the Master taught,—arts (*Wen*),[101] conduct (*Hsing*),[102] loyalty (*Chung*),[103] and faithfulness (*Hsin*)."[104] (*The Analects*, 7,24) Among the four things which Confucius taught, three deal with moral conduct. To put it in modern language, the teaching of Confucius can be divided into two schools, the school of arts and the school of ethics. In the school of ethics, all the moral teachings of Confucius as given above were taught and put into practice as far as possible. The following discussion about the intellectual teaching of Confucius will include only those courses of study as taught in Confucius' school of arts. In the school of arts it is sometimes recorded as having contained three departments, namely, dialectics (*Yen-yu*),[105] politics (*Cheng-shih*),[106] and literature (*Wen-hsueh*).[107] (*The Analects*, 11,2) The chief subjects to be taught in all these departments can be grouped under the four headings: poetry (*Shih*),[108] history (*Shu*),[109] rules of proper conduct (*Li*),[110] and music (*Yueh*).[111]

"The Master's frequent themes of discourse were—the Poetry,

the History, and the maintenance of the Rules of Proper Conduct." (*The Analects*, 7,17)

"The Master said, 'It is by the Poetry that the mind is aroused. It is by the Rules of Proper Conduct that the character is established. It is from Music that the finish is received.' " (*The Analects*, 8,8)

1. Poetry

(a) The use of poetry at the time of Confucius

At the time of Confucius there was a certain collection of songs very similar to the present *The Book of Poetry*. It was exceedingly popular, and soon became one of the most important written records of that time. It was widely used on important occasions, such as feasting, sacrificing, etc., and also often used by scholars in daily conversations or in letter and essay writing. Curiously enough, it was also frequently used as a very important medium of exchange of opinions in diplomatic relationships. Much of the diplomatic exchanges were carried on during the time of feasting, and it was a very common practice to have singers sing songs while feasting in order to entertain the guests. Individuals at the feast were often asked to select one or more songs from the collection of songs, to be sung by professional singers. The following quotation from *Tso Chuan*, under the 16th year of Duke Chao of Lu, 526 B.C., when Confucius was 25 years old, is one of many similar passages about the special diplomatic usage of poetry.

"In summer, in the fourth month, the six ministers of Cheng gave a parting feast to Hsuan-tzu, in the suburbs, when he said to them, 'Let me ask all you gentlemen to sing from the songs, and I will thence understand the views of Cheng'. Tzu-tso then sang the *Yie-yu-man-ts'ao*[112] (*The Book of Poetry*, 1,7,20), and Hsuan-tzu said 'Good, young sir, I have the same desire'. Tzu-ch'an sang the *Cheng-chih-kao-ch'iu*[113] (*The Book of Poetry*, 1,7,6); and Hsuan-tzu said, 'I am not equal to this.' Tzu Ta Shu sang the *Chien-shang*[114] (*The Book of Poetry*, 1,7,13), and Hsuan-tzu, said, 'I am here. Dare I trouble you to go to any other body?'—on which the other bowed to him. Hsuan-tzu then said, 'Good! your song is right. If there were not such an understanding, could (the good relations of your states) continue?' Tzu-Yu sang the *Fung-yu*[115] (*The Book of Poetry*,

1,7,16), Tzu-ch'i sang the *Yu-nu-t'ung-chu*[116] (*The Book of Poetry*, 1,7,9), Tzu-liu sang the *T'uo-chi*[117] (*The Book of Poetry*, 1,7,11). Hsuan-tzu was glad, and said, 'Cheng may be pronounced near to a flourishing condition! You, gentlemen, received the orders of your ruler to confer on me this honour, and the songs you have sung are all those of Cheng, and all suitable to this festive friendliness. You are all heads of clans that will continue for several generations; you may be without any apprehension.' He then presented them all with horses, and sang the *Wo-chiang*.[118] (*The Book of Poetry*, 4,1,1,7) Tzu-ch'an bowed in acknowledgement, and made the other ministers do the same, saying, 'You have quieted the confusion (of the states), must we not acknowledge your virtuous services.' "

It was of supreme importance that those songs should be suitable to the situations. They should be able to express the desires of those who chose them, and at the same time they should not hurt the feelings of others. Very often owing to inability to select songs, or to select the right and appropriate ones, serious national disgrace and calamity resulted. The following are two of such examples.

Tso Chuan under the 12th year of Duke Chao, 530 B.C., states, "In the summer, Hua-t'ing of Sung came to visit (Lu), to open communications (between Sung and Lu). (The duke of Lu) gave him an entertainment, and there was sung for him the *Liao-hsiao*[119] (*The Book of Poetry*, 2,2,9); but he did not understand it, and sang nothing in reply. Chao-tzu said, 'He is sure to be driven into exile. He cherished not that "we feast and talk"; and declared not his sense of that "they favour me, they brighten me"; he understood not that "excellent virtue"; he accepted not that "common happiness";—how should he continue to be in Sung?' "

Again, under the 16th year of Duke Hsiang, 557 B.C., *Tso Chuan* states: "The Marquis of Chin feasted with other princes in Wen, and made their great officers dance before them, telling them that the songs which they sang must be befitting the occasion. They sung by Kao-hou of Ch'i was not so, which enraged Hsun-yen, so that he said, 'The states are cherishing a disaffected spirit', and proposed that all the great officers should make a covenant with Kao-hou, who, however, stole away back to Ch'i. On this, Shu Sun-pao, Hsun-yen of Chin, Hsiang-hsu of Sung, ning-chih of Wei, Kung-sun Chie of Cheng, and a great officer of Little Chu, made a covenant, engaging that they should together punish the state which did not appear at the court of Chin."

Owing to the importance of poetry in diplomatic relationships, the diplomats were always very carefully chosen to be those who were qualified by wit, and familiarity in using the Songs. *Tso-Chuan* under the 23rd year of Duke Hsi, 6, 7, B.C., states:

"The duke of Ch'in invited Ch'ung-erh, a prince of Chin, to a feast, when Tzu-fan said, 'I am not so accomplished as Shuai; pray make him attend you. The prince sang the *Ho-shui*[120] (*The Book of Poetry*, 2,3,9,), and the duke, the *Liu-yueh*[121] (*The Book of Poetry*, 2,3,2). Chao-shuai said, 'Ch'ung-erh render thanks for the duke's gift.' The prince then descended the steps, and bowed with his head to the ground. The duke also descended a step, and declined such a demonstration. Shuai said, 'When your lordship laid your charge on Ch'ung-erh as to how he should assist the Son of Heaven, he dared not but make so humble an acknowledgement.' "

(b) The teaching of Confucius on Poetry (*Shih*)

a) The values of poetry

Confucius paid much attention to his teaching on poetry; he recognized its social, moral and intellectual values.

a. The social value of poetry

As mentioned above, poetry was commonly used in social and political relationship so that Confucius, in order to meet the needs of his disciples, had to pay attention to the teaching of poetry. Poetry gives beauty and authority to conversation, wherein lies its chief social value. As Confucius once said to his son, Po-yu, "If you do not learn poetry, you will not be fit to converse with." (*The Analects*, 16,13,2)

b. The moral value

All songs, according to Confucius, have a common characteristic, namely, "no depraved thoughts"; they are expressive of enjoyment or grief, but without being licentious or hurtfully excessive.

"The Master said, 'In *The Book of Poetry* are three hundred pieces, but the design of them all may be embraced in one sentence —Having no depraved thoughts.' " (*The Analects*, 2,2)

"The Master said, 'The Kuan Tsu (the first song in *The Book of Poetry*) is expressive of enjoyment without being licentious, and of grief without being hurtfully excessive.' " (*The Analects*, 3,20)

c. The intellectual value

"The Master said, 'My children, why do you not study *The Book of Poetry*? Poetry serves to stimulate the mind. It may be used for purposes of observation. It teaches sociability and regulates the feeling of resentment. It not only has lessons for the duties of serving one's father and of serving the sovereign, but also makes us acquainted with names of birds, beasts and plants." (*The Analects*, 17,9)

Using modern terms, poetry (*Shih*) covers lessons in psychology, sociology, political science, and natural science; it explains the nature of mind, society, government, and the nature of organic and inorganic matters.

b) The ways of using poetry

Having realized the values of poetry, Confucius encouraged the full use of poetry in all its customary ways, such as, in all forms of writing and conversation or singing, either private or public, friendly or formal. One typical way of using poetry was specially emphasized by Confucius, that is, by infering certain ideas or principles from those songs and applying them to specific life situations. Those ideas may be far from being the original ideas of the composers of those songs, yet, if the songs can give certain suggestions applicable to certain situations, they are to be cited as references to meet the situations concerned. Confucius is recorded by his immediate disciples as being much pleased when his disciples knew how to use the poetry in such a way. The following are two examples of this nature:

"Tzu Kung said, 'What do you pronounce concerning the poor man who yet does not flatter, and the rich man who is not proud?' The Master replied, 'They will do; but they are not equal to him, who, though poor, is yet cheerful, and to him, who, though rich, loves the rules of proper conduct (*Li*)'. Tzu Kung replied, 'It is said in *The Book of Poetry*, "As you cut and file, as you carve and then polish." (*The Book of Poetry*, 1,5,1,1) The meaning is the same, I apprehend, as that which you have just expressed.' The Master said, 'With one like Tzu (Tzu Kung), I can begin to talk about the poetry, I told him one point, and he knew its proper sequence.' " (*The Analects*, 1,15)

"Tzu-hsia asked, 'What is the meaning of:

> *"Her cunning smiles,*
> *Her dimples light,*
> *Her lovely eyes,*
> *So clear and bright,*
> *All unadorned,*
> *The background white."?'*
>   (*The Book of Poetry*, 1,5,3)

'Colouring,' said the Master, 'is second to the plain ground.' 'Then *Li* is a subsequent thing,' said Tzu Hsia. 'Shang (Tzu Hsia),' said the Master, 'thou hast hit my meaning! Now I can begin to talk poetry with thee.' " (*The Analects*, 3,8)

The practical reason for emphasizing the ability of a ready inference from poetry to other situations, or from other situations to poetry, can easily be seen from the social needs of the time of Confucius. The purpose of most of the students of Confucius was to enter politics, and the knowledge of poetry and tact in using it were very important qualifications of an accomplished and successful politician. The mere ability to recite all these songs has no practical value, according to Confucius, if one has not acquired the art of using them with tact in practical situations.

"The Master said, 'Though a man may be able to recite the three hundred songs, yet if, when instructed with a governmental charge, he knows not how to act, or if, when sent to any quarter on a mission, he cannot give his replies unassisted, notwithstanding the extent of his learning, of what practical use is it?' " (*The Analects*, 13,5)

2. History

The practice of keeping historical records of the great events in certain times and places began very early in China. In the Spring and Autumn Period, at the time of Confucius, there seemed to be a group of official historians in every state. Their chief business was to keep careful records of the important events that happened, especially in their respective states. They appeared to be men of principles and learning, caring only for the right and truth and not for private safety or benefit. The following are two of such examples recorded in *Tso Chuan*.

Under the second year of Duke Hsuan of Lu, 607 B.C., at the time when Duke Ling of Chin was murdered, *Tso Chuan* states:

"The Grand Historian (of Chin) wrote the entry, 'Chao Tun has murdered his prince,' and showed it to the court. Hsuan Tzu (i.e., Chao Tun) said that this was not true. (The historian) replied: 'Sir, you are the highest minister. Flying from the state, you did not go beyond its frontiers. When you returned you did not punish the assassin. If it is not you (who are responsible), who is it?'. . . . Confucius said of this: 'Of old, Tung Hu was an excellent historian. In his writings he had the rule of not concealing (the truth).' "

Again, under the 25th year of Duke Hsiang, 548 B.C., when Duke Chuang of Ch'i was murdered:

"The Grand Historian (of Ch'i) made a record of the fact which said: 'Ts'ui Tzu has murdered his prince.' Tsui Tzu thereupon had him executed. Two of his brothers did the same after him, and were also executed. A third wrote the same and was spared. The historian in the south, learning that the Grand Historian and his two brothers had died in this way, took his tablets and went (to record also that Ts'ui Tzu had murdered his prince). But learning on the way that the affair had already been recorded (by the third brother), he returned."

There seemed to have been quite a number of written historical records existing during the time of Confucius, from which he derived much of his teaching materials. There were very ancient historical materials, recording the great events of the remote past, somewhat like the present *Shu Ching, The Book of History*. Some of them appeared credible to Confucius, and some of them he honestly doubted.

"The Master said, 'I could describe the rules of proper conduct (*Li*) of the Hsia Dynasty, but Chi cannot sufficiently attest my words. I could describe the rules of proper conduct (*Li*) of the Yin Dynasty, but Sung cannot sufficiently attest my words. (They cannot do so) because of the insufficiency of their records and wise men. If those were sufficient, I could adduce them in support of my words.' " (*The Analects*, 3,9)

There were also historical records of different states, such as, the *Ch'eng*[122] of Chin, the *Tao Wu*[123] of Ch'u, and the *Ch'un Ch'iu of Lu*. Mencius said:

"The *Ch'eng* of Chin, the *Tao Wu* of Ch'u, and the *Ch'un Ch'iu* of Lu were books of the same character. Their subject was the affairs of (Dukes) Huan of Ch'i and Wen of Chin, and their style was historical. Confucius said: 'Their righteous principles I ventured to take.' " (*Mencius*, 4,2,21)

When the question arose as to what should be taught to the crown prince of Ch'u, son of King Chuang (613-591 B.C.), the answer came:

"Teach him the *Ch'un Ch'iu* and by it encourage goodness and censure evil, so as to refrain and admonish his mind." (*Kuo Yu*, Ch'u Yu, 1,1)

As a citizen of Lu, Confucius was naturally more interested in the *Ch'un Ch'iu*, the historical record of his native state. Very likely he offered to his disciples a special course of instruction on the history of the State of Lu. For that course, probably he had taken the existing historical records of his state, the *Ch'un Ch'iu of Lu*, as a basis, and used the "righteous principles" which he deduced from all the historical records of his day, to expound or rectify the older materials of the *Ch'un Ch'iu* annals. Hence the name Confucius has been specially connected with the *Ch'un Ch'iu of Lu*, which has long been supposed to have been written by him.

To be a historian was a very honourable and important calling, so Confucius, in order to meet the need of his time, used special efforts to instruct his disciples to be good historians. He lamented over the moral degeneracy of the historians of his time, saying,

"Even in my (early) days, a historian would leave a blank in his text (in case of doubt). . . . Now, alas! there are no such things." (*The Analects*, 15,25)

Teaching history would naturally include also the arts of writing and composing. For example, the chief purpose of the *Ch'un Ch'iu* is supposed to be the "rectification of names". Every term or word has its special usage. So sometimes the governmental notifications, in the days of Confucius, which were to be preserved as historical records, had to pass through many hands.

"The Master said, 'In preparing the governmental notifications, P'i Shen first made the rough draught; Shih Shu examined and discussed its contents; Tzu Yu, the manager of foreign intercourse, then polished the style, Tzu Ch'an of Tung-li gave it the proper elegance and finish.' " (*The Analects*, 14,9)

As those formal documents or historical records had to be so carefully done there was always a great demand for scholars, and this probably is one of the reasons why Confucius was so popular as a teacher in his day.

3. The rules of Proper Conduct (*Li*)

The teaching of Confucius on the rules of proper conduct (*Li*) has already been discussed in this chapter, so it will·be sufficient simply to reiterate a few lines here.

The importance of *Li* had been recognized long before Confucius as a kind of unwritten law in political administration. It was supposed to be observed by everybody, even kings and princes were no exceptions. One rhymester spoke of the man who did not observe *Li* as being inferior to a rat, and he wished that such a man had been dead rather than alive. He said:

> *"Look at a rat,—it has its limbs;*
> *But a man shall be without the* Li.
> *If a man observe no* Li,
> *Why does he not quickly die?''*
> (*The Book of Poetry*, 1,4,8)

Owing to the importance of being recognized by the people, in general, during the time of Confucius, teaching on it became essential and in great demand. Confucius, as already pointed out, was famous in his day for his extensive knowledge of *Li*. There was much written material about the *Li* of the remote periods of Chinese history, with which Confucius was very familiar.

"Confucius said, 'The Yin Dynasty followed the *Li* of the Hsia: wherein it took from or added to them may be known. The Chou Dynasty had followed the *Li* of the Yin: wherein it took from or added to them may be known.' " (*The Analects*, 2,23)

"The Master said, 'I could describe the *Li* of the Hsia Dynasty, but Chi cannot sufficiently attest my words. I could describe the *Li* of the Yin Dynasty, but Sung cannot sufficiently attest my words. (They cannot do so) because of the insufficiency of their records and wise men. If those were sufficient, I could adduce them in support of my words.' " (*The Analects*, 3,9)

"Yen Yuan asked how the government of a country should be administered. The Master said, 'Follow the seasons of Hsia. Ride in the state carriage of Yin. Wear the ceremonial cap of Chou. . . .' " (*The Analects*, 15,10,1-4)

Confucius very probably took the traditional materials on *Li* as the basis of his instruction. He selected the best, and expounded and rectified them. He put new meaning into them, by emphasizing the spirit as well as the form of *Li*. He was conscious of the fact that the rules, rites or any other external restraints imposed upon individual conduct were not enough. They were merely outward forms and had no real value without the proper response from the heart and mind of the individual.

"The Master said, 'It is according to the rules of proper conduct (*Li*),' they say, 'It is according to the rules of proper conduct (*Li*),' they say. Are gems and silk all that is meant (by) the rules of proper conduct?" (*The Analects*, 17,11)

"Gems and silk" are the outward forms or appearance of *Li*. They are important, but they are not all that is meant by *Li*. A complete observance of *Li*, according to Confucius, is both the proper outward expression or form, and the sincere inward heart or spirit.

"The Master said, 'Where the substance (*Chih*,[124] the reality or basic stuff of human nature) exceeds the form (*Wen*[125] the culture, training, or accomplishments), we have rusticity; where the form exceeds the substance, we have the manners of a clerk. When the form and substance are equally blended, we have the Superior Man.' " (*The Analects*, 6,16)

4. Music

It includes instrumental and vocal music, the words as well as the tune, and also the dancing which sometimes accompanies and expresses it. The Chinese word has a much broader connotation than the English word music, and is much closer to the ancient Greek concept of "music".

(a) Confucius' interest in music

Confucius was artistic and musical by nature and was especially fond of music. He both played musical instruments and sang songs, and indeed the two usually went together in his day. He was so much interested and versed in music, that it was but natural that he should take music as one of the important courses of his teaching.

"When the Master was in Ch'i, he heard the Shao music and for three months did not know the taste of flesh. 'I did not think,' he said, 'that music could have been made so excellent as this.' " (*The Analects*, 7,13)

"The Master instructing the Grand music-master of Lu said, 'How to play music may be known. At the commencement of the piece, all the parts should sound together. As it proceeds, they should be in harmony, while severally distinct and flowing without break, and thus on to the conclusion.' " (*The Analects*, 3,23)

"When the Master was in company with a person who was singing, if he sang well, he would make him repeat the song, while he accompanied it with his own voice." (*The Analects*, 7,31)

"The Master was playing, one day, on the *Ch'ing*[126] (a musical stone) in Wei, when a man, carrying a straw basket passed the door of the house where Confucius was, and said, 'His heart is full who so beats the *Ch'ing*." (*The Analects*, 14,42,1)

(b) Confucius' conception of music—traditional viewpoint

Confucius, in the main, shared the traditional conception of music, as recorded in the written materials, supposed to have handed down to his day from the past. The following are some examples.

"The Emperor (Shun) said, . . . 'I appoint you to be canon of music, to teach the youth to be upright but mild, gentle but firm, strong but without tyranny, and direct but without arrogance. Poetry expresses ideas and singing prolongs the utterance. The tones go with the utterance, while the notes harmonize the tones. The eight sounds can be brought together so that no one detracts from the others. Spirits and men are thus harmonized.' " (*The Book of History*, "Shun Tien")[127]

"The duties of the minister of education (*Ta-szu-t'u*)[128] are . . . to teach harmony with music and the rules of proper conduct (*Li*), so that the people will not oppose one another. . . ; to make use of the six forms of music to control the emotions of the people, and to teach them harmony. . . ." (*Chou Li*, "Ti Kuan",[129] pp. 14-15)

a) To promote the music of *Ya*,[130] and to banish the music of *Cheng*[131]

Confucius cherished the same traditional idea that music should harmonize one's emotions according to the doctrine of the Mean —"to be upright but mild, gentle but firm, strong but without tyranny, and direct but without arrogance." For this reason, in his teaching of music, he tried very hard to promote the music of *Ya*, and banish the music of *Cheng*.

"The Master said, . . . 'I hate the way in which the sounds of *Cheng (Cheng Sheng)*[132] confound the music of *Ya (Ya Yueh)*.[133] I hate those who with their sharp months overthrow kingdoms and families.' " (*The Analects*, 17,18)

"The Master said of the *Shao*,[134] (the music made by Shun) that it was perfectly beautiful and also perfectly good. He said of the *Wu*,[135] (the music of King Wu) that it was perfectly beautiful but not perfectly good." (*The Analects*, 3,25)

"Yen Yuan asked how the government of a country should be administered. The Master said, . . . 'Let the music be the Shao with its pantomines. Banish the sound of *Cheng*, and keep far from specious talkers. The sound of *Cheng* is licentious; specious talkers are dangerous.' " (*The Analects*, 15,10,5-6)

"The Master said, 'I returned from Wei to Lu, and then the music was reformed, and the pieces in the *Ya* (Royal songs) and *Sung* (Praise songs)[136] all found their proper places.' " (*The Analects*, 9,14)

"The Master said, 'When the music-master Chih first entered on his office, the finish of the Kuan Chu was magnificent;—how it filled the ears!' " (*The Analects*, 8,15)

"The Master said, 'The Kuan Chu is expressive of enjoyment without being licentious, and of grief without being hurtfully excessive.' " (*The Analects*, 3,20)

From the above quotations certain conclusions may be drawn, such as, that the music of *Cheng* is licentious, excessively attractive and stimulating; while the music of *Ya* is peaceful, harmonious, and edifying. The former is compared with the 'specious talkers' or 'those who with their sharp mouths', and with their beautiful talks can so attract the audience that they become 'dangerous' and able 'to overthrow kingdoms and families'; while the latter is like the Kuan Chu, which strikes at the Mean of one's emotion,— 'expressive of enjoyment without being licentious, and of grief without being hurtfully excessive.' The peaceful and melodious music of *Shao* is to be preferred to that of *Wu*, because the latter, though in perfect melody, breathes the martial air, indicative of its author.

In short, the music which Confucius advocated and taught is that which is both beautiful and good, melodious and edifying, and is expressive of one's emotions, but always harmonious and moderate. This is why he promoted the music of *Ya* and banished the music of *Cheng*.

b) The rectification of music

Confucius, believing in the doctrine of the "rectification of names" and the rules of proper conduct (*Li*) for different classes or ranks of people, followed also the traditional view of the function of music, that it should be used to harmonize different classes of people so that they 'will not oppose one another'. During the time of Confucius there was a tendency towards the improper use of music. Many a time, the royal music and songs were played and sung in the homes of the ministers, and Confucius was recorded to have been very indignant at this unlawful usurption.

"Confucius said of the head of the Chi family, who had eight rows of pantomines in his ancestral court, 'If he can bear to do this, what may he not bear to do?' " (*The Analects*, 3,1)

"The three families used the *Yung* song, while the vessels were being removed, (at the conclusion of the sacrifice). The Master said, 'Assisting are the princes;—the son of heaven looks profound and grave':—what application can these words have in the hall of the three families?' " (*The Analects*, 3,2)

Eight rows of pantomines with music could only be used by the king in his ancestral temples, and the *Yung* song could properly only be sung in the royal temples, and neither the Chi nor the three families, according to Confucius, had any right to use them. In the teaching of music, Confucius tried also to rectify the proper use of different pieces of music, and put to them in their proper places.

"The Master said, 'I returned from Wei to Lu, and then the music was reformed, and the pieces in the *Ya* and *Sung* all found their proper places.' " (*The Analects*, 9,14)

Ya[137] means 'elegant' or 'correct'. They are the songs to be used with music at royal ceremonies and festivals, so were known to be Royal songs. *Sung* means 'praise'[138] and they were songs praising the virtues of the founders of different dynasties, and were used in the services of the ancestral temples. Here is a clear instance of Confucius' service in correcting and rectifying the music of his own state. But despite the effort of Confucius in selecting and rectifying the proper and the *Ya* music, and banishing and condemning the *Cheng* and the improper or usurping music, very little result was achieved. Different kinds of the so-called "modern" music and songs sprang up very rapidly in the period of the Warring States. They were much more complicated and popular than the so-called "ancient" music and songs, as advocated by Confucius and his followers. This will be discussed later.

(c) The musical instruments possibly used by Confucius

Confucius, as shown above, was only interested in sacred or classical music. *Yo-chi*[139] gives the following list of musical instruments as made long before Confucius, and used in sacred music. Confucius might have used such to teach in his course on music.

"The (ancient) sages made the musical instruments, the Yao (a small drum with two beads suspended on both sides and a handle —when the handle is rolled between the palms, the beads strike the drum itself), the drum,[140] the K'ung[141] and the Ch'ia[142] (varieties of square wooden drums with wooden tops with a hole in the center), the Hsuan,[143] and the Ch'ih[144] (varieties of mouth organs, the Hsuan being a broad oval-shaped clay pot with six holes (ocarina) and the Ch'ih being made of bamboo with different pipes provided with reeds). These six instruments produce sounds used in sacred music. In addition, they are accompanied by the bells,[145] the Ch'ing[146] (a sonorous stone), the Yu[147] (a kind of bagpipe with 36 reeds) and the Seh[148] (a long horizontal string instrument with fifth or less strings). With the dance were used shields and hatchets (military dance) and pennants of ox-tails and long pheasant tails (civil dance). This was the kind of music used at the ceremonies of ancient kings and at drinking ceremonies. It is the kind of music by which a sense of social order between the different ranks was established, and the sense of discipline between elders and juniors and superiors and inferiors was taught to the following generations." (Li-chi, chap. 19; The Wisdom of Confucius, pp. 264-265; cp. The Book of Poetry, 4,1,2,5)

The following are some references concerning musical instruments mentioned in The Book of Poetry, for the sacred music connected, in most cases, with ancestor worship. They must have been familiar to Confucius, and most of them are similar to those musical instruments mentioned above in Yo-chi.

a) Metal and stone instruments:
  a. Bells:
    Chung[149] (2,3,1,1), Yung[150] (3,1,8,3)
    Cheng[151] (3,3,4,3), Ling [152](4,1,2,8)
  b. Stone and jade, sonorous plagues:
    Ch'ing[153] (2,6,4,4; 4,3,1)
b) Vibrating instruments:
  Ku[154] or drums (2,3,1,1; 2,6,5,5)
  T'ao or hand-drum (4,1,2,5)
  Ch'un or a wooden instrument for giving signal

to musicians to commence (4,1,2,5)
Yu[155] or a wooden instrument for stopping the music (4,1,2,5)
c) Wind instruments:
Hsuan[156] or a pottery ocarina (2,5,5,7)
Yo[157] or a kind of flute (1,3,13,3)
Ch'ih[158] another kind of flute (2,5,5,7)
Hsiao[159] or the pan-pipes (4,1,2,5)
Sheng[160] or pipe mouth-organ (2,1,1,1)
d) String instruments:
Ch'in[161] or a kind of flute of five or seven strings (1,4,6,1)
Seh[162] or lute of 25 to 50 strings (1,1,1,3)

(B) According to Mencius and Hsun-tzu

1. According to Mencius

The greatness of Confucius, as Mencius saw it, primarily lies in his moral character and moral teaching. He, as with the seventy famous disciples of Confucius, submitted to Confucius chiefly through the influence of the virtue of the master. He says, "When one subdues men by virtue, in their hearts' core they are pleased, and sincerely submit, as was the case with the seventy disciples in their submission to Confucius. What is said in *The Book of Poetry*,

> '*From the east, from the west,*
> *From the south, from the north,*
> *There was no one who thought of refusing submission.*'

Is an illustration of this." (*Mencius*, 2,1,3,2) It was chiefly the moral teaching of Confucius, especially on love (*Jen*) that Mencius was interested in. He states,"Confucius said, 'There are but two courses (which can be pursued), that of love and not-love.' " (*Mencius*, 4,1,2,3) He was not specially keen on the intellectual teachings of Confucius, which were to him, all secondary things. He regarded, for example, the function of wisdom as merely to know and hold fast the virtues of filial piety and fraternal duties, the roots of love and righteousness respectively; the function of the rules of proper conduct (*Li*), as "the ordering and adorning those two things"; and the function of music, as "the rejoicing in those two things." (*Mencius*, 4,1,27)

As a Confucianist, he was also interested in education, the object of which was essentially moral, "to illustrate the human relations." He says:

"Establish Hsiang, Hsu, Hsueh, Hsiao—(all those educational institutions),—for the instruction of (the people). . . . The object of them all is to illustrate the human relations." (*Mencius*, 3,1,3,10)

Being primarily an idealist, believing that the truth lies essentially in the human mind, Mencius paid more attention to the psychological development of the individual in the educational process, rather than to the impartation of knowledge, and not even to those traditional classical writings as taught, revised, or written by Confucius. To him, books are fallible, and should not be entirely believed, and should be taught with emphasis on the general aims and thoughts of the writers instead of on their specific terms or sentences in the books.

"Mencius said, 'It would be better to be without books than to give entire credit to them. In the "Completion of the war" (Wu Ch'eng),[163] I select two or three passages only, which I believe.' " (*Mencius*, 7,2,3,1-2)

"Those who explain the songs (in *The Book of Poetry*), may not insist on one term so as to do violence to the general aim (of the writer). They must try with their thoughts to meet the aim, and then we shall apprehend it. If we simply take single sentences, there is that in the song called 'The Milky Way',—

> *'Of the black haired people of the remnant of Chou,*
> *There is not half a one left.'*

If it had been really as thus expressed, then not an individual of the people of Chou was left." (*Mencius*, 5,1,4,2)

Mencius, however, esteemed one book very highly, namely, the *Ch'un Ch'iu* or *The Spring and Autumn Annals*. He attributed its authorship directly to Confucius. It is chiefly through his commendation that the *Ch'un Ch'iu* has obtained its unique place in

Chinese classical literature, and has been regarded as containing the most important intellectual teaching of Confucius. Mencius says:

"The world fell into decay, and principles faded away. Perverse speakings and oppressive deeds waxed rife again. There were instances of ministers who murdered their sovereigns, and of sons who murdered their fathers. Confucius was afraid, and made the *Ch'un Ch'iu*. What the *Ch'un Ch'iu* contains are matters proper to the emperor. On this account Confucius said, 'Yes! It is the *Ch'un Ch'iu* which will make men know me, and it is the *Ch'un Ch'iu* which will make men condemn me.' " (*Mencius*, 3,2,9,7-8)

"The traces of imperial rule were extinguished, and the poetry ceased to be made. When the poetry ceased to be made, then the *Ch'un Ch'iu* was produced. The *Sheng* of *Chin*, the *Tao-wu* of Ch'u, and the *Ch'un Ch'iu* of Lu, were books of the same character. The subject was the affairs of Huan of Ch'i and Wen of Chin, and its style was the historical. Confucius said, 'Its righteous principles I ventured to make.' " (*Mencius*, 4,2,21)

2. According to Hsun-tzu

The greatness of Confucius, according to Mencius, as pointed out above, lies chiefly in his moral qualities, but to Hsun-tzu, his greatness chiefly lies in his intellectual qualities, such as his wisdom, scholarship, and his intellectual power of overcoming prejudice. Hsun-tzu says:

"Confucius possessed the qualities of love (*Jen*) and wisdom, and was not prejudiced; hence his scholarship and mastery over all teachings were sufficient to make him equal with the ancient kings. He possessed the whole of the right Way (*Tao*); he brought it to people's notice, and he used it; he was not prejudiced nor unable to carry it out. Hence his virtue was equal to that of Duke Chou; his reputation is abreast to that of the three Kings; this is the happiness which comes from not being prejudiced." (*The Works of Hsun-tzu*, p. 265)

Being primarily an empirical philosopher, believing that the truth only comes from human experience, Hsun-tzu paid more attention to the impartation of knowledge, more especially that which was stored up in those classics as taught, revised or written by Confucius, such as *The Book of Poetry (Shih)*, *The Book of History (Shu)*, *The Book of Rites (Li)*, *The Book of Music (Yueh)*, and *The Spring and Autumn Annals (Ch'un Ch'iu)*. Among these courses of study, Hsun-tzu, as mentioned above, paid most attention to *Li*.

"What should one study? How should one begin? The art begins by reciting the Classics and ends in learning the rites *(Li)*. . . . *The Book of History* records political events. *The Book of Poetry* regulates sounds so that they should attain the normal and not go beyond it. *The Book of Rites (Li)* deals with the great distinctions of society through rules; it is the unifying principle of general classes of action. Study advances to *The Book of Rites (Li)*, and stops there. That is what is meant by the extreme of virtue. The reverence and love of elegance of *The Book of Rites (Li)*, the harmony of *The Book of Music*, the broad knowledge of *The Book of Poetry* and *The Book of History*, the subtleties of *The Spring and Autumn* are the completion of all creation." *(The Works of Hsun-tzu*, pp. 36-37)

"In studying there is nothing better than being intimate with a worthy teacher. The *Rites (Li)* and *Music* give principles and no false teaching. The *Poetry* and *History* tell about the ancients, and are not familiar. The teaching of *The Spring and Autumn* is suggestive rather than expressive." *(The Works of Hsun-tzu*, p. 38)

"Unless a person thoroughly cultivates himself so as to be a Superior Man, he cannot have knowledge. Hence it is said: A short rope cannot draw water from a deep well; he whose knowledge is limited cannot converse with those who reach to the status of a Sage. Then the function of the *Poetry*, the *History*, the *Rites (Li)*, and the Music is certainly not for the ordinary man to understand. Hence it is said, Concentrate on them and then you can know more; possess them, and you can be enduring; be versed in them and you can be successful; think on them and you can be peaceful; repeatedly follow and investigate them and you will love them the more. By them control your passions and you will gain benefit; by them make a reputation, and you will have honour; by them live in society and you will have harmony; by them live alone and you will be satisfied." *(The Works of Hsun-tzu*, pp. 64-65)

Beside special emphasis on *Li*, Hsun-tzu also paid great attention to *Music*, to which he dedicated one of his books in *The Works of Hsun-tzu*. The importance of music, according to that book, can be summarized as follows:

(a) Music is the expression of joyful emotion.

"Music is the expression of joy. Men's feelings make this inevitable. . . . Man must needs be joyous; if joyous, then he must needs embody his feelings; if they are embodied, but without conforming to any principles, then they cannot avoid being disordered." (*The Works of Hsun-tzu*, pp. 247-248)

(b) Music harmonizes and unites the people.

"Music is the greatest unifier in the world, the bond of inner harmony, the inevitable consequence of human emotion." (p. 249)

(c) Music turns the people's hearts to virtue.

"When music plays, the will is clear, the rules of proper conduct (*Li*) are cultivated and the character is perfected; the ear and eye are acute, the body and mind are tranquil, the customs and habits are altered, the whole country is peaceful, beautiful, good, and joyous. . . . Hence music is that whereby joy is conformed to principle. 'Metal, stone, string, bamboo' (materials for musical instruments) are the things which induce virtue. When music is played, the people turn towards it. Hence music is the greatest power in ruling." (pp. 253-254)

(d) Music and *Li* embrace the whole heart of man.

"Music is unchanging concord. *Li* is undying principles. Music unites; *Li* distinguishes. The union of *Li* and music embraces the whole heart of man." (p. 254)

(e) Music reflects the universe.

"The drum is like heaven; the bells are like earth; the stone chimes like water; the organs, the flageolet, the flutes are like the stars, the sun and the moon; the hand drum, the tub clapper, the "fu" drum, the bell-frame, the notched sounding board, and the time maker, are like the ten-thousand things." (p. 255)

Hsun-tzu and his school of Confucianism followed the efforts of Confucius and tried to promote ancient or classical music, and banish the new music.

The new music included the music of Cheng, Sung, Wei, and Ch'i. These four kinds of music, according to Hsun-tzu and his school, were sensual and able to undermine the people's character and put the country in disorder, therefore they ought to be banished. *The Book of Music (Yo-chi)*[164] states:

"The music of Cheng is lewd and corrupting, the music of Sung is soft and makes one effeminate, the music of Wei is repetitious and annoying, and the music of Ch'i is harsh and makes one haughty. These four kinds of music are all sensual music and undermine the people's character, and that is why they cannot be used at the sacrifices." (*Yo-chi, Li-chi,* Chap. 19; tr. by Lin Yu-tang in *The Wisdom of Confucius,* p. 264)

"The music of Cheng and Wei is the music of countries in turmoil, coming very near to a general discord. The music of 'In the Mulberry Field', upon the banks of River P'u (in Wei) is the music of a destroyed country. . . ." (*The Wisdom of Confucius,* p. 254)

Hsun-tzu says in the same manner:

"Pretty and fascinating appearance, the music of Cheng and Wei makes men's hearts licentious." (*The Works of Hsun-tzu,* p. 252)

"When the music is pretty and fascinating, it is dangerous; then the people degenerate, are negligent, mean, and low. If they lose self-restraint and are negligent, turmoil will begin; if they are mean and low, they will wrangle. If they are in turmoil and wrangle among themselves, then the armies will be weak, cities will be attacked and enemy states will be dangerous." (*The Works of Hsun-tzu,* p. 251)

The Classical music includes *Shu,*[165] *Yung,*[166] *Shao,*[167] *Wu,*[168] *Ya,*[169] *Sung,*[170] etc. They are, according to Hsun-tzu and his school, both beautiful and good, expressive and edifying, and should be promoted. Hsun-tzu says:

"The early Kings hated the disorder, hence established the music of the *Ya* and *Sung* to conform it to principle, so as to cause its music to produce joy and not to degenerate, so as to cause its beauty to change but not stop, so as to cause its indirect and direct appeals, its manifoldness and simplicity, its frugality and richness, its rests and notes, to stir up the goodness in men's mind, and to prevent evil feelings from gaining any foothold." (*The Works of Hsun-tzu*, p. 248) Again he says:

"When I hear the music of *Ya* and *Sung*, my purposes are broadened." (*ibid.*, p. 249) Again:

"Posturing the *Shao*, singing the *Wu*, make men's heart dignified." (*ibid.*, p. 252)

Yo-chi states:

"*The Book of Poetry* says, 'The harmonious sounds are *Shu* and *Yung* and my ancestor listened to them'. *Shu* means 'pious' and *Yung* means 'peaceful'. If you have piety and peacefulness of character, you can do everything you want with a country." (*Li-chi*, Chap. 19; *The Wisdom of Confucius*, Lin Yu-tang, p. 264)

"In the ancient music the dancers move in formation forward and backward in an atmosphere of peace and order and a certain luxury of movement. The 'hsuan' (a string instrument), the gourd and 'sheng' (a kind of mouth organ with bamboo reed-pipes, resembling the pipe-organ in principle), are held in readiness until the drum gives the signal for the start. The music begins with the civil dance movements and ends with the military dance movements, and there is a continuity of movement from the beginning to the end, while the measure of the classical music prevents or checks the dancers who are inclined to go too fast. After listening to such music, the Superior Man will be in a proper atmosphere to discuss the music and the ways of the ancients, the cultivation of personal life and the ordering of national life. This is the main sentiment or character of ancient music." (*The Wisdom of Confucius*, pp. 262-263)

Despite the efforts of Confucius and his believers, including Mencius and Hsun-tzu, the ancient classical music could not maintain its original position, the new music gradually won its way and became very popular. For example, King Hui of Liang told Mencius that, 'I am unable to love the music of the ancient sovereigns; I only love the music that suits the manners of the present age." (*Mencius*, 1,2,1,2) Again, *Yo-chi* states:

"Baron Wen of Wei asked Tzu Hsia, the disciple of Confucius, 'why is it that I feel sleepy every time I listen to classical music in my official dress, and never feel tired when I listen to the music of (the states of) Cheng and Wei? Why is it that the classical music is like that and the new music is like this?" (*Li-chi*, Chap. 19; *The Wisdom of Confucius*, p. 262)

There was also a great increase in the variety of musical instruments in the period of the Warring States, in which Mencius and Hsun-tzu lived. The music and poetry began to be separated, and to be developed each along its own line, and they were no longer required to go together as in the earlier periods. The styles of poetry began to be varied, such as the long pieces of poetry which we call Hsao,[171] and Fu,[172] which are supposed to be read only and not to be sung. In music, Han Fei Tzu said: "there had to be three hundred men to blow the flutes, whenever King Hsuan of Ch'i asked for music." (Chapter on Nei Chu, part one)[173] *Shih Chi* records an incident when music was played without the accompaniment of vocal songs:

"When the king of Chau ... met the king of Ch'in at Chen Ch'in. the king of Ch'in, after drinking much wine, said, 'I have heard that the king of Chau is fond of music, may I beg you, sir, to play the lute.' So the king of Chau played the lute. . . ." (The Biographies of Lien-po and Lin Hsiang-ju)[174]

The classical music is too simple in character to compete with the 'new' music. But Hsun-tzu and his school made the distinction between music and the sounds of music. "Music and sounds are of course related, but they are two different things." (*Yo-chi*, see *The Wisdom of Confucius*, p. 263) Hsun-tzu said, "Sound and music enter deeply into people, their influence is rapid." (p. 250) "Sound is the form of music." (*Hsun-tzu*, p. 254); it is not the whole of music. In listening to music one should not only listen to its sound, but rather listen to the significance proper to the different sounds. *Yo-chi* gives the following statement about the sounds of different instruments and the proper significance of the different sounds:

"The sound of the bell is clear and resonant; its clarity and resonance make it especially suitable for serving as signals, such signals create an impression of majesty, and the impression of majesty inspires a sense of military power. Therefore when the sovereign hears the bell, he thinks of his military officials. The sound of the musical stone is sharp and clear-cut; its sharpness and clear-cut quality tend to foster the sense of decision, and the sense of decision makes it easy for the generals to die in battle. Therefore when the sovereign hears the musical stone he thinks of his military officers who die in battle at the border. The sound of the string is plaintive; its plaintive quality cleanses the soul, and the cleansed state of mind makes for a sense of righteousness. Therefore, when the sovereign hears the sound of the string instrument, the Ch'in and the Seh (both horizontal string instruments on a flat sounding board), he thinks of his righteous ministers. The sound of bamboo (corresponding to the Western woodwind instruments) has a floating quality; its floating quality tends to spread everywhere and bring together the masses of the people. Therefore when the sovereign hears the sound of bamboo instruments, he thinks of his ministers of the interior. The sound of the big and small drums is noisy; its noisy quality tends to arouse and excite, and the excitement tends to prepare the masses for action. Therefore when the sovereign hears the sound of the big and small drums, he thinks of his great generals. It is seen, therefore, that in hearing music, the sovereign does not hear their sounds only, but also hears the significance proper to the, different sounds." (*The Wisdom of Confucius*, pp. 265-266)

It is because the "significance proper to the different sounds" interested those Confucianists, that naturally they should oppose the music which is "pretty and fascinating", which attracted the listeners too much to its sounds, so that they forget its real meaning and significance.

In short, Hsun-tzu and his school of Confucianism paid much attention to the intellectual teachings of Confucius especially *Li* and music, and it is probably due to the efforts of Hsun-tzu and his school that both *Li* and music have occupied such an important place in the thoughts and practices of Confucianism.

C. Religious Teaching of Confucius

(A) According to *The Analects* and Other Classics

1. Confucius was not a Teacher of Religion, but a Religious Teacher.

Confucius, according to the records of his immediate disciples, taught very little about the metaphysical problems of religion. In his teachings, he chiefly concerned himself with the essential human relationships, and not with the world of spirits or immortality or other metaphysical problems. One of his disciples said, "The subjects on which the Master did not talk, were—extraordinary things, feats of strength, disorder, and spiritual beings." (*The Analects*, 7,20) Another one of his disciples remarked, "The Masters' personal displays of his principles and ordinary descriptions of them may be heard. His discourses about man's nature, and the way of Heaven, cannot be heard." (*The Analects*, 5,13)

This does not mean that Confucius was not a religious person. He did not discountenance or alter very much the traditional religious belief, though occasionally he did give comments on religious problems when he was asked about them. He was, in fact, a true heir of best religious heritage that came to him from the remote past. All he did was to transmit that heritage to later generations with some of his own important remarks. He was deeply religious by nature, and had a firm belief in the one supreme, all-ruling, and personal God whom he called T'ien or Heaven. When he was a boy, he was reported to have been fond of religious matters; he "used to play at making sacrificial offerings and performing the ceremonies." (*Shih Chi*, "The Life of Confucius") Throughout his life he had the highest regard for religious things. For example, the reason which he gave for the resignation of his position as the Chief Minister of Lu was, according to *Shih Chi*, that the Duke of Lu "did not remember to send the burnt offering to the ministers." ("The Life of Confucius") He would not bow to his friends no matter what gifts they sent him, "the only present for which he wanted was that of the flesh of sacrifice." (*The Analects*, 10,15,2) He prayed, (*The Analects*, 7,34) fasted (10,7), and attended public worship regularly and reverently. (*The Analects*, 3,12) He knew the ordinances of God (*The Analects*, 2,4), stood in awe of them (16,8), obeyed them faithfully and carried them out enthusiastically. He regarded his work as a divine mission, and constantly renewed his strength with comfort from God, especially when confronted by difficulties and dangers. Once he was heard to say in despair, "Alas! there is no one who knows me!" to which he immediately subjoined, "But there is Heaven, He knows me!" (*The Analects*, 14,37) When he was in danger of being killed by Huan T'ui, a high officer of Sung, he said calmly, "Heaven produced the virtue that is in me. Huan T'ui—what can he do to me?" (*The Analects*, 7,22) Again, "When the Master was put in peril in K'uang, he said, 'After the death of King Wen, was not the cause of truth lodged here in me? If Heaven had wished to let this cause of truth perish, then I, a future moral, should not have got such a relation to that cause. While Heaven does not let the cause of truth perish, what can the people of K'uang do to me?' " (*The Analects*, 9,5)

He did not, however, share much of the contemporary superstitious belief. He was rather sceptical about the spirits or demons who were commonly believed to inhabit everywhere in the air, rivers, mountains, trees, etc. He did not let his disciples pray for him when he was seriously ill to "the spirits of the upper and lower worlds." (*The Analects*, 7,34) He discountenanced the popular belief that the will of God could be changed through prayers given to the spirits who were supposed to carry out the will of God. "Wang-sun asked, saying, 'What is the meaning of the saying "It is better to pay court to (the spirit of) the furnace than to that of the South-west corner?' " The Master said, 'Not so, He who offends against Heaven has none to whom he can pray.' " (*The Analects*, 3,13) His practical advice concerning the attitude towards the spirits was "to respect spiritual beings, but keep aloof from them." (*The Analects*, 6,20)

In short, Confucius was not a teacher of religion, but a religious teacher, accepting unquestionably the best of the traditional religious beliefs, and transmitting them to his disciples. Those beliefs, having been approved by Confucius, became incorporated and perpetuated in the Confucian system, as if they were a part of the teaching of Confucius. So to-day when we speak about Confucian Religion, we really mean the traditional religion which Confucius accepted and transmitted to his disciples with a few notable alterations. The following are some of the traditional religious beliefs which have become the religion of Confucius.

2. The Doctrine of God

God, in the pre-Chou period, was generally called Ti,[175] the Supreme One, who was conceived to be the all-ruling personal spirit, able to receive burnt offerings and other sacrifices from men and to bless them with prosperity and happiness. Though His chief abode was in Heaven, yet He was always present, so that no image of Him was possible or necessary. From the Chou period onward T'ien[176] or Heaven, and Ti, have been used interchangeably to denote the one God who is all-ruling, intelligent, all-knowing, almighty, full of love and justice. (For more detailed discussion on the nature of God, see chap. 2, "The Religious Background of the Teaching of Confucius")

Confucius, as recorded in *The Analects*, always used the name T'ien and avoided the more personal name Ti to denote the one personal God, the only supreme ruler over heaven and earth. That probably has something to do with the more naturalistic interpretation of Confucian religion given by many great Confucian thinkers in later periods.

3. The doctrine of Man

(a) Man is the creature of God.

That man as the creature of God is one of the most fundamental of the original Chinese beliefs. It is an important tenet of the traditional religion of China which Confucius apparently accepted. A poem of the ninth century B.C., with which Confucius was familiar, says,

> *"Heaven, in giving birth to the multitudes of the people,*
> *To every faculty and relationship annexed its law.*
> *The people possess this normal nature,*
> *And they (consequently) love its normal virtue."*
> *(The Book of Poetry,* 3,3,6,1)

Mencius, after quoting this poem to defend his theory of the goodness of human nature, said, "Confucius said, 'The maker of this poem knew indeed the principle (of our nature).' " (*Mencius,* 6,1,6,8)

There are many other places in *The Book of Poetry* that can be mentioned to show that the doctrine of man as the creature of Heaven or God was a common belief in the early Chou period. For example:

"Oh vast and distant Heaven, who art called our parent." (2,5,4,1)

"Heaven gave me birth." (2,5,3,3)

The Book of History, one of the chief textbooks which Confucius used for his course on history, also gives the same doctrine. For example, King Wu, the first sovereign of the Chou Dynasty (B.C. 1122) in a "Great Declaration" made to his adherents when he had taken the field against the last ruler of Shang, said, "Heaven and Earth is the parent (lit., the father and mother) of all creatures, and of all creatures man is the most intelligent. The sincerely intelligent (among men) becomes the great sovereign, and the great sovereign is the parent (lit., the father and mother) of the people. "But now, Chou, the king of Shang, does not reverence Heaven above, and inflicts calamities on the people below." (5,11,3-4) "Heaven and Earth" is no more plural, than the sovereign, who also is "father and mother", is plural. They pass immediately, in the above quotation, into the one name Heaven;—notwithstanding the dualistic form of the expression, it is only one that is the parent of all creatures.

(b) The original nature of man

Confucius did not talk explicitly about man's original nature. One of his disciples recorded that "his discourses about man's nature, and the way of Heaven, cannot be heard." (*The Analects* 5,13) But he gave many suggestions in his teachings and in the textbooks which he selected and commented upon that the original nature, being conferred by Heaven or God is good, or at least has the tendency to be good. The same idea was later on fully developed by Mencius. For example, Confucius says, "By nature, men are nearly alike; by practice, they get to be wide apart." (*The Analects*, 17,2) Again, he says, "Man is born for uprightness. If a man lose his uprightness, and yet live, his escape (from death) is the effect of mere good fortune." (*The Analects*, 6,17) In the Classics there are many suggestions of the goodness of human nature. King T'ang says in *The Book of History*:

"The great God has conferred (even) on the inferior people a moral sense, compliance with which would show their nature invariably right. To make them tranquilly pursue the course which it would indicate is the work of the sovereign." (*Shu Ching*, 4,3,2)

It is recorded in *The Book of Poetry* that King Wen of Chou gave a warning to the last sovereign of the Shang Dynasty, saying:

"*How great is God, who ruleth men below!*
In awful terrors now arrayed.
His dealings seem a recklessness to show,
From which we shuddering shrink, dismayed.
But men at first from Heaven their being drew,
With nature liable to change.
All hearts in infancy are good and true,
But time and things those hearts derange."
(*Shih Ching*, 3,3,1)

There is no such doctrine as the Fall or Original Sin in the traditional Chinese religion. Chinese thinkers, including Confucius, as a whole, have dwelt more on the healthy aspect of human life. It is the problem of the duty of man in human relationships, and not that of the depravity of human nature, that has drawn their primary attention. They have assumed that "man is the most intelligent" of all the creatures created by God, "to every faculty and relationship He annexed His law." "But men at first from

Heaven their being drew, with nature liable to change", so there is the need of rulers and teachers to instruct them, and to keep them from going astray from their good divine nature. "Heaven", said King Wu, "to help the inferior people, made for them rulers, and made for them teachers, who should be assisting God, and help to secure tranquility throughout the realm." (*The Book of Poetry*, 5,1,7) This is what Mencius means when he says that "the great end of education is nothing else but to "seek for the lost mind." (*Mencius*, 6,1,11,4) The mind which is "ensnared and drowned in evil" owing to its daily contact with the evil environment. (*Mencius*, 6,1,7,1)

(c) The duty of man

To state it briefly, the duty of man consists in the compliance with his moral nature and its appliance to the five constituent relationships of society. The five relationships are the relations of ruler and subject, father and son, husband and wife, elder brother and younger, friend and friend. But the divine law "annexed in every faculty and relationship of man" serves as the most important combining factor to hold those five relationships in proper order, without which, indeed, all relations would be impossible, and a chaotic condition within one's own self and in society would be the result. So the duty of man should be first to comply with his moral nature which is conferred by God, and then to apply it to human relationships. In other words, he has his first duty towards God and then his duty towards man. The duty towards man has been shown in the moral teachings of Confucius, and his duty towards God will be shown later as consisting in prayers and sacrifices, the chief aim of which is to offer praise and thanksgiving to God, and in the carrying out of his will in this world.

(d) The destiny of man

The Chinese were among the first to believe in an afterlife. There was P'an-keng, one of the kings of the Shang Dynasty in the 14th century B.C., about whose life we now know much that is definite, from the Honan oracle bones, which verify to a great extent the literary record of the moving of his capital city, as given in *The Book of History*. He was irritated by the opposition of the wealthy and powerful houses to his measures, and threatened them with calamities to be sent down by his ancestor, T'ang the Successful. He told his ministers that their ancestors and fathers, who had loyally served his predecessors, were now urgently entreating T'ang to punish their descendants. Not only, therefore, did good sovereigns continue to have a happy existence in Heaven, but their good ministers shared their happiness with them, and were round about them, as they had been on earth, and took an interest in the progress of the concerns which had occupied them during their lifetime. (See, Chapters on P'an-keng, *The Book of History*). Indeed, the practice of ancestor-worship which presumably may be traced to prehistoric times, presupposed the existence of the dead ancestors in a spiritual form.

Although the traditional Chinese religion believes in immortality, or life after death, yet it gives no explicit utterances on the state of man after death. It holds, and has always held, that, though disembodied, he continues to live on; but it says very little, and nothing definite, as to the conditions of his future life.

Confucius, in emphasizing that "one should respect the spirits, but keep them at a distance," (*The Analects*, 6,20) and "sacrificed (to his ancestors) as if they were present and sacrificed to the spirits as if they were present," (*The Analects*, 3,12) must have shared the traditional belief in the life after death. But Confucius was only interested in this life, and he added nothing to the traditional belief of the conditions on the life after death. The following conversation between Confucius and one of his disciples shows very clearly the attitude of Confucius on such a problem.

"Chi Lu asked about serving the spirits (of the dead). The Master said, 'While you are not able to serve men, how can you serve (their spirits)?' (Chi Lu added), 'I venture to ask about death?' He was answered, 'While you do not know life, how can you know about death?' " (*The Analects*, 11,11)

To know life here and now, and serve men while they are living should be our chief concern. If we can live a beautiful and helpful life, death is nothing to be afraid of, and indeed we shall have no time nor inclination to brood over our personal future.

"The Master said, . . . 'From of old, death has been the lot of all men; but if the people have no faith they cannot stand.' " (*The Analects*, 12,7,3)

"The Master said, 'If a man in the morning hear the Right Way (*Tao*), he may die in the evening without regret.' " (*The Analects*, 4,8)

"The Master said, 'The determined scholar and the man of love will not seek to live at the expense of injuring their love (*Jen*). They will even sacrifice their lives to preserve their love (*Jen*) complete.' " (*The Analects*, 15,8)

"The Master said, 'The Superior Man dislikes the thought of his name not being mentioned after his death.' " (*The Analects*, 15,19)

"Homo liber de nulla re minus quam de morte cogitat", says Spinoza; "there is nothing on which the free man lets his thoughts dwell less than on death." (*Ethics*, 4,67) "Et ejus sapientia," he adds, with an obvious allusion to Plato, "non mortis sed vitae meditatio est"; "the free man's wisdom is not a meditation of death but of life". In the same spirit Goethe would have us substitute for the old maxim, "memento mori", the truer motto, "gedenke zu leben", —"memento vivere",—remember to live.

> *"In the very world, which is the world*
> *Of all of us,—the place where in the end*
> *We find our happiness, or not at all."*
> (Wordsworth, *The Prelude*, Book II)

4. The Communication Between God and Man

(a) The revelation of God to Man

a) Through natural phenomena

"The Master said, 'Does Heaven speak? The four seasons pursue their courses, and all things are continually being produced, but does heaven say anything?' " (*The Analects*, 17,19,3)

King Ch'eng, the son of King Wu, in the eleventh century B.C., prayed in his ancestral temple, saying:

> *"With reverence I will go*
> *Where duty's path is plain.*
> *Heaven's will I clearly know;*
> *Its favour to retain*

Is hard;—let me not say
  'Heaven is remote on high,
Nor notices men's way.'
  There in the starlit sky
It round about us moves,
  Inspecting all we do,
And daily disapproves
  What is not just and true."
    (*The Book of Poetry*, 4,1,3,3)

b) Through the moral nature of man

"Heaven, in giving birth to the multitudes of the people,
To every faculty and relationship annexed its law.
The people possess this normal nature,
And they (consequently) love its moral virtue."
    (*The Book of Poetry*, 3,3,6,1)

c) Through rulers and teachers

"Heaven to help the inferior people, made for them rulers, and made for them teachers, who should be assisting God, and help to secure tranquility throughout the realm." (*The Book of History*, 5,1,7)

Confucius believed that he was such a teacher to assist God to carry out His will and preach the truth so that tranquility throughout the realm would be secured.

"The Master was put in peril in K'uang. he said, 'After the death of King Wen, was not the cause of truth lodged here in me? If Heaven had wished to let this cause of truth perish, then I, a future mortal, should not have got such a relation to that cause. While Heaven does not let the cause of truth perish, what can the people of K'uang do to me?' " (*The Analects*, 9,5)

d) Through the spirits as the agents of God, that is, the spirits of natural objects, such as the sun, moon, stars, mountains, rivers, trees, etc., and the spirits, of departed men, especially the departed great, such as national heroes, faithful ministers, great kings, etc., and the departed ancestors as tutelary spirits, to whom generally were sacrifices offered by ordinary people. (See the section on Sacrifices). Subordinate to God and fulfilling the will of God, these spirits were actively involved in the affairs of their people or descendants, to whom they were infinitely superior. They would, however, show no partiality in favour of their people or descendants who did evil, but, on the contrary, would join in their chastisement. That is why Confucius said, "He who offends against Heaven has none to whom he can pray." (*The Analects*, 3,13,2)

Although Confucius had a great confidence in the one supreme Heaven or God, yet he was rather sceptical about the spirits. For example, he said:

"To give one's self earnestly to the duties due to men, and, while respecting spiritual beings, to keep aloof from them, may be called wisdom." (*The Analects*, 6,20) Again he said,

"For a man to sacrifice to a spirit which does not belong to him is flattery." (*The Analects*, 2,24)

In the time of Confucius there were also a few literati who were more enlightened and shared with Confucius the same sceptical view of the popular belief in spiritual beings. *Tso Chuan* records speeches by several such men, as for example, under the 32nd year of Duke Chuang of Lu, 662 B.C.—"It is when a state is about to flourish that (its ruler) listens to his people; when it is about to perish, he listens to the spirits." Under the first year of Duke Ting, 509 B.C., "The state of Hsieh makes its appeal to man, while that of Sung makes its appeal to spirits, the offence of Sung is great."

Through the influence of the sceptical views of those more enlightened people, including Confucius, the belief in spirits later diminished. Mo-tzu, in his section "On Ghosts" (Chap. 31), lamented that in his time men's unbelief in spirits had led the world into grave disorder, thus necessitating his spending much effort in attempting to prove their existence.

(b) Man's attempt to enter into communion with God, or spirits

a) Through prayer

"The Master being very sick, Tzu Lu asked leave to pray for him. He said, 'May such a thing be done?' Tzu Lu replied, 'It may. In the Lei,[177] (or Eulogies), it is said "Prayer has been made for thee to the spirits of the upper and lower worlds" '. The Master said, 'My praying has been for a long time.' " (*The Analects*, 7,34)

b) Through sacrifice (*Chi*)[178]

a. The meaning of the word *Chi*

The Chinese word *Chi* really covers a much wider meaning than sacrifice. The Morrison's Dictionary, for example, quoting mainly from the *K'ang Hsi Dictionary*, speaks of *Chi* as "To carry human affairs before the Gods (i.e., spirits). That which is the medium between, or brings together, men and God. To offer flesh in the rites of worship; to sacrifice with victims." The most general idea symbolised by the character *Chi* is—an offering whereby communication and communion with spiritual beings is effected.

b. Twofold sacrifice

The Chinese character for God, Ti,[179] as pointed out in the second chapter under the section of the religious background to the teaching of Confucius, suggests the idea of the One Above to whom sacrifices are offered. The sacrifice to God was, no doubt, the first, and for a time, probably, the only worship or sacrifice. By and by all nature was conceived to be a manifestation of God, and to be peopled by His spirits, or the spirits of men were supposed to have come from the spirits of God, superintending and controlling its different parts, such as mountains, rivers, all heavenly bodies, different individual homes, etc., in subordination to the one supreme God. So there grew up sacrifices to these spirits in connexion with the sacrifice to God. The name of God was not given to them, but honour was done to them as ministers of God, and help might be sought from them as mediators with Him, through prayer or sacrifice. But the common people were debarred from sacrificing to God and His spirits, that was done for them vicariously by the ruler of the state and his ministers. They were allowed, however, to sacrifice to their ancestors who became the tutelary spirits of individual families. Thus we have the twofold sacrifice. On the one hand, we have the sacrifice to God and His subordinate spirits, in which the ruler of the state and his ministers should be the officiators. Usually the ruler of the state was the only officiator in the sacrifice to God, and his ministers as officiators in the sacrifice to the subordinate spirits of God according to the rank of ministers and the grade of the spirits; the higher ministers offered to the higher spirits while the lower ministers officiated in the sacrifice to the lower spirits. These are the sacrifices for all people by a few representatives, led by the head of the state. On the other hand, we have the sacrifice to the ancestors by all people, or at least by the heads of families, for themselves and all the members in their relative circle. There was no priesthood in such traditional religion. The rulers of the state and the heads of the families acted only as representatives of their people or children and not as hierarchy.

From the Chou Dynasty down to the end of the Manchu empire, sacrifices had always been offered to Heaven with its celestial spirits, and to Earth with its earthly spirits at the two places distinguished as the altars of heaven and to earth;—at the round altar to heaven on the day of the winter solstice, and at the square altar to earth on the day of the summer soltice. There was danger of such a practice leading to serious misconception concerning the traditional monotheistic belief—a danger which Confucius himself happily came in to avert. We have from him the clear statement, "The ceremonies of the sacrifices to Heaven and Earth are those by which we serve Shang Ti (God)." (*The Doctrine of the Mean*, 19,6) The worship offered in them was to the one and the same God. Again, there was a danger at the time of Confucius for the common people to be too superstitious by offering sacrifices to different spirits besides those of their ancestors—a danger which Confucius also tried to avert, saying, "For a man to sacrifice to a spirit which does not belong to him is flattery." (*The Analects*, 2,24)

c. Sacrifices as oblations rather than propitiation

Sacrifices were generally conceived as the tributes of duty and gratitude, accompanied with petitions and thanksgivings. There never was any idea of propitiation or expiation in them. They did not express a sense of guilt, but a feeling of dependence, and thanksgiving. The book called "The Laws of Sacrifice" (*Chi Fa*)[180] in *The Book of Rites*" (*Li Chi*), states:

"The rule observed by the Sage-kings in instituting sacrifices was this,—that those who had legislated for the people should be sacrificed to, also those who had died in the diligent discharge of their duties, those whose toils had established states, and those who warded off, or given succor in, great calamities." Then follows a list of ancient worthies, distinguished by such achievements, and the book concludes: "As to the sun, moon, and constellations of the zodiac, they are looked up to by men with admiration; and as to mountains, forests, rivers, and valleys, the people derive from them their material resources. It is only such beneficial services that give a place in the sacrificial canon."

The idea of substitution is not unknown in Chinese history, but as Chinese thinkers have dwelt chiefly on the positive aspect of life, "to give one's self earnestly to the duties of men" (*The Analects*, 6,20), and not on the negative aspect of life, death or sin, so they have not developed the idea of substitution in religious services.

"T'ang (the first king of the Shang Dynasty) said, 'I, the child *Li*, presume to use a dark-coloured victim, and presume to announce to thee, O most great and sovereign God, that the sinner I dare not pardon, and thy ministers, O God, I do not keep in obscurity. The examination of them is by thy mind, O God. If in my person I commit offences, they are not to be attributed to you, the people of the myriad regions. If you in the myriad regions commit offences, these offences must rest on my person.' " (*The Analects*, 20,1,1-3) In harmony with this generous utterance was an incident in the life of T'ang, which has been handed down by the historian Ssu-ma Ch'ien and others. For seven years after his accession (*c.* 1776-1760 B.C.) there was a great drought and famine. It was suggested at last by some one that a human victim should be offered in sacrifice to Heaven, and prayer made for rain. T'ang said, 'If a man must be the victim, I will be he." He fasted, cut off his hair and nails, and in a plain carriage, drawn by white horses, clad in rushes, in the guise of a sacrificial victim, he proceeded to a forest of mulberry trees, and there prayed, asking to what error or crime of his life the calamity was owing. He had not done speaking when a copious rain fell. The ideas of substitution and consecration are thus to be found in Chinese history, but they have not been dwelt upon in religious ceremonies.

d. Reverence as the most important attitude in sacrifices

"In sacrificing his thoughts are reverential, in mourning his thoughts are about the grief (which he should feel); such a man commands our approbation indeed." (*The Analects*, 19,1)

"He sacrificed (to the dead), as if they were present. He sacrificed to the spirits, as if the spirits were present." (*The Analects*, 3,12)

To have such a religious spirit of reverent fear in daily life is recorded in *The Book of Poetry* as the secret of the success of the good King Wen.

> *"Wen formed himself upon his sire,*
> *Nor gave their spirits pain.*
> *Well pleased were they. Next he inspires*
> *His wife. His brethren fain*
> *To follow there. In every state*
> *The chiefs on his example wait.*
> *In a palace see him,—bland, serene;*
> *In fane,—with rev'rent fear.*
> *Unseen by men, he still felt seen*
> *By spirits always near.*
> *Unweariedly did he maintain*
> *His virtue pure, and free from stain."*
> (*Shih Ching*, 3,2,6)

c) Through divination and magic

Divination and magic of various kinds began very early among the ancient Chinese people, and some of their methods have been carried down to the present day. In the Chinese thought there has been no clear consciousness by the ego of itself, and so there had been little attention paid to the division between the ego and the non-ego, or the distinction between the individual and the universe. The concepts 'Spirit', 'Nature' and 'Man' have usually been blended. Such blending can be seen in various ways in Chinese thoughts and practices, and the wide use of divination and magic is one of them. Through the methods of divination or by observing certain noteworthy natural phenomena, the wills of the spiritual beings, or the courses of human affairs can be seen and foreseen. The enormous quantity of the oracle bones of the Shang people recently discovered shows that the practice of divination was already common at least a thousand years before the Christian era. According to *I-wen Chih*, the "Catalogue of the Imperial Han Dynasty Library," found in *Ch'ien Han Shu*, Chapter 30, the arts of divination and magic fall into six classes: a. Astrology (T'ien Wen),[181] b. Almanacs (*Li pu*),[182] c. The Five Elements (Wu Hsing),[183] d. Divination plants (Shih)[184] and tortoise shell (Kuei),[185] e. Miscellaneous divination (Tsa Chan),[186] and f. The system of forms (Hsing).[187] (See *A History of Chinese Philosophy*, by Fung Yu-lan, translated by Derke Bodde, pp. 43-50)

Confucius, according to *The Analects* of the Ancient Text School, was very fond of *Yi*,[188] the divination book of his day, and said, "If some years were added to my life, I would give fifty to the study of *Yi*, and then I might come to be without great faults." (*The Analects*, 7,16) Chinese scholars have doubted the authenticity of this saying of Confucius, but it seems probable that Confucius, having "extensively studied all learning", was familiar with *Yi*, which in his time was one of the most popular and important written documents. In the time of Chuang-tzu *Yi*, or *The Book of Changes*, had already become one of the Six Classics of the Confucian school.

(B) According to Mencius and Hsun-tzu and Their Schools

1. According to Mencius and His School of Confucianism.

Mencius and his school followed pretty closely the traditional religious beliefs as transmitted and commented on by Confucius. He quoted from *The Book of History* that "Heaven having produced the people below, appointed for them rulers and teachers, with the purpose that they should be assisting God. . . ." (*Mencius*, 1,2,3,7; see *Shu Ching*, 5,1,1,7) Like Confucius, he believed that he was one of those teachers appointed by God to teach the people; he also regarded his mission as a divine mission. He says,

"Heaven's plan in the production of mankind is this,—that they who are first informed should instruct those who are later on being informed, and they who first apprehend principles should instruct those who are slower to do so. I am one of Heaven's people who have first apprehended;—I will take these principles and instruct this people in them. If I do not instruct them, who will do so?" (*Mencius*, 5,1,7,5) Again:

"But Heaven does not yet wish that the empire should enjoy tranquility and good order. If it wished this, who is there besides me to bring it about? How should I be otherwise than dissatisfied?" (*Mencius*, 2,2,13,5)

He believed with Confucius that God is the supreme, moral, and personal Deity. He reveals Himself through his works in the universe, through the rulers and teachers appointed by Him, and through the moral nature of man.

"Wan Chang said, 'Was it the case that Yao gave the empire to Shun?' Mencius said, 'No, The emperor cannot give the empire to another.' 'Yes, but Shun had the empire. Who gave it to him?' 'Heaven gave it to him', was the answer. 'Heaven gave it to him; did Heaven confer its appointment on him with specific injunctions?' Mencius replied, 'No. Heaven does not speak. It simply showed its will by its conduct and doings." (*Mencius*, 5,1,5,1-4)

The great contribution of Mencius to moral as well as religious teachings was his exemplification of the traditional doctrine of the moral or divine nature of man. The nature of man, as pointed out above, is directly conferred by God and so is entirely good. It should be the true measure of all things, since it represents the nature of God. Confucius also said that "Man can enlarge the principles which he follows (*Tao*);[189] those principles (*Tao*) do not enlarge the man." (*The Analects*, 15,28) But Mencius went a step further by attributing the right of man to the authority of the Divine. He quoted from "The Great Declaration" (*T'ai Shih*)[190] of *The Book of History*, saying, "Heaven sees according as my people see; Heaven hears according as my people hear." (*Mencius*, 5,1,5,8; see *Shu Ching*, 4,1,2,7) Again he said, "He who exercises his mind to the utmost knows his nature. Knowing his nature, he knows Heaven." (*Mencius*, 7,1,1,1)

Although human nature is divine, yet it is often "ensnared and drowned in evil" when in contact with evil environment. Hence there is the difference between a good man and a bad man. Mencius says:

"The bodily organs with their functions belong to our Heaven-conferred nature. But a man must be a sage before he can satisfy the design of his bodily organization." (*Mencius*, 7,1,28)

Man when he has "lost his mind" in evil, comes short of "the design of his bodily organization" as conferred by God; but if he repents his sins he may be restored to his former normal state of mind, and be worthy to sacrifice to God. Mencius says:

"Though a man may be wicked, yet if he adjust his thoughts fast, and bathe, he may sacrifice to God." (*Mencius*, 4,2,25,2)

As Mencius emphasized the sanctity of the individual, he believed that to sacrifice to God was not to be limited to the ruler of the state alone, but it might be performed by anybody who was pure in mind and body.

Like Confucius again, Mencius was also sceptical about spiritual beings. He regarded them as less important than the people. They are to be sacrificed to only when they are worthy, if they have been proved to be unworthy they are to be changed. Mencius says:

"The people are the most important element (in a nation); the spirits of the land and grain are the next; the sovereign is the lightest. . . . When a prince endangers the altars of the spirits of the land and grain, he is changed, and another appointed in his place. When the sacrificial victims have been perfect, the millit in its vessels all pure, and the sacrifices offered at their proper seasons, if yet there ensue drought, or the waters overflow, the spirits of the land and grain are changed, and others appointed in their place." (*Mencius*, 7,2,14)

Both Confucius and Mencius, though sceptical about spirits, did not deny their existence. They recognized the usefulness of such a traditional belief in the life of a believer. They always thought of man first, and the belief in the spirits was rationalized for its desirable results wrought upon the life of man. The existence of the spirit was thus justified for the sake of expediency.

"The Master said, 'How abundantly do spiritual beings display the powers that belong to them! We look for them, but do not see them; we listen to, but do not hear them; yet they enter into all things, and there is nothing without them. They cause all the people in the kingdom to fast and purify themselves, and array themselves in their richest dresses, in order to attend at their sacrifices. Then, like overflowing water, they seem to be over the heads, and on the right and left (of their worshippers). It is said in The Book of Poetry, 'The approaches of the spirits, you cannot surmise;—and can you treat them with indifference?' Such is the manifestness of what is minute! Such is the impossibility of repressing the outgoings of sincerity!' " (*The Doctrine of the Mean*, Chap. 16)

Here the spirits were compared with the doctrine of the "manifestness of what is minute", and the virtue of "sincerity". The doctrine of spirits became more of the subjective moral and social usefulness rather than the strictly objective reality. This rationalistic aspect of the religious teachings of Confucius and Mencius was carried much further by Hsun-tzu and his school of Confucianism.

2. **According to Hsun-tzu and His School of Confucianism**

(a) The idea of God

To Hsun-tzu God is identified with the impersonal natural law of the universe which governs everything including Heaven, Earth, and Man. To that supreme natural law everything must conform.

"Heaven does not suspend the winter because men dislike cold; the Earth does not suspend its spaciousness because men dislike distances; the Superior Man does not suspend his good actions because of the railings of little-minded men. Heaven has a constant way of action; Earth has a constant numerical size; the Superior Man has a constant decorous demeanour." (*The Works of Hsun-tzu*, p. 178)

The natural law which governs mankind is called *Tao* or *Li* which everybody should obey. Man needs only to know and comply with the law of man which governs his destiny, and it is not necessary to go beyond in seeking to know and obey the laws which govern Heaven and Earth. For a man to know and obey the law of man is the same as to know and obey the ultimate law which governs everything, including himself as well as the laws of Heaven and Earth. The following quotations from the *Works of Hsun-tzu* will help to make clear these points.

"The Way (*Tao*) is not primarily the Way (*Tao*) of Heaven; it is not the Way (*Tao*) to Earth, it is the Way (*Tao*) man acts, the Way (*Tao*) the Superior Man acts." (p. 96)

"Heaven and Earth are the source of life. The rules of proper conduct (*Li*) and justice (*Yi*) are the source of good government; the Superior Man is the source of the rules of proper conduct (*Li*) and justice (*Yi*). . . . The Superior Man forms a triad with Heaven and Earth; he is the controller of all things, the father and mother of the people." (p. 135)

"The rules of proper conduct (*Li*) are those whereby Heaven and Earth unite, whereby the sun and moon are bright, whereby the four seasons are ordered, whereby the stars move in their courses, whereby rivers flow, whereby all things prosper, whereby love and hatred are tempered, whereby joy and anger keep their proper place. It causes the lower orders to obey, and the upper orders to be illustrious; through a myriad changes it prevents going astray. But if one departs from them, he will be destroyed. Are not *Li* the greatest of all principles?" (pp. 223-224)

"The rules of proper conduct (*Li*) are the utmost of human Way (*Tao*)." (p. 225)

"If a person neglects what men can do and seeks for what Heaven does, he fails to understand the nature of things." (p. 183)

"The Superior Man is anxious about what is within his power, and does not seek for what is from Heaven." (p. 179)

"When the actions of the Sage are completely governed, the nourishment for the people is completely obtained, and in his life he injures none—this is what is meant by knowing Heaven." (p. 176)

"Heaven has a constant regularity of action. . . . If the Way (*Tao*) is cultivated and not opposed, then Heaven cannot send misfortune. . . . If a person rebels against the Way (*Tao*) and acts unseemly, then Heaven cannot make him fortunate. . . . Heaven has its seasons, Earth has its wealth, Man has his government. The foregoing is what is meant by being able to form a triad with Heaven and Earth. To give up that wherewith one can form such a triad, and to desire to know those with whom he forms a triad, is to be led into error." (pp. 173-175)

According to Hsun-tzu there is no spiritual principle in the universe. The so-called spirits are but the causes of the effects in natural phenomena which are unknown to man. They do not really cause anything; everything goes by the impersonal natural law of the universe. Hsun-tzu says:

"The fixed stars make their round; the sun and moon alternately shine; the four seasons come in succession; the Yin and Yang go through their great mutations; the wind and rain widely affect things; all things acquire their germinating principle, and are brought into existence; each gets its nourishing principle and develops to its completed state. We do not see the cause of these occurrences, but we do see their effects—this is what is meant by the influence of the spirits. The results of all these changes are known, but we do not know the invisible source—that is, what is meant by the work of Heaven. Only the Sage does not seek to know Heaven. . . . What is known about Heaven is that we see its phenomena have their regular sequences; what is known about Earth is that it is seen that it meets the conditions of life and can produce; what is known about the four seasons is that it is seen that they have a definite number, and can be used to serve humanity; what is known about the Yin and Yang is that it is seen that they interact and can be used in ruling a country." (pp. 175-7)

(b) Religious ceremonies

Although Hsun-tzu did not believe in the existence of spiritual beings, not even in the spirits of one's ancestors, for "once dead", said Hsun-tzu, "a person cannot be resurrected again" (p. 228), yet he found a place in his teachings for the existence of the traditional religious ceremonies, such as, prayer, divination, funeral rites, sacrifices, etc. All these religious ceremonies were rationalized as being "human practices", or able to serve certain human purposes, such as to beautify human life, or to unite the people together in society. Hsun-tzu says:

"Ceremonies were established in accordance with the strength of the emotions in order to beautify the ceremonies relating to social relations, to friends and strangers, to kindred and those who are not related, and to the noble and base. They cannot be added to or diminished." (p. 239)

a) Prayer and divination

When Hsun-tzu was asked, "If people pray for rain and get rain, why is that?" Hsun-tzu answered, "There is no reason for it. If people do not pray for rain, it will nevertheless rain. When people save the sun or moon from being eaten (in an eclipse), or when they pray for rain in a drought, or when they decide an important affair only after divination—this is not because they think in this way they will get what they seek, but only to gloss over the matter. Hence the prince thinks it is glossing over the matter, but the people think it supernatural. He who thinks it is glossing over the matter is fortunate; he who thinks it is supernatural is unfortunate." (pp. 181-182)

b) Funeral rites

"Funeral rites are the beautification of the dead by the living; they are sending off the dead very similarly to that in their life. Hence we should treat the dead like the living, the absent like the present. . . . All rites, if for the service of the living, are to beautify joy; or if to send off the dead, they are to beautify sorrow; or if for sacrifice, they are to beautify reverence; or if they are military, they are to beautify majesty." (pp. 235-237)

c) Sacrifices

Sacrifices were regarded as human practices, used for the serving of certain human purposes and not for serving the spirits. They were regarded as release channels of human emotions, to be performed with great reverence to the different grades of gods in the celestial order, according to the different ranks of people in the social order.

"The emotions produced in him who performs sacrifice by his memories, ideas, thoughts, and longings, cause him to change countenance and pant; it cannot be that such feelings should never come to him. . . . Hence I say: Sacrifice is because of the emotions produced by memories, ideas, thoughts, and longings; it is the extreme of loyalty, faithfulness, love and reverence; it is the greatest thing of the rites (*Li*) and of beautiful actions. If there were no Sages, no one could have understood this. The Sage plainly understands it; the scholar and Superior Man accordingly perform it; the official observes it; among the people it becomes an established custom. Among Superior Men it is considered to be a human practice (*Tao*); among the common people it is considered to be serving the spirits." (pp. 244-245)

"The sacrifice to Heaven is limited to the Emperor; the sacrifices to the gods of the land belong to the feudal nobles down to the officers and prefects. That whereby the honourable are distinguished is that they serve the honourable deities; and the lowly serve the lowly deities. It is proper that the great should have the great deities, and the small the small deities." (p. 220)

In short, Hsun-tzu tried to give new rationalistic interpretations of the traditional beliefs in God, Heaven, Earth, spirits, and all the religious ceremonies. He gave new and different meanings to them, while still retaining the use of those terms and practices. He justified their existence not because of their objective realities or truths, but because of their subjective usefulness or expediency. The age in which he lived was a very sceptical age. Mo-tzu, for example, protested, saying, "Those who deny the existence of spirits proclaim: 'Of course there are no spirits'. And from morning till evening they teach this doctrine to the people of the empire. They bewilder the people, causing them all to doubt the existence of ghosts and spirits. In this way the empire becomes disorderly." (*Mo-tzu*, Chap. 31, "On Ghosts") From this we can see somewhat the reason why Hsun-tzu should use so much effort in trying to explain, in a rational way, those traditional religious beliefs and practices, so as to justify their existence. He was one of the greatest leaders of the "left" party of the school of Confucianism, and has had a tremendous influence over the more sceptical Confucian scholars of later periods.

D. Conclusion

As a great teacher, Confucius not only transmitted the best traditional cultural heritage from the past, but also gave new emphasis and interpretations to the old teachings, and transformed the whole into his new system of thought, which entitled him to be the acknowledged Founder of the great school of Confucianism. In him was summed up all the best Chinese cultural heritages, and from him began the era of Chinese thought which has outgrown all other rival ideologies, and dominated the Chinese intellectual world for over two thousand years.

He was the first Chinese thinker who brought into prominence the universal virtue of love (*Jen*), and since then it has become the most important virtue in Chinese ethics. He gave new meanings and life to the traditional doctrine of the rules of proper conduct (*Li*) and filial piety (*Hsiao*), by emphasizing both the inward spirit and outward form of those two kinds of conduct. He always paid attention to balanced life and thought, and evaded the extreme, thus both individual and social heritage, discipline and freedom, adaptation and individualism were equally emphasized and marvellously harmonized in his teachings.

He was primarily a moral teacher, but he was conscious of the fact that morality cannot and should not be divorced from intellect and religion. They are essentially complementary to one another. Thus his interest in moral problems led him also to educate his disciples in the traditional intellectual and religious heritages of his days. He selected, expunged, rectified, and commented upon the existent materials of history, poetry, music, and different rules of proper conduct (*Li*), and used them all as textbooks for his intellectual teaching. He gave new interpretations to traditional literature and utilized them to exemplify his moral teachings. He was not a profound teacher of religion, but he was a deeply religious person. He accepted in general the traditional religious beliefs, but sometimes he gave specific and important comments. His teachings were developed into two distinct schools of thought, that of Mencius and that of Hsun-tzu. Mencius developed more the individual and psychological aspects of Confucius' teachings, while Hsun-tzu emphasized more the social and intellectual aspects of the teachings of the Master. William James, in his *Pluralistic Universe*, divides philosophical schools into those that are "tough-minded" and those that are "tender-minded". Mencius belongs to the "tender-minded" group, with a philosophy of idealistic tendencies, while Hsun-tzu is of the "tough-minded" school, with a philosophy having materialistic tendencies. But if we compare the teachings of these two schools of Confucianism with the life and teachings of Confucius as recorded by his immediate disciples in *The Analects* and other classics, we have a fairly good and reliable account of the substance of the teachings of this great Master, Confucius. (See also the conclusion at the end of the section, "The Moral Teaching of Confucius")

CHAPTER VI

THE METHODS OF THE TEACHING OF CONFUCIUS

OUTLINE

A. Democratic Method
1. Opportunity of education for all
2. Popularization of education and culture
3. Catholic curriculum

B. Modern Principles of Teaching-method Utilized
1. Apperception
2. Activity
3. Individualization
4. Motivation
5. An example—a lesson taught by Confucius, showing how those principles were utilized

C. The Method of Example: He Practised What He Taught
1. Love (*Jen*)
(1) His love for all
(2) His love for his disciples
(3) His love for the poor and needy
(4) He mourned with those who mourned, and rejoiced with those who rejoiced
2. The rules of proper conduct (*Li*)
He practised himself the principles which he taught about *Li*, namely, Economy, Sincerity, and Reverence
3. Filial Piety
4. The Doctrine of the Mean

D. Methods of Learning
1. Men are teachable—a basic conception of Confucius
2. Five steps of learning
(1) Study extensively

(2) Inquire accurately
(3) Think carefully
(4) Discriminate clearly
(5) Practise earnestly
3. Two essentials of learning
(1) Diligence
(2) Humility

E. Sociological Method of Education
1. Education in relation to government
2. Education in relation to the family
3. Education in relation to religion
4. Education in relation to rites
5. Education in relation to ethics
6. Education in relation to arts

F. Results of His Teaching
(A) His influence upon his disciples
1. Moral and intellectual growth of his disciples
2. The attitude of his disciples towards him
(B) His influence upon society in general
1. Immediate or direct influence
(a) His political career
(b) His educational work
(c) His glorious failure
2. Later or indirect influence through the work of his disciples

G. The Methods of the Teaching of Confucius, According to Mencius, and Hsun-tzu, and Their Schools
(A) Mencius and his school
1. The theory of human nature
(a) The origin of human nature
(b) The goodness of human nature
(c) The difference in human nature
2. Methods of teaching
   The development of human nature

3. Methods of learning
(B) Hsun-tzu and his school
1. The psychology of Hsun-tzu
(a) Some psychological terms defined
(b) The theory of the mind
(c) The theory of human nature
a) The definition of human nature
   a. The origin of human nature
   b. The content of human nature
   c. The expression of human nature
b) The depravity of human nature
(d) The relation between human mind and human nature
(e) The purpose of education
2. The methods of learning
(a) To nourish the mind by the impression through the senses
(b) To investigate thoroughly
(c) To study thoroughly
(d) To think thoroughly
(e) To practise vigorously
(f) To concentrate on one purpose
(g) To learn diligently
3. The methods of teaching
(a) The methods of dealing with subject-matter
(b) The importance of teachers in the process of teaching
(c) The method of arousing the interest of the learners

H. Conclusion

The most helpful lessons that modern education can draw from the teaching of Confucius are along the lines of methods. The teaching procedure of Confucius, is, without a doubt, as effective as any yet contrived. In his manner of instructing his disciples, as recorded in *The Analects*, he has set an excellent example in educational methodology. He seemed to have an intuitive grasp of the laws of learning and of the principles of teaching that are now accepted as basic to teaching effectiveness. For the sake of clearness the methods which Confucius used in his teaching are grouped under the following seven headings: the democratic method, modern principles of teaching-method utilized, method of example, methods of learning, sociological method, results of his teaching, and the methods of his teaching according to Mencius and Hsun-tzu and their schools of Confucianism.

A. Democratic Method

1. Opportunity of Education for All

Confucius advocated public education, particularly free universal education with no distinction of class, sex, or race. He said, "Where there is instruction, there will be no distinction of classes." (*The Analects*, 15,38) As a matter of fact, he was the first great Chinese public teacher, who made his living through teaching. He received everybody as his student who came to him with the intention to study and with a small amount of payment. He said, "From the man bringing his bundle of dried flesh (as payment) upwards, I have never refused instruction to any one." (*The Analects*, 7,7) Such payment was probably not received in any fixed amounts, but given to Confucius in the form of gifts. He was not wholly dependent on the payment from his students for his livelihood, and could also look to the state rulers for a certain amount of support. He owed the support from the state rulers to the very fact that his students were numerous and the results of his teaching were excellent. The government grant was given to him in appreciation of his good work in education. Ssu-ma Ch'ien says, "Confucius taught poetry, history, the rules of proper conduct (*Li*), and music, to 3,000 pupils, of whom 72, like Yen Tu-hsiu, mastered "the Six Classics". There were a great number of people who came to study under him." ("The Life of Confucius", *Shih Chi*) There seems to have been no definite time or place for his teaching. He seized every opportunity possible for teaching, regardless of time or place. Sometimes he taught them in his own home (Shih Chi, "Confucian students studied the rules of proper conduct (*Li*) at his home"), sometimes under the trees, (*The Analects*, 12,21) sometimes by the riverside (9,16), sometimes on the roads during his wandering life from one state to another. (*The Analects*, 11,2)

2. Popularization of Education and Culture

Before the time of Confucius, those cultural heritages known as the Six Disciplinary Arts, namely, *Shih, Shu, Li, Yueh, I*, and *Ch'un Ch'iu*, had been very rare materials, acquired only by a portion of the nobility. Ku Yu tells us that a crown prince of Ch'u, son of King Chuang of Ch'u (613-591 B.C.), was given instruction in such works as *Poetry* (*Shih*), *Rites* (*Li*), *Music* (*Yueh*), *Spring and Autumn* (*Ch'ung Ch'iu*), and the *Old Records* (*Ku Chih*). (*Ch'u Yu* 1,1) *Tso Chuan* tells us that when an envoy from Wu visited Lu "he observed the music of Chou", and that when Han Hsuan Tzu visited Lu, he "examined the books of the Great Historian, and saw the symbols of *I* and the *Ch'un Ch'iu* of Lu, whereupon he said: 'the *Li* of Chou are all in Lu, and now I comprehend the power of the Duke of Chou and how it was that the Chous became kings.' " So these literary possessions were rare and highly prized and were almost inaccessible to the common people. Confucius, so far as we know, was the first person who sought to popularize those precious cultural possessions, by teaching them to a large number of people. He regarded the popularization of education as the best means of carrying out his purpose of bringing about individual regeneration and social reform. When Confucius was asked the way of making people virtuous, he answered, "Advance the good to teach the incompetent then they will eagerly seek to be virtuous." (*The Analects*, 2,20) To have the people educated was counted as one of the three great achievements of government (*The Analects*, 13,9), and to punish the people without having educated them first was condemned as cruelty. (*The Analects*, 20,2) *The Book of History*, which Confucius used as one of his teaching materials, says,

> "*It was the lesson of our great ancestor:—*
> *The people should be cherished;*
> *They should not be down-trodden:*
> *The people are the root of the country;*
> *The root firm, the country is tranquil.*"
> (*Shu Ching*, Pt. 3, Bk. 3, Ch. 4, "T'ai Kung")

Only through popular education could the "root" be made firm, and the country tranquil. Moreover, "Heaven sees as my people see, and hears as my people hear". The highest source of human wisdom was supposed to be the people themselves—VOX POPULI, VOX DEI. It was only through popular education, Confucius believed, that the sacred right of man could be realized, and he was in full conviction that he had a Divine Mission to teach the people. (See *The Religious Teaching of Confucius*, Chapter 5)

3. Catholic Curriculum

Confucius taught all the important subjects that his age could offer, namely, the Six Disciplinary Arts. Unlike other schools which taught the doctrines originating in their own schools, in order to produce scholars for their schools, as, Chuang Tzu (Ch. 33, p. 442) tells us, the disciples of the Mohist School all intoned in "Mohist Canons", Confucius only wished his disciples to become 'men' in the full sense of the term, rather than sectarian scholars belonging to any one particular school. So he offered a catholic curriculum, including all the important literary possessions of his days, and people belonging to any particular school could come and study under him. This is also one of the reasons why the Six Disciplinary Arts, the *Liu I*, though not originated by Confucius, came to be the exclusive possessions of his school shortly after his death. Chuang-tzu, for example, a contemporary of Mencius, says with reference to the Confucianists: "The *Shih* describes aims; the *Shu* describes events; the *Li* depicts conduct; the *Yueh* secures harmony; the *I* shows the principles of Yin and Yang; the *Ch'un Ch'iu* shows distinctions and duties". These were the six works of the *Liu I* which were the subjects of study of the Confucian School. (*Chuang-tzu*, Ch. 33, p. 437)

B. Modern Principles of Teaching-method Utilized

Among the modern principles of teaching-method utilized by Confucius the following four are especially note-worthy.

1. Apperception

By apperception is meant the cognition through relating of new ideas to familiar ideas, or of the unknown to the known. Confucius recognized his principle in his teaching. He drew extensively upon the previous knowledge of his students by frequent reference to the well-known historical events of the past, such as those connected with Yao, Shun, Yu, T'ang, Wen, Wu, Chou Kung, Kuan Chung, Hui of Liu-hsia, Po-i, Shu-ch'i, etc.; and to the famous books that existed in his days, such as *The Book of History*, *The Book of Poetry*, and *The Book of Rites*. He made effective use of the simile, the metaphor, the analogy, and the parable. The following are some examples:

When he was standing by a stream with his disciples, he taught them the great lesson of "change" by comparing it with the ever-changing and yet ever-the-same stream of water which was passing by them, "never ceasing day or night." (*The Analects*, 9,16)

In the winter time when all trees were withered except the pine and the cypress, he pointed out those ever-green trees to his students and taught them the lesson of how men are known in times of adversity. "When the year becomes cold", he said, "then we know how the pine and the cypress are the last to lose their leaves." (*The Analects*, 9,27)

One night when he saw the bright north solar star shine like a prince among the constellations, he said to his disciples, "He who exercises government by means of virtue may be compared to the north polar star, which keeps its place and all the stars turn towards it." (*The Analects*, 2,1)

He compared the importance of truthfulness in a man to the cross-bar for yoking the oxen to a large carriage, or the arrangement for yoking the horses to a small carriage. Those carriages were the chief means of transportation in his days. "The Master said, 'I do not know how a man without truthfulness is to get on. How can a large carriage be made to go without the cross-bar for yoking the oxen to, or a small carriage without the arrangement for yoking the horses?' " (*The Analects*, 2,22)

The influence of the character of the superior to the inferior was analogized with the wind to the grass. "The relation between superiors and inferiors", he said, "is like that between the wind and the grass. The grass must bend, when the wind blows across it." (*The Analects*, 12,19)

He pointed out the fault of his disciples who were not able to prevent their master from wrong-doing by using the parables of a tiger or a rhinoceros which escapes from his cage, and a tortoise shell or piece of jade which is injured in its repository. When the wild animal escapes from the cage, and the precious shell or stone is injured in its repository, the keepers of the sage and repository are certainly those who are to be blamed. Similarly, those disciples of his, being the ministers of their ruler and yet unable to help him to do the right thing or prevent him from doing the wrong thing, were, according to Confucius, responsible for the undesirable results. "Jan Yu and Chi-lu had an interview with Confucius, and said, 'Our chief, Chi, is going to commence operations against Chuang-yu'. Confucius said, 'Ch'iu, is it not you who are in fault here? ... When a tiger or rhinoceros escapes from his cage; when a tortoise shell or piece of jade is injured in its repository:—whose is the fault?' " (*The Analects*, 16,1)

Other common objects like the road, the door, the plant, the flower, the hill, etc., were all taken as his object-lessons. (*The Analects*, 6,15; 9,21; 9,18, etc.) He was fond of using concrete, everyday incidents for his teaching, and was skilful in drawing lessons from the concrete to the abstract, from known to unknown, and from near to the more remote. The Master said, "To be able to give examples from what is near;—this may be called the method of love (*Jen*)." (*The Analects*, 6,28,3) Again, he said, "If a man keeps reviewing the old, so as continually to be acquiring the new, he may be a teacher of others." (*The Analects*, 2,11)

2. Activity

Confucius recognized also the principle of activity in his teaching. He urged his students to be doers and not hearers or learners only. In the opening sentence of *The Analects* this whole idea of the importance of doing or practicing is brought out very clearly:

"The Master said, 'To learn and practice constantly, is that not a pleasure?' " (*The Analects*, 1,1,1)

He asked his disciples to imitate the way of Heaven, because it works all the time, "the four seasons pursue their courses, and all things are continually being produced." (*The Analects*, 17,19,3)

He encouraged again and again his students to put his teaching into action. To be able to talk about the knowledge which he gave them was not to be regarded as of the first importance, but, rather, to put that knowledge into actual practice was of the first importance. Everywhere in the traditional records we can find that it was the fostering of personality rather than the imparting of information that Confucius was primarily interested in. So to do much and to talk little, or to act first and to speak later, was the constant advice given by him to his students. The following are some of the quotations:

"Tzu-kung asked what constituted the Superior Man. The Master said, 'He acts before he speaks, and afterwards speaks according to his actions.' " (*The Analects*, 2,13)

"The Master said, 'The Superior Man . . . is earnest in what he is doing, and careful in his speech. . . .' " (*The Analects*, 1,14)

"The Master said, 'The Superior Man wishes to be slow in his speech and earnest in his action.' " *The Analects*, 4,24)

"The Master said, 'The Superior Man is modest in his speech, but exceeds in his actions.' " (*The Analects*, 14,29)

He also encouraged questions, and gently rebuked his students for not asking questions which they had. He often showed his appreciation when good questions were broached to him. "Fan Ch'ih rambling with the Master under the trees about the rain altars, said, 'I venture to ask how to exalt virtue, to correct cherished evil, and to discover delusions'. The Master said, 'Truly a good question!' " (*The Analects*, 12,21,1-2)

"Lin Fang asked what was the first thing to be attended to in the rules of proper conduct (*Li*). The Master said, 'A great question indeed!' " (*The Analects*, 3,4,1-2)

"The Master said, 'Hue gives me no assistance. There is nothing that I say in which he does not delight.' " (*The Analects*, 11,3)

"The Master said, 'If a man does not ask—"How is it? How is it?" I can indeed do nothing with him!' " (*The Analects*, 15,15)

"The Master said, 'I do not open up the truth to one who is not eager (to get knowledge), nor help out any one who is not anxious to explain himself (or to ask questions). When I have presented one corner of a subject to any one, and he cannot learn it from the other three, I do not repeat my lesson.' " (*The Analects*, 7,8)

Confucius said, 'The Superior Man has nine things which are subjects with him of thoughtful consideration. . . . In regard to what he doubts about, he is anxious to question others. . . .' " (*The Analects*, 16,10)

Confucius regarded the original nature of man as very much the same in all, and it is chiefly due to practice that men become different from each other. "The Master said, 'By nature, men are nearly alike; by practice, they get to be wide apart.' " (*The Analects*, 17,2) Practice, though it does not make one perfect, is the chief factor, according to Confucius, that builds up one's character. So his major task was to help his students form the right kind of habit chiefly through the constant practice of the right thing in the right way. Even when one is alone, one should act carefully with reverence as if "ten eyes were beholding and ten hands were pointing to him." (*The Great Learning*, 6,3)

3. Individualization

He recognized the principle of individual differences and adjusted his teaching methods to the needs, conditions, and capacities of his students. That is one of the reasons why he gave so many different answers to the same problems concerning Love (*Jen*), Government (*Cheng*), Superior Man (*Chun-tzu*), Filial Piety (*Hsiao*), etc., which were brought forward by different persons. He always paid attention to individual differences in teaching his disciples or in solving problems for them. The following is an example of this: "Tzu-lu asked whether he should immediately carry into practice what he heard. The Master said, 'There are your father and elder brothers to be consulted;—why should you act on that principle of immediately carrying into practice what you hear?' Jan Yu asked the same, whether he should immediately carry into practice what he heard, and the Master answered, 'Immediately carry into practice what you hear.' Kung-hsi Hua said, 'Yu (*Tzu-lu*) asked whether he should carry immediately into practice what he heard, and you said, "There are your father and elder brothers to be consulted". Ch'iu (Jan Yu) asked whether he should carry into practice what he heard, and you said, "Carry it immediately into practice". I, Ch'ih, am perplexed, and venture to ask you for an explanation.' The Master said, 'Ch'iu is retiring and slow; therefore I urged him forward. Yu has more than his own share of energy; therefore I kept him back.' " (*The Analects*, 11,21)

Here the same problem was brought up by two of his disciples and was given exactly opposite answers. The reason for this was clearly stated by the Master: the first person who brought up the problem had "more than his share of energy, therefore I kept him back"; while the second person was "retiring and slow, therefore I urged him forward". He was primarily interested in the development of personality, and since no two persons are exactly alike, they are different in their needs, conditions, and capacities, so he had to use different methods and different lessons in teaching different persons. When the talkative Tzu Kung asked, "What constituted the Superior Man, the Master said, 'He acts before he speaks, and afterwards speaks according to his actions.' " (*The Analects*, 2,13) But when the same question was asked by Tzu Lu, a man of impulse rather than reflection, the answer was, "The cultivation of himself in reverential carefulness." (*The Analects*, 14,45) The principle of individualization was fully recognized, and indeed, one cannot fully understand the teachings of Confucius without the recognition of such a principle.

He knew very well the individuality of each of his students. For example, he said, "Ch'ai is simple, Ts'an is dull, Shih is specious, and Yu is coarse." (*The Analects*, 11,17) Again, "Yu is a man of decision. ... Tzu is a man of intelligence. ... Ch'iu is a man of various ability." (*The Analects*, 6,6) He knew his students very well. He mingled with them in their daily lives and observed them carefully in their ways of living. For example, in referring to one of his students, he said, "I have examined his conduct when away from me." (*The Analects*, 2,9) Again he said, "See what a man does. Mark his motives. Examine in what things he rests. How can a man conceal his character? How can a man conceal his character?" (*The Analects*, 2,10) Sometimes he found out the individual differences of his students by asking them to speak about their own ambitions (*The Analects*, 5,25; 11,25), and more often he found them out by the question-answer method.

As a consequence of this individualized teaching, the achievements of his disciples were different along different lines of learning according to their needs, conditions, and capacities.

"The Master said. ... 'Distinguished for their virtuous principles and practice, there were Yen Yuan, Min Tzu-ch'ien, Jan Po-niu, and Chung Kung; for their ability in speech, Tsai Wo and Tzu Kung; for their administrative talents, Jan Yu and Chi Lu; for their literary acquirements, Tzu Yu and Tzu Hsia.' " (*The Analects*, 11,2)

"The Master said, '... In a kingdom of a thousand chariots, Yu might be employed to manage the military levies. ... In a city of a thousand families, or a clan of a hundred chariots, Ch'iu might be employed as a governor. ... With his sash girt and standing in a court, Ch'ih might be employed to converse with the visitors and guests, ...' " (*The Analects*, 5,7)

"Good teaching", says Thorndike, "expects and adapts itself to wide individual differences in original nature" (Edward L. Thorndike, *The Principles of Teaching*, p. 24), and the recognition of such individual differences was one of the reasons of the great success of the teaching of Confucius.

4. Motivation

All effort is impelled by a motive of some sort, and so is the effort of learning. No good teacher should neglect the question of motivation of action. He is generally interested in such problem from two points of view. In the first place, he is interested in the question of how adequate motives may be found to stir up activity of the right sort on the part of the learners. Secondly, he is interested in the problem of what are the best motives to be employed so that the subsequent effects would be desirable. For example, the motives of the hope of reward or the fear of punishment may be practically effective, but they may so sap the independence of the learner as to render him incapable of intelligent self-guidance in later life.

Confucius, being a good teacher, was also keen on the problem of the motivation of action. He often exemplified such a principle in the method of his teaching. He solved very satisfactorily, from the modern educational point of view, both the problems of how and what motives are found to stir up activity of the right sort on the part of the learners.

(1) How can adequate motives be found?

(a) Through able presentation of teaching materials

The words and demonstrations presented by Confucius in the process of his teaching were full of interest and attracted and held the attention of the learners. For example, one of his students said about the teaching of Confucius as follows:

"The Master, by orderly method, skilfully leads men on. He enlarged my mind with learning, and taught me the restraints of the rules of proper conduct (*Li*). When I wish to give over the study of his doctrines, I cannot do so, and having exerted all my ability, there seems something to stand right up before me; but though I wish to follow (and lay hold of it), I really find no way to do so." (*The Analects*, 9,10)

He sometimes taught his disciples the whole day, and they were so much interested that they did not feel tired of listening, but got hold of what he said, and put it into practice.

"The Master said, 'I have talked with Hui for a whole day, and he has not made any objection (to anything I said);—as if he were stupid. He has retired, and I have examined his conduct when away from me, and found him able to illustrate (my teachings). Hui!—He is not stupid.' " (*The Analects*, 2,9)

(b) Through the encouraging of a thinking activity

Learning frequently becomes dull when no thinking on the part of the learner is motivated. "The Master said, 'Learning without thought is labour lost; thought without learning is perilous.' " (*The Analects*, 2,15) Both learning and thought were emphasized. He told his disciple Shen that "my doctrine is that of an all-pervading unity", but he did not go on to say what his "all-pervading unity" was, and left the whole matter to be reasoned out by his disciple.

"The Master said, 'I do not open up the truth to one who is not eager (to get knowledge), nor help out any one who is not anxious to explain himself. When I have presented the corner of a subject to any one, and he cannot from it learn the other three, I do not repeat my lesson.' " (*The Analects*, 7,8)

To help cultivate a thinking activity or clear intellectual insight, he suggested to his disciples that they should read extensively, hear much, and see much.

"The Master said, 'The Superior Man, extensively studying all learning. . . .' " (*The Analects*, 6,25)

"Tzu Kung asked, saying, 'On what ground did K'ung Wen Tzu get the title of "accomplished" (*Wen*)?' The Master said, 'He was of an active nature and yet fond of learning, and was not ashamed to ask (and learn of) his inferiors!—On these grounds he has been styled "accomplished" (*Wen*).' " (*The Analects*, 5,14)

"Hear much and select what is good and follow it; see much and keep it in memory." (*The Analects*, 7,27)

"The Master said, 'Hear much and put aside the points of which you stand in doubt. . . . See much and put aside the things which seem perilous. . . .' " (*The Analects*, 2,18,2)

(c) Through formulating clear and definite objectives

To crown all, Confucius successfully found adequate motives of study among his disciples through giving them clear and definite objectives of the lessons which he taught. For example:

"The Master said, 'In *The Book of Poetry* there are three hundred pieces, but the design of them all may be embraced in one sentence —"Having no depraved thoughts.' " (*The Analects*, 2,2) "Having no depraved thoughts" was then taken as the objective of his course on Poetry.

"Lin Fang asked what was the essence in the ceremonies (*Li*). The Master said, 'A great question indeed! In ceremonies (*Li*), it is better to be sparing than extravagant. In the ceremonies of mourning, it is better that there be deeper sorrow than a minute attention to observances.' " (*The Analects*, 3,4)

Here the objective of his course on *Li* was to put a premium on the sincere expression of personal feeling, and in those ceremonies "It is better to be sparing than extravagant." The personal or subjective element was regarded as more important than the formality of the ceremony itself.

"The *Sheng* of Chin, the *Tao wu* of Ch'u, and the *Ch'un Ch'iu* of Lu were books of the same character. The subject of them was the affairs of Huan of Ch'i and Wen of Chin, and its style was historical. Confucius said, 'Its righteous principles I venture to take.' " (*Mencius*, 4,2,21)

The objective of his course on History was its "righteous principles."

He mentioned again and again that there was "an all-pervading unity" in all his teachings.

"The Master said, 'Ts'an, my doctrine is that of an all-pervading unity.' The disciple Tseng (Ts'an) replied, 'Yes.' The Master went out, and the other disciples asked, saying, 'What do his words mean? Tseng said, 'The doctrine of our master is to be *Chung* (faithful) and *Shu* (like-minded),—this and nothing more.' " (*The Analects*, 4,15)

"The Master said, 'Tzu, you think, I suppose, that I am one who learns many things and keeps them in memory?' Tzu Kung replied, 'Yes,—but perhaps it is not so?' 'No' was the answer; 'I seek a unity all-pervading.' " (*The Analects*, 15,2)

"Tzu Kung asked, saying, 'Is there one word which may serve as a rule of practice for all one's life? The Master said, 'Is not *Shu* (like-mindedness) such a word? What you do not want done to yourself, do not do to others.' " (*The Analects,* 15,23)

The general aim of all learning for an individual was clearly set forth before his disciples as that of a Chun-tzu or Superior Man. Much of his teaching was centered around the character of such an ideal personality. "The Master said to Tzu Hsia, 'Do you be a scholar after the style of the Superior Man, and not after that of the mean man.' " (*The Analects,* 6,11)

To make the learners understand and be interested in the aims of teaching has been regarded as the best means of defining the motives of study. An interest in a problem, a topic, a subject, is evidence that there is a vital union between the student and his study. The etymology of the word "interest", namely, *inter* and *esse,* to be between, suggests that if a student is really interested in his study, there will be no gulf existing between his concrete mind and the material to be learned. Similarly, the adequate motives of study can be found when there is a vital union between the end of study and the means of accomplishing it. When an individual is intensely and sincerely interested in an end, the sense of separation between the means and the end tends to disappear. The means becomes saturated with a sense of the value of the end; and the end is so identified with the means of achieving it that it ceases to seem remote and far away; every one of the present means represents and embodies it. "Good teaching," says Professor Thorndike, "decides what is to be learned by an appeal not to interest, but to the general aim of education. Having so decided, it secures interest—the most, the best and the steadiest possible." (Edward L. Thorndike, *The Principles of Teaching,* p. 58)

"Firmly believe in good learning, hold fast even unto death the good doctrine"—that was the strong appeal of Confucius to the aims of the learning of his disciples, and that did successfully secure their interests or motives of study—"the most, the best and the steadiest possible."

(2) What are the adequate motives to be found?

Confucius made no use of such instinctive motives as competition and acquisition, the hope of reward and the fear of punishment.

"The Master said, 'He who aims to be a Superior Man in his food does not seek to gratify his appetite, nor in his dwelling-place does he seek the appliances of ease. . . .' " (*The Analects*, 1,14)

"The Master said, 'The determined scholar and the man of love (*Jen*) will not seek to live at the expense of injuring their love (*Jen*). They will even sacrifice their lives to preserve their love (*Jen*) complete.' " (*The Analects*, 15,8)

"Is he not a Superior Man, who feels no discomposure though men take no note of him?" (*The Analects*, 1,1,3)

"The Master said, 'The Superior Man has no contentions. If it be said he cannot avoid them, shall this be in archery?' " (*The Analects*, 3,7)

"Ssu-ma Niu asked about the Superior Man. The Master said, 'The Superior Man has neither anxiety nor fear.' 'Being without anxiety and fear! said Niu;—'does this constitute what we call the Superior Man?' The Master said, 'When internal examination discovers nothing wrong, what is there to be anxious about, what is there to fear?' " (*The Analects*, 12,4)

"The Master said, 'A scholar, whose mind is set on truth, and who is ashamed of bad clothes and bad food, is not fit to be discoursed with.' " (*The Analects*, 4,9)

"The Master said, 'The Superior Man thinks of virtue; the small man thinks of comfort. The Superior Man thinks of the sanctions of law; the small man thinks of favours (which he may receive).' " (*The Analects*, 4,11)

Love, especially the love of the parents, was the chief motive he offered as the positive stimulus. Love (*Jen*) was the chief virtue of a Superior Man, and the best policy of government.

"The Master said, 'If the will be set on love (*Jen*), there will be no practice of wickedness.' " (*The Analects*, 4,4)

"Filial piety and fraternity!—are they not the root of love (*Jen*)?" (*The Analects*, 1,2,2)

(See the aims and substance of the teachings of Confucius, Chapters 4 and 5)

5. An Example

The following is a concrete example of the teaching of Confucius as recorded in *The Analects*, to show how those principles mentioned above were recognized in one of the lessons taught by this ideal teacher.

"Tzu Lu, Tseng Hsi, Jan Yu, and Kung-hsi Hua were sitting by the Master. He said to them, 'Though I am a day or so older than you, do not think of that. From day to day you are saying, "We are not known". If some ruler were to know you, what would you like to do?' "

"Tzu Lu hastily and lightly replied. 'Suppose the case of a state of ten thousand chariots; let it be straitened between other large states; let it be suffering from invading armies; and to this let there be added a famine in corn and in all vegetables:—if I were entrusted with the government of it, in three years' time I could make the people to be bold, and to recognize the rules of right conduct. "

The Master smiled at him.

Turning to Yen Yu, he said, 'Ch'iu, what are your wishes?' Ch'iu replied, 'Suppose a state of sixty or seventy li square, or one of fifty or sixty, and let me have the government of it;—in three years' time, I could make plenty to abound among the people. As to teaching them the rules of proper conduct (*Li*), and music, I must wait for the rise of a Superior Man to do that.'

'What are your wishes, Ch'ih, said the Master next to Kung-hsi Hai. Ch'ih replied, 'I do not say that my ability extends to these things, but I should wish to learn them. At the services of the ancestral temple, and at the audiences of the princes with the sovereign, I should like, dressed in the dark square-made robe and the black linen cap, to act as a small assistant.'

Last of all, the Master asked Tseng Hsi, 'Tien, what are your wishes?' Tien, pausing as he was playing on his lute, while it was yet twanging, laid the instrument aside, and rose. 'My wishes', he said, 'are different from the cherished purposes of these three gentlemen.' 'What harm is there in that?' said the Master; 'do you also, as well as they, speak out your wishes.' Tien then said, 'In this, the last month of spring, with the dress of the season all complete, along with five or six young men who have assumed the cap, and six or seven boys, I would wash in the I, enjoy the breeze among the rain-altars, and return home singing.'

"The Master heaved a sigh and said, 'I give my approval to Tien.'

"The three others having gone out, Tseng Hsi remained behind, and said, 'What do you think of the words of these three friends?' The Master replied, 'They simply told each one his wishes.' Hsi pursued, 'Master, why did you smile at Yu?' He was answered, 'The management of a state demands the rules of proper conduct (*Li*). His words were not humble; therefore I smiled at him.'

"Hsi again said, 'But was it not a state which Ch'iu proposed for himself?' The reply was, 'Yes; did you ever see a territory of sixty or seventy li, or one of fifty or sixty, which was not a state?' Once more, Hsi inquired, 'And was it not a state which Ch'ih proposed for himself?' The Master again replied, 'Yes; who but princes have to do with ancestral temples, and with audiences but the sovereign? If Ch'ih were to be a small assistant in these services, who could be a great one?' " (*The Analects*, 11,25)

(1) Motivation

(a) A very favourable environment of learning was created

a) A proper physical environment

There were not too many in one room and they were all properly seated. They "were sitting by the Master."

b) A homogeneous group

This group of students was composed of men of similar intellectual standards and high ambitions. They were all favourite disciples of the Master.

c) The sincerity and friendliness of the Master

"Though I am a day or so older than you, do not think of that." How noble these words are! They must have touched the hearts of his disciples and moved them to thought. He seemed to have said, "Let us discuss together in a friendly way. Forget our position and our age. I am but one of you, so let us express our ideas frankly and without reserve." This certainly could only come from the mouth of a very noble and excellent teacher.

(b) A life-situation approach

He approached the whole discussion with the life-situation of his disciples in mind. He told them, "From day to day you are saying, 'We are not known'. If some ruler were to know you, what would you like to do?" This appealed to the very end or aim of the study which they had laboured on "from day to day", and at once stimulated their activity and motivated their thinking.

(2) Apperception

He built up his whole lesson here upon the past knowledge and attitude of his disciples. "From day to day you are saying, 'We are not known' ". From that past experience he led them a step further to a new situation, "If some ruler were to know you, what would you like to do?" This is indeed a problem which requires all the best part of the past experiences of his disciples that they had so far acquired.

(3) Activity

He seemed to have recognized the principle that "there is no impression without expression." He encouraged his disciples to express their own ideas, each one of them. When one of them was timid to express his idea, he urged him on in the most friendly manner, and did not command him with the severity which usually characterizes the old-style Chinese teacher.

(4) Individualization

He respected the individual differences of his students. He did not dictate his own idea or neglect their individual differences of opinion, though he did pronounce his own personal preference and opinion in the end of the discussion. He simply gave a sceptical smile at one of the students, who made some remarks with which he did not agree. "His words were not humble," said the Master, "therefore I smiled at him." This also shows the tact which was used by Confucius in the process of his teaching.

As a whole, this gives an excellent example of the discussion method of teaching which was constantly used by Confucius. Another favourite method of teaching which Confucius used very often was the dialectic method. He encouraged his disciples to ask questions, and frequently in the process of question-and-answer the general truth was brought to light. Beyond all else, he taught by the method of example, which is now to be discussed in the following section.

C. The Method of Example

One of the important reasons for the success of the teaching of Confucius was that he taught by the method of example. His own life ever exemplified his teachings. He always practiced what he taught, and where can one find a better method?

"Tzu Kung asked what constituted the Superior Man. The Master said, 'He acts before he speaks, and afterwards speaks according to his actions.' " (*The Analects*, 2,13)

"The Master said, 'The Superior Man is modest in his speech, but exceeds in his actions.' " (*The Analects*, 14,29)

The four main moral teachings as mentioned in chapter 5 exemplify the teachings of the Master in his own life.

1. Love (Jen)

Confucius was a very kind-hearted, sympathetic, self-sacrificing educationist and social reformer. He spent his whole life drifting here and there, preaching, teaching and helping all kinds of people. He was sometimes compared to a homeless dog wandering among the different states. Once he and his disciples lost track of each other. The disciples finally heard from the crowd that there was a tall man standing at the East Gate with a high forehead resembling some of the ancient emperors, but that he looked crestfallen like a homeless wandering dog. The disciples finally found him and told him about this remark and Confucius replied, "I don't know about my resembling those ancient emperors, but as for resembling a homeless wandering dog, he is quite right! He is quite right!" (Shih Chi, "The Life of Confucius") His intense love of his fellow beings gave him a positive and persistent urge to help them, irrespective of the consequences or of his own personal sufferings. Once it was remarked of him, "Oh, is he the fellow who knows that a thing can't be done and still wants to do it?" (*The Analects*, 14,41) There

was a high moral idealism in Confucius, a consciousness of a
Divine Mission, that made him completely believe in himself, and
enabled him to endure any kind of difficulty with cheerfulness.

"The Master said, 'With coarse rice to eat, with water to drink,
and my bended arm for a pillow;—I have still joy in the midst of
these things. Riches and honours acquired by unrighteousness are
to me as a floating cloud.' " (*The Analects*, 7,15)

The following are some instances in the life of Confucius as
recorded in *The Analects* that show something of the loving kindness of this great Master.

(1) Love for all

His love for all people is shown in the indiscrimination he
manifested in receiving his students. "Where there is instruction,
there will be no distinction of classes." (*The Analects*, 15,38) "From
the man bringing his bundle of dried flesh (as payment) upwards,
I have never refused instruction to any one." (*The Analects*, 7,7) His
geniality and hospitality towards all desiring to learn is recorded
in the following incident, resembling a story in the Bible when
Jesus said, "Suffer the little children to come unto me." The people
of a certain village were given to mischief, and one day some
children from that village came to see Confucius, and the disciples
were surprised that Confucius saw them. Confucius remarked,
"Why be so harsh on them? What concerns me is the fact of their
coming and not the matter of their leaving. When a man approaches me with pure intentions, I respect his pure intentions, although
I cannot guarantee what he does afterwards." (*The Analects*, 7,28)

(2) Love for his disciples

There was a complete understanding and deep affection between the Master and his disciples. He regarded them as his own
children and they loved him as their own parents.

"When Yen Yuan died, the Master bewailed him exceedingly,
and the disciples who were with him said, 'Master, your grief is
excessive?' " (*The Analects*, 11,9,1)

"The Master said, 'Hui behaved towards me as his father. . . .' "
(*The Analects*, 11,10,3)

"The Master said, 'Do you think, my disciples, that I have any concealments? I conceal nothing from you. There is nothing which I do that is not shown to you, my disciples;—that is my way.' " (*The Analects*, 7, 23)

"The Master having visited Nan-tzu, Tzu Lu was displeased, on which the Master swore to him saying, 'If I have done improperly, may Heaven reject me! May Heaven reject me!' " (*The Analects*, 6,26)

"The Master was put in peril in K'uang, and Yen Yuan fell behind. The Master, on his rejoining him, said, 'I thought you had died.' Hui replied, 'While you were alive, how should I presume to die?' " (*The Analects*, 11,22)

(3) Love for the poor and needy

"When any of his friends died, if he had no relations who could be depended on for the necessary offices, he would say, 'I will bury him.' " (*The Analects*, 10,15,1)

"Tzu Hua being employed on a mission to Ch'i, the disciple Jan requested grain for his mother. The Master said, 'Give her a *fu*.' Yen requested more. 'Give her an *Yu*', said the Master. Yen gave her *ping*. The Master said, 'When Ch'ih was proceeding to Ch'i, he had fat horses to his carriage, and wore light furs. I have heard that a Superior Man helps the distressed, but does not add to the wealth of the rich.' Yuan Ssu being made governor of his town by the Master, he have him nine hundred measures of grain, but Ssu declined them. The Master said, 'Do not decline them. May you not give them away in the neighbourhoods, hamlets, towns, and villages?' " (*The Analects*, 6,3)

(4) He mourned with those who mourned, and rejoiced with those who rejoiced

"When the Master was eating by the side of a mourner, he never ate to the full. He did not sing on the same day in which he had been weeping." (*The Analects*, 7,9)

"When he saw any one in a mourning dress, though it might be an acquaintance, he would change countenance. . . . To any person in mourning he bowed forward to the cross-bar of his carriage." (*The Analects*, 10,16)

"When the Master was in company with a person who was singing, if he sang well, he would make him repeat the song, while he accompanied it with his own voice." (*The Analects*, 7,31)

2. **The Rules of Proper Conduct (*Li*)**

"Lin Fang asked what was the essence of *Li*. The Master said, 'A great question indeed! In ceremonies (*Li*), it is better to be sparing than extravagant. In the ceremonies of mourning, it is better that there be deep sorrow than a minute attention to observances.' " (*The Analects*, 3,4)

"The Master said, '. . . Ceremonies (*Li*) performed without reverence; mourning conducted without sorrow—wherewith should I contemplate such ways?' " (*The Analects*, 3,26)

Here Confucius mentioned at least three important principles for the rules of proper conduct (*Li*), namely, economy, reverence, and sincerity.

(1) Economy—"It is better to be sparing than extravagant." "The Master said, 'The linen cap is that prescribed by the rules of proper conduct (*Li*), but now a silk one is worn. It is economical, and I follow the common practice.' " (*The Analects*, 9,3,1)

When his son died, Confucius only gave him a simple burial. He said, "There was Li (his son); when he died, he had a coffin but no outer shell." (*The Analects*, 11,7,2) When Yen Yuan, one of his favourite disciples, died, he disapproved of the idea of his disciples that they should give him a great funeral.

"When Yen Yuan died, the disciples wished to give him a great funeral. The Master said, 'You may not do so.' The disciples did bury him in great style. The Master said, 'Hui behaved towards me as his father, I have not been able to treat him as my son. The fault is not mine; it belongs to you, O disciples.' " (*The Analects*, 11,10)

(2) Sincerity—"In the ceremonies of mourning, it is better that there be deep sorrow than a minute attention to observances."

When Yen Yuan died, he bewailed him with exceeding grief (*The Analects*, 11,9), and he was careful in the observance of conduct befitting an occasion of mourning (*The Analects*, 7,9)

(3) Reverence

"He sacrificed to the dead, as if they were present, He sacrificed to the spirits, as if the spirits were present." (*The Analects*, 3,12,1)

"When he entered the ancestral temple of the state, he asked about everything." (*The Analects*, 10,14) This, he said, "is a rule of proper conduct (*Li*)." (*The Analects*, 3,15)

"When a friend sent him a present, though it might be a carriage and horse, he did not bow. The only present for which he bowed was that of the flesh of sacrifice." (*The Analects*, 10,15)

"When he saw any one wearing a cap of full dress, or a blind person, though he might be in his undress, he would salute them in a ceremonious manner." (*The Analects*, 10,16,2)

"Although his food might be coarse rice and vegetable soup, he would offer (a little of it) in sacrifice with a grave respectful air." (*The Analects*, 10,8,10)

3. Filial Piety

About filial piety Confucius said, "That parents, when alive, should be served according to the rules of proper conduct (*Li*), that, when dead, they should be buried according to *Li*; and that they should be sacrificed to according to *Li*." (*The Analects*, 2,5,3)

About serving his parents when they were alive, we have no record at all. The great historian, Ssu-ma Ch'ien, tells us that his father died soon after Confucius was born, and gives some account about the burial of his parents. He says, "When Confucius' mother died, he buried her temporarily, for caution's sake, in the Street of the Five Fathers, and it was not until an old woman, the mother of Wan-fu of Tsou, informed him of the whereabouts of his father's grave, that he buried his parents together at Fang Shan. Once a Baron of Lu, Chi, was giving a banquet to the scholars of the town, and Confucius went while still in mourning." (*Shih Chi*, "The Life of Confucius")

According to this statement, Confucius buried his parents cautiously, and observed mourning according to the rules of proper conduct (*Li*). About sacrificing to his parents, Confucius must have observed very faithfully and reverently according to the rules of proper conduct (Li). "He sacrificed to the dead, as if they were present. He sacrificed to the spirits, as if the spirits were present. The Master said, 'I consider my not being present at the sacrifice, as if I did not sacrifice.' " (*The Analects*, 3,12) The dead, or the spirits which he sacrificed to were very likely his parents or his other ancestors, because he said, "For a man to sacrifice to a spirit which does not belong to him is flattery." (*The Analects*, 2,24,1)

He regarded his whole educational and social works as primarily the discharging of filial and brotherly duties. "Some one addressed Confucius, saying, 'Sir, why are you not engaged in the government?' The Master said, 'What does *Shu-ching* say of filial piety? —"You are filial, you discharge your brotherly duties. These qualities are displayed in government." This then also constitutes the function of government. Why must there be that—making one be in the government?' " (*The Analects*, 2,21) Indeed, if we consider the end in view of filial piety taken by Confucius as recorded in *The Book of Filial Piety*, that "To establish oneself and walk in the right Way, and spread a name to a later generation, so that one's parents will be glorified," Confucius may be said to be one of the most filial sons that China has produced.

4. The Doctrine of the Golden Mean

Confucius said, "With me there is no inflexible may or may not". (*The Analects*, 18,8,5)

"Mencius said, 'Chung Ni (Confucius) did not do excessive things.' " (*Mencius*, 4,2,10)

"There are four things from which the Master was entirely free. He had no foregone conclusions, no arbitrary predeterminations, no obstinacy, and no egoism." (*The Analects*, 9,4)

"The Master was mild, and yet dignified; majestic, and yet not fierce; respectful, and yet easy." (*The Analects*, 7,37)

In short, he not only taught about love (*Jen*), the rules of proper conduct (*Li*), filial piety, the Golden Mean, and others but he actually exemplified them in his own life. Here lies one of the important reasons for the effectiveness of his teachings. His character is very honestly and vividly described in the following by his own words:

"The duke of Yueh asked Tzu Lu about Confucius, and Tzu Lu did not answer him. The Master said, 'Why did you not say to him, —He is simply a man, who in his enthusiasm (for his work) forgets his food; who is optimistic, forgetful of his sorrows; and who does not perceive that old age is coming on?' " (*The Analects*, 7,18)

"The Master said. . . . 'It may simply be said of me, that I strive to do my work without satiety, and teach others without weariness.' " (*The Analects*, 7,23) Again he said the same about himself, "The silent treasuring up of knowledge; learning without satiety; and instructing others without being wearied;—which one of these things belongs to me?" (*The Analects*, 7,2) Mencius says, "Formerly Tzu Kung asked Confucius, saying, 'Master, are you a Sage?' Confucius answered him, 'A Sage is what I cannot rise to. I learn without satiety, and teach without being tired.' Tzu Kung said, 'You learn without satiety:—that shows your wisdom. You teach without being tired:—that shows your love (*Jen*). Loving and wise: —Master, you ARE a Sage.' " (*Mencius*, 2,1,2,19)

D. Methods of Learning

A good teacher is not only skilful in teaching on various subjects, but he is also skilful in helping and encouraging his students how to learn by themselves. Modern teaching is sometimes regarded as simply the designed arrangement of favourable conditions for effective learning. The principles regarding the teaching process are equally the principles regarding the learning process. The following, however, are some of the methods which Confucius especially emphasized in the learning process that were found useful by his disciples, and are, no doubt, still useful to-day.

1. **Men are Teachable**

He started his whole educational career on the presumption that men are teachable; they are able to learn if they will. Once one of his disciples came to him and said, "It is not that I do not delight in your doctrines, but my strength is insufficient." But Confucius answered, "Those whose strength is insufficient give over in the middle of the way (i.e., they go along as far as they can, and while they are still pursuing they come to a stop), but now you limit yourself." (*The Analects*, 6,10) It is not the problem of insufficiency of personal strength which prevents one from learning a thing, it is rather a problem of self-limitation or lack of personal will that causes the lesson not to be learnt. Men are all teachable, but only those who will, will actually learn.

The Master said, "Is any one able for one day to apply his strength to love (*Jen*)? I have not seen the case in which his strength would be insufficient." (*The Analects*, 4,6,2) Again, he said, "If the will be set on love (*Jen*), there will be no practice of wickedness." (*The Analects*, 4,4)

The original nature of man, which was a favourite subject of discussion for later scholars, did not come prominently into the thought system of Confucius himself. So one of his disciples said, "His discourses about man's nature, and the way of Heaven, cannot be heard." (*The Analects*, 5,12) He took it for granted that "by nature, men are nearly alike; by practice, they get to be wide apart." (*The Analects*, 17,2) Men are made different not by their original nature, but by what they have learnt through practice. Learning which brings the difference between individual persons has not so much to do with the original nature, as the reconstruction of experience through contact with the outside world, such as seeing, hearing and touching which can be controlled by the process of education. That is why Confucius believed so much in education as the best means for individual regeneration and social reform.

Confucius admitted, however, that there are a small group of abnormal persons who are either extraordinarily bright or extraordinarily dull. They were called "the wise of the highest class" (*Shang-chih*),[4] and "the stupid of the lowest class" (*Hsia-yu*).[5] "The Master said, 'There are only the wise of the highest class and the stupid of the lowest class, who cannot be changed.' " (*The Analects*, 17,2) The phrase, "cannot be changed" is difficult to understand. It cannot be taken to mean that those two classes of people are not teachable, or cannot be changed to be better or to be worse through education. "Confucius said, 'Those who are born with the possession of wisdom are the highest class of men. Those who learn, and so, readily, get possession of wisdom, are the next. Those who are dull and stupid, and yet compass learning, are another class next to these. As to those who are dull and stupid and yet do not learn;—they are the lowest of the people.' " (*The Analects*, 16,9) So according to his saying, the lowest class of people are those who do not learn. If they learn they can rise to be the higher class of people. By the phrase "cannot be changed", he seemed to point to the fact that there are certain limits for the changes. "The Master said, 'To those whose talents are above mediocrity, the highest subjects may be announced. To those who are below mediocrity, the highest subjects may not be announced.' " (*The Analects*, 6,19) The 'mediocrity' seemed to be the mark-line between 'the wise of the highest class' and 'the stupid of the lowest class', over which neither of them could pass. That is to say, 'the wise of the first class', if properly educated, cannot degenerate below mediocrity, while 'the stupid of the lowest class', though given the same proper education, cannot rise above the mark of mediocrity. Han Yu, the great Confucian scholar in the T'ang Dynasty commented upon the original nature of man as taught by Confucius, saying, "There are three ranks of human nature; upper, middle, lower. The upper is that which is only good. The middle is that which can be led upwards, the lower is that which is only bad. The upper degree by learning becomes intelligent; the lower by being in fear of authority reduces its offenses. Therefore, the upper grades can be taught and the lower grades can be controlled." (Han Yu, *An Enquiry into Human Nature*, Yuan Hsing)[6]

So all people, no matter what kind of nature they have, can, according to Han Yu, be made better, more or less, through education,—the upper by learning "becomes more intelligent," the middle "can be led upwards", the lower "can be controlled." They are all teachable, and can be changed, though in different degrees, through education.

2. Five Steps to Learning

"The Master said, ... 'Study extensively, inquire accurately, think carefully, discriminate clearly, and practise earnestly. ... Let a man proceed in this way, and, though dull, he will surely become intelligent; though weak, he will surely become strong.' " (*The Doctrine of the Mean*, 20,19-21)

(1) Study extensively

"The Master said, 'The Superior Man, extensively studying all learning. ...' " (*The Analects*, 6,25)

"Hear much ... See much." (*The Analects*, 2,18; 7,27)

"A man of the village of Ta-hsiang said, 'Great indeed is Confucius! His learning is extensive, and yet he does not render his name famous by any particular thing.' " (*The Analects*, 9,2,1)

(2) Inquire accurately

"Tzu Kung asked, saying 'On what ground did Kung Wen-tzu get the title of "accomplished" (*Wen*)?' The Master said, 'He was of an active nature and yet fond of learning, and was not ashamed to ask and learn of his inferiors!—On these grounds he has been styled "accomplished" (*Wen*).' " (*The Analects*, 5,14)

One of the nine things, which, according to Confucius, a Superior Man should take into serious consideration, is "in regard to what he doubts about, he is anxious to question others." (*The Analects*, 16,10)

"The Master said, 'If a man does not ask—"How is it? How is it?" I can indeed do nothing with him!' " (*The Analects*, 15,15)

"The Master, when he entered the grand temple, asked about everything. . . ." (*The Analects*, 3,15)

(3) Think carefully

"The Master said, 'Learning without thought is labour lost; thought without learning is perilous.' " (*The Analects*, 2,15)

"The Master said, 'When we see men of worth, we should think of equalling them; when see men of a contrary character, we should turn inwards and examine ourselves.' " (*The Analects*, 4,17)

"The Master said, 'I do not open up the truth to one who is not eager (to get knowledge), nor help out any one who is not anxious to explain himself. When I have presented one corner of a subject to any one, and he cannot from it learn the other three, I do not repeat my lesson.' " (*The Analects*, 7,8)

(4) Discriminate clearly

"The Master said, . . . 'Hear much and select what is good and follow it; see much and keep it in memory.' " (*The Analects*, 7,27)

"The Master said, . . . 'He who attains to Sincerity (*Ch'eng*),[7] is he who chooses what is good, and firmly holds it fast.' " (The Doctrine of the Mean, 20,18)

"The Master said, 'Believe firmly in good learning, and hold fast the good doctrine even unto death.' " (*The Analects*, 8,13,1)

"The Master said, 'Attack the strange doctrines which are injurious to ourselves.' " (*The Analects*, 2,16)

(5) Practice earnestly

"The Master said, 'To learn and practice constantly, is it not a pleasure?' " (*The Analects*, 1,1,1,)

"The Master said, 'The Superior Man . . . is earnest in what he is doing, and careful in his speech.' " (*The Analects*, 1,14)

According to one of Thorndike's laws of learning, the "Law of Exercise", "Whenever a modifiable connection between situation and response is exercised its strength is increased", so the surest way of acquiring new knowledge, skill, or habit is to put them under constant practice or review. Again, learning is generally understood as the reconstruction of experiences, so a new experience can only be acquired through the reconstruction of past experiences. Confucius says,

"If a man keeps reviewing his old (knowledge, skill, or habit), so as continually to be acquiring the new, he may be a teacher of others." (*The Analects*, 2,11)

3. Two Essentials of Learning
The two essentials of learning, according to Confucius, are diligence and humility. "Tzu Kung asked, saying, 'On what ground did Kung Wen-tzu get the title of "accomplished" (*Wen*)?' The Master said, 'He was of an active nature and yet fond of learning, and was not ashamed to ask and learn of his inferiors!—on these grounds he has been styled "accomplished" (*Wen*).' " (*The Analects*, 5,14) This idea of diligence and humility as the two essentials of learning has long been recognized by Chinese thinkers before the time of Confucius. It is mentioned in one of the oldest traditional documents preserved in *The Book of History* which Confucius selected and taught to his disciples. The "Charge to Yueh" (*Yueh Ming*)[8] in *The Book of Shang* states:

"In learning there should be a humble will, and a striving to maintain a constant diligence. In such a case the learner's cultivation will surely come. He who sincerely cherishes these things will find all truth accumulating in his person. To teach is one half of learning. When a man's thoughts from first to last are constantly fixed on such learning his virtuous cultivation comes unperceived." (*The Book of History*, 4,3,3,4-5)

(1) Diligence
"The Master said, 'In a hamlet of ten families, there may be found one honourable and sincere as I am, but not one so fond of learning.' " (*The Analects*, 5,27)

"The Master said, 'I have been the whole day without eating, and the whole night without sleeping;—occupied with thinking. It was of no use. The better plan is to learn.' " (*The Analects*, 15,30)

"When the Master was in Ch'i he heard the *Shao*, and for three months did not know the taste of flesh. 'I did not think', he said, 'that music could have been made so excellent as this.' " (*The Analects*, 7,13)

(2) Humility

"The Master said, 'Learn as if you had not reached your object, and were always fearing also lest you lose it.' " (*The Analects*, 8,17)

"When you have faults, do not fear to abandon them." (*The Analects*, 1,8,4; 9,24)

"The Master said, 'To have faults and not to reform them,—this, indeed should be pronounced as having faults.' " (*The Analects*, 15,29)

"The Master said, 'Yu, shall I teach you what knowledge is? When you know a thing, to hold that you know it; and when you do not know a thing, to allow that you do not know it;—this is knowledge.' " (*The Analects*, 2,17)

"The Master said, 'When I walk along with two others, they may serve me as my teachers. I will select their good qualities and follow them, their bad qualities and avoid them.' " (*The Analects*, 7,21)

"The Master said, 'Am I indeed possessed of knowledge? I am not knowing.' " (*The Analects*, 9,7)

E. Sociological Method of Education

A modern writer on sociology has pointed out that the social process as a whole, and that part of it which is formally educative, are essentially the same in procedure and result. (C. A. Ellwood, The Educative Nature of the Social Process, *Teachers College Record*, May 1921) This truth is very well exemplified in the teaching of Confucius. He not only cared for the individual development of his disciples through utilizing the principles of apperception, activity, individualization, and motivation; through his own personal example; and through his teaching about methods of learning; he also cared for the needs of society. So he tried to relate as closely as possible education and society, and to adjust his disciples as far as possible to the social needs, without, however, infringing upon their individualities. Of social life during the time of Confucius, to which he endeavoured to bring his teaching in close relation, the following six major aspects will be considered, namely, government, family, religion, rites, ethics, and arts.

1. **Education in Relation to Government**
The definition which Confucius gave to government, is that, "To govern means to put things right."[9] (*The Analects*, 12,17) He aimed at social reform or "putting things right" through education. So he believed in government as one of the most effective means of serving the purpose of putting right the evils of society, and bringing to pass the perfect order of his ideal society. He was very much interested in politics. He studied carefully the political problems of every state which he visited. "When our Master comes to any country," said Tzu Ch'in, one of the disciples of Confucius, "he does not fail to learn all about its government." (*The Analects*, 1,10,1) He held governmental offices for certain periods of time, and awaited opportunities to be of real use in the government.

"Tzu Kung said, 'There is a beautiful gem here. Should I lay it up in a case and keep it? or should I seek for a good price and sell it? The Master said, ' Sell it! Sell it! But I would wait for one to offer the price.' " (The Analects, 9,12) He encouraged his disciples to enter into politics, and recommended them to the rulers of different states for various offices. For example, he recommended his disciples Yu, Ch'iu and Ch'ih to Meng Wu-po, saying,

"In a kingdom of a thousand chariots, Yu might be employed to manage the military levies. . . . In a city of a thousand families; or a clan of a hundred chariots, Ch'iu might be employed as governor. . . . With his sash girt and standing in a court, Ch'ih might be employed to converse with the visitors and guests. . . ." (The Analects, 5,7)

In the same manner he recommended his disciples to Chi K'ang Tzu, saying,

"Yu is a man of decision; what difficulty would he find in being an officer of the government? . . . Tz'u is a man of intelligence; what difficulty would he find in being an officer of government? . . . Ch'iu is a man of various ability; what difficulty would he find in being an officer of government?" (The Analects, 6,6)

The idea that "the student, having completed his learning, should apply himself to be an officer" (The Analects, 19,13) was generally conceived by scholars during the time of Confucius.

All the teachings of Confucius, both moral and intellectual, had something to do with teaching his students how to run governmental offices.

(1) Moral teaching

Since moral character is the most important qualification for being an officer, Confucius paid most attention to moral teaching. Once he told one of the political leaders of his native state, Lu, about the importance of virtue in government, saying, "Let your (evinced) desires be for what is good, and the people will be good. The relation between superiors and inferiors, is like that between the wind and the grass. The grass must bend, when the wind blows across it." (The Analects, 12,19) Again, he said, "He who exercises government by means of his virtue may be compared to the north

polar star, which keeps its place and all the stars turn towards it."
(*The Analects*, 2,1) He advised his disciple, "Do you be a scholar
after the style of the Superior Man, and not after that of the mean
man." (*The Analects*, 6,11)

(2) Intellectual teaching

a) Poetry

One of the objectives of his course on Poetry was political.

"The Master said, 'Though a man may be able to recite the three
hundred odes, yet if, when intrusted with a governmental charge,
he knows not how to act, or if, when sent to any quarter on a
mission, he cannot give his replies unassisted, notwithstanding the
extent of his learning, of what practical use is it?' " (*The Analects*,
13,5)

b) History

History was one of the important courses for the officer or ruler
in ancient China. So when the question arose as to what should be
taught to the crown prince of Ch'u, son of King Chuang (613-591
B.C.), the answer came: "Teach him *Ch'un Ch'iu* (the historical
records of Lu) and by it encourage goodness and censure evil, so
as to restrain and admonish his mind." (*Kuo Yu*, Ch'u Yu, 1,1)
Mencius also mentioned that the aim of *Ch'un Ch'iu* which Confucius edited was mainly political. He says,

"The world fell into decay, and principles faded away. Perverse
speakings and oppressive deeds waxed rife again. There were
instances of ministers who murdered their sovereigns, and of sons
who murdered their fathers. Confucius was afraid, and made *Ch'un
Ch'iu.* . . . When *Ch'un Ch'iu* was completed, the rebellious ministers and villainous sons were struck with terror." (Mencius,
3,2,9,7-11)

c) The rules of proper conduct (*Li*)

One of the important objectives of his teaching on *Li* was also
to train his disciples to meet the political needs.

Confucius said, "The management of a state demands the rules
of proper conduct (*Li*)" (*The Analects*, 11,25,10)

"The Master said, 'If a kingdom is governed with the complaisance proper to *Li*, what difficulty will it have?' " (*The Analects*,

4,13)

d) Music

Music was also regarded as one of the best means for governmental control. Once Confucius was asked about government by his disciple, he said,

"Ah Shih, didn't I tell you before? All that one needs to do is simply for the Superior Man fully to understand *Li* and music and then apply them to government!" (*Li-chi*, Chap. 28)

So one of his disciples when he was in charge of a city at once put the idea into practice, trying to govern the city by means of music.

"The Master having come to Wu city, heard there the sound of stringed instruments and singing. Well pleased and smiling, he said, 'Why use an ox-knife to kill a fowl?' Tzu-lu replied, 'Formerly, Master, I heard you say.—"When the Superior Man has learnt the right Way (*Tao*), he loves men; when the Small Man has learnt the Way (*Tao*), he is easily ruled.' " The Master said, 'My disciples, Yen's words are right. What I said was only in sport.' " (*The Analects*, 17,4)

2. In Relation to the Family

It has been mentioned above that Confucius had no sympathy with the nationalistic and legalistic theories of a military system which was developing rapidly in his days. He was rather in favour of the Feudal System of the early Chou Dynasty with its primary virtues of loyalty and rules of proper conduct (*Li*), and he remedied the evils of class distinctions of that system by means of the family virtues, especially love and filial piety, which characterized the Patriarchal System of the period of the Sage-kings before the Chou Dynasty. So he paid much attention in his system of education to family relationships. The duties towards the members of one's family were very much emphasized, and the virtue of filial piety was esteemed to be the root of all virtues. (See chapter 5, section on Filial Piety) In due time *The Book of Filial Piety* (*Hsiao Ching*) was written by his disciples, who attributed all the content of the book to their Master, and it became a textbook for elementary schools through all subsequent generations. Thus family virtues, especially that of the son in relation to his father, were made the basis of the system of education in China.

3. In Relation to Religion

As has been pointed out above, although Confucius was not primarily a teacher of religion, yet he was a deeply religious person. He was specially interested in religious ceremonies, which already attracted much of his attention when he was just a small boy. We can imagine that one of the departments of his course on the rules of proper conduct (*Li*) must have been on the rules of proper conduct for religious ceremonies, or rites. Once he refused to talk about military tactics with Duke Ling of Wei, saying, "I have heard all about sacrificial vessels, but I have not learned military matters." (*The Analects*, 15,1,1) Although in the original Chinese religion there never was a separate class of priesthood, consecrated specially for religious services, yet there seemed to have been a special class of officers of State who were versed in religious ceremonies, and whose duty it was primarily to attend to the sacrificial rites and other religious matters. That is why Tseng Tzu said, "As to such matters as attending to the sacrificial vessels, there are the proper officers for them." (*The Analects*, 8,4,3) As society needed men for religious functions, Confucius, therefore, trained his followers for those duties. One of his famous disciples expressed his cherished wish to attend to religious matters. He said, "At the services of the ancestral temple, and at the audiences of the princes with the sovereign, I should like, dressed in the dark square-made robe and the black linen cap, to act as a small assistant." (*The Analects*, 11,25,6) "Tzu Kung asked 'What do you say of me?' The Master said, 'You are a utensil.' 'What utensil?' 'A gemmed sacrificial utensil.' " (*The Analects*, 5,3) It may well be that this disciple also was interested in religious matters and that he was thus compared to a "sacrificial utensil".

4. In Relation to Rites (*Li*)

As has been mentioned, at the time of Confucius, everything was governed by rites or the fixed rules of proper conduct. They were the standards of proper conduct in government, society, or in the daily life of an individual. Formality, superstition, wasteful extravagance, and hypocrisy were some of the prevailing evils of the time. Confucius being a great revolutionary teacher with regard to the traditional rites, scolded those "good careful people of the villages" who carefully observed the traditional rites, but were really "the thieves of virtues." (*The Analects*, 17,13; *Mencius*, 7,2,37,8) In order to meet the social needs, he taught various rites or rules of proper conduct to his disciples, but he emphasized more their spirit rather than their form. (See Chap. 5, section on *Li*)

5. In Relation to Ethics

His disciples recorded that "there were four things which the Master taught,—arts, ethics, loyalty, and truthfulness." Among the four things, three of them dealt with the problems of ethics. The development of the moral character of the individual to bring peace and order and prosperity to society was the chief aim of the teaching of Confucius. The individual problem was, to his, essentially the same as the social problem; the problems of ethics and politics were identical. His definition of government as aiming "to put things right" was primarily an ethical definition. He was aiming at the moral basis for peace in society, out of which political peace should naturally ensue. "Some one addressed Confucius, saying, 'Sir, why are you not engaged in the government?' The Master said, 'What does *Shu-ching* say of filial piety?—"You are filial, you discharge your brotherly duties. These qualities are displayed in government." This then also constitutes the function of government. Why must there be that,—to make one be in the government?' " (*The Analects*, 2,21) Politics was regarded to be the same as ethics. Confucius was never quite satisfied with the kind of social order achieved by a rigorous administration of enforcement of the criminal law. He would prefer the slow but steady method of the moral conversion of the heart of the people. The government run by virtue was more preferable than that run by legal regulations. Politics to him should be identified with ethics.

"The Master said, 'If the people be led by laws, and uniformity sought to be given them by punishments, they will try to avoid the punishment, but have no sense of shame. If they be led by virtue, the uniformity sought to be given them by the rules of proper conduct (*Li*), they will have the sense of shame, and moreover will become good.' " (*The Analects*, 2,3)

Confucius, as mentioned above, was primarily a moral teacher.

(f) In relation to arts

A passage in the *Chou Li* explaining the duties of the Minister of Education says that he was to teach the people "the Six Arts, namely, rites (*Li*), music, archery, chariot driving, writing, and arithmetic." (*Chou Li*, section on Ti Kuan, p. 14) This term "the six arts" is a common term in classical literature for the content of education. The term "rite" (*Li*) here probably covered all classical literature which was taught by Confucius, such as, poetry, history, and the rituals (*Li*). Music was a favourite subject of instruction by Confucius. He was skilful in archery and chariot driving, though they were not the major subjects of his teaching. "The Master shot —but not at birds perching" (*The Analects*, 7,26), that is, he was sportsman enough to shoot at birds only when they were flying. He was also interested in charioteering. For example, he said, "What shall I practise? Shall I practise charioteering, or shall I practise archery? I will practise charioteering." (*The Analects*, 9,2,2) He taught something about the manner of these arts to his disciples, as recorded in *The Analects*.

"The Master said, 'The Superior Man has no contentions. If it be said he cannot avoid them, shall this be in archery? But he bows complaisantly to his competitors; thus he ascends the hall, descends, and exacts the forfeit of drinking. In his contentions, he is still the Superior Man.' " (*The Analects*, 3,7)

"The Master said, 'In archery it is not going through the leather which is the principal thing;—because people's strength is not equal. This was the old way.' " (*The Analects*, 3,16)

"When he was about to mount his carriage, he would stand straight, holding the cord. When he was in the carriage, he did not turn his head quite round, he did not talk hastily, he did not point with his hands." (*The Analects*, 10,17)

As to the arts of writing and arithmetic, they belonged more to the elementary education which Confucius was not so much concerned with, for he dealt primarily with the adult or higher education.

F. Results of His Teaching

The efficiency of his teaching methods can best be seen in the results of his teaching: his influence upon his disciples, and upon society in general.

(A) His Influence Upon His Disciples

This can be clearly seen from their moral and intellectual growth, and from their attitudes towards their master.

1. Moral and Intellectual Growth of His Disciples

Owing to his great respect for individuals, he never despised the free growth of his disciples, but let them grow fully according to their capacities and interests. Consequently their achievements were not the same, but varied along the different lines of their work. For example:

"Distinguished for their virtuous principles and practice, there were:

Yen Yuan, Min Tzu Ch'ien, Jan Po Niu, and Chung Kung;
Distinguished for their ability in speech, there were:
Tsai Wo and Tzu Kung;
Distinguished for their administrative talents, there were:
Jan Yu and Chi Lu;
Distinguished for their literary acquirements, there were:
Tzu Yu and Tzu Hsia."
(The Analects, 11,2)

In order to show the growth of his disciples morally and intellectually along different lines of life, one of each group may be taken as an example.

(a) Distinguished for virtuous principles and practice:—Yen Yuan.

"The Master said, 'Admirable indeed was the virtue of Hui (Yen Yuan)! With a single bamboo dish of rice, a single gourd dish of drink, and living in his mean narrow lane, while others could not have endured the distress, he did not allow his joy to be affected by it. Admirable indeed was the virtue of Hui!' " (*The Analects*, 6,9)

"The Master said to Yen Yuan, 'When called to office, to undertake its duties; when not so called, to lie retired;—it is only I and you who have attained to this.' " (*The Analects*, 7,10,1)

"The Master said, 'Such was Hui that for three months there would be nothing in his mind contrary to Love (*Jen*). The others may attain to this on some days or in some months, but nothing more.' " (*The Analects*, 6,5)

(b) Distinguished for ability in speech:—Tzu Kung

"Tzu Kung said, 'What do you pronounce concerning the poor man who yet does not flatter, and the rich man who is not proud?' The Master replied, 'They will do; but they are not equal to him, who, though poor, is yet cheerful, and to him, who, though rich, loves the rules of proper conduct (*Li*).' Tzu Kung replied, 'It is said in *The Book of Poetry*, "As you cut and then file, as you carve and then polish." The meaning is the same, I apprehend, as that which you have just expressed. The Master said, 'With one like Tz'u, I can begin to talk about the Odes. I told you one point, and he knew its proper sequence.' " (*The Analects*, 1,15)

He was sometimes thought to be superior to Confucius.

"Shu-sun Wu-shu observed to the great officers in the court, saying, 'Tzu Kung is superior to Chung Ni (Confucius).' " (*The Analects*, 19,23,1)

"Ch'en Tzu Ch'in, addressing Tzu Kung, said, 'You are too modest. How can Chung Ni be said to be superior to you?' " (*The Analects*, 19,25,1)

This shows somewhat his great advancement both morally and intellectually. He also shared with Confucius the critical spirit and the scientific attitude towards traditional literature. "Tzu Kung said, 'Chou's wickedness was not so great (as that name implies).

Therefore, the Superior Man hates to dwell in a low-lying situation, where all the evil of the world will flow in upon him.' " (*The Analects*, 19,20)

"The Master said, 'Tz'u is a man of intelligence; what difficulty would he find in being an officer of government?' " (*The Analects*, 6,6)

(c) Distinguished for administrative talents:—Jan Yu

Jan Yu, named Ch'iu, and by designation, Tzu Yu. He was a man of ability and resource. "The Master said, 'In a city of a thousand families, or a clan of a hundred chariots, Ch'iu might be employed as a governor. . . .' " (*The Analects*, 5,7,3) He entered the service of the Chi family, the family of the greatest power in the State of Lu. With his great ability and foresight, he helped the head of the Chi family to be rich and strong. "The head of the Chi family was richer than the duke of Chou, and Ch'iu collected his imposts for him, and increased his wealth." (*The Analects*, 11,16,1) He persuaded the head of the Chi family to attack Chuan-yu, for, he said, "At present, Chuan-yu is strong and near to Pi; if (our chief) do not now take it, it will hereafter be a sorrow to his descendants." (*The Analects*, 16,1,8)

(d) Distinguished for literary acquirements:—Tzu Hsia

Tzu Hsia was the designation of Pu Shang. He was famous for his learning, and had many disciples. His views on *Shih-ching* and *Ch'un Ch'iu* are said to be preserved in the commentaries of Mao,[10] and of Kung-yung Kao,[11] and Ku-liang Ch'ih.[12] He lived to a great age, and was much esteemed by the people and princes of the time.

a) His views on the substance of learning

He regarded right conduct as of primary importance in learning. It was the practical action rather than book-learning that was emphasized in his school of study. Once his friend Tzu Yu criticized him saying,

"The disciples and followers of Tzu Hsia, in sprinkling and sweeping the ground, in answering and replying, in advancing and receding, are sufficiently accomplished. But these are only the branches of learning, and they are left ignorant of what is essential. How can they be acknowledged as sufficiently taught?" (*The*

Analects, 19,12,1)

"Tzu Hsia said, 'If a man withdraws his mind from the love of beauty, and applies it as sincerely to the love of the virtuous; if, in serving his parents, he can exert his utmost strength; if, in serving his prince, he can devote his life; if, in his intercourse with his friends, his words are sincere:—although men say that he has not learned, I will certainly say that he has.' " (*The Analects,* 1,7)

(b) His views on the method of learning

"Learn extensively, hold firmly and sincerely the aim of learning, inquire earnestly, and think clearly." (*The Analects,* 19,6)

"He, who from day to day recognizes what has not yet, and from month to month does not forget what he has attained to, may be said indeed to love to learn." (*The Analects,* 19,5)

c) His views on the aim of learning

"Mechanics have their shops to dwell in, in order to accomplish their works. The Superior Man learns, in order to reach to the utmost of the Way (*Tao*)." (*The Analects,* 19,7)

"The student, having completed his learning, should apply himself to be an officer." (*The Analects,* 19,13)

d) His view on universal brotherhood

"Ssu-ma Niu, full of anxiety, said, 'Other men all have their brothers, I only have not.' Tzu Hsia said, 'There is the following saying which I have heard:—"Death and life have their determined appointment; riches and honours depend upon Heaven". Let the Superior Man never fail to be reverent and let him be respectful to others and observant of the rules of proper conduct (*Li*):—then all within the four seas will be his brothers. What has the Superior Man to do with being distressed because he has no brothers?' " (*The Analects,* 12,5)

e) His deep understanding in traditional literature, such as the Poetry and the Rituals.

"Tzu Hsia asked, 'What is the meaning of:

> *"Her cunning smiles,*
> *Her dimples light,*
> *Her lovely eyes,*

So clear and bright,
All unadorned,
The background white.''?'
(*The Book of Poetry,* 1,5,3)

'Colouring,' said the Master, 'is second to the plain ground.' 'Then good form (*Li*) is second,' said Tzu Hsia. 'Shang,' said the Master, 'thou hast hit my meaning! Now I can begin to talk poetry with thee.' " (*The Analects,* 3,8)

2. The Attitudes of His Disciples Towards Him

Mencius spoke about the sincere submission of the disciples of Confucius to their master, not by severe discipline or external force, but by the discipline of loving-kindness or virtue, saying,

"When one subdues men by virtue, in their hearts' core they are pleased, and sincerely submit, as was the case with the seventy disciples in their submission to Confucius." (*Mencius,* 2,1,3,2)

The love of his disciples towards him was fully shown in the following statement written by Ssu-ma Ch'ien, about the three years' mourning observed by his disciples at his tomb. They regarded him as their own father, and observed the rites which were only due to one's parents.

"Confucius was buried in Lu, on the River Szu in the north of the city. His disciples all observed the regular mourning of three years (due to parents), and after the three years of mourning were over, they said good-bye to each other and left, weeping again at the grave before they departed. Some stayed on, but only Tzu Kung remained in a hut near the tomb for six years before he left. Over a hundred families, consisting of Confucius' disciples and natives of Lu, went to live near the tomb ground, and there grew up a village known as K'ung Li (K'ung village). For generations sacrifices were offered at the temple of Confucius at proper times, and the Confucianists also held academic discussions and village festivals and archery contests at the tomb." (*Shih-chi,* "The Life of Confucius")

The following are the sayings from some of his disciples, showing their attitudes towards their beloved Master, Confucius:

(a) Yen Yuan

"Yen Yuan, (in admiration of the Master's doctrines), sighed and said, 'I looked up to them, and they (seemed to become) more high; I tried to penetrate them, and they (seemed to become) more firm; I looked at them before me, and suddenly they (seemed to be) behind. The Master, by orderly method, skilfully leads men on. He enlarged my mind with learning, and taught me the restraints of the rules of proper conduct (*Li*). When I wish to give over (the study of his doctrines), I cannot do so, and having exerted all my ability, something seems to stand right before me; but though I wish to follow (and lay hold of it), really I find no way to do so.' " (*The Analects*, 9,10)

Tzu Kung

"Tzu Kung said, 'Chung Ni (Confucius) cannot be reviled. The talents and virtue of other men are hillocks and mounds, which may be stepped over. Chung Ni is the sun or moon, which it is not possible to step over. Although a man may wish to cut himself off (from the sage), what harm can he do to the sun or moon? He only shows that he does not know his own capacity.' " (*The Analects*, 19,24)

"Our Master cannot be attained to, just in the same way as the heavens cannot be gone up to by the steps of a stair." (*The Analects*, 19,25,3)

"Shu-sun Wu-shu observed to the great officers in the court saying, 'Tzu Kung is superior to Chung Ni.' Tzu-fu Ching-po reported the observation to Tzu Kung, who said, 'Let me use the comparison of a house and its (encompassing) wall. My wall only reaches to the shoulders. One may peep over it, and see whatever is valuable in the apartments. The wall of my master is several fathoms high. If one do not find the door and enter by it, he cannot see the ancestral temple with its beauties, nor all the officers in their rich array. But I may assume that they are few who find the door. Was not the observation of the chief only what might have been expected?' " (*The Analects*, 19,23)

"Tzu Kung said, . . . 'From the distance of a hundred ages after, I can arrange, according to their merits, the kings of a hundred ages;—not one of them can escape me. From the birth of mankind till now, there has never been another like our Master.' " (*Mencius,* 2,1,2,27)

"Tzu Kung asked Confucius, saying, 'Master, are you a Sage?' Confucius answered him. 'A Sage is what I cannot rise to. I learn without satiety, and teach without being tired.' Tzu Kung said,'You learn without satiety:—that shows your wisdom. You teach without being tired:—that shows your love (*Jen*). Loving and wise:—Master, you are a Sage.' " (*Mencius,* 2,1,2,19)

(c) Tsai Wo

"Tsai Wo said, 'According to my view of our Master, he is far superior to Yao and Shun (the two ancient ideal kings).' " (*Mencius,* 2,1,2,26)

(d) Yu Jo

"Yu Jo said, 'Is it only among men that it is so? There is the Chi-lin among quadrupeds; the Feng-huang among birds, the T'ai Mountain among mounds and ant-hills, and rivers and seas among rainpools. (Though different in degree), they are the same in kind. So the sages among mankind are also the same in kind. But they stand out from their fellows, and rise above the level, and from the birth of mankind till now, there never has been one so complete as Confucius.' " (*Mencius,* 2,1,2,28)

(B) His Influence Upon Society in General

He exercised a great influence upon society, either directly by himself—his immediate influence, or indirectly through his disciples—his subsequent influence.

1. Immediate or Direct Influence

During his lifetime his influence upon society was great, either through his political activities, or through his teaching work.

(a) Political career

Ssu-ma Ch'ien recorded some of the political activities carried out by Confucius:

a) When he was a youth, "he was put in charge of the granary of the house of the Baron of Chi, and there he was noted for the fairness of his measures. He also was appointed to take charge of the cattle and sheep, and the cattle and sheep rapidly multiplied. He was then promoted to be a minister of public works."

b) The period of great political power (502-496 B.C.)

In the 8th year of Duke Ting of Lu (502 B.C.), when Confucius was fifty years old, he was made magistrate of Chung-tu by the Duke. "After a year the town became a model city for all its neighbours. From the magistracy of Chung-tu, he was promoted to the office of Secretary of Public Works and finally became Grand Secretary of Justice." When Duke Ting went to a good-will conference at Chia-ku with Ch'i, Confucius was appointed to act as Chief Minister, and through the effort of Confucius, "the Duke of Ch'i returned the lands of Yun, Wen-yang, and Kuei-t'ien which he had taken away from Lu." He also helped the Duke to strengthen his position, by weakening some of the powerful families in his state. "In the 14th year of Duke Ting (496 B.C.), Confucius was 56 years old. From the position of Grand Secretary of Justice, he was promoted to that of Chief Minister. . . . After three months of his premiership, the mutton and pork butchers did not adulterate their meat, and men and women followed different lanes in the streets. Things lost on the streets were not stolen, and foreigners visiting the country did not have to go to the police, but all came to Lu like a country of their own." But he soon resigned his premiership, and spent the rest of his life in travelling, teaching and editing.

(b) Educational work

He spent most of his life in doing educational work, teaching and editing. He had disciples all over China, and many of them held important offices while he was still living. For example, Jan Yu and Chi Lu held important positions under Baron Chi of the state of Lu (*The Analects*, 16,1); Yuan Ssu was made governor of his own town (*The Analects*, 6,3,3); Tzu Hua was employed on a mission to the state of Ch'i (*The Analects*, 6,3,1); Tzu Kao was appointed governor of Pi (*The Analects*, 11,24); Tzu Yu was made governor of Wu-ch'eng; Jan Ch'iu "assisted in the administration of the government of Lu" (*Shih Chi*, "Life of Confucius"); "Confucius had many disciples in the government of Wei", including Tzu Lu who was killed in the civil war in Wei (*Shih Chi, ibid.*); etc. It was chiefly through the disciples whom he taught and the books which he edited that his influence was deeply felt in society. He was constantly summoned to the courts of heads of the states of Lu, Ch'i, and Wei, to consult with them about governmental matters. When he died, "Duke Ai sent a prayer to the funeral of Confucius, which said, 'Alas! Heaven has no mercy on me, and has not spared me the Grand Old Man. He has left me, the poor self, alone and helpless at the head of the state, and I am a sick person now. Alas! Father Ni (Chung Ni—Confucius' Name)! Great is my sorrow! Do not forget me (literally 'do not mind yourself')!' " (*Shih-chi*, "Life of Confucius")

(c) His failure

Although he had accomplished a great deal, both politically and educationally, which caused the dukes in different states to pay a high tribute to him, yet he regarded his life-work as a failure. His high and lofty aims of both the individual life and the social order were not attained during his life-time, and, indeed, have never been completely realized in Chinese history, nor in the history of the world. One day, in despair, he composed a ballad which he sang to his disciples:

> *"We Must climb the hill though the slopes are steep,*
> *Travel the road though the brambles are deep.*
> *What seems near at hand retreats in the way,*
> *And so lengthens our vain labour for another day.*
> *We must onward go though in pain and sorrow,*
> *And expect no easier route to-morrow.*
> *There stands T'ai Shan, a majestic height,*
> *Our symbol of wisdom, virtue and right.*
> *No axe cuts the thorns which flourish apace,*
> *When the way is blocked (beyond recall),*
> *   where will the traveller face?*
> *Alas for a black despair so deep,*
> *That all one can do is sigh and weep."*

"All is over," he declared, "I have not yet seen one who perceives his faults, and inwardly accuses himself." (*The Analects*, 5,26) Again, he said to one of his disciples, "Yu, those who know virtue are few." (*The Analects*, 15,3) When he was going to die, he looked back on the work which he had accomplished, and he certainly received little encouragement: the country was measurably nearer to moral ruin and political anarchy than it had been when he first began his teachings. "He then shed tears and spoke to Tzu Kung, 'For a long time the world has been living in moral chaos, and no ruler has been able to follow me.' " (*Shih Chi*, "The Life of Confucius") Indeed, the world was not ready to receive his doctrine. His failure only shows his greatness. "He knows that a thing can't be done, and still wants to do it." (*The Analects*, 14,41). It was a glorious failure. One day, Confucius asked Yen Yuan, his favourite disciple, "Are my teachings wrong? How is it that I find myself now in this situation?" And Yen Yuan replied, "The Master's teachings are so great. That is why the world cannot accept them. However, you should just do your best to spread the ideas. What do you care if they are not accepted? The very fact that your teachings are not accepted shows that you are a Superior Man. If the truth is not cultivated, the shame is ours; but if we have already strenuously cultivated the teachings of a moral order and they are not accepted by the people, it is the shame of those in power. What do you care if you are not accepted? The very fact that you are not accepted shows that you are a Superior Man." (*Shih Chi*, "The Life of Confucius")

2. Later or Indirect Influence Through the Work of His Disciples

Like Jesus, Socrates, Gautama Buddha, Mohammed, and other great teachers of the world, Confucius had to depend upon his disciples to carry out and exemplify his doctrines. The most important reason for the success of Confucianism in China has been its traditional emphasis put upon the work of education. It has almost monopolized Chinese education for over two thousand years. So the greatness of Confucius lies primarily in his enthusiasm in education, "teaching without being tired", and his methods of teaching which won the hearts of his disciples, who remained faithful to him and his teachings in all circumstances. It was due to him that education and politics began to be separated, private schools began to spring up rapidly, and "scholars"[13] (Shih) began to be distinguished from public officers.

All the ancient Chinese classical writings seem to bear out the fact that in ancient China, long before Confucius, education had been one of the most important functions of the government, it had been run by the government under the direct control of the minister of education, called Shih Tu who was one of the most important officers in the central government. *The Charge of Yueh*,[14] traditionally about 1324 B.C., states, "The thoughts (of the sovereign) from first to last should be fixed on education." (*The Book of History*, 4,8,3,5) A passage in *Chou Li*, explaining the duties of the minister of education (Ta Shih Tu) in ancient China, says that he was to teach the people "the Six Arts, namely, rituals, music, archery, chariot driving, writing and arithmetic." (*Ti Kuan*, p. 14) *Li Chi* also gives a passage about the duties of the minister of instruction (Shih Tu), saying, "The minister of instruction prepared the six rites to restrain the nature of the people. He made clear the seven teachings in order to stimulate the virtue of the people. . . ." (*Wang Chih*,[15] p. 19) It was from the Spring and Autumn Period when "the world fell into decay, and principles faded away", that education was neglected by the government. All the states were too busy preparing armaments and other political measures for offensive and defensive wars to pay attention to education. When Confucius inaugurated, or at least developed, the private school movement, private schools began to spring up very rapidly in the following period. His disciples like Tzu Hsia, Tseng Tzu, Yu Tzu, Tzu Chang, Tzu Yu, Tzu Kung, and others had all private schools of their own. Two very important social effects resulted from such an educational movement.

(a) The competition between different schools

Most of the Confucian schools tried to preserve the best of the traditional cultural heritage, but they disagreed among themselves about the interpretations of the traditional literature as selected, expunged, rectified, and handed down by Confucius, and the methods of teaching them. For example, the school run by Tzu Hsia was much criticized by Tzu Yu about the methods and essentials of learning. (*The Analects*, 19,12) Later on there arose rival schools which criticized or opposed the Confucian schools, and criticized and opposed one another. They all gave reasons for their criticisms and their defences. They all had their textbooks for their arguments or apologetics in order to teach their own students, or to attract students from other schools. In such an atmosphere, the greatest intellectual activity, coupled with the greatest freedom of thought, brought about great richness and variety in Chinese philosophy.

(b) The formation of a new social class of people, called "scholars" (Shih)[16]

Prior to Confucius, the Shih generally meant those who held official positions, or were military officers. But as the private schools flourished, the supply of scholars exceeded the official demand, and there resulted many unemployed scholars, who could do nothing but hold governmental office, and teach. Gradually they became a class of society as distinguished from the farmer, the artisan and merchant classes. Fung Yu-lan says, "It was he (Confucius) who opened the way for the many travelling scholars and philosophers of succeeding centuries. It was also he who inaugurated, or at least developed, that class of gentleman (Shih, or "scholar") in ancient China, who was neither farmer, artisan, merchant, nor actual official, but was professional teacher and potential official." (*A History of Chinese Philosophy*, tr. by Derke Bodde, p. 48)

For further discussion about the indirect influence of the teaching of Confucius through his disciples, see Chapter 1, the Introduction.

G. The Methods of the Teaching of Confucius According to Mencius, and Hsun-tzu and their Schools of Confucianism

The methods of the teaching of Confucius were traditionally believed to have been summarized in *The Great Learning (Ta Hsueh)* and *The Doctrine of the Mean (Chung Yung)*, two of the "Four Books" of Confucianism. *The Great Learning* has been regarded as "a book transmitted by the Confucian school, and forms the gate by which first learners enter into virtue." (See the introductory remarks to *Ta Hsueh*). *The Doctrine of the Mean* has been believed to be a work which "contains the law of the mind, which was handed down from one to another, in the Confucian school, till Tzu Ssu, fearing lest in the course of time errors should arise about it committed it to writing, and delivered it to Mencius." (See the introductory remarks to *Chung-yung*) But as has been mentioned in Chapter 1, *The Great Learning* contains, in general, the views of Hsun-tzu and his school in the interpretation of the teachings of Confucius; and *The Doctrine of the Mean* contains, in general, the views of Mencius and his school in their interpretation of the teachings of Confucius. Nevertheless, both of them may have based their materials upon the teachings of the immediate disciples of Confucius, or upon the teaching of Confucius himself.

(A) Mencius and His School

1. The Theory of Human Nature

As has been pointed out, Mencius and his school conceived that human nature is fundamentally good, and this conception was

taken as the basis of all their important teachings, including the
teaching-method.

(a) The origin of human nature

The origin of human nature is Heaven or God. Since Heaven is
believed to be ethical, nature which is conferred from Heaven must
also be ethical.

"What Heaven confers is called the Nature. The following of this
nature is called the Way (*Tao*). The cultivation of this way is called
instruction." (*Chung Yung*, 1,1)

"Mencius said, 'He who exercises his mind to the utmost knows
his nature. Knowing his nature, he knows Heaven. To preserve
one's mental constitution, and nourish one's nature, is the way to
serve Heaven.' " (*Mencius*, 7,1,1,1-2)

(b) The goodness of human nature

By saying that human nature is good, Mencius only means that
all men possess the "beginnings" (tuan)[17] of goodness, conferred
by Heaven, such as *Jen*,[18] *I*,[19] *Li*,[20] and *Chih*[21] (*Mencius*, 2,1,6) All
human relationships are but the manifestations of these "begin-
nings" in the organization of human society. (*Mencius*, 4,1,27) "The
Sage is the apogee of the human relationships" (*Mencius*, 4,1,2), in
him all the "beginnings" are allowed to reach their complete
development.

When Mencius speaks of nature as good, he draws special
attention to the fact that this nature which he speaks of is "human
nature." (*Mencius*, 6,1,3) "Human nature" implies all that whereby
man is human, and whereby he differs from the lower animals,
therefore, there is no alternative but to say that "human nature" is
wholly good. Love (*Jen*), as pointed in Chap. 5, is regarded as the
primary and comprehensive virtue of the Confucian school, so
both Mencius and the writer of *Chung Yung* say, "Love is (the
distinguishing characteristic of) man." (*Mencius*, 7,2,10; *Chung
Yung*, 20,5) Mencius says again, "Love (*Jen*) is the mind of man;
righteousness (*I*) is man's path." (*Mencius*, 6,1,11) That is, love (*Jen*)
is the mind that man as man should possess; righteousness (*I*) is
the path that he should follow. If he does not "dwell in love (*Jen*)
and proceed from righteousness (*I*)" (*Mencius*, 4,1,10), he is not a

real man. Although everybody has the "beginnings" of goodness that make him human, yet it is not that every human being is good in the same degree, nor is it that everybody is human, in the strict sense of the word. If he loses his human nature he becomes a mere animal. Mencius says, "That whereby man differs from the birds and beasts is but slight. The mass of people cast it away, whereas the Superior Man preserves it." (*Mencius*, 4,2,19)

(c) The difference in human nature

The difference in human nature between different human persons depends upon the degrees of development of the "beginnings" of the goodness of human nature, or the degrees of loss of the original goodness of human nature. Mencius says:

"The feeling of commiseration belongs to all men; so does that of shame and dislike; that of reverence and respect; and that of right and wrong. The feeling of commiseration is love (*Jen*); that of shame and dislike is righteousness (*I*); that of reverence and respect is propriety (*Li*); and that of right and wrong is wisdom (*Chih*). These are not fused into us from without. We originally are possessed of them. (We neglect them) simply because we lack reflection. Hence I say, 'Seek and you will find them; neglect and you will lose them.' (Men differ from one another), some twice as much as others, some five times as much, and some to an incalculable amount. It is because they cannot fully carry out their natural powers." (*Mencius*, 6,1,6)

Why are people not able to "carry out their natural powers"? How do they lose their human nature and not to develop it?

a) Through the influence of environment

"Mencius said, 'In good years the children of the people are most of them good, while in bad years most of them abandon themselves to evil. It is not owing to their natural powers conferred by Heaven that they are thus different. The abandonment is owing to the circumstances through which they allow their minds to be ensnared and drowned in evil." (*Mencius*, 6,1,7,1)

b) Through following the part of man which is small (*Hsiao T'i*)[22] and not the part of man which is great (*Ta T'i*).[23]

"Kung Tu Tzu asked: 'All are equally men, yet some are great men and some are small men. How is it?' Mencius replied: 'Those who follow that part of themselves which is great are great men, and those who follow that part of themselves which is small are small men.' (Kung Tu Tzu) continued: 'All are equally men, but some follow that part of themselves which is great, and some follow that part which is small. How is this?' (Mencius) answered: 'The senses of hearing and seeing do not think, but are obscured by things (of the outside world). When a thing comes into contact with another (i.e., with one of our senses), it simply leads it away (from the right path). But the faculty of the mind is thinking. By thinking, it seizes (the correct view of things), whereas by not thinking it fails to do this. This (i.e., the mind) is what Heaven has given to us. Let a man first firmly establish the nobler part of his constitution, and the inferior part will not be able to take it from him. It is simply this which constitutes the great man.' " (*Mencius*, 6,1,15)

In short, although men are originally the same, endowed with the human nature which is conferred by Heaven, yet through differences in the way of developing that nature they become different morally, intellectually and physically. Some men let their mind or "the part of man which is great" be "ensnared and drowned in evil", some follow their senses or "the part of man which is small' and are led astray by the environment; thus, they lose their mind or their good human nature, and become inferior men. Mencius says, "The way in which a man loses his proper goodness of mind is like the way in which the trees are denuded by axes and bills. Hewn down day after day, can it (the mind) retain its beauty?" (*Mencius*, 6,1,8,2) Others develop fully the "part of man which is great", that is, the mind or the true human nature, and become superior men. Mencius says: "Confucius said, 'Hold it fast, and it remains with you. Let it go, and you lose it. Its outgoing and incoming cannot be defined as to time and place.' It is the mind of which this is said." (*Mencius*, 6,1,8,4)

2. Methods of Teaching

Since human nature, being originated from ethical Heaven, is good, and its differences between different persons depend upon the degrees of its development; so the good teaching method is one which leads to the development or unfolding of the nature of the learners. Mencius says:

"The great end of learning is nothing else but to seek for the lost mind" (*Mencius*, 6,1,11,4), or to develop the mind which is lost through being neglected or "ensnared and drowned in evil."

In order to develop the nature, Mencius and his school exemplified many of the teaching methods of Confucius. "Mencius said, 'There are many arts in teaching. I refuse, as inconsistent with my character, to teach a man, but I am only thereby still teaching him.' " (*Mencius*, 6,2,16) He mentioned five teaching methods which a Superior Man, such as Confucius, had used:

"Mencius said, 'There are five ways in which the Superior Man effects his teaching.

'There are some on whom his influence descends like seasonable rain.

'There are some whose virtue he perfects, and some of whose talents he assists the development.

'There are some whose questions he answers.

'There are some who privately cultivate and correct themselves.

'These five ways are the methods in which the Superior Man effects his teaching.' " (*Mencius*, 7,1,40)

In other words, the Superior teacher, like Confucius, would make use of the following teaching methods:

(a) He would influence his students with his personality,—his patience, loving kindness, moral character, sound knowledge, etc., would descend upon his students like the seasonable rain, helping quietly but effectively the growth of all lovely things in their lives.

(b) He would recognize the individual differences,—some students may have higher intelligence, while others may have better moral capacities, etc.

(c) The major job of a teacher is to assist his students to develop or unfold their capacities or potential abilities, like the seasonable rain which helps the growth of the plants.

(d) He would effectively use the question-and-answer method to stimulate the thought of the learners.

(e) He would stress the practice of self-study and self-activity on the part of the learners. They would be given the greatest opportunity to learn by actual practising and experiencing themselves. In short, the whole emphasis of these methods is put on the development of the nature of the learners.

Like Confucius, Mencius received everybody to be his disciple, who came to him with the mind to learn, without distinction of class, or any inquiry into the past experiences of the learner.

"When Mencius went to T'ang, he was lodged in the upper palace. A sandal in the process of making had been placed there in a window, and when the keeper of the place came to look for it, he could not find it. On this, some one asked Mencius, saying, 'Is it thus that your followers pilfer?' Mencius replied, 'Do you think that they came here to pilfer the sandal?' The man said, 'I apprehend not. But you, Master, having arranged to give lessons, do not go back to inquire into the past, and you do not reject those who come to you. If they come with the mind to learn, you receive them without any more ado.' " (*Mencius* 7,2,30)

3. Methods of Learning

It has been pointed out in *The Doctrine of the Mean* that there were five steps of learning as taught by Confucius:

"The Master (Confucius) said, '. . . Study extensively, inquire accurately, think carefully, discriminate clearly, and practice earnestly. . . . Let a man proceed in this way, and, though dull, he will surely become intelligent; though weak, he will surely become strong.' " (*The Doctrine of the Mean*, 20,19-20)

(B) Hsun-tzu and His School

1. The Psychology of Hsun-tzu

Hsun-tzu was perhaps the first Chinese philosopher who had a clear system of psychology, and his psychology did, in many respects, resemble that of the modern educationist, John Frederick Herbart (1776-1841). In order to understand more clearly the interpretation of the teaching methods of Confucius given by

Hsun-tzu and his school of Confucianism, we must have a general idea of Hsun-tzu's psychology.

(a) Some psychological terms defined

"In miscellaneous psychological terms the essential factor at birth is man's original nature (*Hsing*).[24] That which at birth is produced by the concord of the Yin and Yang, whose essence is suitable for the stimulus and response relation, which is not produced by training, but exists spontaneously, is called original nature (*Hsing*). The love, hate, joy, anger, sorrow, and pleasure of original nature are called the emotions (*Ch'ing*).[25] When the mind selects from among the emotions by which it is moved—this is called cogitation (*Lu*).[26] When the mind cogitates and can act accordingly—this is called acquired training (*Wei*).[27] When, after accumulated cogitation, and the training of abilities, there results completion—this is called acquired character (*Wei*).[28] To act for the sake of righteous gain is what is meant by having a proper occupation. To act correctly according to justice (*I*) is good conduct. That in man by which he knows is (called the faculty of) knowing (*Chih*).[29] That in (the faculty of) knowing which corresponds to (external things) is called knowledge (*Chih*).[30] That in man which he can do something is called his ability (*Neng*).[31] An injury to the nature is called a defect. What one meets with by chance is called destiny (*Ming*)"[32] (*The Work of Hsun-tzu*, pp. 281-282)

(b) The theory of the mind

The mind from birth has the capacity to receive and store away impressions from the outside world through the senses. These impressions received and stored away become collected data (which Herbart would call the apperceptive mass) of the mind. Through the collected data, the mind can distinguish and give meaning to various impressions sent in to the mind through the senses. Hsun-tzu says:

"How can a person know the right (*Tao*)? By the mind. How does the mind know? By emptiness, unity and unperturbedness. The mind never ceases to store away (*Ts'ang*)[33] impressions, yet there is that which may be called emptiness (*Hsu*,[34] receptiveness to new impressions, lack of prejudice). The mind has always a multiplicity (of objects of the mind), yet there is that which may be called a unity (I,[35] unity of mind or concentration). The mind is always active, yet there is that which may be called quiescence or unperturbedness (*Ching*,[36] the quality of not being disturbed by emotion). A man from birth has the capacity to know things; this capacity to know things has its collected data (the apperceptive mass, or the items of memory, *Chih*);[37] these collected data are what are meant by stored away impressions. Moreover he has that which may be called emptiness. That which does not allow what is already stored away to injure that which is about to be received, is called the mind's emptiness. The mind from birth has the capacity for knowledge; this knowledge contains distinctions; these distinctions consist of at the same time perceiving more than one thing. To perceive more than one thing at the same time is plurality. Yet the mind has that which may be called a unity. That which does not allow that impression to harm this impression is called the mind's unity. When the mind sleeps, it dreams; when it takes its ease, it indulges in reverie; when it is used it reflects. Hence the mind is always in motion. Yet it has that which may be called unperturbedness. That which does not permit dreams to disturb one's knowledge is called the mind's unperturbedness." (*The Work of Hsun-tzu*, pp. 267-268) Again, he says:

"By what means are similarities and differences found? The means are the senses given by nature. Whenever anything is judged to be the same sort or the same emotion, it is because the perception of the senses given by nature is that the thing is the same. Hence for example, the reason that similarities are universally recognized to be such everywhere is because their agreed upon names have become universal, and so they can be recognized. Form and colour are distinctions made by the eyes. Clear and confused sound, harmony, musical time, and other sounds are distinctions made by the ear. Sweet and bitter, salty and fresh, peppery and sour, and other flavours are distinctions made by the mouth. Perfumes and smells, fragrant and putrid, the smell of fresh meat and fetid smells, the smell of the mole-cricket and the smell of decayed wood, and other smells are distinctions made by the nose. Pain and itching, cold and heat, smooth and rough, light and heavy, are distinctions made by the body. Doing things from a liking to do them and forcing oneself to do things; joy and anger, sorrow and pleasure, love, hatred, and desire are distinctions made by the mind. The mind also gives meaning to impressions. It gives meaning to impressions, and only then, by means of the ear, sound can be known; by means of the eye, forms can be known. But the giving of meaning to impressions must depend on the senses given by nature, each noting its particular kind of sensations, and then only can knowledge be had. When the five senses note something but do not comprehend it, and the mind tries to give it a meaning but has no explanation; nobody would differ, everyone would call this ignorance. These are the means by which similarities and differences are found." (*The Work of Hsun-tzu*, pp. 284-285)

(c) The theory of human nature

a) The definition of the original nature of man

"That which at birth is produced by the concord of the Yin and Yang, whose essence is suitable for the stimulus and respond relation, which is not produced by training, but exists spontaneously, is called original nature." (*The Work of Hsun-tzu*, p. 281)

"The original nature of man is the product of Heaven. The emotions (*Ch'ing*) are the materials of the original nature. Desires (*Yu*)[38] are the reactions of the emotions (to external stimuli)." (*The Work of Hsun-tzu*, p. 295)

"The love, hate, joy, anger, sorrow, and pleasure of original nature are called the emotions (*Ch'ing*)." (*The Work of Hsun-tzu*, p. 281)

Three conceptions about the original nature of man are brought out by the above definitions, namely, the origin, the content and the expression of the original nature.

a. The origin of human nature

Like Mencius, Hsun-tzu also traced back the origin of human nature to Heaven—"The original nature of man is the product of Heaven." But Mencius' conception of Heaven differs entirely from Hsun-tzu's conception. To Mencius, Heaven is ethical and often personal, but to Hsun-tzu, Heaven is a naturalistic one, more or less the same as the universal law of the cosmos, the invisible and impersonal source of all things. (*The Work of Hsun-tzu*, pp. 173-175)

Thus, to say that human nature is originated in Heaven is the same as to say that it "is the product of Nature", and it "is not produced by training, but exists spontaneously."

b. The content of human nature

The content of the original nature is called the "emotions" (*Ch'ing*), such as the emotions of love, hate, joy, anger, sorrow, and pleasure. "The emotions are the materials of the original nature."

c. The expression of human nature

The expression of the original nature is called "desire", which "is suitable for the stimulus and respond relation." It "is the reaction of the emotion (to external stimulus)."

b) The depravity (*Wu*)[39] of human nature

"The original nature (*Hsing*)[40] of man is evil (*Wu*); his goodness is only acquired by training (*Wei*)[41]." (*The Work of Hsun-tzu*, p. 301)

Since Heaven is naturalistic, and lacks any ideal or ethical principle, the original nature of man, being "the product of Heaven", likewise cannot contain any ethical principle. Morality is something made by man, and so is called "acquired." *The Work of Hsun-tzu* (Ch. 23) says:

"The original nature of man to-day is to seek for gain. If this desire is followed, strife and rapacity result, and courtesy and yielding disappear. Man originally is envious and naturally hates others. If these tendencies are followed, injury and destruction follow; loyalty and faithfulness are destroyed. Man originally possesses the desires of the ear and eye; he likes sound and women. If these are followed, impurity and disorder result, and the rules of proper conduct (*Li*), the standards of justice (*I*), and finish and orderliness disappear. Therefore to give rein to man's original nature and to follow man's feelings, mean inevitable strife and rapacity, together with violations of etiquette and confusion in the proper way of doing things, and a reversion to a state of violence. Therefore the civilizing influence of teachers and laws, and the guidance of the rules of proper conduct (*Li*) and standards of justice (*I*) are absolutely necessary. Thereupon courtesy results, culture is developed, and good government is the consequence. By this line of reasoning it is evident that the nature of man is evil, and his goodness is acquired." (p. 301)

In other words, human nature is not good as Mencius thought it was; it contains evil emotions, and expresses desires which tend to be evil.

(d) The relation between human mind and human nature

If human nature is evil, how can man become good? If his original desires all tend to do evil, how can he sometimes respond to what is good? The answer is that man has not only evil nature which expresses itself in the desires which always tend to be evil, but also he has the mind, which, through its "collected data" or "accumulated impressions" (*Chi*),[42] is able to "cognate" (*Lu*), or to "distinguish" (*Pien*)[43] between the good and bad, and select the good from the bad. So a man can become good by putting his desires under the restraints of the mind. Hsun-tzu says:

"Desire does not depend upon whether satisfaction is possible, whereas its gratification seeks what is possible. That desire does not depend upon whether attainment is possible, is something received from Heaven (*Tien*). That gratification seeks what is possible is something brought about by the mind. The nature possesses desires, for which the mind devises regulations and restraints. . . . What men desire most is life, and what they dislike most is death. Yet there are men who cling to life and find death, not because they do not desire life and do desire death, but because they cannot live but can only die. Therefore, if a person's action stops short of his desires, it is the mind which has arrested it. . . . If a person's desires are weak, while his actions go beyond them, it is the mind which has caused this. . . ." (*The Work of Hsun-tzu*, pp. 294-295)

Desires are permissible and need not be wholly eliminated. What is needed is that they be kept in proper restraint by the mind, through its power of cogitation. Hsun-tzu says:

"Every doctrine of self-control which depends on the removal of desire, has no way of guiding the desires and is hampered by the presence of desire. Every doctrine of self-control which waits for the lessening of desires has no way to curb the desires and is hampered by the numerousness of desires. . . . The necessary beginning of knowledge is to consider that desires are permissible and so to guide (but not wholly repress) them. . . ." (pp. 293-295)

Why can the mind restrain the desires and select the good? Because it knows that if the desires are given free rein, the result will inevitably be undesirable. The Way (*Tao*) or the rules of proper conduct (*Li*) gives the correct standard by which the mind is able to distinguish the good from the evil, or the beneficial from the harmful. Hsin-tzu says:

"The Way (*Tao*) was the correct standard for ancient times as it is for the present. If you depart from the Way to choose your own inner standard, then you will not know what will lead to calamity or happiness. If a trader barters one thing for one thing, people say, 'He has neither loss nor gain.' If he barters one for two, people say, 'There is no loss, but a gain.' If he barters two for one, people say, 'There is no gain but a loss.' The schemer gets as much as he can; the man who plans takes all that he can: no one will exchange two for one because they know the art of evaluating things. To start following the Way (*Tao*) is like exchanging one for two; how can there be a loss? To leave the Way (*Tao*) and pick one's own inner standards is like exchanging two for one; how can there be any gain?" (p. 297)

Thus, according to Hsun-tzu and his school, everybody has the capacity of becoming a Sage, because he has the mind with its capacity of controlling the evil desires of human nature, and select what is the best course to take. Not every man, however, exercises his capacity to its fullest extent, so that not every man has the ability to become a Sage. Herein lies the difference between the good and the bad, the skilful and the less skilful, the strong and the weak, the wise and the foolish, or the sage and "the man on the street." Hsun-tzu says:

"It is evident that the man on the street possesses the power of knowing and the ability to practise these virtues. Now if the man on the street uses his power of knowledge and his ability of acting on the nascent ability of knowing love (*Jen*) and justice (*I*) and the means of becoming so, then it is clear that he can become a *Yu* (A Sage). . . . It is true that the man on the street can become a *Yu*, but it is probably not true that the man on the street has the ability to become a *Yu*. Although he does not have the ability to make himself a *Yu*, that does not destroy the possibility that he could become a *Yu*. . . ." (*The Work of Hsun-tzu*, pp. 313-314)

(e) The chief purpose of education

The chief purpose of education is, from the psychological point of view, "to nourish the mind" so that it is able to put the desires under perfect control, and to think and act freely according to what is right. Hsun-tzu says:

"If a person's animal feelings are strong and severe, then let him weaken them so that he may harmonize himself. If his thoughts are crafty and secretive, then let him unify them so that they may easily be good. If he is bold and violent, then let him guide his feelings, so as to control them. If he is hasty, talkative, and seeking for gain, then let him moderate himself so as to be large-minded. If he is inferior, tardy in important matters, and avaricious, then let him raise himself to a high purpose. If his talents are ordinary or inferior, then let him be importunate to make friends with a teacher. If he is impertinent and proud, then let him reflect on the calamities that will ensue. If he is simple, sincere, upright, and ingenuous, then let him make himself harmonious by the rules of proper conduct (*Li*) and music. Of all the methods of controlling the body and nourishing the mind, there is none more direct than *Li*, none more important than getting a teacher, none more divine than to have but one desire. These are what I mean by the methods of controlling the body and nourishing the mind. If a person's will is cultivated then he can be prouder than the rich and the honourable; if he has emphasized the Way (*Tao*) and justice (*I*) then he can despise kings and dukes; he can contemplate that which is within him and despise outer things. It is said: The Superior Man employs things; the small-minded man is the servant of things—this expresses what I mean." (pp. 46-47)

2. **The Methods of Learning**

The methods of nourishing the mind are the methods of learning and teaching. How can the mind be nourished?

a) To nourish the mind through sense impressions

Mind, as has has been pointed out, "never ceases to store away impressions" which make up what is called "the collected data" of the mind. Through these "collected data", the mind is able to fuse similar ideas, combine disparate ideas, and repel contrary ideas; it is able to cogitate, or distinguish between what is true and what is false, and between what is right and what is wrong. The mind can only get the data through the senses. Hsun-tzu mentioned five senses through which the impressions of the outside world come to the mind and form the "collected data": the senses of hearing, seeing, smelling, tasting, and the sense of touch. "Form and colour are distinctions made by the eyes. Clear and confused sound, harmony, musical time, and other sounds are distinctions made by the ear. Sweet and bitter, salty and fresh, peppery and sour, and other flavours are distinctions made by the mouth. Perfumes and smells, fragrant and putrid, the smell of fresh meat and fetid smells, the smell of the mole-cricket and the smell of decayed wood, and other smells are distinctions made by the nose. Pain and itching, cold and heat, smooth and rough, light and heavy, are distinctions made by the body (the sense of touch)". The mind "gives meaning to impressions", but "the giving of meaning to impressions must depend on the senses given by nature". Thus, to nourish the mind through sense impressions forms the basis for all learning.

Hsun-tzu in the following paragraph gives a clear summary of the methods of learning which enable "the man on the street" to become a Sage. He says:

"If the man on the street uses his power of knowledge and his ability of acting on the nascent ability of knowing love (*Jen*) and justice (*I*) and the means of becoming so, then it is clear that he can become a *Yu*; if he concentrates his mind on one purpose, if he thinks and studies and investigates thoroughly, daily adding to his knowledge and retaining it long, if he accumulates goodness and does not stop, then he will become as wise as the gods, a third with Heaven and Earth. For the Sage is the man who has attained to that state by accumulative effort." (p. 313)

If we put the methods of learning as mentioned in the above quotation in more logical order, we have the following learning methods:

> To investigate thoroughly,
> To study thoroughly,
> To think thoroughly,
> To practise vigorously,
> To concentrate on one purpose, and
> To form without ceasing new "collected data" with accumulative effort.

All these methods are constantly mentioned in the writings of Hsun-tzu and his school of Confucianism. One or two quotations for each of the above methods will help to make clear the views of this school of Confucianism.

b) To investigate thoroughly

"The investigation of things" is the first thing supposed to be taught in the Confucian school according to *The Great Learning (Ta Hsueh)*,[44] which says:

"Things have their root and their branches. Affairs have their end and beginning. To know what is first and what is last will lead near to what is taught in (*The Great Learning*). The ancients who wished to illustrate illustrious virtue throughout the kingdom, first ordered well their own states. Wishing to order well their states, they first regulated their families. Wishing to regulate their families, they cultivated their persons. Wishing to cultivate their persons, they first rectified their minds. Wishing to rectify their minds, they first sought to be sincere in their thoughts. Wishing to be sincere in their thoughts, they first extended to the utmost their knowledge. Such extension of knowledge lay in the investigation of things.

"Things being investigated, knowledge became complete. Their knowledge being complete, their thoughts were sincere. Their thoughts being sincere, their minds were then rectified. Their minds being rectified, their persons were cultivated. Their persons being cultivated, their families were regulated. Their families being regulated, their states were rightly governed. Their states being rightly governed, the whole kingdom was made tranquil and happy." (*The Texts of Confucius*, 3-5)

c) To study thoroughly

To study means, according to Hsun-tzu, to study primarily the Five Classics: *The Book of History, The Book of Poetry, The Book of Rites, The Book of Music*, and *The Spring and Autumn Annals*. The Rites, or the rules of proper conduct (*Li*) was regarded as the most important subject of study.

"What should one study? How should one begin? The art begins by reciting the Classics and ends in learning the Rites (*Li*). Its purpose begins with making the scholar, and ends in making the sage. Sincerely put forth your efforts, and finally you will progress. Study until death and do not stop before. For the art of study occupies the whole life; to arrive at its purpose, you cannot stop for an instant. To do that is to be a man; to stop is to be a bird or beast." (*The Work of Hsun-tzu*, p. 36)

d) To think thoroughly

"This is the manner of the Superior Man's learning; it goes into his ears, it is taken into his mind, it spreads through his entire body, it shows itself in every movement. . . . This is the manner of the little-minded man's learning; it goes into his ears and comes out of his mouth; between mouth and ear there are only four inches; how can that be sufficient to make his seven feet of body beautiful?" (*The Work of Hsun-tzu*, P.37)

e) To practise vigorously

"Not having learned it is not as good as having learned it; having learned it is not as good as having seen it carried out; having seen it is not as good as understanding it; understanding it is not as good as doing it. The development of scholarship is to the extreme of doing it, and that is its end and goal." (*Ibid.*, p. 113)

In one incident, Hsun-tzu mentions that the perfection of scholarship is to be secured through the above three methods of learning; to study the Classics diligently, to think thoroughly, and to practise vigorously. Hsun-tzu says:

"The Superior Man knows that his knowledge is not complete

or perspicuous, insufficient to be classed as fine; so he recites the Classics sentence by sentence in order to make them a part of himself (i.e., to study thoroughly); he seeks to search into them in order to understand them, he puts himself into the places of the writers in order to understand their view-point (i.e., to think thoroughly); he expels any wrong from his nature in order to grasp and mature his knowledge: he makes his eye unwilling to see what is not right; he makes his ears unwilling to hear what is not right; he makes his mouth unwilling to speak what is not right; he makes his mind unwilling to think what is not right; until he obtains what he must desire (i.e., to practise vigorously)." (*Ibid.*, pp. 40-41)

f) To concentrate on one purpose

"He who has not a very deep purpose, nor a very clear perception, nor continuously strives towards a goal, is without illustrious merit. The man who tries to travel along both paths of a forked road will never get there; he who serves two masters will not be employed. The eye cannot look in two directions at once and see clearly; the ear cannot hear two things at once and hear clearly. The T'ang-she dragon has no feet but flies; the squirrel has five talents, but cannot perform any one of them to satisfaction. The ode says:

'The turtledove is in the mulberry tree;
    Its little ones are seven.
The virtuous man, my prince,
    Is uniform in his deportment.
He is uniform in his deportment;
    His heart is as a knot (tied to one aim).'

So the Superior Man, too, knots everything into one (i.e., concentration and unity of aim are essential)." (*The Work of Hsun-tzu*, pp. 35-36)

"Scholarship is to know things thoroughly and to unify them; to be unified in learning and unified in teaching." (*Ibid.*, p. 40)

g) To learn diligently

A scholar must learn diligently using all the methods as mentioned above, namely, to nourish the mind through sense impressions, to investigate thoroughly, to study thoroughly, to think thoroughly, to practise vigorously, to concentrate on one purpose. If he uses all these methods of learning with diligence, "daily adding to his knowledge and retaining it long, accumulating goodness without stopping, then he will become as wise as the gods, a third with Heaven and Earth. For the Sage is the man who has attained to that state by accumulative effort." (See the quotation on page 589)

"Unless a person adds steps and half-steps to each other, he cannot go a thousand *li*, unless little streams are gathered, rivers and seas cannot be formed. A fast horse in one leap cannot go a thousand paces; but an old broken down nag can do it in ten days —its merit consists in not losing time. If you lose your sickle, you cannot cut down a rotten tree; if you do not lose your sickle, you can carve metal or stone. The earthworm has not the benefit of claws or teeth, nor has it the strength of sinews or bones: on the one hand it eats dirt, and on the other it drinks muddy water; it has only one thing—diligence. The crab has six legs and two pincers. It has not a hole like the earthworm, nor has it any place it can trust for security; but it pays strict attention to being fierce. Therefore he who has not a very deep purpose, nor a very clear perception, nor very continuously strives towards a goal is without illustrious merit." (*The Work of Hsun-tzu*, pp. 34-35)

3. The Methods of Teaching

"Of all the methods of controlling the body and nourishing the mind (the chief purpose of education), there is none more direct than the rules of proper conduct (*Li*), none more important than getting a teacher, none more divine than to have but one desire. These are what I mean by the methods of controlling the body and nourishing the mind." (*The Work of Hsun-tzu*, p. 47)

Three major factors in the process of teaching are mentioned in the above quotation, namely, the subject matter to be taught, the teacher, and the learner; there is no subject matter which is more direct to meet the need of the learner than *Li*, there is "none more important than getting a teacher," there is "none more divine", on the part of the learner, "than to have but one desire." In connection with the three major factors in the process of teaching, there are three major problems in the method of teaching, namely, the method of dealing with the subject matter, the method of teaching by the example of the teacher, and the method of creating the interest of the learner.

(a) The method of dealing with subject matter

Since the mind, according to Hsun-tzu, is built up with the "collected data" of the impressions through the senses from without, and the new impressions or ideas can only be formed or interpreted through the old impressions or ideas which have already formed the "collected data" of the mind; so the chief educational problem becomes how to present the teaching materials to the learner in such a way that it can be apperceived or incorporated with the old. The methods of presenting the teaching materials are carefully outlined in the Great Learning (*Ta Hsueh*), in its Introductory Chapter, "The Texts of Confucius", supposed to be "the words of Confucius, handed down by Tseng Tzu."

The subject matter should be presented to the learner from the concrete to the abstract, from the near to the remote; from matters dealing with the individual person, to those dealing with society in general. About matters dealing with the individuals person, teaching should begin from those which deal with sense perception, or concrete things. This stage of learning is called "the investigation of things" (*Ke Wu*),[45] which forms the basis for all other ways of learning. The process of the cultivation of the individual mind cultimates in the "rectification of the mind" (*Cheng Hsin*) which is able to control evil desires, and differentiate the right from the wrong, the good from the evil, or the true from the false. About the subject matter dealing with society in general, teaching should begin from the family to the nation, and from the nation to the world. "The Text of Confucius" says:

"Things have their root and their branches. Affairs have their end and their beginning. To know what is first and what is last will lead near to what is taught (in *The Great Learning*)."

(b) The importance of teachers in the process of teaching

Since the mind of the learner is practically built up by environment, it must be largely in the hands of the teacher to make or modify the "collected data" of the mind of his pupil. So Hsun-tzu and his school gave a very important place to teachers in the process of education.

"Of all the methods of controlling the body and nourishing the mind there is . . . none more important than getting a teacher. . . ." (*The Work of Hsun tzu*, p. 47)

"In studying there is nothing better than being intimate with a worthy teacher. . . . Associate yourself closely with the teacher; familiarize yourself with his teaching; reverence it as universal and common to every age. Hence it is said: in studying there is nothing better than being intimate with a worthy teacher. According to the laws of learning there is nothing which gives quicker results than esteeming a worthy teacher." (*Ibid.*, p. 38)

"The rules of proper conduct (*Li*) is that whereby a person's character is corrected; a teacher is that whereby *Li* is corrected. Without *Li* how can I correct myself? Without a teacher how can I know what particular action is according to *Li*? (*Ibid.*, p. 51)

"A person can become a Yao or Yu; he can become a Ch'ie or a Chih (a notorious robber); he can become a day labourer or an artisan; he can become a farmer or a merchant; it depends on what training he has accumulated from his ways of looking at things, and his habits. . . . Man by birth is a small-minded man. Without a teacher or a set of principles, he can only think of profit. . . . If a man has no teacher or set of principles, his mind is just like his mouth or belly." (*Ibid.*, pp. 60-61)

"If a man is without a teacher or precepts, then if he is intelligent, he will certainly become a robber. . . . If he has a teacher and precepts, then if he is intelligent, he will quickly become learned. . . . Therefore the possession of a teacher and of precepts is the greatest treasure a man can have; the lack of a teacher and of precepts is the greatest calamity a man can have. If a man is without a teacher or precepts, he will exalt his original nature; if he has a teacher and precepts, he will exalt self-cultivation." (*Ibid.*, pp. 113-114)

"Now the people who are influenced by good teachers and laws, who accumulate literature and knowledge, who are led by *Li* and justice (*I*) become Superior Men." (*Ibid.*, p. 302)

(c) The method of creating the interest of the learner

The chief method of creating the interest of the learner emphasized by Hsun-tzu is to unify their desires, and the subject matters which they study, by the objectives of general purposes of study. Like Herbart again, Hsun-tzu believes that while the "many-sided-interest" is desirable, all studies must be unified, and scattering avoided. Hsun-tzu says:

"Scholarship is to know things thoroughly and to unify them; to be unified in learning and unified in teaching. . . . Scholarship must be complete and exhaustive." (*Ibid.*, p. 40)

"Of all the methods of controlling the body and nourishing the mind, there is. . . none more divine than to have but one desire." (p. 47)

The aim of education which unifies all desires and studies is the attainment of character. "When", says Hsun-tzu, "after accumulated cogitation, and the training of abilities, there results completion —this is called acquired character." (p. 281) Such character is embodied in the ideal personality, called the "sage" (Sheng-jen). "The purpose of study begins with making the scholar, and ends in making the 'sage'." (*The Work of Hsun-tzu*, p. 36) One of the chief characteristics of the Sage or Superior Man is that he enjoys what Herbart calls "inner freedom"; he is free in his thought and action, and has no difficulty in controlling his desires or arousing his interest in his study. Hsun-tzu says:

"If a person's will is cultivated, then he can be prouder than the rich and the honourable; if he has emphasized the Way (*Tao*) and justice (*I*), then he can despise kings and dukes; he can contemplate that which is within him and despite outer things. It is said: the Superior Man employs things; the small-minded man is the servant of things—this expresses what I mean." (p. 47)

The 'small-minded man' has not the 'inner freedom' to 'employ things', but rather 'is the servant of things.' He has not cultivated the will to follow the right Way (*Tao*) and justice (*I*), the chief purposes which govern the life of a Superior Man. Hsun-tzu says, "He who has not a very deep purpose, nor a very clear perception, nor very continuously strives towards a goal is without illustrious merit. A man who tries to travel along two paths of a forked road will never get there; he who serves two masters will not be employed" (p. 35), because his interest is divided, and weakened by such division. The saying of Professor Thorndike has been mentioned in this chapter, that "Good teaching decides what is to be learned by an appeal not to interest, but to the general aim of education. Having so decided it secures interest—the most, and the best and the steadiest possible." This has been found to be a great pedagogical truth. It is the method used by Confucius, and the same method is used by Hsun-tzu, in order to secure the best interest of the learner.

H. Conclusion

The methods of the teaching of Confucius, like his aims of teaching, emphasized both the individual and society. On the one hand, he laid stress on the individual development from within, and on the other hand, he also emphasized the humanizing influence of social and natural environments from without. He recognized the modern principles of teaching method, such as, apperception, activity, individualization, and motivation, and utilized them to develop the capacities of his disciples to their fullest extent. His democratic method of teaching everybody "without the distinction of class", and his ideal personality, especially his excellent spirit of "learning without satiety, and teaching without weariness." This spirit of his which is constantly mentioned in the Classics (*The Analects*, 7,23; 72; *Mencius*, 2,1,2,19) had the most abiding influence upon his followers.

He emphasized also the sociological method of education, by intimately relating education to the existing social orders, such as, government, family, religion, social rites, ethics and arts. He tried to adjust his disciples to the needs, habits, an regulations of society, without, however, infringing upon their individual rights and personalities.

His ambiguity in his teaching about human nature caused the split of his school into two diametrically opposite schools, headed by Mencius and Hsun-tzu. Confucius taught "By nature, men are nearly alike; by practice, they get to be wide apart." He only emphasized the importance of practice or education, and did not state very clearly or explicitly in what respect men are nearly alike by nature. Thus he left a great gap in his educational theory and caused much speculation and controversy among the later Confucian scholars. Mencius and his school believed that "by nature, men are nearly alike" in goodness; "by practice" some men "allow their mind to be ensnared and drowned in the evil", so "they get to be wide apart". Hsun-tzu and his school took the opposite point of view, and held that by nature men are evil, they "are nearly alike" in depravity, "by practice, they get to be wide apart", because some men learn to control the evil desires of their original nature, and "nourish the mind" with the impressions from the outside world, especially the teachings of the ancient sages, such as, the rules of proper conduct (*Li*).

With the opposite theories of human nature, these two schools adopted also entirely different views of education. Confucius as already mentioned, emphasized both the development of the individual from within, and the influence of the environment or social control from without. Having assumed that human nature is good, Mencius, like Froebel, emphasized the aspect of education as natural development from within, and laid stress upon the individual and his activities. Hsun-tzu, on the other hand, having assumed that the original nature of men is evil, emphasized the aspect of education as impressions from without or the influences of the environment, and concerned himself mainly with the teachings of the ancient sages, especially about *Li*, and with teachers who are supposed to be largely responsible for building up the contents or the "collected data" of the mind. Like Herbart, Hsun-tzu taught concerning the mind that it was made up of the "apperceptive mass", formed by the impressions from without through the senses, the importance of teachers, and their methods of teaching, the moral character as the aim of education, and the unification of studies, etc.

Both of them claimed that they were faithful followers of Confucius and that their interpretations were true to the teaching of their common Master. They may have been prejudiced in favour of one extreme or the other, but, in general, they have contributed a great deal towards the formation of fuller and clearer views of the teaching methods of Confucius.

CHAPTER VII

CONCLUSION

The main objective of this thesis is to bring out the fact that Confucius was, above all else, an ideal teacher. His masterly ways of dealing with the text-books which he used, his lofty aims of education, his rich substance of teaching, and his ideal methods of teaching—all show that he was an educationalist of the first rank. He transmitted the best of the traditional literary heritage and social regulations; but with his masterly touches, his "expunging, and rectifying", he transformed the old into the new, and the traditional textbooks of the "six disciplinary arts" (*Liao I*) into the "six classics" of his own school. He was both a transmitter and an originator, both a creator and a conserver, of ancient Chinese culture. He aimed at social reform through education, at bringing about an ideal social order through cultivating ideal individuals. In his ideal society both individual and social rights would be perfectly developed and harmonized; it would be the state of "great harmony." The major course of study which he offered was along the line of ethics, especially love (*Jen*), and the rules of proper conduct (*Li*); the former emphasizing more of the individualistic quality, while the latter more of social control. He had a thorough knowledge of the lessons which he taught, and from which he could draw his own unified system of thought and action. "The Master said, 'Shen, my doctrine is that of an all-pervading unity.' " (*The Analects*, 4,15,1; 15,2,3) He had definite teachings to contribute to the world, and he taught them earnestly "without being tired", and with excellent teaching methods.

Perhaps the greatest factor which contributed to the success of Confucius was his methods of teaching, especially his emphasis on the principle that "in teaching there should be no distinction of classes", and his own greatness of character. Owing to his enthusiasm in education, his followers have always paid much attention to teaching and editing. Throughout the ages, Confucian scholars, through the inspiration of their master, have practically monopolized the educational field in China. Few great persons in world history have been more misunderstood and misinterpreted to the West than the person of Confucius. In general, "he has been represented as having been, personally, almost entirely negative, an inhuman, formal, stiff, timid prig". (*Sinicism*, by H. G. Creel p. 72) As Dr. Creel points out, nothing could be farther from the truth. To him, he says, the greatness of character of Confucius could not be "exceeded by any figure in world history". There was evidently in him a certain charm of personality and a prestige that won the hearts of his disciples, and accounted, to a large extent, for his great influence and success.

After his death, his group was divided into many different schools, among them the school of Mencius and that of Hsun-tzu being the best known. They represented different aspects of the teaching of their common master. Mencius and his school emphasized more the individualistic side of the teaching of Confucius, while Hsun-tzu and his school laid more stress upon the social side. Both of them taken together contributed much towards the exemplification of the teaching of the Master.

For the summing up of the teachings of Confucius, and for the rating of Confucius as a teacher, the items as put down in the Teacher-efficiency Score Card (page 48), in *The Principal and His School*, written by Ellwood P. Cubberley, are to be applied here, in these concluding remarks, to Confucius as a teacher.

A. Personal Equipment

1. General Appearance

"The Master (Confucius) was mild and yet dignified, majestic and yet not fierce, respectful and yet easy." (*The Analects*, 7,37)

"His forehead is like that of Emperor Yao, his neck resembles that of the ancient minister Kao-yao, and his shoulders resemble those of Tzu-ch'an; but from the waist down, he is smaller than Emperor Yu by three inches." (Ssu-ma Ch'ien, "Life of Confucius")

"Tzu-kung said, 'Our Master is benign, upright, courteous, temperate, and complaisant.' " (*The Analects*, 1,10,2)

2. Health

He was healthy and unusually tall. (Ssu-ma Ch'ien, "Life of Confucius") He lived 73 years.

3. Voice

His voice was musical. (*The Analects*, 7,31) and yet "firm and decided." (*The Analects*, 19,9)

4. Intellectual Capacity

"Tzu-kung said, 'Certainly Heaven has endowed him unlimitedly. He is about a sage. And, moreover, his ability is various.' " (*The Analects*, 9,6,2)

"The Master said, 'Heaven produced the virtue that is in me.' " (*The Analects*, 7,22)

5. Initiative and Self-reliance

He was confident of his Divine Mission—to proclaim, through teaching, the eternal Truth of God. When the people of K'uang threatened to kill him, he said, 'After the death of King Wen, was not the cause of truth lodged here in me? If Heaven had wished to let this cause of truth perish, then I, a future moral, should not have got such a relation to that cause. While Heaven does not let the cause of truth perish, what can the people of K'uang do to me?" (*The Analects*, 9,5)

6. Adaptability and Resourcefulness

"There were four things from which the Master was entirely free. He had no arbitrariness of opinion, no dogmatism, no obstinacy, and no egoism." (*The Analects*, 9,4)

He rejoiced with those who rejoiced, and mourned with those who mourned. (*The Analects*, 10,16; 9,9; 7,31)

7. Accuracy

"When you know a thing, to hold that you know it; and when you do not know a thing, to allow that you do not know it—this is knowledge." (*The Analects*, 2,17)

8. Industry

He was industrious both working and learning throughout his life. Sometimes "in his enthusiasm (of his work) he forgot his food" (*The Analects*, 7,18,2); sometimes, he said, 'I have been the whole day without eating, and the whole night without sleeping—occupied with thinking' " (*The Analects*, 15,30); and once he told his disciples that he was so much involved in his learning that "for three months he did not know the taste of flesh." (*The Analects*, 7,13)

"The Master said, 'In a hamlet of ten families, there may be found one honourable and sincere as I am, but not one so fond of learning.' " (*The Analects*, 5,27)

"The Master said. . . . 'It may be said of me, that I strive to work without satiety, and teach others without weariness.' " (*The Analects*, 7,33; 7,2; *Mencius*, 2,1,2,19)

9. Enthusiasm and Optimism

"The duke of Yeh asked Tzu-lu about Confucius, and Tzu-lu did not answer him. The Master said, 'Why did you not say to him, 'He is simply a man, who in his enthusiasm (of his work) forgets his food, who is optimistic, forgetful of his sorrows, and who does not perceive that old age is coming on.' " (*The Analects*, 7,18)

"The Master said, 'With coarse rice to eat, with water to drink, and my bended arm for a pillow, I have still joy in the midst of these things. Riches and honours acquired by unrighteousness are to me as a floating cloud' " (*The Analects*, 7,15)

10. Integrity and Sincerity

"The Master said, 'Do you think, my disciples, that I have any concealments? I conceal nothing from you. There is nothing which I do that is not shown to you, my disciples. That is my way.' " (*The Analects*, 7,23)

"The Master said, 'Fine words, an insinuating appearance, and excessive respect—Tso Ch'iu-ming was ashamed of them. I also am ashamed of them. To conceal resentment against a person, and appear friendly with them—Tso Ch'iu-ming was ashamed of such conduct. I also am ashamed of it.' " (*The Analects*, 5,24)

"The Master said, 'The Superior Man, in the world, does not set his mind either for anything, or against anything; what is right he will follow.' " (*The Analects*, 4,10)

11. Self-control

"In youth, when the physical powers are not yet settled, he

guards against lust. When he is strong and the physical powers are full of vigour, he guards against quarrelsomeness. When he is old, and the animal powers are decayed, he guards against covetousness." (*The Analects*, 16,7)

"The Master angled, but did not use a net. He shot, but not at birds perching." (*The Analects*, 7,26)

"Though there might be a large quantity of meat, he would not allow what he took to exceed the due proportion for the rice. It was only in wine that he laid down no limit for himself, but he did not allow himself to be confused by it. . . . He did not eat too much." (*The Analects*, 10,8,4-7)

12. Promptness

He was prompt in action. He said, "A Superior Man wishes to be slow in his speech but prompt in his conduct." (*The Analects*, 4,24)

He was quick in solving problems which were put forth by his disciples, and in drawing meanings from natural phenomena. (See *The Analects*, 9,16; 17,19)

13. Tact

In many incidents, as recorded in *The Analects*, he showed much tact in his teaching. For example, in one of the discussion meetings with his disciples, one of his disciples said something very proud and arrogant. He showed his tact by simply "smiling at him", and not speaking anything to discourage or embarrass him in the presence of his fellow students. (*The Analects*, 11,25) His tact can also be seen in other incidents recorded in *The Analects*. (*The Analects*, 14,31; 3,8; 5,6; 17,4; etc.)

14. Sense of Justice

He praised those who were worthy to be praised (*The Analects*, 3,4,2; 3,8,3; 12,21,2), and punished those who were worthy to be punished. (*The Analects*, 14,22; 14,46;, 11,16)

"The Master said, 'I do not know how a man without truthfulness (or justice) is to get on. How can a large carriage be made to go without the cross-bar for yoking the oxen to, or a small carriage without the arrangement for yoking the horses?' " (*The Analects*, 2,22)

B. Social and Professional Equipment

1. Academic Preparation

2. Professional Preparation

The ancestors of Confucius were of the royal family of Sung, but his great grandfather had moved to Lu, where the family became impoverished. (Ssu-ma Ch'ien's, "Life of Confucius") Confucius said, "When I was young, my condition was low, and therefore I acquired my ability in many things." (*The Analects*, 9,6,3) He did not receive much formal education, and had no "regular teacher". (*The Analects*, 19,22,2) "At fifteen", he said, "I had my mind bent on learning". From that time on he studied very hard, generally by himself, sometimes in consultation with more elderly and experienced scholars (*The Analects*, 5,27; 3,15; 7,21; 7,19; 3,9; 7,18; etc.) "At thirty", he said, "I stood firm. At forty, I had no doubts. At fifty, I knew the decrees of Heaven. At sixty, my ear was an obedient organ. At seventy, I could follow what my heart desired, without transgressing what was right." (*The Analects*, 2,4) He "studied extensively," and was familiar with the traditional literature of all times. For example, he said,

"The Yin Dynasty followed the regulations of the Hsia: wherein it took from or added to them may be known. The Chou Dynasty has followed the regulations of the Yin: wherein it took from or added to them may be known. Some other may follow the Chou, but though it should be at the distance of a hundred ages, its affairs may be known." (*The Analects*, 2,23)

3. Grasp of Subject Matter

He knew very well what he taught, and had a full grasp of the subject matter. From his extensive and thorough study, he could deduce certain underlying unified principles of the subjects which he taught. (See *The Analects*, 2,2; 3,4; 15,2; 4,15)

"A high officer asked Tzu-kung, saying, 'May we not say that your Master is a sage? How various is his ability!' Tzu-kung said, 'Certainly Heaven has endowed him unlimitedly. He is about a sage. And, moreover, his ability is various.' " (*The Analects*, 9,6,1-2)

"A man of the village of Ta-hsiang said, 'Great indeed is Confucius! His learning is extensive. . . .' " (*The Analects*, 9,2,1)

4. Understanding of Students

He understood his students very well. For example, he said, "Ch'ai is simple, Shen is dull, Shih is specious, and Yu is coarse." (*The Analects*, 11,17) (See also *The Analects*, 5,7; 6,6; 11,15; 11,17; 11,21)

He had a great respect for young people. He said, "A youth is to be regarded with respect. How do we know that his future will not be equal to our present?" (*The Analects*, 9,23)

5. School and Community Interest

He had great interest in his teaching work, and he said about himself that he was never tired in his teaching. (*The Analects*, 7,33;7,2; *Mencius*, 2,1,2,19) He was interested in social reform, and the aim of his teaching was to bring about an ideal society through the teaching of his school. As a matter of fact, most of his followers either took up teaching work or entered into public offices. To him school and government have the same purpose and function, and school and community are one, and he was interested in both.

6. Ability to Meet and Interest Parents

He not only loved and cared for his disciples, but he had a great care also for their parents. Filial piety was one of his most important teachings.

"Tzu-lu asked whether he should immediately carry into practice what he heard. The Master said, 'There are your father and elder brothers (to be consulted); why should you act on that principle of immediately carrying into practice what you hear?' " (*The Analects*, 11,21)

"The Master said, 'While his parents are alive, the son may not go abroad to a distance. If he does go abroad, he must have a fixed place to which he goes.' " (*The Analects*, 4,19)

"Tzu-hua being employed on a mission to Ch'i, the disciple Yen requested grain for his mother. The Master said, 'Give her a *fu*.' Yen requested more. 'Give her an *yu*,' said the Master. Yen gave her five *ping*." (*The Analects*, 6,3)

7. Interest in Lives of Pupils

He was interested in the daily life of his disciples. He taught them the manners of eating, walking, dressing, sleeping, etc. (*The Analects*, bk. 10) He blamed his disciple Tsai Yu for his "sleeping in the day time." (*The Analects*, 5,9) and praised Yen Yuan, saying, "I have examined his conduct when away from me, and found him able to illustrate (my teachings)." (*The Analects*, 2,9) By closely watching the daily life of his disciples, he was able to understand their individualities, and help them to develop their capacities and meet their needs. (*The Analects*, 6,6; 2,9; 2,10)

8. Co-operation and Loyalty

He was most loyal to his higher authorities. (See *The Analects*, 10,1-5) He encouraged and recommended his disciples to hold governmental or other public offices. (*The Analects*, 6,6; 9,15)

9. Professional Interest and Growth

He was very much interested in his teaching work, and never got tired of teaching. He was never satisfied with what he had attained, and always strove to be better.

"The Master said, 'The sage and the man of love (*Jen*); how dare I (rank myself with them)? It may simply be said of me, that I strive to become such without satiety, and teach others without weariness.' Kung-hsi Hua said, 'This is just what we, the disciples, cannot imitate you in.' " (*The Analects*, 7,33; 7,2; *Mencius*, 2,1,2,19)

"The Master said, 'At fifteen, I had my mind bent on learning. At thirty, I stood firm. At forty, I had no doubts. At fifty, I knew the decrees of Heaven, At sixty, my ear was an obedient organ (for the reception of truth). At seventy, I could follow what my heart desired, without transgressing what was right.' " (*The Analects*, 2,4)

10. Daily Preparation

Being a diligent student, a kind-hearted master, and a man deeply interested in education, he must have been very careful in the daily preparation of his lessons.

"The Master said, 'I have been the whole day without eating, and the whole night without sleeping—occupied with thinking. It was of no use. The better plan is to learn.' " (*The Analects*, 15,30)

"Tseng-tzu said, 'I daily examine myself on three points. . . .' " (*The Analects*, 1,4)

11. Use of Language (Chinese)

It has been traditionally believed that the Chinese which Confucius used is the best that the Chinese people have ever attained, for the Confucian Classics have always been the standard and model of the Chinese language.

Ssu-ma Ch'ien, for example, says about *The Spring and Autumn Annals* which Confucius wrote that "In writing *The Spring and Autumn Annals*, he wrote down and deleted exactly as he thought fit, and the disciples like Tzu-hsia were not able to add a word." ("The life of Confucius")

C. School Management

1. Care of Light, Heat and Ventilation—No Record
2. Neatness of Room—No Record
3. Care of Routine—No Record

There was no fixed place or school-building for Confucius to teach his students. he sometimes taught them in his home, sometimes in their homes, sometimes on the hill-top, sometimes by the river-side, sometimes under the trees, and sometimes on the road when they were travelling together.

4. Discipline (Governing Skill)

He was very successful in his discipline, for all his students loved and respected him. What he used was a kindly and loving discipline, treating his students as his friends and regarding them as his own children. (See *The Analects*, 11,9; 11,10,3; 11,22; 19,24; 11,25,2; 9,10; 25; 7,23)

D. Technique of Teaching

1. **Definiteness and Clearness of Aim** (See Chap. 4, above)
(a) Individualistic aim
(1) Practical individualistic aim—Superior Man (Chun-tzu)
(2) Ideal individualistic aim—Sage (Sheng-jen)

"The Master said, 'A Sage (Sheng-jen) is not mine to see; could I see a Superior Man (Chun-tzu), that would satisfy me.' " (*The Analects*, 7,25,1)

(b) Social aim

(1) Practical social aim—The ideal state of Lu, or the stage of "small tranquility" (Hsiao Kung).

(2) Ideal social aim—A state of *Tao*, or the stage of "great harmony" (*Ta Tung*).

"The Master said, 'Ch'i by one change, would come to the State of Lu. Lu, by one change, would come to a State of *Tao*.' " (*The Analects*, 6,22. See *Li Chi*, chap. on Li Yung)

2. Skill in Habit Formation

"The Master said, 'To learn and practise constantly, is that not a pleasure?' " (*The Analects*, 1,1,1)

"The Master said, 'If a man keeps reviewing his old (knowledge, habit and skill), so as continually to be acquiring the new, he may be a teacher of others.' " (*The Analects*, 2,11)

3. Skill of Stimulating Thought

He used the modern principles of teaching, such as, apperception, activity, individualization and motivation, in order to stimulate the thought of his disciples. (See Chap. 6, above)

"The Master said, 'I do not open up the truth to one who is not eager (to get knowledge), nor help out any one who is not anxious to explain himself. When I have presented one corner of a subject to any one, and he cannot from it learn the other three, I do not repeat my lesson.' " (*The Analects*, 7,8)

4. Skill in Teaching How to Study

"The Master said. . . . 'Study extensively, inquire accurately, reflect carefully, discriminate clearly, and practise earnestly." (*The Doctrine of the Mean*, 20,19)

Learn diligently and with humility

"Tzu-kung asked, saying, 'On what ground did Kung-wen get the title of 'accomplished' (*Wen*)?' The Master said, 'He was of an

active nature and yet fond of learning, and was not ashamed to ask (and learn of) his inferiors! On these grounds he has been styled 'Accomplished' (*Wen*).' " (*The Analects*, 5,14)
(See Chap. 6, above, Methods of Learning)

5. Skill in Questioning

Often by the skilful question-and-answer method he led his disciples gradually to see the truth. (See *The Analects*, 16,1; 12,20; 15,2; 5,8)

"The Master, by orderly method, skilfully leads me on." (*The Analects*, 9,10,2)

6. Choice of Subject-matter

He chose the best of the traditional cultural heritage, and "expunged and rectified" it, in order to meet the needs of the individual and the demands of society. (See Chaps. 3 and 5, above)

7. Organization of Subject-matter

(a) Through "correlation" or "concentration"

"The Master said, 'Shen, my doctrine is that of an all-pervading unity.' " (*The Analects*, 4,15,1; 15,2,3)

(b) From near to remote

"The Master said, '. . . To be able to give examples from what is near—this may be called the method of love (*Jen*).' " (*The Analects*, 6,28,3)

(c) From known to unknown

(See the principle of apperception, chap. 6, above)

(d) From concrete to abstract, from individual to social

(See *The Great Learning*, "The text of Confucius")

"Things have their root and their branches. Affairs have their end and their beginning. To know what is first and what is last will lead near to what is taught (in *The Great Learning*)," (*Ibid.*)

8. Skill and Care of Assignment

When he assigned certain lessons he would describe something about their nature or content so as to stir up the interest of his students. (*The Analects*, 17,9)

9. Skill in Motivating Work
(See the principle of motivation, Chap. 6, above)
10. Attention to Individual Needs
(See the principle of individualization, Chap. 6, above)

E. Results (See Results of the Teachings of Confucius, Chap. 6, above)

1. Attention and Response of the Class

His students were so much interested in his teaching that they could not give over their study, and many of them did follow his teaching of "believing firmly the good learning, and holding fast even unto death the admirable teaching." (*The Analects*, 8,13,1)

"Yen Yuan said, '. . . When I wish to give over (the study of his doctrine), I cannot do so.' " (*The Analects*, 9,10,3)

2. Growth of Pupils in Study

He often tested the growth of his students by asking them to speak out their own ambitions. (*The Analects*, 5,25; 11,25) Sometimes, his students grew too fast in study, so that he could only wish that they would go slower. "Alas!" he said, about one of his students, "I saw his constant advance; I never saw him stop in his progress." (*The Analects*, 9,20) They all grew rapidly both morally and intellectually.

3. Social Development of Pupils

Most of his disciples held important public positions in the state and society. He spoke thus of the social development of some of his disciples: "In a kingdom of a thousand chariots, Yu might be employed to manage the military levies. . . . In the city of a thousand families, or a clan of a hundred chariots, Chiu might be employed as a governor. . . . With his sash girt and standing in a court, Chih might be employed to converse with the visitors and guests. . . . (*The Analects*, 5,7)

4. Stimulation of Community

His immediate stimulation of community, and his later influence on society.

5. Moral Influence

Mencius said, "When one subdues men by virtue, in their hearts' core they are pleased, and sincerely submit, as was the case with the seventy disciples in their submission to Confucius. What is said in *The Book of Poetry*,

> *'From the west, from the east,*
> *From the south, from the north,*
> *There was not one who thought of refusing submission.'*

is an illustration of this." (*Mencius*, 2,1,3,2)

Finally, we quote from the last paragraph of Ssu-ma Ch'ien's "life of Confucius" in his appreciation of the character of Confucius.

"The Master Historian (Ssu-ma Ch'ien) says: 'The Book of Poetry says, "High is the mountain I look up to, and bright is the example for our emulation! Although I cannot reach the top, my heart leaps up to it." As I read the books of Confucius, I thought to myself how he must have looked. When visiting Lu, I saw the carriages, robes, and sacred vessels displayed at the Temple, and watched how the Confucian students studied the historical systems at his home, and lingered on unable to tear myself away from the place. There have been many kings, emperors and great men in history, who enjoyed fame and honour while they lived and came to nothing at their death. But Confucius, though only a humble member of the cotton-clothed masses, remains among us as the acknowledged Master of scholars for over ten generations. By all, from the emperors, kings and princes down, who discuss the 'Six Arts,' the final authority of the Master is fully and freely admitted. He, indeed, may be pronounced the 'Most Holy.' "

NOTES

CHAPTER ONE

1. 集大成
2. 尧
3. 舜
4. 禹
5. 汤
6. 文
7. 武
8. 周公
9. 《中庸》
10. 《史记》
11. 《汉书·艺文志》
12. 儒
13. 墨家
14. 秦始皇
15. 阴阳家
16. 儒家
17. 墨家
18. 名家
19. 法家
20. 道德家

21. 刘歆
22. 农家
23. 纵横家
24. 小说家
25. 杂家
26. 《汉书》
27. 杨朱
28. 许行
29. 陈相
30. 杨朱
31. 墨家
32. 儒家
33. 《六艺》
34. 《前汉书·艺文志》
35. 将圣
36. 君子
37. 尼父
38. 《史记·孔子世家》
39. 宰我

40. 有若

41. 韩非

42. "五蠹"

43. "五蠹"

44. 高祖

45. 曲阜

46. 平帝

47. 褒成侯宣尼公

48. 永平

49. 明帝

50.《七经纬》

51. 大圣

52. 杀辟

53.《金石萃编》

54. 沙丘

55.《论衡》

56. 鲁恭王

57. 黑帝

58. 颜氏

59. 素王

60. 永寿

61. 建宁

62.《金石萃编》

63. 永平

64. 魏文帝

65. 命世大圣亿载师表

66. 魏正始

67. 先圣

68. 颜渊

69. 先师

70.《魏志》

71. 太和

72. 孝文

73. 文圣尼父

74.《北魏书》

75. 兴和

76. 孝静帝

77.《阙里志》

78. 大成

79. 宣帝

80. 北周

81. 邹国公

82. 《北周书》

83. 开皇

84. 隋文帝

85. 先师尼父

86. 《隋志》

87. 大业

88. 大圣宣尼

89. 百王师表

90. 武德

91. 高祖

92. 先圣

93. 先师

94. 贞观

95. 太宗

96. 《唐书》

97. 州

98. 县

99. 颜子

100. 《唐书》

101. 宣父

102. 永徽

103. 高宗

104. 《阙里志》

105. 显庆

106. 乾封

107. 太师鲁国孔宣公

108. 开元

109. 玄宗

111. 大中祥符

112. 元圣文宣王

113. 齐国公

114. 鲁国太夫人

115. 郓国夫人

116. 曲阜

117. 仙源

118. 《宋史》

119. 至圣文宣王
120. 元
121. 至
122. 至圣
123. 貞宗
124. 赵元明
125. 大德
126. 大成
127. 《明史》
128. 先师孔子
129. 洪武
130. 朱子
131. 《朱子语录》
132. 嘉靖
133. 至圣先师孔子
134. 先师庙
135. 《明纪》
136. 大清会典·礼》
137. 顺治
138. 大成至圣文宣先

师孔子
139. 至圣先师孔子
140. 康熙
141. 万世师表
142. 大成殿
143. 文庙
144. 雍正
145. 今文家
146. 《孔子改制考》
147. 教主
148. 汉武帝
149. 孔教会
150. 《真实报》
151. 袁世凯
152. 张勋
153. 宣统
154. 陈济棠
155. 段祺瑞
156. 张宗昌
157. 《雄辉文存》

158. 张作霖
159. 戴季陶
160. 《孙文主义之哲
　　 学的基础》
161. 礼义廉耻
162. 忠孝仁爱信义
　　 和平
163. 孔祥熙
164. 《洪钟财报》
165. 君子
166. 圣人
167. 教主
168. 《古史辨》
169. 《美国哈佛大学
　　 哈佛燕京学社
　　 汉和图书馆汉
　　 籍分类目录》
170. 《古论》
171. 《齐论》
172. 《鲁论》

173. 《汉书·艺文志》
174. 《论语注序》
175. 易
176. 亦
177. 郭绍渔
178. 务外
179. 主内
180. 朱子
181. 陆香山
182. 王阳明
183. 万章
184. 子思
185. 《史记·孔子世
　　 家》
186. 荀子·非十二子》
187. 《大学为荀学》
188. 《小戴礼记》
189. 《大戴礼记》

CHAPTER TWO

1. 征		21. 孟献子	
2. 伐		22. 襄公	
3. 戚		23. 范宣子	
4. 围		24. 子驷	
5. 入		25. 晋倬公	
6. 武王		26. 曹	
7. 季		27. 鲁宣公	
8. 孟		28. 宋华元	
9. 叔孙		29. 子反	
10. 齐		30. 襄公	
11. 宋		31. 盟	
12. 晋		32. 向戌	
13. 秦		33. 葵丘	
14. 楚		34. 鲁倬公	
15. 五霸		35. 鲁公	
16. 韩非子		36. 宰周公	
17. 庄公		37. 齐侯	
18. 齐恒公		38. 宋子	
19. 有度		39. 卫侯	
20. 宣公		40. 郑伯	

41. 许男

42. 曹伯

43. 楚

44. 晋

45. 秦

46. 山戎

47. 襄公

48. 向戌

49. 韩宣子

50. 陈文子

51. 郑

52. 滕

53. 辛巳

54. 伯州犁

55. 子木

56. 孝

57. 《书经·舜典》

58. 魏子

59. 成鱄

60. 武王

61. 姬

62. 周公

63. 《荀子·儒说》

64. 昭公

65. 王

66. 公

67. 大夫

68. 士

69. 皂

70. 舆

71. 隶

72. 僚

73. 仆

74. 臺

75. 圉

76. 牧

77. 管仲

78. "作内政而寄军令"

79. 航

80. 伍
81. 軌長
82. 里
83. 小戎
84. 里有司
85. 連
86. 卒
87. 連長
88. 多
89. 旅
90. 多良人
91. 師
92. 軍
93. 帥
94. 莊公
95. 獻公
96. 晉
97. 楚
98. 宣公
99. 麗姬

100. 文公
101. "以六卿兼六軍"
102. 先軫
103. 中軍
104. 原
105. 食邑
106. 趙衰
107. 大夫
108. 魯僖公
109. 縣
110. 宣公
111. 昭公
112. 魯成公
113. 宣公
114. 子重
115. 申
116. 呂
117. "償田"
118. 巫臣
119. 申公

120. 鲁隐公
121. 郑庄公
122. 京
123. 鲁闵公
124. 无亏王
125. 曹
126. 鲁庄公
127. 子元
128. 楚令尹
129. 郑
130. 僖公
131. 城濮
132. 鲁成公
133. 郤克
134. 鲁襄公
135. 郑子产
136. 昭公
137. 邾
138. 叔向
139. 哀公

140. 晷翟
141. 赵盾
142. 昭公
143. 郑子产
144. 赵鞅
145. 荀寅
146. 汝滨
147. 鼓
148. 范宣子
149. "礼"
150. "礼"
151. 栾
152. 郤
153. 胥
154. 原
155. 狐
156. 续
157. 庆
158. 伯
159. 宁喜

160. 伯里奚
161. "六艺"
162. "礼"
163. 吕不韦
164. 铜鞮
165. 伯有
166. 章华
667. 晋叔向
168. 齐晏平仲
169. 晋叔向
170. 晋士文伯
171. 郑子产
172. 昭公
173. 班固
174. 城
175. 子贡
176. 昭公
177. 公如晋
178. 公至自晋
179. 班固

180. 士
181. 杨朱
182. 庄子
183. 杞
184. 宋
185. 颜渊
186. "六艺"
187. 《诗经》
188. 《书经》
189. 《仪礼》
190. 铙
191. 钲
192. 镯
193. 镈
194. 铃
195. 铎
196. 《乐经》
197. 《易经》
198. 曹劌
199. 莊公

200. 宣公
201. 灵公
202. 太史
203. 赵盾
204. 襄公
205. 崔子
206. 《乘》
207. 《梼杌》
208. 《春秋》
209. 《故志》
210. 《仪礼》
211. 塾
212. 小学
213. 大学
214. 辟雍
215. 頖宫
216. 校
217. 序
218. 庠
219. 学
220. 朱子
221. 国学
222. 《礼记·学记》
223. 塾
224. 家
225. 庠
226. 序
227. 党
228. 术
229. 学
230. 国
231. 王制
232. 小学
233. 大学
234. 辟雍
235. 頖宫
236. 《汉书·艺文志》
237. 小学
238. "保傅"
239. 白虎通

240.《礼记·内则》

241.《玉海》

242. 大司徒

243.“六德”

244. 智

245. 仁

246. 圣

247. 义

248. 忠

249. 和

250.“六行”

251. 孝

252. 友

253. 睦

254. 姻

255. 任

256. 恤

257.“六艺”

258. 礼

259. 乐

260. 射

261. 御

262. 书

263. 数

264.《周礼·地官司徒》

265. 吉礼

266. 宾礼

267. 军礼

268. 嘉礼

269. 凶礼

270.《佩文韵府》

271. 武王

272.《书经·泰誓》(上)

273.《礼记·学记》

274. 墨子

275.“诸子不出王家”

276. 少正卯

277.《孔子家语》

278.《列子》

279.《道德经》

280. 罗根泽

281. 接与

282. 长咀

283. 桀溺

284. 伯夷

285. 叔齐

286. 虞仲

287. 夷逸

288. 朱张

289. 柳下惠

290. 少连

291. 老子

292. 贤人

293. 匡

294. 多原

295. 多原

296. 经

297.《古诗》

298. 君子

299. 贼

300. 原壤

301. 吴季札

302. 叔孙穆子

303. 晏平仲

304. 郑子产

305. 卫

306. 蘧瑗

307. 史狗

308. 史蝤

309. 公子荆

310. 公子发

311. 公子朝

312. 执圭字

313. 韩宣子

314. 魏献子

315. 晋叔向

316. 宋向戌

317. 芍掩

318. 子木

319.《孝经》

320.《诗经》

321.《易经》

322.《仪礼》

323.《古史新证》

324. 季札

325. 礼

326. 冤

327. 舜

328. 禹

329. 汤

330. 文

331. 武

332. 周公

333. 晋叔向

334. 叔向

335. 叔鱼

336. 平丘

337. 季孙

338. 邢侯

339. 商任

340. 来

341. 郑子产

342. 郑子产

343. 法家

344. 庐

345. 井

346. 宽

347. 子大叔

348. 协

349. 子大叔

350. 赵简子

351. 晏平仲

352.《史记》

353. 信

354. 伯州犁

355. 子牧

356. 商任

357. 来

358. 陈丈子

359. 孟僖子
360. 仪
361. 女叔齐
362. 仪
363. 子家羁
364. 叔倪
365. 子木
366. 向戍
367. 子罕
368. 大
369. 皇天上帝
370. 伊训
371. 鬼
372. 神
373. 史嚚
374. 虢
375. 子尹
376. 伯
377. 韩简子
378. 《书经·说命》

379. 《书经·泰誓》(上)
380. 《书经·泰誓》(中)
381. 《书经·泰誓》(下)
382. 周公
383. 旦
384. 《书经·金縢》
385. 荀子
386. 庙
387. 《前汉书·艺文志》
388. 《天文》
389. 《历谱》
390. 《五行》
391. 《蓍龟》
392. 《杂占》
393. 《形》
394. 孔夫子
395. 丘
396. 仲尼
397. 陬邑
398. 季札

399. 郊 子
400. 孟僖子
401. 孟懿子
402. 南宮敬叔
403. 齊
404. 季平子
405. 孟
406. 叔孫
407. 定公
408. 晏嬰
409. 定公
410. 陽貨
411. 費
412. 夾谷
413. 鄆
414. 汶陽
415. 龜田
416. 費
417. 成
418. 衛

419. 陳
420. 蔡
421. 曹
422. 宋
423. 鄭
424. 晉
425. 哀公
426. 陳恆
427. 簡公
428. 顏回
429. 宰予
430. 仲由
431. 子路

CHAPTER THREE

1. 郑罕

2. 国子监

3. 乾隆

4. 《十三经注疏》

5. 崇祯

6. 赵岐

7. 王弼 (魏)

8. 韩康伯 (晋)

9. 《孔安国传》(汉)

10. 《毛亨传》

11. 《郑玄笺》(汉)

12. 《郑玄笺》

13. 《郑玄注》

14. 《郑玄注》

15. 《杜预注》(晋)

16. 《何休解诂》(汉)

17. 《范甯集解》(晋)

18. 《何晏集解》(魏)

19. 《清世祖注》(晋)

20. 《郭璞注》(晋)

21. 《朱熹注》(宋)

22. 《孝经·逸礼》

23. 龚胜

24. 公孙禄

25. 师丹

26. 范升

27. 李育

28. 何休

29. 临硕

30. 张兴

31. 陈元

32. 贾逵

33. 马融

34. 许慎

35. 卢植

36. 郑玄

37. 汉平帝

38. 张兴

39. 蔡元

40. 楼望

41. 郑玄
42. 刘逢禄
43. 皮锡瑞
44. 龚自珍
45. 魏源
46. 廖平
47. 崔适
48. 康有为
49. 许慎
50. 《说文解字》
51. 张苍
52. 北平
53. 鼎
54. 彝
55. 《七略》
56. 鲁
57. 申公
58. 文帝
59. 韩
60. 韩婴

61. 燕
62. 赵
63. 齐
64. 辕固生
65. 景帝
66. 毛公
67. 赵
68. 平帝
69. 陈侠
70. 徐整
71. 小毛公
72. 毛苌
73. 子夏
74. "我说"
75. 大毛公
76. 子夏
77. 荀卿
78. 郑公
79. 贾逵
80. 马融

81. 郑玄

82. 南陔

83. 白华

84. 华黍

85. 由庚

86. 崇丘

87. 由仪

88. 伏生

89. 济南

90. 欧阳生

91. 张生

92. 夏侯胜

93. 大夏侯

94. 夏侯建

95. 小夏侯

96. 《汉书·大小夏侯
    章句》

97. 《解故》

98. 《欧阳经》

99. 《欧阳章句》

100. 《泰誓》

101. 河内

102. 孔安国

103. 《孔氏古文尚书》

104. 《九共》

105. 《舜典》

106. 《汩作》

107. 《九共》

108. 《大禹谟》

109. 《弃稷》

110. 《五子之歌》

111. 《胤征》

112. 《汤诰》

113. 《咸有德》

114. 《典宝》

115. 《伊训》

116. 《肆命》

117. 《原命》

118. 《武成》

119. 《旅獒》

120.《问命》

121.《孔惠》

122. 礼

123.《论语》

124.《孝经》

125. 科斗

126. 伏生

127.《隶古》

128. 田何《易》

129. 商瞿

130. 杨何《易》

131. 王同

132. 施《易》

133. 施雠

134. 田王孙

135. 丁宽

136. 孟《易》

137. 孟喜

138. 梁丘《易》

139. 京氏《易》

140. 京房

141. 焦延寿

142. 费氏《易》

143. 费直

144. 王璜

145. 费氏《易》

146. 古文《易》

147. 高氏《易》

148. 高相

149. 刘向

150. 施

151. 孟

152. 梁丘

153. "无咎"

154. "悔无"

155. 费氏

156. 高堂生《礼》

157.《经》

158.《士礼》

159.《仪礼》

160. 徐生《礼》

161. 文帝

162. 礼官大夫

163. 后苍《礼》

164.《后氏曲台记》

165. 大戴《礼》

166. 戴德

167. 大戴

168. 小戴《礼》

169. 戴圣

170. 小戴

171.《郑六艺论》

172.《礼经》

173.《礼记》

174. "或曰"

175. 李氏

176.《周官》

177. 事官

178. 金

179.《考工记》

180.《逸礼》

181.《古礼经》

182. 后苍

183. 通儒

184. 子思(级)

185. 缁衣

186. 公孙尼子

187. 月令

188.《周礼论》

189. 陈邵

190. 戴德

191.《古礼》

192.《大戴礼》

193. 戴圣

194.《小戴礼》

195. 马融

196. 庐植

197.《三礼》

198. 公羊学派

199.《公羊春秋》

200. 胡毋生
201. 景帝
202. 《董仲舒》
203. 严頔
204. 严彭祖
205. 颜安乐
206. 《谷梁春秋》
207. 江生
208. 瑕丘
209. 宣帝
210. 《左传》
211. 张苍
212. 荀卿
213. 《鲁论》
214. 《齐论》
215. 《古文论语》
216. 尧曰
217. 子张
218. 曾子
219. 颜芝

220. 长孙氏
221. 江翁
222. 后苍
223. 翼奉
224. 张禹
225. 《孔传》
226. 孔鲋
227. 刘炫
228. 文帝
229. 太宰纯
230. 《知不足斋丛书》
231. 广扬名
232. 庶人
233. 圣治
234. 尧
235. 舜
236. 禹
237. 汤
238. 文
239. 武

240. 周公
241. 伏羲
242. 廖平
243. 《知圣篇》
244. 《佚书》
245. 博士
246. "六艺"
247. 刘知几
248. "整理国故"
249. 敦煌
250. 王国维
251. 马衡
252. 容庚
253. 韩非子
254. "显学"
255. "五蠹"
256. 王充
257. 刘知几
258. "感经"
259. "疑古"

260. 《史通》
261. 欧阳修
262. "十翼"
263. "系词"
264. "文言"
265. "说卦"
266. "杂卦"
267. 朱熹
268. 《语类》
269. 《文集》
270. 孔安国《尚书》
271. 叶适
272. 《习学记言》
273. 王柏
274. 《书疑》
275. 《诗疑》
276. 工宏
277. 阎若璩
278. 《尚书·古文疏证》
279. 姚际恒

280. 崔东壁
281. "层累地造成的
　　　中国古史"
282. 《诗序》
283. 《东壁遗书》
284. 康有为
285. 罗根泽
286. 新文化运动
287. 胡适
288. 顾颉刚
289. 钱玄同
290. 冯友兰
291. 罗根泽
292. 周予同
293. 钱穆
294. 傅斯年
295. 郭沫若
296. 张荫麟
297. 魏建功
298. 梅思平

299. 于鹤年
300. "十翼"
301. 冯友兰
302. 《孔子在中国历
　　　史中之地位》
303. 《燕京学报》
304. "意志的上帝"
305. 主宰之天
306. "宇宙力量"
307. "义理之天"
308. 《彖象》
309. 《尚书纬》
310. 《慈经》
311. 刘知几
312. 万斯同
313. 《易教》
314. 章学诚
315. 钱玄同
316. 疑古先生
317. 总集

318.《断烂朝报》

319. 流水账簿

320. 周予同

321. 罗根泽

322.《国语》

323. 庄王

324. 楚

325. 楚语

326. 襄公

327. 季札

328. 吴

329. 昭

330. 韩宣子

331. 晋

332. 太史

333. "六艺"

334. "义"

335. 晋之"乘"

336. 楚之《梼杌》

337. 罗根泽

338. "战国前无私家
　　著作"

339. 墨家

340. "六艺"

341. 张寿林

342.《古史新证》

343.《虞夏书》

344.《尧典》

345. 皋陶谟》

346.《禹贡》

347.《甘誓》

348.《汤誓》

349.《商书》

350.《商书·盘庚》

351.《商书·高宗肜日》

352. "西伯戡黎"

353. "微子"

354.《周书》

355. "牧誓"

356. "洪范"

357. "金縢"

358. "大诰"

359. "康诰"

360. "酒诰"

361. "梓材"

362. "召诰"

363. "洛诰"

364. "多士"

365. "无逸"

366. "君奭"

367. "多方"

368. "立政"

369. "顾命"

370. "康王之诰"

371. "吕刑"

372. "文侯之命"

373. "费誓"

374. "秦誓"

375. "商颂"

376. 宋人

377. 宗周

378. 卦辞

379. "爻辞"

380. "十翼"

381. 《国语》

CHAPTER FOUR

1. 圣人	21. 子张
2. 君子	22. 子贡
3. 圣人	23. 齐
4. 尧	24. 鲁
5. 舜	25. 道
6. 仁	26. 王霸
7. 子路	27. 尧
8. 君子	28. 舜
9. 君子	29. 禹
10. 君	30. 汤
11. 子	31. 文
12. 仁	32. 武
13. 义	33. 周公
14. 天命	34. 《孔子托古改制考》
15. 礼	35. 罗根泽
16. 礼	36. 《晚周诸子反古考》
17. 礼	37. 《汉书·艺文志》
18. 道	38. 诚
19. 道	
20. 曾子	

39. 仁

40. 让

41. 小康

42. 《礼记·礼运》

43. 小康

44. 大同

45. 仁

46. 仁

47. 仁

48. 命

49. "不仁"

50. "神"

51. 爱

52. 仁

53. 亲

54. 仁政

55. 王政

56. 圣人之政

57. 天吏

58. 井

59. 井

60. 礼

61. 义

62. 士

63. 君子

64. 圣人

65. 道

CHAPTER FIVE

1. 仁	21. 义
2. 礼	22. 道
3. 孝	23.《韩愈·原道》
4. 中庸	24. 博
5. 仁	25. 亲
6. 仁	26. 仁
7. 礼	27. 爱
8. 孝	28. 好
9. 中庸	29. "好德"
10. 智	30. "好色"
11. 勇	31. "好舍"
12. 达德	32. 好
13.《识仁》	33. 女
14.《二程全书》,卷二	34. 子
15. 爱	35. 亲
16. 汎爱	36. 仁
17. 兼爱	37.《淮南子》
18. 墨子	38. 季路
19. 博爱	39. 冉有
20. 韩愈	40. 公西华

41. 仲弓
42. 忠
43. 恕
44. 朱子
45. "尽己之谓忠，
  推己之谓恕。"
46. "良知"
47. 叔向
48. 叔举
49. 叔齐
50. 仪
51. 叔向
52. 孟僖子
53. 大经
54. 昭子
55. 子大叔
56. 赵简子
57. 仪
58. 子产
59. 晏平仲
60. 子贡
61. 《史记·孔子世家》
62. "知礼"
63. 孝
64. 教
65. 孝
66. 文
67. 教
68. 《孝经·天子》
69. 《孝经·开宗明义》
70. 《孝经》
71. 《大戴礼·事父母篇》
72. "微谏不倦"
73. 《大戴礼·立孝篇》
74. "养志"
75. "养口体"
76. 《尚书·舜典》
77. 《中庸》
78. 养心

79. 心

80. 理

81. "大体"

82. "小体"

83. "尽心"

84. "为我"

85. "兼爱"

86. 全生

87. 杨朱

88. 墨翟

89. 天志

90. "四端"

91. 爱

92. 亲

93. "推恩"

94. "仁政"

95. 霸

96. 王

97. 五霸

98. 《中庸》

99. "中和"

100. 乡原

101. 文

102. 竹

103. 忠

104. 信

105. 言语

106. 政事

107. 文学

108. 诗

109. 书

110. 礼

111. 乐

112. 《诗经·野有蔓草》

113. 《诗经·郑之羔裘》

114. 《诗经·褰裳》

115. "风雨"

116. "有女同车"

117. "肆夏"

118. "我将"

119. 笙箫

120. "河水"

121. "六月"

122. "象"

123. 《梼杌》

124. 质

125. 文

126. 馨

127. 《尚书·舜典》

128. 大司徒

129. 《周礼·地官》

130. 雅乐

131. 郑声

132. 郑声

133. 雅乐

134. 韶

135. 武

136. 颂

137. 雅

138. 颂

139. 《乐记》

140. 鼓

141. 椌

142. 楬

143. 埙

144. 篪

145. 钟

146. 磬

147. 竽

148. 瑟

149. 镈

150. 镛

151. 钲

152. 铃

153. 磬

154. 鼓

155. 竽

156. 埙

157. 籥

158. 筳

159. 簫

160. 望

161. 琴

162. 瑟

163. "武城"

164. 《乐记》

165. 肃

166. 雍

167. "韶"

168. "武"

169. "雅"

170. "颂"

171. 骚

172. 赋

173. 《内储》(上)

174. 《廉颇蔺相如列传》

175. 帝

176. 天

177. 诛

178. 祭

179. 帝

180. 《礼记·祭法》

181. 《天文》

182. 《历谱》

183. 《五行》

185. 《耆》

186. 《龟》

187. 《杂占》

187. 形

188. 易

189. 道

190. 《尚书·泰誓》

CHAPTER SIX

1. 柳下惠
2. 伯夷
3. 叔齐
4. "上智"
5. "下愚"
6. "原性"
7. "诚"
8. "说命"
9. "政者正也"
10. 毛
11. 公羊高
12. 穀梁赤
13. 士
14. "说命"
15. 《王制》
16. 士
17. "端"
18. 仁
19. 义
20. 礼
21. 智
22. "小体"
23. "大体"
24. 性
25. 情
26. 虑
27. 伪
28. 伪
29. 知
30. 智
31. 能
32. 命
33. 臧
34. 产
35. 壹
36. 静
37. 志
38. 欲
39. 恶
40. 性

41. 伪

42. 积

43. 辨

44.《大学》

45.“格物”

CHAPTER SEVEN

八"亻六 毛"

SELECTED BIBLIOGRAPHY

1.《四书》

2.《论语》

3.《大学》

4.《中庸》

5.《孟子》

6.《五经》

7.《诗经》

8.《书经》

9.《易经》

10.《礼记》

11.《春秋》

12. 三礼

13.《周礼》

14.《仪礼》

15.《戴礼》

16.《大戴礼》

17.《小戴礼》

18. 三传

19.《左传》

20.《榖梁传》

21.《公羊传》

22.《尔雅》

23.《孝经》

24.《史记》

25.《国语》

26.《二十四史》

27.《吕氏春秋》

28.《荀子》

29.《孔子家语》

30.《经典释文》

SELECTED BIBLIOGRAPHY

A. Primary Sources

1. The Four Books, Ssu Shu[1]

The Analects or *Lun Yu*[2] J. Legge's translation in Chinese Classics, Vol. 1

The Great Learning or *Ta Hsueh*[3] Legge's tran., Vol 1

The Doctrine of the Mean or *Chung Yung*[4] Legge's tran., Vol. 1

Mencius or *Works of Meng Tzu*[5] Legge's tran., Vol. 2

2. The Five Classics, Wu Ching[6]

The Book of Poetry or *Shih Ching*[7] Legge's tran., Vol. 4

The Book of History or *Shu Ching*[8] Legge's tran., Vol. 3

The Book of Changes or *I Ching*[9] Legge's tran.

The Book of Rites or *Li Chi*[10] Legge's tran.

The Spring and Autumn Annals, or *Ch'un Ch'iu*[11] Legge's tran., Vol. 5

3. Three Rites, San Li[12]

Chun Li, The Official Rites of Chou[13]

I Li, The Rites[14] Steele's tran.

Tai Li, The Tais' Records of Rites[15]

(a) *Ta Tai Li, The Elder Tai's Record of Rites*[16]

(b) *Hsiao Tai Li, The Younger Tai's Record of Rites* or *Li Chi*[17]

4. Three Commentaries, San Shuan[18]

Tso Chuan, Tso's Commentary on the Spring and Autumn Legge's tran.[19]

Ku-Liang Chuan, Ku-Liang's Commentary on the Spring and Autumn[20]

Kung-Yang Chuan, Kung-yang's Commentary on the Spring And Autumn[21]

5. Other Works

Er Ya or *Encyclopaedia of Confucian Literature*[22]
Hsiao Ching or *Book of Filial Piety*[23]
Ssu-Ma Ch'ien: Shih Chi or *The Historical Records*[24]
Kuo Yu or *The Narratives of the States*[25]
The Twenty-four Histories[26]
Lu Shih Ch'un Ch'iu or *Lu's Annals of Spring and Autumn*[27]
The Works of Hsun-tzu,[28] translated by H.H. Dubs
The Family Conversations of Confucius[29]
Ching Tien Shih Wan by Lu Teh-ming[30]

B. Secondary Sources (in Chinese)

Ch'en An-Jen: *The History of Chinese Civilization, Ancient, Mediae-val and Modern,* Shanghai, 1938
Ch'en Ching-Chih: *History of Chinese Education,* Shanghai, 1936
Chin Shih Ts'ui Pien
Ch'ueh Li Chih
Feng Yu-Lan: *A History of Chinese Philosophy,* Shanghai, 1934
Feng Yu-Lan: *A Comparative Study of the Philosophies of Life,* Shanghai
Hu Shih: *Outlines of the History of Chinese Philosophy,* Vol. 1
Hung, William: Introduction, *The Combined Concordances to Ch'un Ch'iu, Kung-Yang, Ku-Liang, and Tso Chuan*
Hung, William: Introduction, *Index to I Li*
Hung, William: Introduction, *Index to Li Chi*
K'ang Yu-Wei: *Research on the False Classics of the School of Hsin*
K'ang Yu-Wei: *A study of Confucius' Effort to Revolutionize the System of Chou by Attributing His System to the Ancient System*
Ku Chieh-Kang: *Discussion on Ancient Histories,* volumes 1-4
Lo Ken-Tse: *Discussion on Ancient Histories,* volumes 5-6
Liang Shao-Ming: *Oriental and Occidental Cultures and their Philosophies*
Pi Hsi-Jui: *A History of Classical Learning*
Pi Hsi-Jui: *A Treatise on Classics*

Wang Chih-hsin: *The Philosophy of Confucius*

C. Secondary Sources (in English)

Bergan, P.D.: *The Sages of Shantung,* 1913
Chen, Chin-Chuan: *The Economic Principles of Confucius and his School,* 1911
Chi, Ssu-Ho: *Chinese Feudalism during the Ch'un Ch'iu Period,* Ph. D. Thesis, Harvard, 1935
Creel, H.G.: *The Birth of China,* 1936
Creel, H.G.: *Sinicism,* Ph. D. Thesis, University of Chicago
Crow, Carl: *Master K'ung (The Story of Confucius),* 1938
Cubberley, Ellwood P.: *The principal and his school*
Dawson, M.M.: *The Ethics of Confucius,* 1915
Douglas, R.K.: *Confucianism and Taoism,* 1900
Faber, Ernst: *Systematical Digest of the Doctrine of Confucius,* 1902 (Tran. from the German by P.G. Von Mollendoff, 1875)
Galt, Howard, S.: *The Development of Chinese Educational Theory* (to the close of the Han Dynasty), Ph. D. Thesis, Harvard, 1929
Giles, H.A.: *Confucianism and its Rivals,* 1915
Hsu, Leonard Shihlien: *The Political Philosophy of Confucianism,* 1932
Hsu, Pao C.: *Ethical Realism in Neo-Confucian Thought,* Ph. D. Thesis, Columbia, 1933
Hu, Shih: *The Development of the Logical Method in Ancient China,* Ph. D. Thesis, Columbia, 1920
Johnson, R.F.: *Confucianism and Modern China*
Legge, James: *The Life and Teachings of Confucius,* 1875
Kuo, P.W.: *The Chinese System of Public Education,* Ph. D. Thesis, Columbia University, 1915
Liang, Ch'i-Ch'ao: *History of Chinese Political Thought during the Early Tsin Period,* 1930
Lin, Yu-Tang: *The Wisdom of Confucius,* 1938
Lin, Yu-Tang: *My Country and My People,* 1936
Loh, Rowland Jung-Tsung: *Social Organization during the Shang*

Dynasty of Ancient China, Ph. D. Thesis, 1936

Lyon, D.W.: *Religious Values in Confucianism,* 1938

Mei, I.P.: *Micius*

Pott, W.S.A.: *Chinese Political Philosophy,* 1925

Stewart, J.L.: *Chinese Culture and Christianity,* 1926

Walshe, W.G.: *Confucius and Confucianism,* 1911

Wang, Yueh-Ting: *The Comparison between the Ethics of Confucius and the Ethics of Jesus,* 1932

Wei, Wilson Shih-Seng: *The History of Educational Philosophy in China,* Ph. D. Thesis, N.Y.U., 1931

Wen, Lieu-Chung: *Changing Ideals in Chinese Education,* 1927

Wu, Mi: *Confucius, Confucianism, China and the World To-day,* 1927

Zi, Dung-Hwe: *The Idea of God in the Chinese Classics: The Development of the Idea of Tien and Shan-ti in the Chinese Classics,* Ph. D. Thesis, 1930

Zia, K.Z.: *The Confucian Civilization*

OTHER PUBLICATIONS ON CONFUCIUS
BY DR. CHEN JINGPAN
AFTER THE FOUNDING OF THE
PEOPLE'S REPUBLIC OF CHINA

1. "Place of Confucius in the History of Chinese Education"
(*Journal of Beijing Normal University,* Social Science Edition, No.
3, 1957; *Selected Works on Social Science,* edited by Beijing Normal
University in celebration of the Tenth Anniversary of the People's
Republic of China, Oct. 1, 1959, pp. 59-61)

2. *Confucius' Ideas on Education*
(1957, Hubei People's Press)
"The Hundred Flowers also saw the appearance of the first book
since 1949 specifically on Confucius' educational thought written
by Chen Jingpan of Beijing Normal University . . ." —a comment
on the book by KamLouie in "Salvaging Confucian Education"
(1949-1983), *Comparative Education* Vol. 20, No. 1, 1984.

3. "The Education of the Spring and Autumn Period of China—The
Educational Ideas of Confucius and Mo Zi"
(Teaching Materials on History of Chinese Education, Chap. 2:
Education in Ancient China, Jan. 1961, printed by the Dept. of
Education, Beijing Normal University; *Journal of Beijing Normal
University,* Social Science Edition, No. 1, 1961

4. *History of Modern Chinese Education*
(1979, People's Education Press; second edition 1983; eighth
printing 1986)—A considerable part of this book makes reference
to the place of Confucius' educational thought in modern Chinese
education. Together with *Confucius' Ideas of Education* (1985), this
book was on display in the Hong Kong Exhibition of Chinese
Books of in 1985. In 1988 this book was awarded the honour of
"An Outstanding Textbook for Higher Educational Institutions" by
the State Education Commission of the Peopoe's Republic of China.

5. "On Confucius' Ideas on Moral Education"

(*Journal of Beijing Normal University*, Social Science Edition, No. 4, 1980)

6. "Views of Some Western Scholars—Paul Monroe, H.G. Creel, etc. —on Confucius' Ideas on Education"
(*Journal of Beijing Normal University*, Social Science Edition, No. 1 1981; *Selected Essays on Education*—Special Issue, 1982, edited by the Department of Education of Beijing Normal University in Commemoration of the 80th anniversary of the University; *Selected Works on the Study of Confucius in Recent Forty Years.* Jul. 1987, pp. 439-474, edited by the Academic Committee of the China Confucius Foundation, Qilu Press)

7. Confucius' Ideas on Education, revised edition (1985, Hubei, Education Press)
This new edition was displayed in the Hong Kong Exhibition of Chinese Books in 1985.

8. "A Priliminary Research on Confucius' Idea on 'REN' and Jesus' Idea on 'LOVE'—a thesis presented to and discussed in the Academic Symposium on Confucianism held in Qufu, September 1984
(Excerpts of this thesis are published in *Qilu Journal*, No. 6, 1984; in *Research Papers on Chinese History*, Issues Jul.-Dec. 1984; in the *Social Science Journal of Chinese Higher Educational Institutions*, No. 2, 1985, etc.)

9. "Research on Confucius' Concept of Great Harmony"
(*Studies on Confucianism*, quarterly, first issue, 1986)